STUDIES IN INDIAN AGRICULTURE
THE ART OF THE POSSIBLE

GILBERT ETIENNE

STUDIES IN

INDIAN

AGRICULTURE

The Art of the Possible

Translated from the French by
MEGAN MOTHERSOLE

UNIVERSITY OF CALIFORNIA PRESS
BERKELEY AND LOS ANGELES 1968

University of California Press
Berkeley and Los Angeles, California
Cambridge University Press
London, England

*To the farmers of Khandoï
their fine traditions and
their friendship*

PREFACE

What lies ahead for Indian agriculture? This question must be asked straightaway. The answer could be stagnation, with an absence of agrarian reform resulting in scarcity or famine. This pessimistic view is reinforced by the limited performance of agriculture during the Third Five-Year Plan, 1961–1966, particularly after the catastrophic droughts of 1965 and 1966, when a serious famine involving heavy human loss would have occurred but for the large and timely supply of wheat from America.

A close look at the facts leads us to less pessimistic, and also less definite, conclusions, bringing to mind the old alchemists' formula, *Solve et coagula.* In one place, for example, old, established habits may tend to give way to new ideas; elsewhere they remain entrenched, creating insuperable barriers. Important regions have become involved—some have been so for a long time—in a broad process of economic growth, while others have remained dormant, seemingly unable to rouse themselves from their torpor.

Although I have dealt with several technical problems, I have not attempted any kind of agronomic treatise—which, in any case, I should not be capable of. My aim has been to analyze the rural economy of India, and in particular the factors that influence agricultural production. This has been the guiding line of my inquiries in the rural areas. Although I have been principally concerned with economic development, I have also entered into the fields of political science and sociology wherever they seemed essential to the understanding of economic phenomena. For similar reasons I have taken into account both administrative and educational problems.

There is nothing unusual about my conclusions; however, since they run counter to some firmly established "myths," I must clarify my position and my method. Too many economists approach the study of agriculture by basing themselves in large towns and making only fleeting visits to rural areas. I followed the same pattern myself during several visits to India between 1952 and 1963; but during the last one in 1963–1964 I chose rather to spend most of my time in the villages of four districts. I also covered thirty thousand kilometers of road by car.

Close contact with rural communities enabled me to get away from preconceived ideologies and doctrines and to reach conclusions based on the knowledge of what is practicable. The value of every remedy or solution depends upon the extent to which it is viable and effective, a point that is often overlooked. This elementary truth has enabled me to select the basic ideas for changes which are practicable now or in the immediate future. Some are confined to India; others could apply to a number of underdeveloped countries.

This book was first published in French, in June, 1966, under the title *L'Agriculture indienne ou l'art du possible*. The present version has been enlarged and brought up to date in order to give some conclusions on the Third Five-Year Plan and some discussion of trends in agriculture beginning to appear in the Fourth Plan.

GILBERT ETIENNE

Geneva, *April 1967*

ACKNOWLEDGMENTS

This work has been made possible by a grant from the Swiss National Fund for Scientific Research, to which I should like to express my gratitude.

It gives me equal pleasure to thank Mr. Tarlok Singh, former member of the Planning Commission of India, and Mr. Y. D. Gundevia, former Secretary of the Ministry of External Affairs and, until the end of 1966, Secretary of the President of the Republic of India. I should also like to acknowledge the services rendered by the Swiss Embassy at New Delhi which helped me a great deal at every stage in the organization of my work. Mr. D. P. Singh, former Joint-Secretary (Agriculture) of the Planning Commission, at present Vice-Chancellor of the Uttar Pradesh Agricultural University, Pantnagar; Dr. J. P. Bhattacharjee, former Director of the Program Evaluation Organization, at present with the F.A.O. in Rome; and Dr. D. Hopper, of the Rockefeller Foundation at New Delhi, were unsparing of both the time and the assistance which they gave me. Their knowledge of Indian agriculture has been particularly useful to me. Surendra Pal Singh, M.P., member of the Lok Sabha and deputy foreign minister since 1967, was, during my stay in the Bulandshahr district, both a generous and an able friend, with his deep knowledge of his native soil.

My acknowledgments are due all officials who welcomed me so readily and with such unusual kindness. As for the farmers, if I have made particular mention of those from Khandoï, I have not forgotten the briefer, but equally friendly contacts that I was fortunate to make in other villages.

Professor Louis Dumont, Director of Studies (Indian Sociology) at the École Pratique des Hautes Études in Paris, was good enough to allow me to profit from his experience, particularly of the Tamil areas. The agricultural engineer M. Jacques Carluy, formerly Agricultural Attaché to the French Embassy at New Delhi, made it possible for me to work out certain technical questions. My old friend Jean-Luc Chambard, Professor of Contemporary Indian Civilization at the School of

Oriental Languages, Paris, has made my task very much easier through his knowledge of the Indian rural environment. I am much indebted to him for his help in my preparation both for this mission and for the book.

Finally I should like to thank Mrs. Shirley R. Taylor for her remarkable editing of the manuscript and my sister, Marceline de Montmollin, for her very kind support during the writing of this book. As for my wife, she has taken an active part, both in my researches on the spot, and in their compilation.

If I have been able to profit from a great deal of support from many people, it goes without saying that I alone am responsible for the facts and conclusions presented.

G. E.

CONTENTS

PART I

The Basic Framework

1

SCOPE AND METHOD OF THE INQUIRY

"Don't go to Etawah,[1] that's a showpiece." This remark made by a young official in the presence of his chief, who is responsible for planning in Uttar Pradesh, sums up the scope of inquiry in India.

In many underdeveloped countries the foreign, or native, research worker comes up against all sorts of restrictions, but in India I had complete freedom of action. Thanks to my friends on the Planning Commission and in the Ministry of External Affairs, I received a cordial welcome at all levels. I was allowed to attend meetings of the village councils as well as staff meetings of the block and the district. I was given access to archives, to reports on development, and to files containing records of specific, and sometimes critical, matters. Ministers of the central government and of provincial departments, high-ranking officials and their subordinates alike took me into their confidence, talking to me with much frankness. Although it has not always been possible to mention private and confidential conversations, they have nonetheless played their part in enlightening my judgment and have thus become integrated into my work.

In every region in which I stayed, the people welcomed me warmly, without a trace of xenophobia or mistrust, and the villagers readily submitted themselves to my sometimes irksome and puzzling questions.

Sources

Naturally I referred a great deal to the usual sources such as the central government's reports, and works of Indian and foreign economists. I paid equal attention to the press, a justified step in a country whose newspapers still retain a serious and even slightly Victorian aspect, a quality seldom found elsewhere these days.

In the main part of my work I have relied on documents that are generally little used, at least by foreigners; these are the states' plans and those of the districts, the development blocks, and the villages. I

---

[1] Pilot district where the program of community development was started.

also consulted the minutes of the *panchayats,* which are councils of the village, the block, and the district.

The land records (which are absolute gold mines, and are not used nearly enough) enabled me to get a picture of the general situation, such as the area cultivated, or irrigated, the types of cultivation, the size of landholdings, and the manner in which land is owned or cultivated.

In addition to written sources, among the farmers I usually employed a questionnaire type of interview recorded on cards, taking care to secure a characteristic sample by choosing representatives of different castes, large as well as medium and small landowners, and agricultural laborers.

In this kind of study the question of language is of prime importance. The main part of my research was concentrated on Uttar Pradesh where my knowledge of Hindi, and to a smaller extent of Urdu, enabled me to talk with the farmers directly rather than through an interpreter. At the village level all the documents are in the local language and it is not usual to find anyone with a knowledge of English. Even two steps higher in the scale, at the development block or district level, a knowledge of the local language is indispensable if one is to follow the officials' discussions and to understand documents. (In Uttar Pradesh some documents are in Hindi and others are in English.) In the state of Madras English is more widespread and only in the villages did I have to make use of an interpreter. In Maharashtra I studied, with the aid of a translator, sources written in Marathi. This same translator [2] accompanied me when I interviewed the farmers who did not know Hindi.

Choice of Regions

I was faced at the outset with an awkward problem: India has, according to the 1961 census, a total of 564,718 villages spread over more than three million square kilometers. These figures alone make it difficult to conduct a fully comprehensive study, not to mention the variety of people, customs, and climate. Should I, I wondered, try to cover the greatest possible area of India, visiting as many villages as possible, or should I make a special study of one area only?

Neither of these solutions seemed satisfactory. The first results in a superficial analysis, for it is impossible to assimilate the economic life of a village in a few days. An experienced research worker must be able

[2] Since Marathi employs the same alphabet as Hindi, I was at least able to make some check.

to stay in a place for about two weeks if he is going to *begin* to do any serious work on it. The second solution has the disadvantages of ignoring the immense variety of India. I tried to reach a compromise, beginning with a study as comprehensive as possible of a village where I stayed for five months (September, 1963, to February, 1964) followed by another brief visit in August, 1964. Thus I was able to analyze in depth the mechanisms that determined the economic evolution of one limited region. Having completed this task, I undertook three briefer investigations of contrasting regions in order to underline their differences and similarities.

Although I carried out the main part of my research at village level, I also included the field of Indian administration and planning in villages, blocks of development, districts, and states (provinces).

The Regions Studied

I had to make my first choice: with its 73,746,000 inhabitants (1961), Uttar Pradesh is the largest state in India, which has a total population of 439,000,000. I chose two completely different districts: in the west, Bulandshahr, which is primarily devoted to the cultivation of wheat, and in the east, Benares, where wheat and rice are cultivated.

From the Ganges basin I went toward the delta area in the south, to the Tanjore (state of Madras) district where rice is the main crop. Here I found another interesting pattern of farming, for this was a district where the program of intensive development (package program) was being carried out with the support of the Ford Foundation.

Following these three alluvial and densely populated regions, I needed an example of the Deccan with its poor soil and less dense population: the Satara district in Maharashtra was the answer.

My choice of villages was based on the criteria of their size and their situation in the region. Three of the villages have 1,200 to 1,500 inhabitants; the fourth has 2,500. These figures are fairly representative, since 25 percent of the rural population live in villages containing 1,000 to 2,000 inhabitants, and a little more than 20 percent live in villages with 2,000 to 5,000 inhabitants (1961 census).

Most of the villages in India are far from the main roads. It is difficult to get by car to Khandoï, the village in Bulandshahr: on leaving the district road, which is asphalted, one enters fifteen kilometers of metaled road,[3] which is followed by four kilometers of track that is passable for vehicles only in the dry season. Nahiyan is about

---

[3] A road which, in contrast to a track, has a foundation made of stones. Sometimes the surface is asphalted, sometimes not.

thirty kilometers from Benares, in an area hardly touched by the
influences of urbanization (metaled road and rude tracks for two
kilometers). Kila Ulur, in the Tanjore district, is one and a half
kilometers by foot from the district road. Eksal (Satara) is the only
one of the villages served by bus.

In the four villages, the numerous variety of castes, the size of the
holdings, the relationship between the landowners and the agricultural workers are all representative of conditions widespread in India.
So far as development is concerned, our villages differ little from
thousands of other villages in India which have similar problems and
deal with them, or try to deal with them, in the same ways.[4]

Administration and Politics

The political situation in the Indian states and the quality of administration have an influence of prime importance on rural development.
In this field also I had to choose a varied sample.

For several years now Uttar Pradesh has been the victim of a
political instability that has had serious repercussions on administration and on development. The same instability is found, with slight
variation, in Bihar or in Madhya Pradesh, for example. There are, of
course, more stable and better governed states in India in which the
administration functions more effectively: Madras and Maharashtra
are cases in point.

The picture thus seen is obviously limited. It leaves out extensive
areas and takes no account of tea plantations or the major irrigation
projects. The reader will perhaps regret the fact that I have not dealt
with the Gujarat example, or with some of the regions of the central
Deccan, east and west. My answer to this would be that a marked
increase in the production of tea does not seem likely in the short term
and that the big irrigation projects are essentially long-term operations
even if we are today beginning to enjoy their benefits.

And what of the thinly populated regions of Deccan? It is doubtful
whether they are going to play any major role in the near future. The
soil is often of poor quality, facilities for irrigation are limited, and the
peasants are often slow in waking up to modern techniques.

India is faced with a serious food problem. The decisive factor for
the immediate future lies in the Ganges basin, the coastal strips, and
the relatively prosperous regions of the Deccan—hence my choice.

---

[4] Except, to a certain extent, Kila Ulur.

Principal Themes

Owing to my method of work, in which I tried to stick to facts as closely as possible, I encountered some difficulties that were not wholly unavoidable. The changing faces of reality that I describe make it impossible at times to arrive at clear-cut conclusions.

I was not able to keep strictly to the same plan in all four cases. The first village was the object of a more detailed study than the others. Moreover, neither the sources and documents at my disposal nor the administrative and legislative systems were the same in every state, to say nothing of the differences in languages and in other means of obtaining information.

It seemed best to observe the following principles: (1) to put oneself in the position of the peasant, showing his living conditions, his problems, and his reactions toward measures carried out in his favor by the government and the administration; (2) to put oneself in the position of the authorities and of the services responsible for helping the peasants, to study the workings of the administrative machinery and the ideas of politicians and of those in administrative circles, so far as agricultural development was concerned.

In the course of my inquiry certain ideas gradually emerged: the peasants' attitude toward economic progress, the conditions necessary for an accelerated increase in production while following a strict order of priorities with the concentration of means on the decisive points. Seen in this perspective, the role and organization of the administration are of prime importance. It is equally necessary to have a realistic appreciation of the incidence of *social* factors, particularly education,[5] on agriculture.

Before coming to the heart of the matter I shall try to establish the general framework within which Indian agriculture is developing, noting at the outset the characteristic traits of the Indian political milieu and of economic planning. In parts 2 and 3 I present facts that I had the opportunity to observe. As I have already indicated, the chapters devoted to Uttar Pradesh deal with two rural areas and contain a study of the administrative machinery from village level to development block and district, ending finally at Lucknow, the state capital. Part 3 follows a similar approach but in less detail. In both cases I deal first with the general problems of the state and then

---

[5] This subject was studied in Madras and Maharashtra, where efforts at education are especially intensive.

go on to study at village, block, and district levels. Part 4 is an attempt at synthesis in which I have tried to see how the facts I have analyzed fit into the picture of India as a whole. My purpose is to see by what means production can be further increased, and what lessons can be learned from the accumulated experience since the beginning of the First Five-Year Plan.

2

POLITICAL INSTITUTIONS AND
ECONOMIC PLANNING

If the last phase of decolonization was swift,[1] the political and economic foundations of contemporary India are the product of a long
period of gestation derived from her geographical framework and her
traditional institutions as well as from the British regime. Itself complex, this heritage is made even more so by the size of the territory and
population (439 million in 1961 and over 500 million in 1967) and
by the extraordinary diversity of customs, races, religions, languages,
and climates. Above all, the rhythm of India's history has been determined by the alternation of centrifugal forces leading to the crumbling
of political power and tendencies to regroup. The British helped to
reinforce the latter tendencies without going so far as to eliminate any
risk of division.[2]

A Regime of Parliamentary Democracy

The majority of Asian and African states have, either immediately or
within a short time after their independence, adopted a dictatorial or
authoritarian type of political regime of varying hue: in one place
individual liberty has shrunk like shagreen and the press has been
severely controlled, while in another the system is firm without being
too oppressive. Despite these examples, and contrary to the oversimple
reasoning that one so often hears, it is false to associate authoritarian,
even dictatorial, regimes with rapid economic development. There are
countless examples where the former does not lead to the latter, but to
stagnation, insufficient progress, or economic decline. This does not
mean, however, that democracy alone holds the secret of development:
witness Ceylon. Quite simply, there exists no automatic correlation
between the form of regime chosen and the rate of economic growth.

[1] Independence was announced by Lord Mountbatten on June 3, 1947, and brought
into effect on the following August 15.
[2] See especially Selig S. Harrison, *India, The Most Dangerous Decades* (Princeton,
1960).

India, inspired by Western ideologies in which there is wide freedom of opinion and of the press, chose parliamentary democracy. The government is in itself an example of this by the effort it makes at self-criticism, a phenomenon not often met in underdeveloped countries. General elections with universal suffrage have taken place every five years since 1952. With the exception of a few irregularities, there has never been any question of gerrymandering on a large scale in the counting of votes, nor in pressure on the voters.

So far as economic policy is concerned, this type of regime poses two problems: the rejection of authoritarian formulas, of which there are many laid down in the Constitution and in countless official declarations, and the necessity to take account of the electorate.

There have been many declarations. In the course of a private conversation that I had with Prime Minister Nehru in September, 1959, he said, "Yes, we are in favor of cooperatives"—a subject then provoking lively controversy—but he quickly added, "We are trying to introduce them freely, without any compulsion."

As we shall see, it is possible to have a more elaborate development without altering the democratic system. But one must not lose sight of the existence of a judicial and political framework that may sometimes bar the way to the most practical solutions. Laws and statutes are not made for the convenience of technocrats, and at election time the legislators have accounts to render.

One example will clarify this point. India has quite a considerable system of rural taxation. Today the peasants pay the same amount that they paid forty years ago, despite the fall in the purchasing power of the rupee and the increase in production. Why has the land tax not been increased? In the present social and political context of the rural areas it would be very difficult to get such a measure passed by a legislative assembly, because the politicians would be afraid of jeopardizing their chances of re-election. (Only certain states have succeeded in carrying it through.)

The same phenomenon is repeated in the district, where the politician will willingly cheapen necessary, but unpopular, economic measures for the sole purpose of keeping or winning votes. He runs the risk of having this attitude turn against him one day, and as for the immediate future it makes further development very complicated.

The Federal Framework

Many Asian states lack homogeneity. They need to create a central power that is strong enough to ensure a minimum amount of national cohesion and to establish ties that are flexible enough not to alienate part of the population. In varying degrees, Burma, Ceylon, and Indonesia have not yet solved this problem. The historical and sociological background of India imposed upon the new republic a federal framework in which the prerogatives of a central government and of the various states were carefully proportioned. Side by side with the cabinet and the Parliament, account must be taken of the state governments and their legislative assemblies.

A detailed analysis of India's constitutional law and its application does not come within the scope of a work devoted to development. We shall confine ourselves to its repercussions on the growth of the economy.

One seldom encounters criticism of India's federal system as such. Communalism, however, is very pronounced: the intricate ties of religion, language, customs, and caste would blow up like so many power kegs if centralization were too rigorous. From the economic point of view, also, decentralization is sensible. It would have been impossible to set in motion and to direct the cumbersome planning machinery from New Delhi alone. Delegation of power to local authorities was indispensable.[3]

But along with these advantages, the federal system does have some weaknesses, in part inevitable. According to the Constitution, the central power can intervene in extreme cases when the local executive and legislature, impeded by party political struggles, lack a sufficient majority to govern. (This has happened in Kerala on three occasions.) The state is then administered by the central government, under the President's rule, until new elections can be held. When local political instability and the ineffectiveness of the legislature stop short of total chaos, however, New Delhi is powerless to intervene, even though the local economy may be unhealthy or even approaching bankruptcy.

Since the internal situations of the states are not uniform, their rhythms of development and of achievements are different. Compared with Madras and Maharashtra, which have efficient administrations, the unwieldy mass of Uttar Pradesh is semiparalyzed by factions within the Congress party. Development has been slow, indicating that, at a provincial level, at least a minimum amount of political stability and continuity is necessary for genuine economic progress.

The political powers of the states are consistent with their large responsibilities in matters of planning, which makes it difficult to give a global analysis of the Indian economy. A study of the national

[3] Although China lends itself more readily than India to a centralized form of government, it has encountered certain problems with regard to planning.

economy must be accompanied by a study of the local economies, within the framework of the states, and sometimes even within the districts. This is particularly true in studying the economy of agriculture.

The Division of Economic Activities

The broad outlines of planning are drawn up by the Planning Commission in liaison with the central government; they cover size and distribution of investments, ways of financing, foreign aid, large hydroelectric and other infrastructure projects, and several industries in the public sector. In these fields New Delhi has a relatively free hand subject only to sometimes powerful political pressure for the localization of projects in case of competing areas.

The states themselves are masters of their own agrarian legislation and rural taxation, with the central government confining itself to suggestions (Clause 7 of the Constitution). The interests of local politicians, which are subject to the approval of the electorate, are thus directly opposed to the rigors of development on a national scale.

In addition to projects administered by the central government, the four successive Five-Year Plans have been divided into plans drawn up by each state with the approval of New Delhi. As the following table shows, agriculture occupies a special place in these:

	Public Sector Investments *			Investments in Agriculture (Public Sector)	
		Central Govt.	States	Central Govt.	States
	Total				
1st Plan	20,124	11,149	8,975	1,289	1,553
2nd Plan	47,990	25,590	22,400	650	5,020
3rd Plan	75,000 †	36,000	39,000	1,250	9,430
4th Plan	160,000	85,300	74,640	4,320	19,780

* Figures in millions of rupees; one U.S. dollar = 4.75 rupees before devaluation in June, 1966, after which one U.S. dollar = 7.5 rupees. For the First Plan, figures are actual expenditures; for the others, figures are estimates. Actual expenditures do not always correspond to estimates, but the proportions remain the same.

† This figure was in fact 86,300; the increase beyond the estimate was largely offset by a rise in prices. See Fourth Five Year Plan, A Draft Outline, p. 3.

This table clearly reveals the determinant role played by the provincial authorities in agricultural matters. The difference between investments by the central government and by the states is even greater, for the statistics do not include local contributions raised by village administration. The extensive role of the states in investments in irrigation should also be noted: of the 9,600 million estimated by the

Fourth Plan for this expenditure, the states will be responsible for 9,200 million.

Does this mean that the central government has no means available for carrying out its recommended agricultural policy? The states meet only part of their own needs, with the central government making up the balance. Thus for the First Plan, the central government guaranteed to pay 39 percent of the total sum spent by the states. For the Second Plan, the states could raise only 12,800 million rupees out of a total of 22,400 million rupees. For the Third Plan, the states estimated a sum of 14,600 million, with the central government contributing 23,700 million.[4] Despite these contributions, the central government found that the agricultural plans were in trouble. At the beginning of 1964, for instance, the Planning Commission informed the states that aid from the central government would be reduced if funds intended for agriculture and community development were used for other purposes, without previous authorization from New Delhi.[5] Hardly to anyone's surprise, the situation was not put right very quickly, and on July 24, 1964, the Central Ministry of Agriculture and the Planning Commission were obliged to repeat their instructions.[6]

It is clear that the states need to increase their fiscal effort. In November, 1963, the Planning Commission had to call in the arrears of eight states: Uttar Pradesh, Kerala, Bihar, Madhya Pradesh, Andhra, Mysore, Rajasthan, and Assam. (Let it be mentioned in passing that the first four states at least were then, and still are, victims of an unstable political situation.) The following March, the Minister of Finance, T. T. Krishnamachari, expressed the opinion that "There would be cause for anxiety if borrowed funds are utilized to fill revenue gaps and not spent on projects which were economically sound and could be expected to generate the resources for repaying their liabilities." [7]

In its report on the 1961/62 performance, the parliamentary Public Accounts Committee condemned the "lethargy" of some states in fiscal matters. For various reasons, too, it was not unusual for some ministers of finance to underestimate their income and overestimate their expenditures.[8] An editorial in the *Hindustan Times* (Feb. 26, 1964) commenting on the budgets that had just been voted said: "The financial health of the states varies from the near parlous position of

[4] For these figures, see *Review of the First Five Year Plan* (1957) , pp. 19, 24; *Second Five Year Plan* (1956) , pp. 55, 87; *Third Five Year Plan* (1961) , pp. 58, 102.
[5] See *Hindustan Times*, Jan. 2, 1964.
[6] *Ibid.*, July 25, 1964.
[7] Reported by the *Northern Patrika*, March, 1964.
[8] *Hindustan Times*, Mar. 19, 1964.

Bihar . . . to the comparative affluence of Maharashtra and West Bengal."

The report on the 1963 Plan deplores the difference between the progress of central revenue and the "modest beginnings" made by the states in raising additional resources. This document gives the expenditures for the first three years of the Plan (1961–1964). One observes that generally the states that spent the smallest sums of money were precisely those that were the least healthy. Those with expenditures below 50 percent of the Plan were Bihar, 46.8 percent; Uttar Pradesh, 48.5 percent; and Madhya Pradesh, 49.4 percent.[9]

In this complex field of relations between the central government and the states, New Delhi is not wholly blameless. The Uttar Pradesh government, for instance, complains of the abnormally long time taken by the capital to sanction projects that need to be carried out immediately.[10] The question is receiving more and more attention, and the various central ministries and the Planning Commission have begun to send commissions of inquiry into the provinces with a view to improving relations. But since the constitutional system is still opposed to too rigorous a control, the only certain remedy lies in the reinforcement of political power and administration in the weaker states. Here also, however, the margin for initiative and maneuver from New Delhi is somewhat restricted.

The Socialist Pattern of Society

At the end of 1954 the Indian Parliament adopted the formula of the "socialist pattern of society" as the guiding principle in its planning. This inclination toward socialistic formulas was not new: it appeared well before Independence in the speeches and writings of Jawaharlal Nehru and several other nationalist leaders. In this respect, India has been in the nature of an experiment, embarking on a third road which is neither capitalist nor communist, and which many Asian and African states are seeking. Although tinted with Marxist influences, the approach tries above all to be pragmatic and adapted to the needs of the situation. It does not exclude a certain flexibility, as is revealed in the texts: "It is not rooted in any doctrine or dogma. Each country has to develop according to its own genius and traditions." [11]

This ideology has been put into practice: the government has entered vigorously into the field of industry, but this has not hindered

---

[9] *The Third Plan: Mid-Term Appraisal* (1963), pp. 22, 32.
[10] Government of Uttar Pradesh, *Third Five Year Plan* (Lucknow, 1961), I, 25.
[11] *Second Five Year Plan,* p. 23.

private enterprises from progressing in a very substantial way. What is more, after some difficulties, the pendulum seems today to be swinging toward more realistic formulas than those of the Second Plan, as can be seen in the increasing encouragement given to private foreign investors. One senses also a tendency toward a more marked pragmatism than in the past. Therefore the practical problems of implementing the Plan now overshadow some of the political slogans, but, as we shall see in later chapters, we have not heard the last from the dogmatists.

The influence of socialistic ideals can be equally seen in agriculture, beginning with the plans for agrarian reform proposed by the Congress party well before Independence. These proposals suggested not so much the elimination of private ownership of land as, rather, particularly after the session of Congress at Nagpur in 1959, the encouragement of cooperative farms, which were considered "vital for rural progress," [12] along with cooperative credit and marketing societies.

To sum up, the mechanism of agricultural development is determined by a democratic regime that excludes compulsion or excessive pressure but at the same time allows considerable influence to local politicians; It is, in other words, a federal system that accords wide powers to the states and follows a method of planning that, without resorting to the radical formulas of the U.S.S.R. or China, seeks to limit the abuses of private ownership while at the same time encouraging a cooperative system for services and production.

[12] *Third Five Year Plan,* p. 49.

3

AGRICULTURE IN
THE FIVE-YEAR PLANS

The First Five-Year Plan (1951–1956) represents the modest initial stage of a development process which expanded with the end of each five-year period. The rate of investment increased while at the same time the apportionment of expenditure was modified.

Should priority be given to agriculture or to industry? This question can always provide a lively debate between the exponents of the different ideologies when a development program is being prepared. Let us examine how the issue was settled in India.

In 1950–1951, on the eve of the First Plan, the agricultural situation was extremely serious. The echoes of the Bengal famine of 1943 reverberated in the background and only by massive imports could further trouble be held off. This critical state was reflected in the form of the Plan, in which, quite rightly, government officials held that "agriculture, including irrigation and power, must in our view have the topmost priority." [1]

But there were even more profound reasons behind this decision to concentrate on agriculture. Since the beginning of the twentieth century the relationship between population and agricultural production had been deteriorating.[2] The first sign of this was that India gradually stopped exporting cereals. Around 1880 it had exported an average of 1.2 million tons a year. Between 1905 and 1910 the figure fell to 520,000 tons. Subsequently India had to import 160,000 tons a year (1920–1925), then 1.2 million tons (1930–1935). In the postwar years the annual imports reached about 3 million tons. At the same time the lands cultivated per head of population began to fall. The figure dropped more than 20 percent between 1921 and 1951,[3] and the

---

[1] First Five Year Plan (1952), p. 44.

[2] Between 1891 and 1921 a sort of demographic "squeeze" took place, the population remaining more or less stationary as a result of serious famines and epidemics. Since 1921 the increase has been continuous and progressive (see Appendix).

[3] For these and the preceding figures see Census of India, 1951, Vol. I, "General Report," pp. 141, 164, 166.

decrease was not compensated for by an increase in yields; on the contrary, for the nation as a whole, yields hardly varied.[4] All the evidence shows that it was necessary to arrest the decline in a sector which provided half the national income.

By the end of the First Plan the situation had improved appreciably. On the one hand nature had showed herself more kindly from 1952–1953 after exceptionally grave natural calamities at the start of the Plan. On the other hand, the efforts of the authorities and the peasants had produced tangible results.

Food Grain Output
(food grains = cereals and pulses)

	Year	Millions of Tons
	1949/50	54.9
	1950/51	50.8
1st Plan	1951/52	51.2
	1952/53	58.3
	1953/54	68.7
	1954/55	66.6
	1955/56	66.8

SOURCES: *Fourth Five Year Plan*, p. 172, and *Economic Survey, 1965–66*, table 1:3. Throughout the book, tons means metric tons.

This table gives only cereals and pulses, products that constitute basic food and are therefore the least inadequate indication of progress. In the course of the Second and Third Five-Year Plans, production of cereals and pulses developed as follows:

	Year	Millions of Tons
2nd Plan	1956/57	69.8
	1957/58	64.3
	1958/59	77.1
	1959/60	77.6
	1960/61	82.0
3rd Plan	1961/62	82.7
	1962/63	78.4
	1963/64	80.4
	1964/65	88.4
	1965/66	72.3

SOURCES: *Third Five Year Plan*, p. 302, and *Fourth Five Year Plan*, p. 172.

[4] See particularly the figures provided by W. Malenbaum, *Prospects for Indian Development* (London, 1962), pp. 124–125.

Thanks to the priority granted to agriculture in the First Plan, production climbed and the standard of nutrition of at least part of the population was improved. Thus with the wind behind her sails, India tackled a much more tricky stage with its Second Plan, which involved investments twice as large as the First. This expansion was accompanied by a reorientation of the objectives, in favor of industrialization, with particular emphasis on heavy industries. This item accounted for 20 percent of the investments in the public sector (as against 4 percent for the period 1951–1956), whereas expenditures for agriculture were reduced from 15 percent to 11 percent and those for irrigation (major and medium projects) from 16 percent to 9 percent.[5]

Was this slackening of pace on the agricultural front justified? The Planning Commission gave its opinion of the gains achieved in these terms: "While the general trend of food production would appear to be upward, it must be admitted that favourable seasons have played a notable part and there are substantial elements of instability despite the evidence of growth of agricultural production." [6] The report of the First Five-Year Plan drew attention to the very good monsoons of 1953 and 1954. Despite this implied warning, the same Commission did not mention agriculture among its four main objectives for the years 1956–1961: (a) to increase the national income; (b) to proceed with a rapid industrialization, with the main emphasis on heavy industry; (c) to create more employment opportunities; (d) to reduce inequalities in wealth and income.[7] The oversight was, I think, a consequence of the influences of the socialist planning (of the Soviet type) and of the attraction that great industrial projects so often seem to have for the Third World, along with Congress' excessive optimism about India's agricultural future.

Two years later, in 1957–1958, nature reminded man, with uncommon brutality, that she still had the last word. Particularly adverse climatic conditions resulted in a drop in production of nearly 10 percent. In addition to the agricultural crisis, serious difficulties also arose on the financial side. Subsequently nature proved more merciful and indeed conditions were definitely favorable in the last year of the Plan, when harvests slightly exceeded the target of 80 million tons.

The lessons of 1958 were learned. To the four primary objectives of the Second Plan, the Third Plan added a fifth: to free the country from food imports by obtaining an increase of 32 percent in the

[5] See *Third Five Year Plan*, p. 33.
[6] *Review of the First Five Year Plan*, pp. 100–101.
[7] See *Second Five Year Plan*, p. 24.

production of food grains. This objective was placed second in order of priority, after the increase in the national income and before industry. Yet, one should not see in this an evidence of a fundamentally new strategy. It is acknowledged that "the rate of increase in agricultural production is one of the principal brakes on the progress of the economy" and that "it is therefore necessary to push ahead with agriculture as fast as possible." The fact remains that the Plan, and also many politicians including the Prime Minister, continued to advocate as massive an industrialization program as possible. The percentage of industrial investments remained unaltered (20 percent). The proportion of investments in irrigation was likewise the same (9 percent), but agriculture's share rose from 11 percent to 14 percent of the total expenditure of the Third Plan.[8]

During the next three years production marked time. Besides the shortcomings of planning, meteorological conditions were rather bad. Then a generous and widespread monsoon occurred in 1964. It was followed by conditions also favorable for crops in the winter of 1964–1965. As a result there was a very substantial rise in production. But, just at the time when the balance between population and food resources was beginning to improve, there was a catastrophic drought in 1965 which caused an unprecedented drop in the harvests. India was then threatened with a serious famine. The greater part of Deccan faced a grave food shortage. The rice bowls of the Coromandel Coast had only small surpluses, if any. On the other hand, the Ganges basin was little affected. The winter crops, also, were rather poor, partly owing to the weak monsoon, and particularly in nonirrigated areas.

Thanks to a speeding-up in deliveries of American grain, which rose from 10,000 landed tons a day in the middle of 1965 to 30,000 tons around March, 1966, and to the efforts of the authorities in distributing it, the worst was avoided. Only in six districts of Orissa were there reports of some small pockets of famine that involved a number of cases of death by starvation.

The table following shows how imports have developed. Until 1961 the food shortage varied with the monsoons, but there was no sharp increase in imports. From 1961 onward the shortage went from bad to worse. Not only did the increase in production cease, but the pressure of increasing population became more intense.

According to various opinions, the seriousness of the shortage was due not only to insufficient production but also to faults in the system

[8] As before, I refer to expenditure in the public sector; for details of the plans, see Appendix.

Imports of Cereals

Year	Millions of Tons
1951	4.8
1953	2.04
1955	0.60
1957	3.63
1959	3.86
1961	3.49
1963	4.55
1964	6.26
1965	7.45
1966	10–11 (est.)

SOURCE: *Economic Survey, 1965–66.*

of distribution. Often, in fact, as soon as the merchants, or sometimes the farmers, had a surplus at their disposal, they tended to speculate on a price increase by keeping excessive reserves in stock. This matter is worth further research. I am restricting myself to the impressions that I gathered in the regions I visited. From my observation, there is little doubt that the food shortage has been aggravated by speculation, particularly in the large towns. The rural areas, where home consumption and barter are common, are less affected. According to a report made by the Ford Foundation,[9] only 25 percent of the food produced finds its way into the commercial market. The total absence of flour in the market at Koregaon (district of Satara, Maharashtra) on certain days in July, 1964, was probably largely traceable to bad harvests. On the other hand, it is reported that elsewhere (Madhya Pradesh) wheat crops, after an excellent harvest in 1964, were hoarded in villages adjoining rationed towns. In the district of Bulandshahr, at the height of the crisis in August, 1964, a few large proprietors retained stocks, though they were much below those of the preceding years. Farmers who normally had a small surplus to dispose of had only just sufficient, and the smallholders had shortages.

Another aspect of the recent shortages has to do with the supplying of urban markets. Between 1951 and 1961 the urban population rose from 62.3 million to 78.8 million. Part of the gains in food production have, not unnaturally, remained in the rural areas, providing the peasants with slightly better nourishment; but this means that the demand in urban areas is not always met. It is a process that has occurred elsewhere and is giving rise to much anxiety in several devel-

[9] *Report on India's Food Crisis and Steps to Meet It* (1959), p. 12.

oping countries, particularly China.[10] In India, where the ecomomy is more or less free, the impact may be severe.

To sum up, even if one takes into account losses due to speculation (in any case very difficult to eliminate) and a distribution system between town and country that is not always satisfactory, the situation is nonetheless extremely serious. From 1951 to 1961 agricultural production rose faster than the population. Statistics are, as we shall see, rather unreliable, and certain adjustments must be made for the effects of climatic conditions, but it is fair to say that within the decade, whereas population rose 21.5 percent, production was increased by 35 to 40 percent.[11] In the course of the Third Plan, however, the favorable trend in agriculture was reversed and production was outstripped by population. Here, one must take into account conditions of nature, which were extremely unfavorable as compared with the decade 1951–1961. Between 1961 and 1966 there were three rather bad years, one really good one, and one—the last—truly catastrophic.

Given its dependence on the monsoons, it is absolutely imperative for India to take all possible steps to increase production sufficiently to allow the government to have a minimum of stocks on hand in anticipation of bad years. The drought of 1965 may very likely be repeated—as it was to some extent in 1966, particularly in Bihar and eastern Uttar Pradesh. The increasing population makes it even more imperative to increase production at a faster rate. India is only at the start of a rapid demographic increase with an annual rise of about 2.5 percent. Several other Asian countries are increasing at more than 3 percent per year (the Philippines, Malaysia, Taiwan). Others such as Thailand are approaching this figure. Moreover the eventual development of family planning, by means of the intrauterine loop device or other means, is—even on the most optimistic estimate—only likely to produce results in, say, ten years' time.

[10] "During the last three years, the urban population has increased by 20 million in China. The State had not enough grain to meet all the demand." *Takung Pao,* (China) Feb. 2, 1961, as quoted in *Survey of China Mainland Press,* No. 2466, United States Consulate-General, Hong Kong.

[11] See chap. 26. My reservations about agricultural statistics will become plainer by the end of this work. The trend indicated may seem quite near the truth, but the same does not necessarily apply to actual figures. The National Sample Survey, an independent statistical organization, has arrived at figures much at variance with those of the Ministry of Agriculture. In its first survey (December, 1952) it estimated that the official figures were some 25 percent below its own calculations. The N.S.S. Report No. 73 for 1958–1959 shows a similar discrepancy, of 30 percent. For 1960/61 the N.S.S. gives a figure of 96 million tons as opposed to the official figure of 82 million. As suggested by David Hopper of the Rockefeller Foundation in New Delhi, the truth may well lie somewhere between the two.

The Agriculture vs. Industry Debate

Should we, as some economists have suggested, criticize the Indian authorities for having neglected agriculture in favor of industry?

The circumstances surrounding Indian development make me doubt the decisive importance attributed only to the financial provisions. Would agriculture really have progressed much more quickly if it had had the benefit of more capital investment freed by a less hasty industrialization? In other words, could not better results have been obtained even with the distribution of funds between the two sectors remaining unchanged? This is a difficult question to resolve and one that might well be asked also about other underdeveloped countries. For the moment let us at least be careful about considering capital to be the *only* essential factor.

There is reason to draw attention to two types of error. First, there is a psychological error which has engendered in official circles some relaxing of effort with regard to agriculture since the Second Plan. When the politicians and numerous economists stress the need for rapid industrialization, they seem to misunderstand the initial role of agriculture; they forget the truth demonstrated by nineteenth-century Europe and Japan, that true industrialization can only take root in ground prepared by a relatively high level of agricultural production. In Russia also the agricultural development that continued from the end of the nineteenth century to the First World War facilitated the preference given by the Soviets to industry.[12]

A second error of appreciation is the lack of realism in studying agricultural problems. I shall have occasion to return to the subject of the gulf that has grown between the urban intelligentsia and the rural population. Some of those in charge of agricultural policy have not always had the experience required for all development undertakings. Nor have optimistic statements helped to encourage greater efforts. As an example, I might quote the Minister of Food and Agriculture (S. K. Patil) who said in Parliament in 1960 that the imports of American agricultural surplus were temporary. According to him, India would be self-sufficient when, thanks to the Third Plan, production had reached 105 million tons.[13] The experience of recent years did not justify such statements, which made no mention of a possible gap between theoretical aim and actual achievement.

[12] See, e.g., C. K. Eicher and L. W. Witt (eds.) , *Agriculture in Economic Development* (New York, 1964) , p. 23.
[13] Quoted in the *Overseas Hindustan Times*, Mar. 31, 1960.

The psychological climate and excesses of optimism do not provide the complete explanation; other weaknesses appeared at the executive level. These concerned the administration and operation of the organizations responsible for promoting agriculture, in which greater progress could have been achieved without large additional expenditure. The strategy of agricultural development plays an equally essential part. Instead of inflating expenditure at all costs, it would have been better to ensure a judicious distribution of the money. The policy regarding large irrigation projects, for example, should have been re-examined much earlier. Progress would have been more rapid if minor irrigation works that were simple to execute, inexpensive, and likely to bring immediate results, had received maximum encouragement from the start. Another weak point has been the launching of new projects before the completion of the previous ones, which then often have to be held back because of lack of money and qualified staff.[14] These examples and others that I shall recount in detail are sufficient to show the importance of the *organizational* factor in development.

A final problem, to which I shall return in detail in part 4, is the importance that must be given to the industries that sustain agriculture. In some, there have been serious disappointments, notably in the too slow progress of the chemical fertilizer industry. Besides these shortcomings in the planning process, there are others relating to the implementation of the plans, and it is here that the organizational factor is again of the utmost importance. To appreciate this it is relevant to examine the various technical measures taken to stimulate agricultural production. These result from the physical conditions of India and the habits of the farmers.

Natural Obstacles

For thousands of years Indian agriculture has had to face serious handicaps, most importantly a lack of steady and abundant water. The monsoon rains bestow their favors unevenly: on the western Ghats, Mahabaleshwar has an average rainfall of 6,750 mm., the whole of the Indian peninsula from 500 to 1,000 mm., and the Ganges basin from 750 to over 1,250 mm. The rain is distributed just as unevenly in time as it is in area. About 90 percent of it falls with the summer monsoon between June and October.[15] Irrigation is therefore vital: in some areas

[14] *The Third Plan: Mid-Term Appraisal*, p. 103.
[15] There is one notable exception—the Madras region, where the greatest rainfall comes with the autumn monsoon.

with low rainfall it can be the sole means of survival; in others it makes additional cultivation in the dry season possible; and it is an insurance against a scanty or late monsoon.

Indians had recourse to irrigation very early in their history. The canals that cut across the Cauvery delta in Madras go back at least to the glorious dynasty of Cholas (tenth to eleventh centuries), if not earlier. In the second half of the fourteenth century, Firoz Shah, the sultan of Delhi, cut four canals in the Punjab, and the British later completed extensive canal systems in the north, in Sind, and in the southern deltas.

But water, so necessary to life, can also be a peril to life, with years of drought alternating with years of devastating floods. Owing to slight differences in river levels which impede drainage, heavy monsoons can wreak havoc. The Ganges, for example, 1,600 kilometers from the sea, is at an altitude of 150 meters. Thus, measures have to be taken to regulate the flow of rivers and to control their excesses by dams or bunds.

After water comes the problem of soils. Thanks to irrigation, comparatively new alluvial soil can stand a great deal of harvesting: this applies to the Ganges basin, the Coromandel deltas, and the western coastal areas. Other stretches of land, however, are composed of poor soil which has been worn away by an often galloping erosion and dried up through the disappearance of forests. This kind of soil is typical in tropical agriculture, and it covers a large part of the Deccan [16] which in several respects resembles the no less poor lands of the African continent. Certainly this land can be improved, but it can never be made rich.

Man's Behavior

Although the agriculture of India has not reached the high level of Chinese agriculture, it occupies a reputable place among underdeveloped countries. Nor have the techniques of farming remained as static and old-fashioned as might be thought at first sight. In several areas the farmers seem dynamic and ready to adopt new techniques; long before the Five-Year Plans they had improved their irrigation systems and were often using as much manure as they could. But because of the increasing density of the rural population in many districts in the nineteenth century, there was an ever growing need for more intensive cultivation, which was by no means fulfilled in many areas.

[16] The western area of the Deccan where one finds the black soils or *regar* is much more fertile than other parts.

The perplexing question of how to employ and feed the surplus population has thus grown more and more urgent. There has been a large increase in the number of towns—that is, a greater concentration of people in formerly country areas—but the cities and industries are unable to absorb the surplus of rural population.

Two remedies present themselves: the development of new land, and an increased yield per hectare already under cultivation. Since the sparsely populated or underpopulated regions are often regions of poor and not easily irrigated soils, it seems unlikely that there will be long-term strides in the development of new land, even though appreciable gains have been realized so far. Higher yields, on the other hand, give cause for more hope. Here, the differences between the states are striking. In 1955/56 the average rice yield for the whole of India was 850 kg/ha; for Bihar it was 520; for Uttar Pradesh, 700. For wheat, the average national yield was 725 kg/ha; in the Punjab the yield reached 900 kg/ha.[17] One must note, however, that compared with some other Asian countries, notably China, these figures are low. An increase of 50 to 100 percent is not, therefore, an ideal or vain hope, but a reasonable goal well within the scope of achievement—if, that is, certain decisive improvements can be made, none demanding fundamental changes in techniques and social structures.

Hydraulic Policy

The Five-Year Plans make a distinction between minor irrigation, which is carried out mainly by the states, medium irrigation (with each project costing anywhere between one and fifty million rupees), and the major irrigation projects, which are carried out jointly by the central government and the states. By the end of the First Plan, in 1955, the situation could be broken down as shown on the table on p. 26.[18] Roughly 20 percent of the land under cultivation is irrigated, and about 15 percent has double cropping. Ultimately, it should be possible to irrigate by the various means, large and small, 70 million hectares. This would double the amount of land that could bear two or more crops a year.

Twenty or thirty years, at least, would elapse before such a program would be complete and effective, but its fulfillment would without doubt give the rural population, not abundance, but moderate comfort. By this I mean a standard of living that would certainly be frugal,

[17] H. R. Arakeri et al., Soil Management in India (Bombay, 1962), pp. 286, 313.
[18] Third Five Year Plan, p. 381.

Total area	324 million ha.
Total area of arable land	190
Total area of cultivated land	127
Total area of land cultivated more than once a year	18
(Total area cultivated: 145 million ha., including double cropping.)	
Area irrigated:	
by state canals	7.92 million ha.
by private canals	1.36
by tanks	4.36
by wells (including tube-wells)	6.68
by other means	2.16
Area irrigated more than once	2.80
Total area irrigated	25.28 million ha.

but from which the most serious deficiencies would have been eliminated, even when taking into account the increase in population.

In the Second and Third Plans the major and medium irrigation projects absorbed 9 percent of the investments of the public sector against 11 percent (Second Plan) and 14 percent (Third Plan) for agriculture including minor irrigation.[19] We shall see from several examples how slowly minor irrigation has progressed, while major and medium projects have advanced at an even less satisfying pace.

Projects like the network coming from the Bhakra Dam (Punjab), by the Damodar Valley Corporation (D.V.C.), and the Hirakud Dam (Orissa) should each irrigate several hundred thousand hectares, if not more. Now, it is not only a case of building a dam and digging several large canals. One must also provide for the branch canals that lead to the fields. Farmers must in certain cases be persuaded to move to new, virgin land, and they must adapt themselves to a system of irrigated cultivation, learning to use the water in the right way. In short, quite apart from the cost of these large schemes, the resulting production must be *organized;* the fact that the complexity of this organization has often been underestimated has led to numerous delays.

A detailed study of the Hirakud Dam, entitled *The Economics of a Multiple-Purpose River Dam,* reveals several weaknesses in administration that could have been avoided. What is most striking is the extraordinary slowness of irrigation projects. As the report says (p. 137), "An irrigation system takes twenty to twenty-five years to come to full maturity when its benefits are at the maximum level." [20]

[19] *Ibid.,* p. 58.
[20] It is ironic that one of the few districts in which there were authenticated cases of death due to starvation in 1966 was Sambalpur, at the foot of the Hirakud Dam.

Despite the disappointing results of the major irrigation projects so far, it is possible that within the next few years the projects will begin to prove their value. Following preliminary research for the Fourth Plan, 1966–1971, it has been proposed that no new irrigation construction should be undertaken, but that the 540 major and medium projects put into operation from 1951 onward [21] should be completed. This alone is a challenge, since the program has been a heavy one, burdened by continual delays.

In 1961, the planners estimated that by 1966 the cumulative new potential of irrigation achieved since 1951 should be 10 million hectares, out of which 9 million should be utilized. In 1966, the achievements were estimated at 7.2 and 5.5 million hectares, respectively. The particularly wide gap between potential and utilization indicates some serious problems in planning and implementation—a point that the authors of the *Fourth Plan* frankly concede (see pp. 216–217).

Fertilizers

After irrigation, fertilizers constitute another imperative which is closely linked to the first, for, in fact, chemical fertilizers often have little effect, and are sometimes completely ineffective, if the fields lack water.

For want of adequate statistics on organic manure, let us look at the progress of chemical fertilizers:

	Consumption in Tons (production and imports)			
	1950/51	*1955/56*	*1960/61*	*1965/66 (Targets)*
Nitrogenous fertilizers (in terms of N)	55,000	105,000	193,000	1,000,000
Phosphatic fertilizers (in terms of P_2O_5)	7,000	—	70,000	400,000
Potassic fertilizers (in terms of K_2O)	—	—	25,000	200,000

SOURCE: *Third Five Year Plan.* pp. 35, 37, 311.

Notwithstanding the appreciable increases in percentages, the total figures for 1961 were extremely low for a country the size of India. Furthermore, goals for the Third Plan were far from met. In the last year of the Plan, 1965–1966, the consumption of chemical fertilizers was as follows:

[21] *Overseas Hindustan Times,* Nov. 5, 1964.

Nitrogenous (N)	600,000 tons
Phosphatic (P_2O_5)	150,000
Potassic (K_2O)	90,000

It should be noted that the distribution of chemical fertilizers is carried out almost exclusively through government channels and their dependent organizations such as development blocks and cooperatives.

Other Techniques of Agronomy

On a limited basis, India has been attempting to supplement its program of irrigation and fertilizers with other techniques of agronomy long in use in the West. In areas made desolate by erosion, such as the Deccan, or threatened by erosion, contour farming programs are underway. At the block level, work has been done to introduce the farmers to the Japanese high-yield method of growing rice and to more effective methods for wheat. Hybrid varieties of maize are being grown, and efforts are being made to see that local seeds generally are replaced by selected varieties that give a higher yield—in wheat, cotton, and rice. The blocks distribute the seeds, often on credit.

The blocks are also encouraging the use of pesticides, and in some cases the village panchayats collaborate by buying a sprayer. In some areas, too, collective or private measures are being used to protect crops from other pests such as rats, sparrows, and even monkeys.[22]

This survey of techniques and methods constitutes the essential recommendations that any agronomist would make in a tropical country. What matters most for our purposes is how these measures are put into practice, and what results they have. How do those responsible for carrying them out behave, and in what order of priority and urgency does one place these means of progress? Problems of organization, coordination, and subordination arise in each of the different administrative services. How can they be solved? Finally, what are the reactions of the farmers to these changes, and what are the possibilities for progress?

[22] On this last point the Hindu's attitude differs widely in each region. Professor J. L. Chambard tells of the systematic extermination of monkeys in the village of Sirsod, Madhya Pradesh. Elsewhere people are content merely to chase them away, and in some regions they remain taboo.

4

THE BASIS OF
AGRICULTURAL POLICY

The development of Indian agriculture depends on a broad program that falls into three main divisions. After the technical measures already mentioned, these are: the proper kind of agrarian reforms, and the way in which these and the consequent alterations to the legal framework are carried out; and the introduction of new political, administrative, and social structures to encourage the peasant to raise his standard of living.

Even before Independence the Congress party had made a study of these problems. As early as 1931 it drew up an economic program, and in 1936 it prepared an agrarian program. In 1937, when the party constituted the government of several provinces, it took a certain number of concrete measures. The agrarian program of 1947 therefore did not spring *ex nihilo*. Besides, in several provinces the British had even in the nineteenth century begun to pass laws giving some protection to the tenants.

Agrarian Reforms

Agrarian reform has been left to the discretion of the various states, which can create their own legislation, taking into account local conditions as well as possible suggestions from New Delhi. Immediately after Independence the broad lines of agrarian reform were laid down by the central committee of the Congress party, by a decision taken in November, 1947; it was recommended that each state should adapt these broad lines to suit its own conditions and needs.[1] In 1950, after a slow start, often delayed by vested interests, the agrarian laws began to be passed, marking the beginning of an exceedingly large amount of legislative work which is not yet completed today.

Let me select the principle directives from an almost superabundance of texts:

[1] Remember that at that time, power lay with Congress as much in New Delhi as in the states.

(1) Abolition of the *zamindari* system, a form of property ownership predominant in the Ganges basin which has spread into certain southern regions (see chap. 6).

(2) Regulation of different types of tenure and tenancy in order to protect those who cultivate land for somebody else.

(3) The imposition of a ceiling to property with a redistribution of the surplus to those who own none.

(4) Restrictions on moneylending and an attempt to regulate rural credit.

(5) Protection of landless laborers by introduction of minimum wages.

Later, we shall see the effect of these measures "in the field." For the moment let us restrict ourselves to noting that the abolition of the zamindari system has unquestionably produced some positive results. Item 4 has been achieved in part, less by legal provision than by the extension of credit cooperatives. Item 3 has remained only theoretical in many states, and as for 2 and 5, the laws had varying effects depending on the degree of implementation or other circumstances related to economic growth.

Given the existing social and political conditions of India, agrarian legislation could have only a limited impact on production and social structure; this has encouraged the left wing of the Congress party to reopen the whole issue of agrarian policy.

Community Projects

On October 2, 1952, an experiment was begun which, eleven years afterward, had spread to nearly the whole of the country: it took the form of community projects by which the peasants were encouraged to improve their standard of living.

It is important to distinguish the undercurrent of ideas, both Indian and foreign, that inspired this movement. The history of the early experiments is set out in two brochures published by the Ministry of Community Development: *The Evolution of the Community Development Programme in India* and *The Scope of Extension.* One of the earliest projects was that of Rabindranath Tagore, launched in 1922 in the Bengal village of Surul, near Sriniketan, with the help of a young Englishman, M. Helmhirst, who had been trained in the United States. About the same time Dr. Spencer Hatch of the Y.M.C.A. started a similar project in the extreme south at Travancore. A third was undertaken by F. L. Brayne, Deputy Commissioner,[2] in Gurgaon dis-

[2] A high-ranking official in charge of a district, called elsewhere collector or district magistrate.

trict, Punjab. Other movements were begun later in the state of Baroda, owing to the initiative of an Indian, V. T. Krishnamachari, who later became vice-chairman of the Planning Commission. In 1946 the Madras government (composed of Indians) put the final touches to the Firka development program. Finally, shortly after Independence, thanks to the initiative of S. K. Dey (until 1966 Minister of Community Development) the Nilokheri Center in the Punjab was established for the purpose of resettling refugees from West Pakistan.

The launching in 1948 of the pilot project in Etawah (a district in Uttar Pradesh) represents the final stage of these experiments; it was now possible to elaborate the pattern, making it applicable to the whole country. Some young and very able Indian civil servants worked in conjunction with an American, Albert Mayer, whose arrival, to borrow D. P. Singh's words, served to act as a "catalyst by bringing together the divergent ideas and elements." [3]

The dominant idea of American origin is that of extension or the spreading of knowledge to agriculturalists. This method was given a considerable stimulus at the time of President Roosevelt's New Deal. V. T. Krishnamachari defines it in an Indian context: "Extension is a continuous process intended to make the peasants aware of their problems by showing them ways and means of solving them."

The aims are threefold: (a) material: increased production: (b) educational: improving techniques and encouraging peasants to change their "traditional static" attitude into one that is "scientific and dynamic"; (c) social and cultural: developing the community spirit and strengthening cooperatives, panchayats (village councils), and youth clubs. [4]

One should keep in mind the two basic characteristics of the program: the use of education as part of the *means,* and the *multipurpose approach* which takes into considerattion economic, social, and psychological problems. This latter principle is derived from the following reasoning: "The peasant's life is not cut into segments in the way the Government's activities are apt to be; the approach to the villager has, therefore, to be a coordinated one and has to comprehend his whole life." [5]

The present program of community development is essentially the same as the one first set up at Etawah. All the districts are divided into development blocks, each of which consists of a group of 60 to 100

[3] For this quotation and the facts mentioned above, see *The Evolution of the Community Development Programme in India* (1963).

[4] *The Scope of Extension* (1962).

[5] *First Five Year Plan,* p. 223.

villages with a total population of 60,000 to 100,000 inhabitants. A Block Development Officer (B.D.O.) is in charge of a staff of specialists (extension officers) —an agriculture officer, veterinary and health officers, and officials in charge of cooperatives, with one person being responsible in each of these fields. The person ultimately responsible for liaison and for stimulating and supervising the work carried out is the gram sewak (village-level worker), who is in charge of five to ten villages. Like the B.D.O., he is frequently a "generalist" working with the specialists of the block.

The basic principle at all levels is to help the farmers to help themselves. As *The Scope of Extension* points out (p. 5), the aim is not for the government to direct the work, but rather for it to delegate authority to local leaders. Of course, only democratic methods are recognized: "There must be neither coercion nor forced persuasion" (p. 6). It is only by winning the peasants' confidence that the instructors and other block officials can fulfill their functions (p. 15).

Experiments carried out before and after Independence have been remarkably successful. In every region affected, the material conditions of the peasants have improved, great progress has been made in yields per hectare, and certain defects in the social organization have been eliminated. It would appear that the success of the Etawah experiment has been to some extent an incentive to setting agriculture free and to achieving an accelerated rate of growth.

By October, 1952, a total of 55 regions and 27,388 villages (16.7 million inhabitants) were covered by the community projects.[6] By the spring of 1956, at the end of the First Five-Year Plan, these figures had risen to 140,000 villages (77.5 million inhabitants).[7] In 1956 it was envisaged that the whole of rural India would be incorporated in the scheme by the end of the Second Plan, but this achievement was delayed until October, 1963.

From 1957–1958 onward, it was possible to see evidence of the first results. The combination of governmental services and evaluation missions, both foreign and native, brought to light serious defects. The results are not entirely negative, but the program is far behind the original schedule. As we have seen, agricultural production does not move forward in a regular rhythm. With his customary lucidity, Dr. J. P. Bhattacharjee recalls that in 1956 and 1957 one could see in the village communities "a trend to give more emphasis to social programs than to agricultural production."[8] Nor can it be said that the success

[6] The Ford Foundation made a grant of $1,200,000 in addition to providing the help of experts.

[7] *Review of the First Five Year Plan*, pp. 109–110.

[8] "Community Development Programme and the Approach to Agriculture Extension," *Kurukshetra*, October, 1962.

of community development in certain areas has stimulated a mass effort or even one of popular initiative; the program has indeed in this sense failed to achieve its principal objective. In addition, the organization and functioning of the blocks have revealed serious gaps. "We repeatedly heard complaints that the fixing of targets had been arbitrary and unrealistic. . . . A serious cause for dislocation of work and consequent waste is the delay in the issue of financial sanctions." [9]

In 1957 an interesting change took place: *the simultaneous attack* of every social and economic aspect of community development began to be questioned. At its sixth meeting in 1957 at Mussoree, the Conference of Development Commissioners decided that the gram sewaks should devote 70 to 80 percent of their time to agriculture. The *Mehta Report* in 1957 (I, 125) confirms this reorientation: "The emphasis should shift without delay to the more demanding aspects of economic development and the priorities as between the different activities should be: supply of drinking water, improvement of agriculture and animal husbandry, cooperative activities, rural industries, and health, followed by all others." The conclusions of a mission of experts from the United Nations (1958–1959) are more explicit: "Above all, the community development programme of India must put priority during the forthcoming years on increasing agricultural production. The situation seems to be more serious than realized a few years ago." [10] The Ford Foundation comes to the same conclusion in its report. It advocates a more distinct concentration on the part of the block toward productive activities.

The recognition of an order of priorities gradually made headway in New Delhi as well as in the state capitals. But this was not the case at village and block level, and the question recurred again and again. In 1963, at the annual conference on community development and the Panchayati Raj, a study group was set up for the purpose of making proposals for the improvement in the working of blocks and panchayats conditional upon an effective priority being given to programs of agricultural production.

The position at the end of 1964 can be summed up as follows: The original tenets of community development have been partly revised; and an order of priority in favor of agricultural production has indeed been established, but has its importance been sufficiently underlined?

[9] *Reports of the Team for the Study of Community Projects and National Extension Service*, abridged in the *Mehta Report* in the name of the president of the group, I (1957), 24–25. This report is particularly important, for it suggests modifications to the system while at the same time proposing to launch a new movement, the Panchayati Raj.

[10] *Report of a Community Development Evaluation Mission in India* (New York, 1959), p. 47.

On page 93 of the *Guide to Community Development* of 1962 we read that the means of agricultural production must be the first concern. On the other hand, the same guide begins by saying (p.1) : "The community development programme was outlined by the Planning Commission in the first three Five-Year Plans as essential for the improvement of all phases of village life." We look in vain in the first chapter for a clear indication of an order of priorities and of a modification of the initial strategy.

The Panchayati Raj

The Panchayati Raj [11] is an attempt to restore and extend the activities of the old village councils, or panchayats. It is both an outcome of a long evolutionary process as well as a way of remedying the weaknesses of community development. The scheme was first proposed in the *Mehta Report,* which evaluated the work of the blocks, and it amounted to a complete remodeling of the political and administrative organization at district level.

The British sought gradually to fill the administrative gap in the villages. In 1870, the first district local funds committees were set up in certain provinces; these were formed by local leaders nominated by the government. In 1882 Lord Ripon proposed his resolution, still famous today, on the principle of local self-government. It opened the door to the establishment of district boards elected partly by limited suffrage and partly by government nomination. In this connection Lord Ripon writes: "It is not, primarily, with a view to improvement in administration that this measure is put forward . . . It is chiefly desirable as an instrument of political and popular education." [12] The movement finally reached the village level and in the 1920's several provinces adopted legislation that gave powers—albeit very modest—to the panchayats, particularly in connection with petty litigation and the levying of minor taxes. (It must be specified that the traditional panchayats existed only within the caste framework; see Glossary.)

Immediately before and after Independence new laws increased the panchayat's powers and functions. When the Constitution was being drawn up, the extent of these powers became a matter of some debate. Mahatma Gandhi and several Congress members would have liked to give an important place to the panchayats, but largely owing to the

[11] *Panchayat:* council of five (originally, these councils only had five members) ; *raj:* reign.

[12] Quoted in *Report of the Committee on Democratic Decentralisation* (Bombay, 1961) , p. 9.

influence of Dr. Ambedkar, one of the chief authors of the Constitution, their powers were kept fairly limited. Article 40 simply mentions that "the state (province) will take measures to organise village panchayats and to give them the powers and authority necessary to enable them to function autonomously." [13]

The question came up again in 1957 with the publication of the *Mehta Report*. When the report was adopted several months later it set in motion a ground swell that is still shaking the rural areas. Every state decided to promote legislation and to create the means of assuring the efficient functioning of the Panchayati Raj. The district board was replaced by a new council, *zila parishad,* which was given more power. The village councils, *gaon panchayat,* were given considerably wider responsibilities than before. In addition, a change of form took place in that the block was headed by a council, *samiti* block, in which the majority of the powers were concentrated.[14] As the system now functions, the gaon panchayat is elected by universal suffrage except for the seats "reserved" for the ex-untouchables; the samiti block consists of the presidents of the panchayats, and the zila parishad is composed of the presidents of the samitis, and in certain states of members of the Parliament and Legislative Assembly.

The basic principle of the Panchayati Raj is to give the council powers which restrict the authority of the administration. Traditionally, the district magistrate played a predominant role. As part of the elite cadre of the Indian Civil Service (I.C.S.) under the British and of the Indian Administrative Service (I.A.S.) today, he retained wide powers of action, being responsible in practice for all district affairs. Now the district magistrate has to reckon with his council and local political forces. At block level, the B.D.O. (Block Development Officer) has become the executive officer of the samiti, and he is tied to its rules.

What is the purpose of this highly significant change? Under the Panchayati Raj, India now has an administrative machinery that restricts both the responsibilities and the functions of the old administration. The reasons for this change are not all clear, though a few hints are evident in the texts. According to the *Mehta Report* (I, 25) the masses were apathetic toward community development because it

[13] Dr. Ambedkar's lack of enthusiasm was no doubt due to the fact that, as a former untouchable, he feared that granting further power to the panchayats would only help to increase the ascendancy of the upper castes over village life.
[14] Terminology differs in certain states. I have chosen the most widespread expressions. Maharashtra and Gujarat have adopted another system in which the zila parishad is the principal body. Its composition, like that of the samiti, differs from the general pattern.

had been imposed from above and often with little understanding. It is imperative for the villages to have the means of directing their own social and economic affairs. This argument is consistent with a broad current of opinion prevalent in several underdeveloped countries. It means in fact the establishment of a dual movement coming from below as well as from above—an aspect of development that had been partly overlooked.[15] (Here again one is reminded of China, where the same sort of concern helped to create the people's communes.)

The desirability of this dual current is perfectly legitimate; it is only the ways and means of bringing it about that are open to discussion. Returning to the argument of the *Mehta Report,* we see that the Panchayati Raj must boost the activities of community development, in particular its weakest point, agricultural production. Logically, the first aim of the Panchayati Raj ought therefore to be to emphasize activities concerned with production. Now not only does the report not specifically make this correlation but it is still less evident in laws passed by the majority of the states, which show no trace of a new inspiration driving people toward increased production.

As we shall see in detail later on, neither in the new laws passed by the states nor in the minds of the people themselves was there any determination to solve the problems of lagging production. Both the government and the legislators seemed in fact to be acting more for political concerns than for purely economic considerations.[16] The new administrative structures, going beyond the expressed objectives of the *Mehta Report,* were designed in part as a safety valve to control the demands of the peasants, who are emerging from their old isolation and becoming more politically conscious. Some read newspapers written in the vernacular language, and they want to express their needs and state their claims. The Panchayati Raj is a means of channeling these forces within the bounds of the various councils and giving those elected an opportunity to take an active part in local affairs. It is also evident that the Congress party, whose popularity showed signs of waning, may have hoped to strengthen its position by capturing council memberships.[17]

Obviously, since these arguments are based on unofficial, very fragmentary information, I cannot endorse them unreservedly. It is not certain whether they had any influence on the original drafting of the

[15] See Ursula Hicks, *Development from Below* (Oxford, 1961).

[16] The indifference of some politicians to agricultural problems is indicative of the situation; see chap. 26.

[17] It was rather naïve to hope, as some people did, that the Panchayati Raj could remain outside politics. See *Indian Journal of Public Administration,* VIII: 4 (1962), for contradictory articles dealing with this as well as other problems.

Mehta Report, but it is perfectly clear that they had considerable influence upon its fuller, final shape and content.

The Cooperatives

In the second half of the nineteenth century the British authorities began to give their attention to the peasants' indebtness. Commissions of inquiry agreed on the need to allow adequate means of credit to farmers, and after 1871 a certain number of Taccavi Acts—that is, government loan acts—were passed. At about the same time, the rise of the cooperative movement in Europe (Schulz–Pelitzsch, Raiffeisen in Germany, the people's bank Luzzati in Italy) attracted the attention of British administrators. Shortly before the end of the century the Madras government sent an official to study cooperatives in Europe, and similar studies were carried out in northern India. These investigations led to the introduction in 1904 of the cooperative system in India by means of the Cooperative Credit Societies Act. Most of the provinces legislated accordingly, and in several regions, particularly Maharashtra, credit societies were established.

Progress was slow: in 1951 cooperatives secured only 3.1 percent of the rural credit; government loans were represented by the same percentage, with the overwhelming majority of credit coming from professional moneylenders or relatives and friends.[18] Finally, after the launching of the Second Five-Year Plan, the cooperative idea began to grow, following the concept of the socialist pattern of society: "The character of economic development in India with its emphasis on social change, therefore, provides a great deal of scope for the organisation of co-operative activity." [19]

The cooperative system has several aspects: on the one hand we find credit, marketing, and processing, combined or not in the same society; on the other hand there are the cooperative farms—producer cooperatives—where the land is cultivated jointly. The first group of cooperatives have the approval of the majority of public opinion in India, for they are one of the essential agents to agricultural development. Similarly, such cooperatives had much to do with the rise of Danish agriculture in the nineteenth century, or—a closer comparison—with the growth of agriculture in Japan since 1945.

In India, there are still far fewer credit cooperatives than conditions require, but the number and membership have grown steadily:

[18] *Sahakari Samaj,* p. 25.
[19] *Second Five Year Plan,* p. 221.

Year	Number of Primary Agricultural Credit Societies	Membership (in millions)	Short- and Medium-term Loans (in millions of rupees)
1950/51	104,998	4.4	229
1960/61	210,000	17.0	2,000
1965/66	208,000	24.0	4,000 *

SOURCES: *Third Five Year Plan*, p. 204, and *Fourth Five Year Plan*, *A Draft Outline*, pp. 136-138.

* If one includes all short- and medium-term loans granted within the cooperative sector, this figure becomes 6,500.

The cooperative farms gave rise to lively controversy. The official argument observed that about 30 percent of the farmers owned less than 0.4 hectare (one acre) of land, which was generally cultivated on an uneconomic basis; by grouping themselves together, but without giving up any of their property rights, the farmers could increase their productivity. In this way the government would be killing two birds with one stone: social differences would be reduced, and production would be increased. At first this argument met little opposition, but there was evidence of discontent during the Nagpur session of the Congress party in 1959. A resolution was passed calling for the speedy adoption of laws fixing a ceiling on landholdings and handing over the surplus to small holders and agricultural workers to cultivate in cooperatives.

Despite opposition, the government encouraged cooperative farms, though without much conviction. The Third Plan foresaw in each district the formation of a pilot block for such undertakings: "These pilot projects would demonstrate the advantages of cooperative farming to the farmers and act as catalytic agents for further expansion." [20] Clearly, there was no question of resorting to compulsion or to direct pressure. The state confined itself to granting several additional advantages so far as the conditions of loans were concerned, but decisions about their use remained with the farmers.

In 1960, some 1,600 cooperative farms and nearly 900 collective farms were in existence. According to plan,[21] the former should have increased by 3,200 units between 1960 and 1966, but in fact the movement remains limited and cannot be said to have had any marked influence on production. Of some 5,000 societies established between 1961 and 1966, many are hardly working and must be strengthened in order to be at all effective.[22] One nevertheless comes across some

[20] *Sahakari Samaj*, pp. 103–104. We shall see whether this hope has in fact been borne out.

[21] *Ibid.*, p. 105.

[22] See *Fourth Plan*, pp. 143–144.

pockets of successful endeavor in a few districts like Dhulia and Sangli (Maharashtra) and Sambalpur (Orissa).

The Package Program

The report of the Ford Foundation (1959) which has already been mentioned contained several concrete suggestions that were accepted by the government and included in the Third Plan. All these suggestions grew out of the emphasis on an order of priorities which was designed to increase production, particularly within certain key regions. The aim was to concentrate financial resources and administrative machinery on areas that were most likely to make fast and relatively easy progress. The criteria for the selection of these areas were simple: (1) guaranteed irrigation; (2) a minimum of obstacles needing long-term remedies (dangers of flood, acute erosion, and so on; (3) relatively advanced institutions (cooperatives and panchayats); (4) a good potential for speedy progress. Following these criteria, sixteen districts were chosen as the first experimental field (seven to begin with, then nine others).

The novelty of this scheme lies in its pragmatic nature. There are no great principles, merely two fundamental rules: (a) to seek efficiency in general; and (b) to seek efficiency in particular in the most favorable conditions, that is to say in regions where chances of immediate success are greatest, deferring until a later date the attack on major obstacles. But though the scheme is desirable from an economic point of view, it conflicts with certain ideals of Indian planning. The majority of the chosen districts are rich (they have good irrigation and are fairly protected from natural calamities). Offhand, it might seem fairer to reduce the gaps by selecting poor districts, but we shall see later on how illusory such a notion can be.

As for results, the experiment is still too new and too limited to have had any noticeable effect on India as a whole, but its influence can be seen in the way in which the sense of priorities and of choice is becoming stronger and is spreading beyond the districts included in the program. Since 1964, the scheme has been applied to a limited extent in several other districts besides the original sixteen.

The Bhoodan

This chapter would be incomplete if we failed to mention the *Bhoodan* movement—donations of land—which was launched in 1951 by the chief disciple of Gandhi, Vinoba Bhave. Inspired by the ideals and

methods of the Mahatma, Vinoba goes around the countryside on foot
urging the farmers who are rich or reasonably well off to give part of
their land to those who are poor. Since 1957 the movement has been
carried on in the somewhat different form of *Gramdan* (village donations). Vinoba wishes the farmers to renounce the larger part of their
lands in favor of their villages so that lands would be cultivated by the
whole community.

"If a landowner refuses to give, even after he has fully understood
our purpose, we will harbor no resentment against him, for we are sure
that he will give it one day; in other words, once the seed has been
sown it will bear fruit sooner or later." [23] This quotation is typical of
the feeling and spirit that Vinoba has sought to inject into the rural
areas: following the example of Gandhi in his struggle against the British, he believes that by dint of generosity and patience he will triumph
in the end.

Vinoba Bhave began his activity in the region that had just been
badly shaken by the Communist uprising of 1948, Telingana, in Hyderabad. He helped to bring about peace between the rural proletariat
and the landowners who had been dispossessed by the short-lived
village soviets and were intent upon getting back their land. On the
national scale, however, the movement has met with only limited
success. In 1961 Vinoba had secured 1.76 million hectares, of which
only 360,000 had been effectively distributed.[24] Moreover, some of this
land was of very poor quality and there were legal disputes over other
parts. I have no recent figures on the Gramdan, but it seems to be
making very slow progress.

As a symbolic, moral force, Vinoba Bhave's action cannot be over-
looked. On the practical side, however, its results are questionable.
Although Gandhi's ideals were a powerful force for the liberation of
India, they cannot have the same bearing on the agricultural develop-
ment of such a vast country. For this reason, few Indians see the
Bhoodan and the Gramdan as the key to the problem.

*   *   *

During the period from 1951 to 1966 it was inevitable that experiments would not always be successful and that hopes would at times be
unfulfilled; it would have taken supermen, free from all political ties,
to find the right answer straightaway. Nevertheless one wonders
whether it might not have been possible to stick to a more precise
policy instead of steering first in one direction and then in another.

[23] *Bhoodan Yajn̄a*, p. 7.
[24] *Third Five Year Plan*, p. 376.

The First Plan staked itself upon community development, but the inadequacies of this system led to new solutions being widely propounded; first cooperative farming, then the Panchayati Raj. Such changes were perhaps bound to lead to some confusion and dispersal of forces at the operational level, when it would have been preferable to plot and follow one course only, merely adjusting the steering as necessary.

Gradually there emerged the idea of putting efficiency above everything else within the framework of the intensive program and its extensions. What is essential now is that this realistic view should spread, so as to eliminate once and for all the temptation to succumb to the proposals of reckless escapists or devotees of failure—such proposals (often from influential persons) as a re-examination of the issues of agrarian reform, or the inflation of the powers of the panchayats by changing the Constitution.[25] The facts revealed in parts 2 and 3 of this book rule out any illusions of this sort as an answer to India's food problem.

[25] See, for example, the resolution adopted by the All-Indian Panchayat Parishad, *Times of India,* July 19, and 21, 1964.

PART II

Uttar Pradesh

5

UTTAR PRADESH

Uttar Pradesh is composed of three quite separate regions: the Himalayan districts, part of Bundelkhand (the Vindhya Mountains), and the Ganges basin and that of its principal tributary, the Jumna.

The first region is of limited interest: it has an economy typical of a mountain area with soil that is on the whole suitable for cultivation only in the heart of the valleys and on the easy sloping gradients. Because there is not sufficient work for the entire population, many people are forced to seek employment outside the area, either in the towns or in the army.

The four Bundelkhand districts consist of wooded hills, plateaus that are not very productive, belts of land that are fertile when irrigated, and plains south of the Jumna. The possibilities for expansion are relatively limited.

The third region is by far the most interesting. Here people have lived and cultivated the land for thousands of years; it covers forty-three of the fifty-four districts and has 67 million inhabitants out of a total of 74 million (1961 census). The horizon is uninterrupted from its western boundaries as far as Benares in the east; it is a vast plain upon which the large clumps of mango trees and pipals outside every village make but little impression. The density of the population varies from 200 to 600 per square kilometer; thus everywhere the region is thickly populated and often overwhelmingly so.

Owing to its natural resources, Uttar Pradesh has until now concentrated mainly on agriculture, but it is certain that the industrial sector could be developed by attracting the manufacture of consumer goods and by encouraging the industries that process the local raw materials (sugar refineries, textile mills). On the other hand, there is an absence of minerals, which are salient features of West Bengal, Bihar, Orissa, and Madhya Pradesh [1] and are essential for heavy industry.

[1] There are areas rich in minerals (iron, coal, manganese) where iron and steel works of considerable variety and plants manufacturing heavy machinery have been set up.

Planning and Development

Between 1951 and 1956 [2] any planning was of a very improvised
nature, but the second plan set up new administrative machinery
which made work more constructive. An office directed by the development commissioner drew up plans in collaboration with the departments concerned.[3] Numerous discussions took place with the Planning
Commission in New Delhi before the full program was finally elabo-
rated. The program was then carried out on an annual basis, and was
incorporated into the budget accepted by the Legislative Assembly
(Vidhan Sabha) before the beginning of the financial year (April 1 to
March 31).

The successive plans of Uttar Pradesh (public sector) cover the
main aspects of economic and social life. The item dealing with the
agricultural program includes production, minor irrigation, soil conservation, animal husbandry, distribution of milk, forests, fisheries,
silos, and commercial agricultural structures. The other sectors come
within the same department: cooperatives, community development,
and panchayats. Major and medium irrigation, flood control, and
power are included in another department. Then come industries
(major, medium, and artisan) and mines, transport and communications, social services including education, hygiene, and health, aid to
the underprivileged classes, and so on.

Whereas on the national scale the distribution of investments has
been variable, the three Uttar Pradesh plans were conceived with one
and the same idea, and were definitely geared to agricultural development:

Distribution of Investments, Public Sector
(in percentage)

	1st Plan	2nd Plan	3rd Plan
Agricultural program	17.6	14.11	17.54
Cooperatives, community development, panchayats	5.5	12.61	13.26
Irrigation and flood control	23.8	9.	10.
Power	15.2	22.	23.
Industries and mines	4.15	6.49	4.28
Transport and communications	4.47	6.81	6.15
Social services	29.17	27.12	24.85

The first plan pledged investments of 1,530 million rupees; the second,

[2] Several projects already on the point of becoming realized had been united and
coordinated.

[3] In the states the term department is used rather than ministry.

2,531 million, of which 2,230 million were in fact spent; the third, 5,022 million. The central government's contribution (loans and grants) amounted to 1,224 million for the second plan and 3,500 million for the third.[4]

The increase in investments was accompanied by more elaborate planning which sought to define and to isolate problems, encouraging the preparation of programs at district, block, and village level. As early as April 15, 1960, the development commissioner was sending detailed directives from Lucknow concerning ways and means of setting up local plans which were due to be put into execution in a year's time.

The Results

Several studies, in giving results attained since 1951, relate them to the general context of India. Reading the résumé of the report drawn up by Professor Baljit Singh [5] or the official document, the *Third Five Year Plan,* one finds the development disappointing. Despite the approximate nature of the statistics, they do show the main trends:

Index Number of Per Capita Income
(at 1948/49 prices)

Year	India	Uttar Pradesh
1951	100	100
1961	116.7	103.5

SOURCE: Uttar Pradesh, *Third Five Year Plan,* I, 3.

In 1951 the per capita income of Uttar Pradesh was 5 percent higher than the national average. In 1961 it was lower by 7 percent, a drop that is greatly accentuated by the difference in population figures: for India +21.5 percent, for Uttar Pradesh +16.6 percent between 1951 and 1961.

According to Professor Baljit Singh, the most serious failures occurred in the secondary and tertiary sections:

Progress, 1951–1961

	India	Uttar Pradesh
Agricultural production	37.1%	32.3 %
Mines and industries	48.8	4.3
Revenue from commerce and transport	52.5	23.14
Other services	81.5	2

[4] For these figures and the table, see Uttar Pradesh, *Third Five Year Plan,* I, 11, 19, 28–46.

[5] *Problems of Economic Development of U.P.*

Production in Uttar Pradesh (food grains)

1950/51	11.6 million tons
1955/56	11.9
1960/61	14.2

SOURCE: Uttar Pradesh, *Third Five Year Plan*, I, 21.

Since the prospects for heavy industrialization in Uttar Pradesh were relatively unfavorable, it might have been desirable—and perhaps possible—to exceed the national figure for agricultural development.

There are several reasons for this rather slow rate of progress. Private capital is less abundant in Uttar Pradesh than in the big centers of Calcutta, Bombay, and Madras. On the national scale the total amount of private investments was about 49,000 million for the first two plans; for Uttar Pradesh it could hardly have exceeded 3,000 million. The central government is in fact a little more generous with Uttar Pradesh than with the other states in its credits and grants, but the per capita investments there are the lowest in all India: for the Third Plan they amounted to 67.34 rupees per person (as compared with 72.47 in Bihar, 71.43 in West Bengal, and elsewhere 84.72, 100, 110.[6] These variations can be explained partly by the difference in natural resources of the various states and partly by differences in population density. And in population Uttar Pradesh by far exceeds all other states, with 74 million inhabitants. Bihar has 46.4 million, then there are four states with less than 40 million inhabitants, and four others with 20 to 30 million. In 1961, 17 percent of the total population of India was concentrated in Uttar Pradesh.

But lack of capital and heavy population do not explain everything. In official circles as well as in public opinion generally it is recognized that political instability has hindered development. We shall take up this point later on, after looking at its repercussions in the districts.[7]

So far as administration is concerned, Uttar Pradesh is hindered more than any other state by its size: it ranks first in terms of population, and fourth in terms of surface area (291,840 sq. km.). In smaller states like Madras, the secretary of the finance department also acts as the development commissioner and is responsible for planning: this simplifies the administrative work. In Uttar Pradesh the size of the tasks places such a burden on the administration as to risk the weakening of its efficiency. On several occasions consideration has been given

[6] Uttar Pradesh, *Third Five Year Plan*, I, 15.

[7] Until the end of 1954 the situation remained fairly stable thanks to the chief minister, Pandit Pant, a very able man with a great deal of influence, but he left Lucknow to become Home Minister in the central government. He died in 1961.

to the division of the territory into two states, but though this is rational as a technical proposition, it would be difficult to carry out from the political point of view.

The limited industrialization is due to more than these natural obstacles, however. The authorities could have shown more skill and dynamism in attracting factories from the private sector, as was done with such success by that other agricultural state, the Punjab. It must be remembered that, except for those in the west, the natives of Uttar Pradesh do not possess the enterprising spirit that is so characteristic of the Punjabis, who have always been ready to set up all manner of workshop or factory.

The irrigation policy in Uttar Pradesh has been the object of some justified criticism. Between 1951 and 1961 the amount of potentially irrigable land increased by 1.72 million hectares (600 million rupees' worth of investment), whereas the surface effectively irrigated remained almost constant, about 5.6 million hectares.[8] More striking results could have been achieved by extending minor irrigation.

A disturbing picture emerged both from conversations that I had in Lucknow (in September, 1963), and from reading official documents: the size of the problems, the natural factors, and the shortcomings of men all conspired to weave a tight web. The growth of investments provided for the third plan and the experience accumulated since 1951 should have led to a marked increase in the rates of growth, but as we shall see (chap. 17) the results obtained were disappointing, often far below those expected.

What is happening then to make progress today so difficult in this area which was once a veritable nursery for nationalist leaders?

Western and Eastern Uttar Pradesh

Before considering the Bulandshahr district in the west of Uttar Pradesh and that of Benares in the east, we must try to see them in relation to the rest of the state.

Bulandshahr is part of the progressive wing of Uttar Pradesh, that fringe of districts bordering on the Punjab.[9] This is a prosperous area (much more so than in the rest of the state) which for over a century has been engaged in a broad process of development. There is no overwhelming poverty, and irrigation is well advanced; the farmers are

---

[8] See Baljit Singh, *Problems of Economic Development of U.P.* This appraisal of the situation is perhaps a little severe; the official statistics show evidence of progress. One million out of 1.72 million hectares would be effectively irrigated.

[9] The other districts are Meerut, Muzaffarnagar, and Saharanpur.

closer in spirit to the active and forward-looking farmers of the Punjab [10] than they are to their eastern neighbors. Sugar cane is particularly important in comparison to the eastern districts, having higher yields and the advantage of better processing and marketing facilities.

In the interior of this area, Bulandshahr is making less progress than other districts, and certainly less than its neighboring district of Meerut. It is an illustration of the type of district that is forging ahead without achieving an exceptional rate of growth. Although available capital is less abundant, and there are fewer sugar mills than in most of the western region, its prosperity is still fairly high.

The central region of Uttar Pradesh occupies an intermediary position between the two extremes of the west and east. The economy progresses at a slow rate, the standard of living is only fair, although it is better than in the eastern districts, and the farmers do not possess the enterprising spirit of those in Bulandshahr.

From the point of view of the national plan, of course, Uttar Pradesh is an area where it is difficult to achieve high impetus, and it must be remembered that it is much hampered by the fifteen districts in the east [11] which slow down its general rate of progress. The population of these districts reaches 28.3 million, of which there are 2.2 million in the towns and 26.1 million in the rural areas. The average density per square kilometer is 300 as against 253 in the whole of the state. This criterion, as it is, can be misleading, for the Meerut district, which is just as heavily populated as Deoria, Benares, and Jaunpur, is developing very quickly. In fact, what really matters is not the average density of a district but its rural density. The latter is usually higher in the eastern districts because of a slower urbanization.[12]

In the east, the burden of high density of population is aggravated by the lack of land that can be brought under cultivation. In general, 80 percent of the arable land is already being farmed (for the Ballia district the figure is 92 percent). Irrigation is far from adequate, the techniques being less efficient than those of the west, and men lack not only capital but also a strong spirit of enterprise.

A study of one of these districts, Benares, will force us right to the heart of underdevelopment in its most bitter and disturbing aspects. Not only is the example chosen typical of eastern Uttar Pradesh, but

[10] The Indian Punjab had a deficit in cereals when its western districts, at the time of Independence, became Pakistani; today it has a surplus.

[11] These are the districts of Gorakhpur, Deoria, Basti, Azamgarh, Varanasi, Jaunpur, Ghazipur, Ballia, Pratapgarh, Sultanpur, Faizabad, Gonda, Bahraich, Mirzapur, and Allahabad.

[12] See *Census of India, 1961*, pp. 48, 52.

similar conditions of marginal progress overwhelmed by pressure of population also prevail in Bihar and, to a certain extent, in Bengal. Unemployment and underemployment, serious food shortages, exploitation which is sometimes plainly abusive of the Harijan (ex-untouchables) by the higher castes—all these are evils which the most far-seeing government, with twice the amount of highly efficient administration, would have difficulty in eliminating.

6

KHANDOÏ FROM 1860
TO THE PRESENT DAY

"This is an average sized village of ordinary appearance: to the south
the lands are good and temporary wells can be sunk in that direction
and there are some ten at work. To the north and east, however, the
soil is rather light and sandy and quite unirrigated. . . . There are 92
acres of culturable waste,[1] most of which is good and fit for immediate
cultivation. The cultivated and irrigated area has increased 47 acres
since the last settlement. I therefore depart very slightly from the value
opined at [unreadable] deduced rates and continue the *jamma* [tax] at
750 Rs. Enclusive the local cesses and the pay of one *chaukidar* [guard]
at Rs. 36– per annum." So Robert Kurrie, settlement officer, con-
cludes his report on Khandoï dated March 1, 1862.[2]

Khandoï's appearance had changed very little between the date of
Kurrie's visit and that of my arrival in September, 1963. Kurrie's
analysis of the soil is still perfectly valid. Like many of the villages
in the area, Khandoï is situated right in the middle of the fields which,
broken only by clumps of trees, stretch away in unrelieved flatness to
the horizon. Yet appearances are deceptive. Over the last century
profound changes have taken place which have affected the economic
stability and posed problems that formerly did not exist.

Population and Resources

The *First Settlement* and the census which has been carried out every
ten years since 1891 enable us to trace the curve of the population:

1861	451 inhabitants	1941	865 inhabitants
1891	506	1951	1,041
1921	731	1961	1,227 (density of 444
			inhabitants/sq. km.)

[1] In addition to the area already under cultivation.

[2] Extract from the report on the *First Settlement 1859–63*. Every thirty to forty
years the administration would make a new land assessment. Kurrie refers to an
earlier report which has since disappeared.

Growth was very slow in the nineteenth century, but progress gradually forced the pace of increase from 30 percent between 1891 and 1921 to 40 percent in the next thirty years. The 1951 rate marks the beginning of a new phenomenon: 18 percent in a single decade, though this was less than the national rate of +21 percent during the same decade, 1951–1961.

How did men react to this new phenomenon? The total area of the village and its fields had not changed for over a century. It measured 1,106 *bighas,* or 276 hectares, of which according to the *First Settlement* 228 hectares were under cultivation. About 37 hectares had been lying fallow, some for a longer time than others, and could have been cultivated. The amount of irrigated land *(abi)* covered 59 hectares, the method of irrigation being either by tanks *(talab)*, which store water from the monsoon, or more often by wells *(chahi)*.

The Second Settlement (1889), signed by T. Stocker, represents a turning point: forests and land lying fallow for a long period have disappeared, and all cultivable land has now been put to use; this amounts to 263 hectares. *The Third Settlement* (1916), signed Philips, shows signs of further progress: the amount of land under irrigation has reached 131 hectares—that is, 50 percent of the total area, which is a high percentage, since even today the national average is around 20 percent.

In 1962 the consolidation of holdings began (see chap. 7), and this enables us to get a more accurate picture of the situation.[3] The fields were measured again, and the quality of the soil and irrigated areas was re-evaluated. As a result, we have been able to draw up the following table:

Total area	276	ha.
Inhabited	8.5	
Area of unproductive soil (belonging to the village)	1.3	
Tanks	2.3	
Roads and footpaths	2.25	
Orchards	7.5	
Sown area	254.15	

The Khasra land records (a register that enumerates the plots in serial order) of 1963 show 192 hectares irrigated in the following ways:

[3] An accurate picture is almost impossible for villages where the agricultural map and registers do not correspond exactly to the situation in the village, let alone to the surrounding built-up areas.

by one electrically powered well
   (state tube-well)   67 ha.
by 3 wells worked by a motor
   pump (private tube-well)   47
by 26 wells with Persian wheels
   (*rahat*)   48
by the canal dating from the end
   of the last century   30

The state tube-well was constructed by the department of irrigation; the other tube-wells were the result of private effort, the first having been installed in 1949 by the ex-*lambardar* [4] of the village, one of the principal landowners. For forty years the inside and the curbstone of the wells have been made of stonework which ensures both efficiency and durability. At about the same time the Persian wheel replaced the less efficient system of the *mot* (see chap. 17).

Changes have taken place in the form of cultivation. After experiencing a considerable rise toward the middle of the nineteenth century, cotton gave way to sugar cane. The ex-lambardar Tez Pal Singh devotes to cotton only a quarter of the area given it by his grandfather (who, incidentally, lived through the Great Mutiny of 1857–1858). Cotton was not, apparently, well suited to the climate, and in any case sugar cane has a greater yield. At one time the peasants used only local varieties of cane which produced a poor yield, but toward the 1930's they began to use the improved varieties which were originally introduced with much success in Java and Sumatra, and were now being distributed to India by the agricultural services.

The peasants have a good and fairly varied stock of farm implements. Within living memory the plough has been reinforced with an iron nail. Likewise the seed-drill attached to the plough and drawn by a pair of bullocks dates back a long time. For many years they have used a chaff cutter worked by hand instead of the simple chopper which is still used elsewhere for cutting animal fodder.

The utility of cow dung is very well known. Part of it is used as manure on the fields, but a large proportion of animal dejection is used as fuel, since wood is scarce. The opening of the development block in 1954 brought about the introduction of chemical fertilizers.

With the extension of cultivation in the area, pasture land has practically ceased to exist; today Tez Pal Singh owns a dozen head of cattle, whereas his grandfather owned a hundred. This does not mean

---

[4] The lambardar was the principal zamindar. He was responsible for remitting to the state the total amount of the village taxes which he and other zamindars collected.

that at the village level the number of cattle has declined. The opposite has probably taken place, with the increase in population and cultivation provoking a greater need for cattle.

Man's pressure on the land makes it difficult to follow the European practice of changing the type of fodder by a rotation of wheat and lucerne. At Khandoï they try rather to produce two cereal harvests a year, and it is extremely rare for land to lie fallow.

The absence of pastures does not mean that the cattle are neglected. They have a right to all waste products such as wild grass picked from the side of the roads, sugar-cane tops, millet or mustard stalks. Out of the understanding that has grown up between man and animal, a remarkable self-discipline has developed: in the space of more than five months I never once saw cattle loose in the fields; they were invariably in their proper place in front of the puddled-clay feeding troughs, tethered to a stake.

Another change that has taken place has been the opening of the village to the market economy. Even as late as 1920–1925 only a limited amount of ready money was in circulation at Khandoï. The price of a *maund* of *gur* was 1.50 rupees, and that of wheat 2.8 rupees.[5] Today money circulates freely. A weekly market is held in the principal village of the neighborhood, four kilometers away at Unchagaon, where stalls are permanently set up. The market has not eliminated barter economy or home consumption, however; there are only a few shops in Khandoï, selling a small amount of cereals, matches, and salt, and some payments are still made in grain. We shall see later the importance of home consumption.

For many centuries, the region of Khandoï remained cut off from urban centers. Jahangirabad (with a population of 20,000) and Bulandshahr, the district town (with a population of 60,000), are 15 and 44 kilometers away, respectively. The rudimentary road would become flooded by the monsoon rains, and between August and October it was passable only on foot or on horse.[6] It has only been since 1955 that a metaled road, passable for vehicles all the year round, has linked Unchagaon to the neighboring towns. The track leading to Khandoï is still cut off by floods from time to time.

The primary school, founded by the ex-lambardar, has become larger since Independence. It has two teachers for 121 pupils, of whom 75 come from Khandoï and the rest from nearby villages. There are secondary schools within a radius of four to eight kilometers. Of the

[5] One maund = 37.3 kg. Oddly enough, at that time *gur* was cheaper than wheat.
[6] Most of this information was given to me from memory by Tez Pal Singh, who is now about sixty years old.

total number of inhabitants 235 (50 female) have been to school; of these, 138 have not continued beyond the primary stage, 82 have completed their secondary education, and 11 have gone on to a higher grade. Eighteen percent of the population can read and write; this compares favorably with the Uttar Pradesh average of 17.6 percent.[7]

Land Tenure Legislation [8]

Originally the English were baffled by the Indian way of land owner-ship since in no way did it resemble the European system. It was based on two principles: the first man to bring land into cultivation had prior claim to part of its produce; those who had conquered the country also had a right to part of it. In fact, the harvest was divided among the grower, the sovereign, and the workers who gave their services to the growers: the blacksmith, the carpenter, the sweeper, the barber.[9]

In the sixteenth century the Muslims began to introduce new struc-tures, at the same time reorganizing the agrarian system and the land revenue system. The reforms introduced by Sher Shah (ruled 1540–1545) were taken up and developed by Akbar (ruled 1556–1605). His minister, Todar Mal, replaced the sovereign's share, hitherto paid in kind, by a cash payment, the price of which was fixed by the taxation authorities set up for this purpose. The tax was collected by the zamindar, who represented the power at village level. He was a kind of sovereign's vassal, or simply a peasant who was a little more important than the others.

Originally the zamindar was not a landowner, but with the collapse of the Mogul Empire his powers and responsibilities, hence his influ-ence, increased. The British, in applying their judicial concepts, made the zamindar not only a collector of taxes but also a landowner with all the attendant rights.

The *First Settlement* of Khandoï shows that there were two Muslim zamindars living in a nearby village; each of them owned some of the fields and part of the built-up area. The first chapter of the report sets out the zamindar's rights. The land tax (*malguzari*) gave the state a sum amounting to 825 rupees. Rent (*lagan*) levied on the peasants by the zamindars was fixed at 1,604 rupees; the zamindars had no power to change this on their own in any way.[10]

---

[7] *Census of India, 1961*, p. 349.

[8] Walter C. Neale has written an extremely detailed book on this subject: *Economic Change in Rural India: Land Tenure and Reform in Uttar Pradesh, 1800–1955* (New Haven, 1962).

[9] *Ibid.*, pp. 19–20.

[10] This was a considerable protection against the zamindars' arbitrary powers.

The zamindars had other privileges: they approved the choice of the *patwari* (village accountant in charge of the land records), and their consent was needed every time a tenant wished to plant or cut down a tree. They were paid grazing rights at the rate of one rupee for a buffalo and 0.50 rupee for a cow or a bullock. The zamindars also owned the wells, which the peasants sank only with their permission; if it was a masonry well, they levied a tax of 25 rupees. They had a right to the manure of all inhabitants who were not cultivators themselves, and no house could be built without their permission. The term *begar* included various forms of services not included in the payment of rent. It might well have taken the form of forced labor. In addition to all this, the zamindar had the right to borrow the farmers' carts free of charge.

When a girl got married, her father had to give the zamindar 2.5 kg. of rice, 1.5 kg. of sugar, and one rupee. (This rule applied only to lower castes and the untouchables.) The villagers who did not farm paid him an annual sum of 0.75 rupee for each household.

The land was cultivated in three ways: by nonoccupancy tenants (*ghair maurusi*) who could be evicted by the zamindar at will; by occupancy tenants (*maurusi*) who could hand down their land to their sons; or by the zamindars directly, with the help of agricultural laborers (*khudkasht*). The occupancy tenants cultivated an area of 43 hectares.

The right to charge rent and the obligation to levy tax—the two chief prerogatives of the zamindars—were to last until the zamindari system together with several services covered by the *begar* was abolished in 1952. There was a gradual diminution of certain lesser powers, however: by the time of the *Third Settlement,* for example, the peasants no longer needed official permission to build a house or sink a well.

One can readily imagine the amount of influence and power that the zamindar enjoyed, and it was not by a mere stroke of the legal pen that the traditional office was abolished. Sometimes they brought trouble on themselves. One zamindar, now dead, was so bullying that all the barbers (*nais*) left the village and refused to return until they were promised better treatment.

In 1917 one of the Muslim zamindars sold his position and his land for 36,000 rupees to one of his peasants; the peasant's family, which had held occupancy rights since 1860, then disposed of 18 hectares. In this way, by its hard work and spirit of enterprise, Tez Pal Singh's family rose to the rank of zamindar; it acquired the rest of the village for 24,000 rupees in 1924.

The *Third Settlement* (1916) shows how legislation progressed in favor of the tenants.[11] Those who held transferable rights of occupation possessed the major part of the area of land, divided into forty-seven holdings, as against 5.2 hectares for the unprotected tenants.[12]

Tez Pal Singh's family included two brothers and a cousin who between them were directly responsible for the cultivation of 25 hectares (*khudkasht*). In 1921 the joint family was divided into two parts, and following this, yet another division created a third zamindar.

Tax and Rent

The rent imposed by the zamindar and the amount that he paid to the state evolved as follows:

	Rent	*Tax*
First Settlement, 1863	1,604 rs.	825 rs.
Second Settlement, 1889	2,638	1,250
Third Settlement, 1916	2,976	1,860

Since we do not have the necessary statistics to compare the change in rent, tax, production, and purchasing power of money between 1860 and 1916, it is difficult to know whether the charges levied on the peasants have in fact increased. The situation became much clearer after 1916.[13] Increased production, and, more importantly, increased prices alleviated the burden of taxation up to the crisis of 1929, the consequences of which were felt very strongly. Prices fell, but taxes remained the same. Then, during the Second World War and after, prices increased again, going way beyond those of the 1920's. Production also picked up, and this led to the growing undertaxation of which I have already spoken.

Abolition of the Zamindari System

In 1950 the Uttar Pradesh Legislative Assembly passed the Uttar Pradesh Zamindari and Land Reform Act. The law went into effect in

---

[11] *North Western Provinces Tenancy Act, 1901.*

[12] The terminology has changed, with the terms *maurusi* and *ghair maurusi* becoming *dakhilkar* and *ghair dakhilkar*.

[13] Neale cites the following statistics:

	Wholesale Prices	*Rents from Protected Tenants*	*Rents from Nonprotected Tenants*
1901–1905	100	100	100
1924–1929	220	120	149
1930–1934	122	121	163

1952. It introduced the following changes at Khandoï. The three zamindars were allowed to retain the ownership of the land that they themselves cultivated (*khudkasht*) —in this case 36 hectares. There had been instances of zamindars evicting some of their tenants in order to increase their *khudkasht;* at Khandoï, however, the legal provisions for long-term protection of the peasants were respected, and I heard no evidence of complaints. The land records had not been falsified (this was far from true elsewhere) ,[14] and they show that the zamindars had kept within the law in regaining the additional eleven hectares which represented the difference between their *khudkashts* in 1916 and 1951. (Most of the land came from tenant families that had died out; some of it had been taken over because of nonpayment of rent.)

As compensation, the zamindars received, in ready cash and government debentures or bonds, eight times the net annual revenue from the lands on which they were losing their rights. They became *bhumidars* on the *khudkasht,* and paid only half the tax previously levied.

The occupancy tenants became *sirdars* and paid to the state tax equivalent to the amount of rent previously charged by the zamindar. They retained all their former rights: use of land and transference to their heirs. The only restriction related to subletting, which they were prohibited from doing. (This law was an attempt to combat the abuses of parasitism and to prevent cultivation from becoming too fragmented.) As in the past, the *sirdars* were not allowed to sell their land. One very important provision authorized, and even encouraged, the *sirdars* to become *bhumidars* by reducing their tax by half if they agreed to pay an amount ten times the former rent.

The law assured a minimum amount of protection to the nonoccupancy tenants, who until then had no right of occupation; these were the *asamis.* In Khandoï there was only one, who farmed 0.5 hectare.

During the ten years following the abolition of the zamindari system, the peasants showed little inclination to become *bhumidars;* this was no doubt due to lack of money at Khandoï, a situation which was equally true of other parts of the country. The 1963 land records show that 68 hectares of land belonged to *bhumidars,* 36 of which were the *khudkasht* of ex-zamindars, which means that the acquisition of ownership rights had involved only 32 hectares of land. In several cases a peasant in need of ready cash became *bhumidar* of a very small piece of land with the intention of selling it, either immediately or a little later on.

[14] See Neale, p. 245.

Should one repeat what so many writers have said before, that this law changed practically nothing, since it only meant that the tenants changed their name to *sirdars* and paid to the state what they had previously paid to the zamindar? This is a much too narrow point of view. Actually the law did offer larger opportunities to *sirdars* and it introduced one new element—the complete abolition of all the rights by means of which the zamindars had become masters of the village, controlling all activities and bestowing numerous advantages on themselves by levying special taxes and using the *begar* system. Thus the trend toward protecting the tenants was at last completed. Six of the sixty *bhumidars* and *sirdars* who were covered by my questionnaire gave the abolition of the zamindari system as one of the notable achievements of the last fifteen years.

So far as finance was concerned, the law provided for the tax to equal either the rent, in the case of *sirdars,* or, in the case of the *bhumidars,* half the amount charged before 1950. The legislators refused to increase the taxes, but based their assessment on the last settlement, in this case that of 1916. Bound as they were by promises made before Independence, Indian politicians dared not take what was the obvious measure from the economic point of view, that is, the acceleration of the formation of capital by means of an increased taxation of land. Not only did they maintain a rate of tax which had become very low owing to the depreciation of money since 1916, but they pledged themselves to maintain it for the next forty years (Section 251).

As a result of the reduction of the *bhumidars'* rent, Khandoï now has a land revenue lower than the total rent of 1916—2,596 rupees in 1963. There is nothing unusual about this phenomenon; many such examples can be found all over the country.

7

THE LAND AND THE MEN

In 1962, at the instigation of the Block Development Officer, some volunteers undertook an inquiry into several villages. The figures obtained for Khandoï differed somewhat from the census figures of 1961 (1,294 inhabitants as opposed to 1,227),[1] but the data that were collected were accurate enough to be useful.

There is a wide variety of castes:

Jats	386	(an important agricultural caste from the north of India)
Jativs	223	(Harijans: [2] ex-untouchables)
Lodha-Rajputs	137	(an agricultural caste: Sudras)
Brahmins	71	
Bhangis	54	(scavengers, sweepers: Harijans)
Kumhars	51	(potters: Sudras)
Thakurs	51	(Kshatriyas)
Jogis	47	(Sudras)
Vaisyas	46	(tradesmen or cultivators)
Khatiks	44	(cultivators: Sudras)
Nais	41	(barbers: Sudras)
Dhobis	31	(laundrymen: Harijans)
Garayas	10	(shepherds: Sudras)
Dhimars	6	(water carriers: Harijans)
Sunars	5	(goldsmiths: Sudras)
Dhunas	8	(wool carders: Sudras)

and finally 83 Muslims.

According to a tradition which has descended from the Vedas, the castes are divided into four main categories (known as *varna:* color) which, although abstract, serve as a general reference. After these come the outcastes or untouchables. The first category, that of the Brahmins, is responsible for the maintenance of spiritual values; the Kshatriyas are soldiers by profession and concern themselves with temporal powers; the Vaisyas are either tradesmen or cultivators; the Sudras are

---

[1] Our volunteers counted the forty-seven men whose families were in the village but who worked outside it, whereas the 1961 census left them out.

[2] Literally, people of the god Hari, a name given by Ghandi to the untouchables.

agricultural laborers and artisans. As for the untouchables, some are in various forms of service and others are agricultural workers. In actual fact there are 2,500 to 3,000 different endogamous groups or castes (*jati*) which can be classified either into one of the *varnas* or into the untouchable category.

There is an undeniable fluidity, both in time and in space, in this form of classification. It allows some a certain rise in the social scale which, once it has been recognized, creates a higher status. Theory would dispute this, but facts support it. Thus the Jats call themselves Kshatriyas whereas the Brahmins class them as Sudras. In fact, because of its social and economic rank,[3] this agricultural caste can be included among the Kshatriyas. The Lodha-Rajputs, who are a lower agricul-tural caste, were originally called Lodhas, but they added the epithet Rajput (Kshatriyas caste) to facilitate social promotion. Forty years ago the Jativs still bore the name Chamars; by giving themselves a new name they hoped gradually to rid themselves of their inferior status and to make a distinction between themselves and those members of their caste who kept to the traditionally impure trade which deals with everything connected with leather and skins.[4]

One other fact must be made clear: the classification of society into four *varnas* and untouchables is equivalent to a kind of division of labor, but this has not been strictly observed—even less since the modernization of the country. At Khandoï the overwhelming majority of high castes (the first three *varnas*) devote themselves to agriculture, a vocation that is certainly not a recent one. The traditional occupa-tions of the Sudras and the untouchables have changed slightly, and the competition of modern industry has forced a number of artisans into the agricultural workers' bracket.

The correlation between the social rank of the caste and land ownership is a widespread phenomenon, with the principal land-owners in a village belonging to the higher castes. It is quite common to find, as one does at Khandoï, one caste that is dominant in influence, land, and number; here it is the Jats. (See table at the top of p. 63.) (*Sirdars* and *bhumidars* come into the category of farmers as opposed to agricultural workers or landless laborers.) The area of land owned by the Jats, Brahmins, and Thakurs is in fact greater than the table indicates, since many of them own plots in nearby villages (amounting to a total of at least 35 hectares). The Jat group is largest in number as

---

[3] The Jats began to play an influential political role during the eighteenth cen-tury.
[4] The Harijans do not constitute a homogeneous group. They are composed of numerous groups of varied social status.

Caste	Total Area Owned (in hectares)	Area Owned per Head (in hectares)
Jats	150	0.4
Vaisyas	12.25	0.26
Thakurs	13	0.25
Brahmins	16.25	0.23
Lodha-Rajputs	28.5	0.20
Muslims	10	0.12
Kumhars	5.10	0.10
Khatiks	3.85	0.09
Jativs	20.5	0.09
Jogis	2.2	0.04

well as richest in land. The Jativs (Harijans) come second in number and last but one in land ownership.[5]

The connection between caste and land has changed little during the last fifty years, with opportunities for land occupation still remaining very restricted. The *Third Settlement* (1916) gives the following figures:

Jats	122 ha.
Chamars	25
Vaisyas	12.0
Thakurs	14.0
Brahmins	11.5
Lodha-Rajputs	40
Muslims	5.5
Lohars	4.5*
Kumhars	5.0
Khatiks	3.0
Kahars	1.3*

* No longer in existence today.

All the castes have occupancy rights. The zamindars are Jats, and the increase in land ownership by this caste is the result of the extinction of several families and of the appropriation of seven hectares from a Lodha family for failure to pay rent.

A second criterion for classification is the distribution of land according to its dimensions. This can be a very irksome task, for in the *Khatauni* (land records) the same peasant comes under the heading of *bhumidar* for some plots and *sirdar* for others. Also, the Khatauni often show a plot of land as being occupied by one family, whereas in fact the members of the family have by private agreement divided it among themselves.

[5] These figures represent the average per group. Within each group there are some who own land and others who do not.

Five of the 121 holdings must be discounted, these being some five hectares belonging to peasants from other villages. The remaining 116 holdings cover a total acreage of 260.85 hectares [6] which can be broken up as follows:

Number of Holdings	Total Acreage	Average Holding	Classification by Size of Holdings
10	2 ha.	0.2 ha.	0–0.4 ha.
20	15.3	0.76	0.4–1
37	56	1.5	1–2
28	67.5	2.4	2–3
8	29	3.6	3–4
7	32	4.6	4–6
1	6.05	6.05	6–8
2	17	8.5	8–10
1	10	10	10–12
2	26	13	12 and above

A holding of two hectares represents the dividing line between a fairly reasonable, if frugal, standard of living, and conditions of existence which are precarious, to say the least. Forty-nine families come into the first category, a dozen families own nearly two hectares, and a little more than fifty families are in serious need of more land.

There is another consideration to be faced: the future is not yet determined by the present fragmentation of holdings, man's proliferation, and plots of land which are too small to be economic. Of the 256.6 hectares cultivated at Khandoï, 17.3 represent holdings (zero to one hectare) that are too small to support the families who cultivate them. In the third category (one to two hectares) 17.5 of the total of 56 hectares represent holdings of about 1.75 hectares, which is close to the acceptable minimum.

Finally, the uneconomic holdings occupy 55.8 hectares; 17.5 hectares represent marginal holdings; and the major part of the land, about 200 hectares, is cultivated under relatively favorable conditions. The economic role of the very small holdings is still somewhat limited owing to the quality of the soil; many of the uneconomic plots are found in areas where the land is of lesser quality and is insufficiently irrigated.

In conclusion, looking at the situation strictly from the point of view of production, prospects are not bad for owners of two or more hectares of land. Their yields have been rising for a century, and the margin of further increase is fairly appreciable when one takes into account the quality of the soil and the irrigation.

[6] This is the figure given in the land records. In fact the area cultivated amounts to only about 254 hectares owing to the extension of the built-up area since the beginning of the century.

Of the 182 families at Khandoï, 108 own land; [7] a little more than half of the remaining families are landless and work as agricultural laborers. Could a new agrarian reform improve their conditions? An equal distribution among the 116 farming families and the 40 families of agricultural laborers who live without land from day to day would make each holding only 1.60 hectares. This figure alone illustrates the danger, if not the absurdity, of such a measure.

Nor is Khandoï an exceptional case. In the neighboring villages and in several other regions the situation is similar. The "large" land-owners, the "rich" people of the village, own, like our ex-zamindars, from 10 to 20 hectares. During my travels in Uttar Pradesh I met only one really large landowner, who before the 1952 reforms owned several villages. According to Walter C. Neale and the Indian documents which he consulted, only a few thousand of the two million zamindars in Uttar Pradesh owned holdings of more than a hundred (or over a thousand) hectares. Our three Khandoï zamindars paid a total of 1,860 rupees in taxes, which is a sign of their—comparative—affluence, for only 11,000 zamindars in Uttar Pradesh paid an annual sum of between 500 and 2,000 rupees. There are barely 2,500 landowners in the highest income category.[8]

The Ceiling on Holdings

Instead of making a complete redistribution of land, the 1952 Act sought to prevent the formation of new large holdings by limiting the amount of land that could be purchased to 30 acres (12 ha.); if a peasant already owned land his future purchases were not to exceed this ceiling.[9] Following the Nagpur resolution (1959) the Uttar Pradesh Legislative Assembly adopted in 1960—without much enthusiasm—the Uttar Pradesh Imposition of Ceiling on Land Holding Act which fixed the maximum acreage of properties at 40 acres (16 ha.). The surplus would be repurchased by the state and distributed to the agricultural laborers. The Act was hardly put into practice, however; the large landowners simply shared out their land to relatives or to front men. I was told at Lucknow in 1963 that the state ought by then to have regained some 200,000 acres, or 80,000 hectares, out of the 40 million acres cultivated in Uttar Pradesh.

[7] This figure does not agree with the 116 holdings mentioned above, for the census understands by the term "family" all those who live and eat under the same roof; these are entered under the same number on the Khatauni register. But we have already seen that several families are in fact divided up quite differently from the figures shown in the land records.

[8] See Neale, *Economic Change in Rural India,* p. 236.

[9] In 1958 an amendment reduced this limit to 12.5 acres (5 ha.).

Professor Baljit Singh feels—and he is not alone in this—that the limit of 16 hectares is too high. He proposes that it should be 6 hectares (15 acres) .[10] At Khandoï, with such a limit, six holdings would be affected, covering a total area of 59 hectares; 23 hectares would be reclaimed, enough to accommodate eleven families. Now, fifty or so families own less than the economic minimum and about forty others own no land at all. A simple calculation shows that there is just not enough land for everybody.

Fragmentation of Holdings

The formidable results of the population expansion can be seen in another way: the fragmentation of holdings. What were 47 holdings in 1916 became 116 in less than forty years. Under the joint family system of the nineteenth century the sons retained joint ownership of their inheritance; barter and home consumption formed the basis of the economy, and it was relatively easy to share out the harvest produce, ensuring by means of a collective system that everybody's needs were met.

This system cannot coexist with an economy in which money plays an ever increasing role. The rising population, largely due to a lower rate of mortality, put a strain on households and difficulties of accommodation began to be felt. An even more delicate matter was the sharing out of ready cash. Most families lacked the means to send all the children to primary school and especially to secondary school. Which of the numerous cousins should be chosen? Uncles were naturally reluctant to contribute toward the cost of their nephews' education if it meant that their own sons remained illiterate or very superficially educated. How were they to share out the credit from the cooperative, and how were they to repay it? Marriages, too, entailed quite considerable expenditure, and this was another cause for dispute among brothers who had many children and others who had only a few. There is nothing new in these sources of disagreement, but they are accentuated by the more complex living conditions of today.

Generally, as long as a father remains alive his sons work with him. After his death the common way of farming ceases, although the Khatauni makes no mention of this. The consolidation of holdings has made the position much clearer. In Khandoï, previous divisions were registered as well as the breaking up of five new families. The two

[10] *Next Step in Village India* (Bombay, 1961) , p. 77.

sons of Phul Singh (Jat) inherited from their father 2.5 hectares which they divided into two equal parts. Bhola Singh (Jat), who belonged to another family, cultivated, together with his brother, an area of five hectares, which was sufficient to ensure them a reasonable standard of living. Today, however, the brothers have separated, with the result that their respective living standards may be in jeopardy.

Twenty years ago Lila Ram (Brahmin) and his brother cultivated ten hectares which gave them a relatively comfortable standard of living. Today, the holding has been divided into three equal parts. By dint of hard work their sons continue to live fairly well, but what will happen to their children? Khanchand, one of the three sons, has four boys between three and twenty-five who have either completed their education or are about to start school. The eldest of the four has a job with the district administration; the second is on the point of leaving secondary school and shows little inclination toward farming; he has been offered the opportunity of leaving the village. This leaves the two younger sons, who will probably have to live off 3.3 hectares.

These educated Brahmins will eventually be able to work in the tertiary sector, but the case of Sukharam would indeed give cause for alarm. He has succeeded, with a great deal of tenacity, in cultivating his 3.75 hectares of land. His three sons are married and have at the moment four sons and three daughters. They all live under the same roof, and they all work together. Their very survival depends on the maintenance of a good understanding, since a division of the land would give the sons only 1.25 hectares each.[11] As members of a low caste (Khatik), they have had no education, and thus they have very few alternatives to farming.[12]

Ram Chandra (Jat) is an old man who also owns 3.75 hectares. One of his four sons (aged between thirty and forty) has left Khandoï to become a policeman; the other three work with their father and they are threatened with the same fate as Sukharam's sons.

These examples show that the deadline has now been reached. The Khandoï peasants have a reprieve of ten to fifteen years during which they must at all costs improve the yield of their land so that they will be able to live on less than two hectares. The enterprise will be made easier if it is embarked upon before the land is divided up yet again.[13]

[11] Daughters have no traditional rights of inheritance.

[12] Today education is more widespread in the lower castes. All Sukharam's grandchildren go to school.

[13] I shall not at this point raise the question of cooperative farms, which, we shall see, encounter such serious obstacles that it is difficult to imagine how they can form the basis of a policy of agricultural reform.

Consolidation of Holdings

In 1860 the map of Khandoï was composed of 489 plots (known in Hindi as *chak*). The *Second Settlement* (1889) recorded 613, and these existed until 1964. The holdings continued to increase by being broken up and it became more and more difficult to get any value out of them. The peasants wasted time moving from one plot to another for cultivation, and they found it difficult to establish a sound system of water supply, being somewhat reluctant to sink wells if they were not on good terms with their neighbors.

Uttar Pradesh followed the Punjab in undertaking the complicated task of consolidation of holdings (*chakbandi*), that is, the incorporation of the several plots of one holding into one or two larger plots. At Khandoï, the number of plots has fallen to 135 for 121 holdings.

The principal operations are as follows: A group of ten villages is formed under the direction of an assistant consolidation officer and in collaboration with the *lekhpals* of each village.[14] Once the team has been set up it begins by checking the accuracy of the records; it measures the fields,[15] and settles existing lawsuits without prejudice to any appeal to a higher authority. The plots are valued according to the quality of the soil and the extent of irrigation. Then begins the task of dividing the lands anew, and this is a genuine puzzle from the point of view of quality and quantity of the fields. The task is difficult enough on paper, but it becomes even harder when the team comes up against mistrust, quarrels, and corruption, not to mention lawsuits and petitions submitted to the district. For this reason the personality of the officials is of prime importance: some of them give way to the entreaties and allow themselves to be bribed, thus provoking a whole round of complaints which are in part justified.

Khandoï, fortunately, has a remarkably honest official who is devoted to his task. It must be admitted that there have been long delays of more than two years in carrying out the plan of consolidation, but there have been few complaints. As we shall see later, a decisive step has now been taken toward improvement of the agricultural situation.

[14] Since 1954 the *patwari*, the official in charge of the land records of one or more villages, has been called *lekhpal*. It is no longer a hereditary office.

[15] At Khandoï the difference between the original figures for total acreage and the new figures is only 0.5 hectare—a compliment to the accuracy of the cadastral survey of one hundred years' standing.

The Area Under Habitation

The final consequence of the pressure of population has been that the area of the village has expanded. In 1860 the built-up area (*abadi*) of Khandoï covered 2.5 hectares; in 1916 it was 3.5, and later on five more hectares of land were absorbed. Some of this extension, however, has not been related to the increase in population. Some of the better-off farmers enlarged their dwellings: one of them, for instance, enlarged and walled the enclosure for his cattle, and another built a *chaupal*.[16] This expenditure was not absolutely necessary—a strictly utilitarian reasoning would have preferred expenditure on a vegetable patch. But haven't men the right to a minimum amount of comfort?

[16] House or verandah where the men gather in their leisure time to discuss their affairs and, if they belong to the same or equivalent caste, to smoke their *hookahs*. (Jats and Thakurs smoke the same hookah.)

8

AGRICULTURE AND THE FARMERS

A century ago Khandoï began to develop land that was potentially suitable for cultivation but had lain almost idle for hundreds of years. The result was that the increase in production probably exceeded that in population, and many families benefited. What are the conditions under which the land is cultivated?

The Cycle of the Seasons

The agricultural calendar typical of northern India begins with the monsoon in July and consists of two main seasons: the *kharif* until October–November and the *rabi* from November to March–April. Sometimes there is a third harvest in June, but it is of little importance, being merely vegetables and fodder.

Cracked and hardened by the hot, dry weather from April to July when the temperature often exceeds 40° C. in the shade, the soil has to be softened either by irrigation or by the first rainfall before it will respond to the plough. The farmers plough once and sometimes twice for the main crops of the *kharif;* these are generally pulses, maize, *jowar,* and *bajra.*[1] Depending on the strength of the oxen, it takes one man an entire day to plough an area of one to 1.5 *bigha pakka* (0.25 to 0.37 ha.). After each ploughing the soil is leveled with a heavy plank drawn by oxen. Seeds are then sown broadcast.

Since *jowar* and *bajra* are poor crops the farmers devote less care to them than to the others, and they are sown in mixture. Some is harvested "green," from September onward, for cattle feeding; the rest is gathered toward the end of October.[2]

Maize is a much more interesting crop. In addition to farm manure,

[1] These last two crops are varieties of millet: *jowar* is sorghum, *bajra* is pearl millet.

[2] This is frequently the case and one wonders how statistics can be arrived at which give an accurate picture of the present, or make a reasonable prediction of the future of these crops.

it may be given chemical fertilizers. Weeding is one of the most demanding tasks, for the humidity and the inadequate ploughing mean that weeds spring up quickly. The farmer, eager to make the most of the rains and gather in the harvest well before the *rabi,* hasn't the time to turn the soil more than twice, so three times during the maize-growing season he must pull the weeds with a metal tool. From six o'clock in the morning to midday he and six laborers clean 0.25 hectare of land in exceedingly humid heat—often, between rains, as high as 32° to 35° C. in the shade.[3]

October and November are the hardest months, for the *kharif* must be harvested at the same time as the land is being prepared for the *rabi. Jowar* and *bajra* are pulled by hand, and maize is cut with a hand sickle. In fields close to the village the peasants carry in the harvest on their heads.

In the second half of November the sugar cane ripens after a growing period of ten to twelve months. From then until February the cane is harvested and processed. It is cut and made into *gur,* which is a kind of raw sugar, in small open places known as *kolu* (sugar mill). The village of Khandoï has thirteen of these.[4] The juice is squeezed out of the stalk in an iron crusher which is rotated by two bullocks or a camel; it is collected in earthenware jars, and is then poured into a large iron pan placed on a fire of sugar-cane waste (*bagasse*). After several hours' cooking the brown liquid is decanted into a stone mould. While it is still soft it is placed in wooden racks, each one of which holds a piece weighing 5 kg. These will be sold in the neighboring markets of Unchagaon, four kilometers away, and Jahangirabad, fourteen kilometers away.[5]

Farmers can rent the crusher and the pan at 175 to 200 rupees per season; this saves them the expense of maintenance and repair costs. To work the *kolu* it takes one man, or a young boy, to make the bullocks turn, another man to feed the canes, five at a time, into the crusher, one more to tend the fire, and yet another to prepare the *gur.* It takes a whole family, perhaps with the help of friends and laborers, twenty-four hours to make seven vatfuls of *gur.* Quite often the *kolu* works far into the night.

During the sugar-cane harvest, work on the *rabi* must also go on.

---

[3] One weeding is enough for wheat, a *rabi* crop, because the weather is drier and the farmer is able to plough several times before sowing.

[4] Six belong to Jats, two to Lodha-Rajputs, one to Brahmins, one to Vaisyas and Jats, one to Jativs, another to a group of Khatiks, Brahmins, and Thakurs, and another to the cooperative farm. The majority are under co-ownership.

[5] It takes three hours to travel these 15 km. by bullock cart, which is the chief means of transport.

Preparation for the *rabi* comes at the beginning of November—first the ploughing, then the sowing of the principal crops, wheat, barley, *matar* (peas), *chana* (gram), and mustard.

Wheat is often sown in mixture with barley, gram, or mustard,[6] and it requires a considerable amount of work. The farmers prepare the seed bed with extreme care: they plough from seven to twelve times, and between each ploughing they level the ground to preserve its humidity. When the soil is at last aerated, friable, and free from rubbish and roots of weeds, they sow the seeds with a bamboo seed drill attached to the plough. An area of 0.37 hectare can be sown in a day by two persons, one man guiding the plough and another man, or a woman, putting the seeds into the funnel. Once the wheat is up, it is sufficient to weed once and to irrigate three or four times.

Pulses, which are nitrogen-rich and therefore important in crop rotation, are grown after sugar cane, a heavy consumer of nitrogen. Land for pulses needs to be ploughed only two or three times, but the cycle of growing seasons calls for a degree of energy and application which does great credit to the farmers. In October and November the whole village works in the fields, even some of the women and many of the children.[7] At two or three o'clock in the morning the oxen bells herald the beginning of the working day. The farmers yoke the oxen and begin to plough by moonlight. Toward nine or ten o'clock the women bring the men their meal which they eat beside their plough. The working day is broken by a siesta at noon and then continues until dusk comes at about six in the evening. While the ploughing is being done, others harvest the *kharif* and cut the sugar cane.

At the beginning of December the farmers relax a little, for the major part of the work is over and there only remains the sugar cane and *gur*. This relaxation is marked by the pilgrimage to the Ganges, eight kilometers away. Bullock carts pour out of all the villages and pass through Khandoï laden with children and women clad in their finest saris.

---

[6] The mixture is an insurance against eventual drought, which would be fatal for wheat but is less harmful to gram and mustard, which are harvested after several months of growth and before the wheat is ripe. Mustard protects the young shoots against the birds and enriches the soil. But the type of mustard chosen must be one that does not create too much shade.

[7] Women in Khandoï generally take little part in agricultural work. Many of them, particularly in the higher castes, observe the Muslim custom of purdah and do not like going out of their houses; when they do go out they hide part of their face under a flap of their sari (known here as *dhoti* like the dress of the man). They are responsible for looking after the cattle and the home; most of them have to grind the grain by hand, a task that takes from one to two hours a day, do the cooking, and look after the children.

Toward the end of January, the rhythm of work increases again; the soil is prepared for the sugar cane, which, as a cash crop, is the real basis of the economy. Again the farmers plough and level their fields ten or twelve times. Two or three ploughs follow one behind another and open up the furrows in which the sugar-cane plants (20 to 30 cm. long) are laid flat. The rows are covered with earth mounded in two ridges so that the irrigation water can flow between. Families help one another and the farmers who are somewhat better off employ extra laborers. They weed several times in an effort not only to get rid of weeds but also to aerate the soil and combat evaporation.[8]

In March the *rabi* harvests begin—first the pulses, then in April the cereals. The following two months are not so busy; during these the farmers tend the growing sugar cane, cultivate some vegetables and fodder, and gather mangoes from the orchards. Otherwise, they do as little as possible, for May and June are the season of overwhelming heat and sandstorms.

The statistics drawn up by the *gram sewak*[9] for the report of the Third Plan do not give an accurate picture of the crop rotation:[10] the figures for pulses, *jowar,* and *bajra* at the *kharif* are particularly doubtful, since the former crop occupies a very limited area compared with the other two. The figures for pulses might in fact apply to *jowar* and *bajra,* and vice versa. The figures for wheat and sugar cane seem to have been arrived at more accurately.

Table from the Third Plan

Rabi			*Kharif*	
Wheat	60	ha.	*Jowar* and *bajra*	6.4 ha.
Barley	36		Maize	35
Pulses	30		Pulses	60
Potatoes	0.4		Rice	0.4
	126.4 ha.		Cotton[11]	7
				108.8 ha.

Sugar cane		90 ha.
Orchards (mainly mangoes)		7.5[12]

[8] The same plant yields two successive crops before it is pulled up. The second crop requires less effort, but it has a lower yield.

[9] Village-level worker who is a kind of rural organizer in charge of a group of villages within the development block.

[10] *Kendr Naglamadaripur, tisri panchvarshiyayojna, 1961–1966* ["Third Five-Year Plan of the Naglamadaripur Circle, 1961–1966"].

[11] Cotton is of only limited importance despite the large number of spinning wheels (155) in the village. The women spin the thread, but either sell it or exchange it for cloth; most clothes are factory made.

[12] Since I was not in Khandoï during the harvest of mangoes, I cannot judge their economic importance with accuracy. Many trees seem to have a poor yield.

There is a second statistical weakness in cases where the *rabi* follows the *kharif* on the same soil. Not counting the orchards, the lands cultivated in a year are given as 325.5 hectares for a total land area of 254 hectares—in other words, nearly a third of the land bears double cropping. In actuality, the proportion is higher—probably 40 percent. The above table also takes no account of the area covered by kitchen gardens, nor of certain patches devoted to fodder.[13]

Irrigation

The heaviest rainfall occurs between the end of July and the end of September; there is also some precipitation in winter (December and January). This natural watering is not enough, and water is the primary decisive factor for all farming success. Sugar cane, in particular, demands a great deal of moisture, especially in the dry, torrid season between April and July, when irrigation must be carried out every fortnight.

Some wheat is grown on unirrigated land. If the winter rains are not too sporadic and come at the right time, the farmers can expect a fair harvest, but if it does not rain at all, as in the winter of 1963–1964, or if it rains only in March, the crop will be poor. Wheat that has been well irrigated—three or four times between sowing and harvest— produces a good yield, and the use of well water is a sure guarantee of success. Even in the monsoon season, irrigation may be necessary if the rain is late, or if it comes all at once.

According to the Khandoï land records, 191 out of 263 hectares are irrigated, but in reality the situation is not that good: twenty of the forty-eight farmers questioned complained that they either did not get their water in time or were without it altogether. The state tube-well, installed in 1955, is the main source of the delays. It is supposed to irrigate 800 acres (320 ha.) in Khandoï and other villages, but this is much too great an area with such an intensive system of cultivation.[14]

Tez Pal Singh, the ex-lambardar, has a tube-well which supplies water to his fields close by. The surplus water is sold to small land- owners, but at a price that is too high for some of them to afford often: for a period of one hour (time enough to irrigate 0.2 hectare) they pay about 2.5 to 3 rupees to the state tube-well, and 3.75 to Tez Pal.

[13] After the first cutting of sugar cane, the farmers sow broadcast and irrigate *meti*, a fodder plant which is pulled after several months as soon as the cane shoots start to reappear.

[14] This is what is called a "command area." As we shall see (chaps. 14 and 17), this same problem of too great an area occurs frequently.

The two tube-wells with oil engines (see chap. 7) are not satisfactory. Frequent breakdowns, followed by long delays for repair, in addition to the fuel cost, make them more costly to run than the electric pumps. One of them operates infrequently, and the other has been out of action for a year.

Recently, a number of Persian wheels (*rahat*) have been improved: by drilling the bottom of the well the villagers have been able to install a cylinder of baked earth which makes it possible to seek water at a depth of twenty meters. The installation costs 100 rupees. With or without this boring, Persian wheels need two pairs of bullocks and two men working in shifts for twelve hours in order to irrigate 0.25 hectare: a slow method which can be costly.

The real reason for the water shortage is the *simultaneous need* for irrigation, since all the peasants follow roughly the same rotation of crops. In theory, it ought to be possible to work out a rotation system that would allow a better distribution of water needs, but such a solution is actually too complicated, and in some instances is impossible.

Khandoï is scarcely touched by the canals from the Ganges and the Jumna which crisscross the district, except for one branch of the canal that passes through Unchagaon and irrigates an area of thirty hectares. Here as elsewhere there are numerous causes for complaint. The command area has become too big for intensive cultivation (owing to the extension of the practice of double cropping) with the result that there is insufficient irrigation, especially on the banks of the secondary canals (like those of Khandoï) at their tail. In the dry season there is sometimes water enough for only one week in every month; obviously, under such circumstances, the harvest is a risky affair, and the sugar-cane crop may be lost completely.

These facts call for prudence when interpreting national statistics, which for understandable reasons do not distinguish between land that has been well irrigated and land that has been inadequately irrigated.

In Khandoï in August, 1964, many of the fields of maize were in a sorry state, with only a few miserable shoots appearing above ground, but on a neighboring plot, where the soil was the same, the stems might be growing in fairly close rows, giving promise of a decent—if disappointing—harvest. What is the reason for the different results? In this instance it was simply that some farmers did their ploughing and sowing at the time of the rains, which were unusually violent that year and lasted for several days on end, and the seeds rotted in the soggy ground. Some farmers ploughed and sowed again, risking subsequent shortage of water, with a result almost as disastrous as before. The smallest losses (25 percent) occurred with the farmers who did not wait for the monsoon: three weeks before the rain was due, they irrigated, ploughed, and sowed their seeds. When the rains came the maize was far enough advanced to withstand them, and in fact to benefit from them.

Those who waited for the rains either did so without consideration or because they did not have the money to pay for the water, or because the neighboring well was not sufficient to water their plots.

In January, 1964, the same difference was evident in the wheat fields; in one field there were fine stems growing close together about twenty centimeters high, whereas in another there were gaps in the rows, either because the seedling plants had dried up for lack of irrigation, or because the seeds had been sown too deep.

In 1964, also, part of the sugar-cane harvest was lost because the state tube-well broke down and was out of order for nearly the whole of the hot season. Between May and July only one irrigation was possible, which meant a loss estimated by the farmers at 50,000 rupees (cf. chap. 14).

Fertilizers

Owing to the scarcity of fuel in Khandoï, much of the cow dung becomes fuel; it is dried into cakes, which are preserved by being stacked into hutlike heaps and covered with straw and gourds. Only a small part of the dung is used to enrich the soil. Not only is there a limited amount, but what there is is badly preserved. The manure is thrown carelessly into pits and nobody bothers either to make it into proper compost by adding leaf waste and a little water, or to protect it from the weather. Most of the manure is therefore exposed to the sun and dries up, losing much of its richness. This lack of care is surprising because the Khandoï peasants do know a great deal about agriculture. I noticed the same carelessness all over India, however, curiously in contrast to the painstaking way in which the women each morning collect every bit of cattle dung from the ground near the watering troughs where the animals are tethered.

Because of the shortage, farmers can put manure on their fields just once for the *kharif*, or when they plant the sugar cane. They do not do it before the *rabi* because there is not enough manure left, nor is there the time even if they had the manure.

Why not follow the Chinese example and make use of human excrement? The peasants are not unaware of its fertilizing effect, and it is not simply the need for privacy that makes them relieve themselves in the fields; that aside, a methodical system of latrines, collection, and application of excrements seems out of the question in India. Only the Bhangis (ex-untouchables; sweepers) would accept such a task, and there are not enough of them to do it.

The outlook is better for green manure. The Uttar Pradesh technique for wheat consists of ploughing the land in June, planting local species such as *sann* and *dhaincha,* and ploughing these crops under, from mid-August onward, to enrich the soil for *rabi.* Driven as they are by the constant need to produce more, the peasants of Khandoï are reluctant to follow this practice, for they are not convinced that the increased wheat yields compensate for the absence of maize or millet, which these green manures have replaced.

Ultimately, therefore, chemical fertilizers are the most effective, for they produce good results even if the application of farm manure is limited [15] provided there is adequate irrigation. The farmers recognize the problem, and it is not generally because of "ignorance" [16] that they refuse to use chemical fertilizers in plots where they are not sure of obtaining water.

For wheat the best fertilizer is a mixture (mixture No. 1) with a base of nitrogen and phosphate; for sugar cane, the same, or nitrogen only; for maize many of the peasants make one or two applications of ammonium sulphate or urea. Some use chemical fertilizers for peas. The amount of fertilizer used for wheat varies from around 80 to 160 kg/ha. If the first figure is rather low, the second meets the standard recommended by the agricultural handbooks dealing with the region.[17]

Out of fifty-nine farmers questioned in Khandoï, twelve, on account of ignorance or poverty, used no chemical fertilizers at all; thirteen had vague ideas on the subject and sometimes used them; thirty-four knew quite a lot about it and used them often. The majority started using such fertilizers under the influence of the development block which was instituted in 1954.

Seeds, Farm Implements

Another stimulus to progress has been the replacement of local seeds by improved strains or by hybrid plants. An improved strain of sugar cane has been grown for several decades, and wheat has also been

[15] Chemical fertilizers should be used together with a large quantity of farm manure.

[16] As certain theorists from the towns would assert.

[17] See, e.g., Arakeri *et al., Soil Management in India,* p. 321. The amount of nitrogen represents one-fifth of the weight of the fertilizer, and that of phosphate (P_2O_5) one-sixth.

improved by the use of better seed from the Punjab. Today the development block is the principal seed supplier to the farmers. (We shall see later why the results are rather mitigated.)

So far, Khandoï has not been able to replace its old farm implements. The experts would like to introduce cultivators to speed up and improve ploughing, but despite their low price (45 rupees), they are beyond the means of most farmers, because they must be drawn by bullocks heavier than the usual ones. This means selling the old pair worth 600 to 1,000 rupees, and buying a stronger pair at a cost of 1,000 to 1,500 rupees.

At the moment, mechanization is inconceivable. One of the ex-zamindars bought a tractor but he later sold it. Tractors are economic only on farms of fifteen hectares or more, and in Khandoï even the "large" holdings scarcely approach this size.[18] As for the eventual collective use of a tractor, we shall see later what obstacles of a sociological nature this would encounter.

What of the pests, animals, and insects about which one hears so much in connection with India? In Khandoï, the cattle, as we have seen, are never allowed to wander freely. There are few goats and sheep, and an equally strict watch is kept over these. There are no monkeys.[19] This leaves birds, which indeed do serious damage especially to the *jowar* and *bajra*. It is not unusual to see ears completely stripped before the harvest. The depredation caused by rats and insects is difficult to determine. For some years now the sugar cane has been attacked by parasites, with fairly heavy losses. The farmers take no protective measures, lacking the necessary competence, and it remains for the development block, within its limited resources, to give them the needed instruction.

Yields per Hectare

The Khandoï farmers are a far cry from the oversimplified picture of the Indian peasant with his "ignorant" and "fatalistic" ideas. For the most part, their farming techniques, their system of crop rotation, and their implements are well adapted to local conditions and produce respectable results.

Because there is no check made at harvest time, exact figures of the yield are difficult to obtain. Not all the forty-nine farmers I questioned knew even the amount of acreage they had under seed, and often a

[18] Even including land owned in other villages.
[19] While I was in the district I noticed only three areas inhabited by half a score of monkeys.

farmer would give different figures to me in the same discussion. The variation in yield went from 1.5 to 4 maunds of wheat per *bigha kachcha* [20]—that is, from 740 to 2,300 kg/ha. The lower figure was for wheat that had received little or no irrigation, the higher for wheat grown under the best conditions, with plenty of water, fertilizers, and, possibly, green manure. The average yield seems to be about 1,200 or 1,300 kg/ha, though the Third Plan report of the gram sewak gives 930 kg. My figure is, however, based on a study of the most competent farmers in the region.

Indeed, the crop yields achieved in Khandoï and the surrounding villages exceed those of many other areas; the official estimate for wheat production in the whole of India is 810 kg/ha, and for Uttar Pradesh 800 kg/ha.[21] The maize yield for Khandoï is about the same as that of wheat; for all India it is 870 kg/ha, and for Uttar Pradesh, 710 kg/ha.

Even for sugar cane, a crop that is not particularly well suited to the extreme climate of the north, Khandoï figures are quite high. In Uttar Pradesh, temperatures are very high in summer and often quite low in winter, when the thermometer will fall to 4° or 5° C. at night. For this reason, the Uttar Pradesh yields (2,800 kg/ha) are decidedly lower than the national average of 3,340 kg. of *gur* per hectare. In Khandoï, however, they produce an average of nearly 5,000 kg/ha—about 6,000 kg. from the first harvest and 3,600 from the second.

These high levels of production are due not only to the quality of the soil and to irrigation but also to the experience of the peasants, who have a century-old tradition of cultivating the soil with the aid of irrigation, the Khandoï area being the heart of a region where the British in the nineteenth century built a great network of canals and later on government-owned tube-wells. Thus in the race to expand production after Independence, Khandoï began several paces ahead, and during the 1950's production increased 20 to 30 percent.

The role of the farmer himself has been decisive. The Khandoï farmer knows how to make use of land that is naturally favorable to good agriculture. And he works hard. Tez Pal Singh, for example, is always busy, either looking after his sugar cane or his wheat or overseeing his tube-well or his mill, while his widowed sister-in-law looks after the cotton harvest. She is an unusually industrious woman for her class, but her hard-working habits are not rare in Khandoï.

[20] In Khandoï the farmer talks in terms of *bigha kachcha*, whereas the records use the measurement *bigha pakka*, which is equivalent to 4 *bigha kachcha*.

[21] For the average wheat and maize yields for the period 1958/59 to 1960/61, see *Eastern Economist*, Annual No., Jan. 5, 1962; for *gur*, see *Soil Management in India*, p. 358, figures for 1955/56. The ratio of cane to *gur* is ten to one.

The average peasant, who owns between two and six or eight hectares, works with his hands. He ploughs and sows with the help of a friend or his wife, and he turns the wheel of his well. If for some reason he is unable to find a laborer to help him, he simply gets up earlier in the morning.

The Jats, the most numerous caste in the village, are noted for their hard work and enterprising spirit,[22] but the Brahmins, too, are good farmers at Khandoï. Elsewhere, Brahmins often refuse to touch the plough and hire others to cultivate their fields for them, but here no agricultural work is beneath them. The Vaisyas also work hard, and among the Lodha-Rajputs there are excellent farmers who are very resourceful in working out ways of increasing their production. The Thakurs are the only caste which tends to look upon farming with a certain lack of enthusiasm; it is as if their traditional military vocation will not permit them to give themselves wholly to work which they consider ill-fitting to their rank. Cases of sharecropping are met among this caste.

What might be called the "spearhead" is a group of men aged thirty-five to fifty. Many of these men are illiterate, but they know how to farm their lands.

Credit

The extension of agricultural credit is an important part of the farm economy of Khandoï; it has allowed farmers to take advantage of modern chemical fertilizers and selected seeds, and to buy new cattle, to repair their wells, and so on.

Before approaching the question from the point of view of Unchagaon block, let us first look at the progress made during the last ten years in Khandoï. Since 1955 credit advanced by the cooperative societies as well as *taccavis* (government loans) has been based on a relatively moderate interest rate of 8.75 percent; local moneylenders charge 3 percent monthly interest, which amounts to more than 36 percent a year.

I found from my questionnaire that the farmers are sometimes not at all clear about their debts, and in any case they are not always willing to admit how large they are. Certain gaps inevitably appeared; nevertheless the information gathered has an indicative value.

Of the fifty-one farmers questioned, only eighteen had no debts.

[22] This is certainly true in the Punjab, as much among the Indians as among the Pakistanis. It should be made clear that the Jats are not all Hindus; some are Sikhs, some Muslims, but this has nothing to do with their habits.

Others owed sums from between 200 to 3,000 rupees, the average being 900 rupees. In four cases the money had been obtained entirely from moneylenders; but for the rest the total debt, or at least part of it, was owed either to the cooperative or to the government (*taccavi*).

The reasons for these debts are difficult to specify: cooperatives and the government stipulate that loans must be used for agricultural purposes, as a means of increasing production, and a farmer is hardly inclined to admit that he used a loan for some other purpose. But loans of more than 1,000 rupees are particularly suspect and may well have been spent on a marriage rather than on fertilizer.

The total debts incurred by the thirty-three persons in the survey amounted to 30,000 rupees—18,000 rupees in cooperative and *taccavi* loans, and 12,000 rupees from moneylenders, relatives, and friends. I should estimate that probably two-thirds, or 12,000 rupees, of the 18,000 were actually turned to farm-production expenses.[23] Most of the 12,000 rupees advanced by individuals was used to finance marriages and in some cases legal proceedings or even food.

Despite its imperfections, which we shall look at more closely in chapter 12, the cooperative has greatly extended rural credit, freeing farmers from the clutches of professional moneylenders with their exorbitant rates of interest.[24]

The situation could be improved were it possible to curb the lavish sums which custom demands should be spent on weddings. The medium farmers (those owning from two to six hectares of land) may spend between 2,000 and 3,000 rupees on the wedding of one child. The quite exceptional case which proves the rule is that of Harpal, a good Jat farmer who only invited five people, instead of a quarter of the village, to his sister's wedding.

The Weak Spots

In Khandoï, apart from the poor conservation of farmyard manure, a mark of bad husbandry that I found in all the villages I visited, there is one aspect of farming that could be improved, namely, vegetable gardening.

It is the custom for a number of peasants to own a patch of land, either within the village or on the outskirts, which they use for vegetables. Usually, however, instead of careful cultivation, the gardening is

[23] This sort of abuse of loan funds appears to be common all over India, hence the growing tendency to give more loans in kind.

[24] There was only one professional moneylender in Khandoï. He was a tight-fisted, shabbily dressed miser who went around bemoaning his alleged debts! In 1966 he was found murdered in a field. The culprit has not been discovered.

haphazard—a few gourds, aubergines, or peas according to the season. Behind where we lived, for example, our landlord owned a plot of land measuring 200 square meters. It did not lack water, for there was a hand water pump, but only part of this land was being cultivated, and only very casually. There were a few cauliflowers and tomato plants, but for want of attention—including a good application of manure—they produced only a small number of vegetables of very poor quality.

Owing to its distance from the market towns, Khandoï can hardly be expected to take up kitchen gardening on an intensive scale. On the other hand, it seems a reasonable suggestion that it could develop it sufficiently to satisfy local needs—assuming, of course, that vegetables could be brought into the average diet. We shall see later how seldom vegetables come into the diet even of the person of average means. At first, attempts to develop kitchen gardening would no doubt meet certain caste prejudices, but these could be countered with educational propaganda. Oscar Lewis has noted that in a Jat village in the Delhi region, the high-caste Jats scorned vegetable gardening as work suitable only for lower castes. It took some time to rid them of their prejudice.[25]

[25] *Village Life in Northern India* (New York, 1965) , p. 88.

9

THE LANDOWNERS

"Are your living conditions any better than they were ten or fifteen years ago?" In Khandoï, thirty-five of the fifty-four landowners who were asked this question answered in the affirmative. The majority of these own more than two hectares. Those whose standard of living has remained static either do not possess the minimum requirements to raise themselves, or they just lack vitality.

Higher Living Standards

What sort of progress has been made? As we saw in chapter 6, six replies mention, among other improvements, the abolition of the zamindari system. Others mention increased production together with increased prices. Toward the beginning of 1950, they could sell 37.3 kg. of wheat (one maund) for 12 or 13 rupees; a decade later the price had increased to 15 or 20 rupees, and more. The price of *gur* had doubled (30 rupees for 37.3 kg.).

These profits have made it possible for the farmers to improve their dwellings, to build new houses of brick, and to clothe themselves better. Some of them have bought bicycles, others a watch, and all of them are trying to give their sons an education.[1] This generation of farmers will be the last to include a large number of illiterates. It is worth noting, however, that their traditional oral education has not prevented them from improving their standard of living—proof, I think, that mass primary education is not a prerequisite to economic development.[2]

Except for the former zamindars and the few people who own ten or a dozen hectares, the way of life in the village is still very frugal. Most of the farmers work hard for a limited profit—and this is revealed by the type of food they eat. With the exception of some Jats, Thakurs, and Harijans, the whole of the population of the village is vegetarian, even to the point of not eating eggs. Their basic diet is composed of

[1] The education of girls is making slower progress.
[2] See part 4.

chapatis—a pancake made of wheat, maize, or millet—seasoned with spices and vegetable sauce. A few mustard leaves when in season, and different varieties of pulses complete the menu. The average peasant has two meals in winter, when days are short, and three in summer.

The Bulandshahr region is noted for the quality of its cattle. The buffaloes yield an average of five to seven liters of milk a day, and the cows—fewer in number—give a few liters. Part of the milk is used to make *ghee* (clarified butter), which is the main fat used. Of the fifty-six farmers questioned, thirty drank milk regularly; this was true of adults as well as of children. Some adults—those who were well off—drank up to half a liter a day. There were seventeen families who had just enough milk for their children, and three that had none at all.

Only the "big" landowners can afford the luxury of eating vegetables, potatoes, and fruit regularly. Those who farm between two and six hectares rarely eat them. *Gur*, or raw sugar, is a rich food which from November to February in particular helps to relieve the ordinary diet. But most peasants keep only a small quantity of *gur* for themselves, preferring to sell a product which represents their principal source of ready cash.

The diet is strikingly monotonous, though this is true of most diets in Asia. It is also very unbalanced, with a large proportion of cereals and only a small amount of protein. Some peasants—those who get milk—can be said to subsist on a fairly satisfying diet, but these are in distinct contrast to those whose daily diet falls below the normal minimum for the whole of India. The regular consumption of milk generally corresponds to an economic holding and to a progressive farmer; the lack of milk is a further indication of a noneconomic holding and of a stagnant farmer.

The medium farmers—Brahmins, Jats, Vaisyas, and Lodhas—are strong and capable of doing really heavy work, even though their diet hardly corresponds with what is considered a good basic diet in the West. Certainly both their physical bearing and their enterprising spirit are sufficient proof that they are not suffering from serious malnutrition.

Some Examples

For evidence of this physical and mental vigor, let us look at the resources of some of the peasants whose standard of living has either risen or is now undergoing improvement.

The ex-lambardar, Tez Pal Singh, is considered to be a rich man. The fields he owns in Khandoï and the next village have an acreage of fifteen hectares. His main crops are sugar cane (4.5 ha.) and wheat (2.5 ha.), the remainder being lower-grade cereals, a little cotton, and some pulses.

I do not know what his total assets are, but he is not short of savings. In 1949 he spent 30,000 rupees on the installation of his tube-well; on a mill for the grain, and on a sugar-cane crusher. In 1960 he installed an electric engine: the maintenance costs of it come to 800 or 900 rupees a year, and he meets them by selling water and renting the mill. He spent 15,000 rupees on his second daughter's wedding, and he is not in debt.

Tez Pal employs five permanent laborers, to whom he pays wages of thirty rupees a month each; sometimes he allows them interest-free loans and occasionally he gives them a little wheat. When the *gur* is being produced he engages four additional men, whom he pays at a rate of two rupees a day for a period of four months.

His yields are higher than those of most of the village. He is a prudent and enterprising farmer, having been the only one to make use of artificial fertilizers before the creation of the development block. His fields are well irrigated, and he sells half his wheat—some 1,900 kg.—for between 750 and 1,000 rupees, and most of his *gur* for about 15,000 to 18,000 rupees. The other cereals and the pulses are partly for family consumption and partly for payment to laborers at harvest time. Six good bullocks take care of the agricultural work, and two buffaloes yield ten liters of milk each a day. Tez Pal also has a little horse which he rides to survey his fields.

Under the one-family roof live our landowner, his wife, and his widowed sister-in-law, and one son with his wife and three children. Another son works outside the village and the two daughters are married.[3]

Tez Pal Singh does not enjoy the luxuries of one who possesses over a hundred hectares; he has no car and his way of life is simple compared with Western standards, but in the eyes of the village he enjoys a comfortable existence, and he knows how to work in order to get a living from the land.

Diwan, a Brahmin, owns 3.3 hectares: he has a quarter in wheat, a quarter in sugar cane, and the rest in poorer cereals and pulses. He and his two cousins own two Persian wheels which irrigate some of their fields; the remainder are close to the state tube-well. He owns two bullocks and one buffalo which yields four liters of milk a day.

His standard of living has improved, mainly because the land tax

[3] Tradition requires that husband and wife should belong to the same caste but must come from different villages.

has remained the same while productivity and prices have risen. He does, however, have difficulties in that the wedding of his elder son, a minor civil servant in another village, and that of one of his daughters have run him heavily into debt. At the moment he owes 2,000 rupees. His mother and his six other children, the eldest of whom goes to a secondary school, all live under his roof.

Like most of the peasants of Khandoï, Diwan keeps all his *kharif* cereals for home consumption. If he happens to have an exceptionally good harvest he may sell a little wheat, but most years *gur* is his main cash crop. After deducting his main costs of production, his net income amounts to about 1,500 rupees a year.

For Bhola Singh, a Jat, the standard of living is a little higher. Before the consolidation of holdings he and his brother used to cultivate five hectares, of which one and a quarter were in sugar cane and nearly two in wheat, with the remainder used for other cereals. The land is carefully cultivated, with chemical fertilizers and selected seeds. The yield of some of the plots would be improved if the canal from Unchagaon and the Ganges worked more efficiently. Bhola and his brother have four bullocks, one cow which gives five liters of milk a day, and two buffaloes, each of which gives ten liters of milk a day. These figures are higher than the average for the locality.

Bhola Singh and his wife with their four daughters (a fifth daughter is married), one of their sons, and Bhola's brother and sister-in-law (who have no children) all live together in the same house. This family lives as a community,[4] and consumes all the *kharif* and half of the wheat harvest. The remaining 1,400 kg. are sold for 600 to 800 rupees. The *gur* brings in 4,000 rupees. This relative affluence enables Bhola Singh to cover the cost of his eldest son's education, which amounts to 1,300 rupees a year: he is at a university reading for a B.A. degree.[5] Despite this heavy sacrifice, Bhola has been able to enlarge his house, cultivate a kitchen garden, sink a well with a Persian wheel, and renew his cattle without getting into debt.

It is evident from figures obtained that farmers who own at least 2.75 hectares generally dispose of surplus cereal by selling it in town. This applies mainly to wheat; other cereals and pulses never leave the village. Except in the case of very large families, the amount sold represents a third, or sometimes half, of the total gross product. Those who cultivate smaller acreages—two hectares or so—have only a small

[4] Remember that the joint family holding has been broken up by the process of consolidation of holdings.

[5] This is one of the exceptional cases in the village.

surplus of wheat, which means that *gur* is often the only source of ready cash.

The Enterprising Spirit

The mere fact that he is denied the minimum necessary land and a proper diet doesn't necessarily condemn the peasant to stagnation. By dint of ability and tenacity, some manage to escape their harsh fate.

Hulassi, a Lodha-Rajput, is a case in point. For a long time he worked as a laborer for Tez Pal Singh. His total cattle consisted of one buffalo. After the abolition of the zamindari system he managed to buy 0.3 hectare of land of which he is a *bhumidar*. It is a mark of his intelligence that he has made sugar cane his main crop, for this is more profitable than cereals. In addition he cultivates 0.5 hectare of a field and 0.4 hectare of an orchard for a Jat. Half the cost of cultivation is paid by the landowner, and Hulassi receives a quarter of the harvest.

Cattle provide a third source of income for Hulassi, who now has two buffaloes. They are second-rate stock (each yielding three liters of milk a day) because he could not afford to pay more than 550 rupees for them; but they have had four calves, and by turning most of the milk into *ghee*, Hulassi can earn another 60 rupees a month (120–150 liters of milk produce 12 kg. of *ghee*).

By these various activities, Hulassi has raised his standard of living from what it was fifteen years ago, despite his large family: his wife, four boys aged ten to eighteen, and three daughters, one still unmarried and at home.[6]

Stagnation

How do the small landowners exist, who own only a hectare of land, or less? A man who owns at least 1.75 hectares is able to subsist with his cereal crops, which his family consumes, and the sale of *gur*. But a man who has less land has an extremely hard time, especially if he has a family of several children.

Baljit Singh and his brother, who are Jats, cultivate 1.35 hectares, half of which is in wheat. The joint family consists of their two wives and four children, as well as the third brother's wife and her three children. They own a bullock, a calf, a heifer, and a buffalo which gives between four and five liters of milk a day (all of which is

---

[6] A married daughter is still some cost to her parents, since she often visits them and on returning home must take presents to her in-laws.

consumed by the children). Because of the small wheat crop, the family must buy much of the grain it needs, and even in summer they seldom eat more than two meals a day.

The fact that they do somehow manage to live is due to the financial help of the third brother, who works outside as operator of a state tube-well. Thanks to the contribution that he makes, they can sometimes use artificial fertilizers. Their debts to the cooperative exceed 1,000 rupees.

Sukha and his two brothers (Jativs) cultivate a similar area of land. Sukha is a widower, with one married child and three children under twenty-one. The second brother lives with his wife and three very young children, the third with his wife and five children. The three brothers own jointly two bullocks and two buffaloes, which give three to four liters of milk a day. Some of the milk is kept for the children, but throughout the year the adults have only two daily meals consisting mainly of *chapatis*. By selling *gur* they make enough money to buy grain, but any expenditure on production (chemical fertilizers, or selected seeds) is quite out of the question.

I know two brothers, both of whom are in the prime of life. "Has your lot improved at all?" I asked them. *"Kuchh nahin* [Not at all]," they answered wearily and sadly. These men live a stagnant existence, weighed down by the poverty and the prejudices that have overwhelmed the untouchables for centuries.

It is the same with Kirpal, a Jativ, and his wife and two children. Kirpal has inherited 0.35 hectare of land which he does not cultivate himself because he has no bullocks and no knowledge of ploughing. His crop-sharer gives him about 150 kg. of grain which is enough to live on for a few months. He has no cattle at all. For four months of the year he works at a *kolu* for a seasonal wage of 120 to 150 rupees. He also helps with the harvest, at a wage of one rupee a day.

So lives Kirpal, in uncomplaining acceptance of his lot.

Roshan, a Muslim, owns 1.5 hectares of land. He is an old man, and he and his wife live with their two married sons, a total household of six adults and six young children. Half his fields are devoted to wheat, a third to sugar cane, and the remainder to other cereals. His cattle consist of a pair of bullocks and two buffaloes, each producing five or six liters of milk a day. The cereals that Roshan grows meet about three-fifths of his needs. He buys an average of 750 kg. of wheat a year (at a cost of 300–400 rupees) which he is able to pay for out of income from the sale of *gur,* and the two kilos of *ghee* [7] that he sells each week for ten rupees.

[7] One kilo of *ghee* sells at five rupees.

Roshan's family has a slightly better standard of living than our Jativs. In addition to cereals, their diet includes a little milk and some *ghee*. But they live on a very tight budget; once they have paid their taxes and water rates they have practically nothing left for buying fertilizers and selected seeds, or for improving their farm implements. For two years Roshan has had a debt of 200 rupees outstanding with the dealer who buys his *gur*. He borrowed this sum to finance the wedding of one of his daughters, at an interest rate of 3 percent a month.

The Figures and Decisive Factors

The reader will no doubt be disappointed that I have not given an example of a family budget together with the cost of agricultural production, but local conditions do not permit an exact statistical analysis, as Professor Louis Dumont has so rightly shown in his investigations into southern India: "Since it is not sufficient merely to observe, one is largely dependent on oral information. Now a systematic quantitative analysis would in my opinion give an exaggerated picture of the situation. To express in terms of money such assets as foodstuffs produced on the farm or to try to calculate precisely what is the average expenditure, etc., it is necessary to make quite a number of arbitrary assumptions." [8]

With maize, *jowar, bajra,* more than half the wheat, and most of the pulses never leaving the village, home consumption plays an important part in the economy of Khandoï. But the farmers do not weigh what they have harvested, and so we must be content with approximate figures.

The amount of wheat that goes into the market economy varies a great deal according to good and bad years. In 1964, for example, the cold weather destroyed a large part of the harvest. Also, the selling price of wheat varies with the season: at harvest time wheat brings 15 rupees for 37.3 kg., but later on it may bring as much as 20 rupees. [9] The farmer does not always remember how much income he gets from each sale.

Gur is, in fact, the only product that can be assessed with accuracy. The small holders' other sources of income, such as that from the sale of *ghee* or from the wages they earn as casual laborers, are never

[8] Louis Dumont, *Une Sous-caste de l'Inde du Sud* (Paris, 1957), pp. 107–108.

[9] In December, 1963, the selling price at the bazaar was 24 rupees per maund, already rather a high figure which was due to rise still higher the following year (see chap. 10).

recorded, nor can one accurately know their expenditures, since they live largely off their own produce, particularly cereals, pulses, and milk, and the cattle feed off the farm waste.

Even the farm implements, which are for the most part of the traditional kind, are a vague item in total costs, since they are made either by the farmers themselves or by the carpenter who receives grain in return for his labor. As for seeds, the farmers may get them from their own crops; if they obtain selected seeds from the development block, they buy them on credit, which they repay after the harvest in the form of grain corresponding to the amount borrowed, plus a quarter by way of interest.

Whenever possible, the farmers buy chemical products to supplement their farm manure; this costs between 40 and 80 rupees for one hectare of wheat and between 60 and 120 rupees for the same area of sugar cane.

One can be fairly precise about the cost of water obtained from the state tube-well or from Tez Pal Singh's tube-well. Every three or four successive irrigations of wheat cost from 13 to 20 rupees per hectare. The *rahat* can be used at no cost to the owner; others pay two rupees a day, but even so the amount of water purchased varies so much that no accurate account can be kept.

Land taxes are very low: Diwan, for example, is taxed 20 rupees a year for his 3.3 hectares, Bhola 71 rupees for nearly five hectares, the tax varying according to the quality of the soil.

Labor costs are particularly difficult to assess. With the exception of some "large" landowners, hired labor is used only sporadically. Women and children are recruited to help at harvest time, and the peasants help one another when the need arises. Casual laborers are usually paid one rupee a day for ploughing, sowing, or weeding, or from five to seven kilos of wheat for harvesting; for maize, the pay is one kilo of maize for every maund harvested (37.3 kg.) and one kilo per maund when it is threshed.

As we have already seen, the cost of the *kolu* for sugar cane includes the rent of the crusher and the vat, which amounts to 175 to 200 rupees, shared between the co-owners. It is more difficult to be precise about the other expenses: in some cases processing is carried out by the landowner's family and in others one or more casual laborers are hired and paid in *gur,* the monetary equivalent being from one and a half to three and a half rupees a day according to the work done.

The net result of our questionnaire makes it possible to distinguish between the landowners whose income just covers their working expenses and those who manage to make a profit. The first only just make ends meet. Unless, like our Lodha Hulassi, they are full of energy and are willing to make heavy sacrifices, they have nothing to spare for improvements, either in their irrigation or in the quality of their fertilizers and seeds, and they therefore have great difficulty in laying a kind of "take off" basis for progress. Would a more liberal rural credit help them to make a start? Those who own one or two hectares might benefit, but for those with less land a solution is much more difficult.

The second category includes those farmers who own at least two hectares. The margin within which they work and can invest is determined as much by irrigation and the size of their families and their lands as by their own abilities as farmers. A Diwan is beginning to feel the pinch, while another, Bhola, lives more comfortably.

An analysis of the size of the holdings (chap. 7) and of the revenue from them leads us to the same conclusion. The days are numbered for the farmers of Khandoï. The major part of the land yields a surplus which can be reinvested in order to increase production. In ten years' time, unless a new stage in the progress of farming has been reached, the increased population will absorb most of today's hard-earned surplus.

10

THE PEOPLE WITHOUT LAND

Census returns have drawn up a detailed classification of the population according to its occupation: [1]

	Men	Women
(1) Cultivators of land wholly or mainly owned	318	289
(2) Cultivators of land wholly or mainly unowned	17	12
(3) Cultivating or landless laborers	16	10
(4) Artisans	57	37
(5) Traders	13	11
(6) Transport	16	19
(7) Other services	108	106
(8) Noncultivating owners	1	11

The first and the last categories are, of course easy to define. The others are less clear cut. The private inquiry made in 1962 (see chap. 7) accounted for 108 landowners (categories 1 and 8) and this confirms the total of 619 people accounted for in the 1951 census.

The 1962 inquiry does not analyze in detail the other categories, which include seventy-four families. It makes no distinction between tradesmen and people engaged in transport, nor does it give the number of agricultural workers. These lacunae are even more unsatisfactory than the census figures, which in this connection are below reality. A good part of categories 5 and 7 should be included in category 3.

Many families have more than one means of livelihood. For instance, Jasram, a Jativ, owns a rope-making machine, and he also spends a lot of time working in the fields. Should he be classified as an artisan or as an agricultural worker? Kanaram, another Jativ, is a mason when he is not working as a casual laborer. A third sells cattle hides as well as working as a woodsman or a harvester according to season. Husseini, a Muslim, is an oil worker for part of the year and an

[1] From the *Census of India, 1951, District Census Handbook, U.P. Bulandshahr District;* the 1961 figures have not yet been published. Children are included in each column.

agricultural laborer for the rest of the time. Mirchani, a Jativ, owns a horse and *tanga;* [2] he himself is a laborer and his son is the coachman, but both of them may have been classified under the heading of transport.

In order to obtain a better idea of the true position I have followed another criterion: about thirty of the seventy-four families find their main source of living outside agriculture, as artisans, in trade, or in service; the others, about forty, are mainly employed as agricultural laborers. Some of those in the first category just about manage to make ends meet; those in the second live a very precarious existence.

Very Hard Conditions

Despite some nuances, of which we shall give examples, the common trait of agricultural workers and artisans is the precariousness of their standard of living. What a contrast there is between the Jats or Brahmins whose lively appearance gives way to the air of depression among the Jativs who comprise the majority of the landless people. How many times have I been given the same, sad, rather bitter answer "*Kuchh nahin* [Nothing]" when I have questioned them on the progress made during the last ten or fifteen years. Twenty out of 22 agricultural laborers, together with 18 of the artisans and tradesmen questioned, gave this reply.

Nearly all of them incur debts; 19 of the 22 agricultural workers could not exist without borrowing, and the same applies to 15 of the 18 artisans and tradesmen. The total debt of the former amounts to 10,300 rupees, an average sum of 542 rupees per person; the latter owe a total sum of 6,600 rupees, which is 440 rupees each, and is evidence of rather less acute poverty. The farmers obtain three-fifths of their loans from the cooperative or the government at a rate of 8.75 percent. But those who have neither the land nor the security to guarantee their loans have to resort to moneylenders, whose interest rate is generally 36 percent a year.

Sources of Credit (in rupees)

	Moneylenders	Cooperative Societies and Government
Landless laborers	9,500	800
Artisans, traders, services	6,000	600

[2] A two-wheeled horse-drawn carriage which provides transport to the bus station at Jahangirabad.

Some Examples

Ram Singh, a Khatik, has been working for Tez Pal Singh for twelve years. He is one of the permanent laborers at Khandoï, and he earns fixed monthly wages of 30 rupees, in addition to a little grain when the opportunity offers. He is married, with two children. Since he owns no cattle, the family has to go without milk and make do with *chapatis,* pulses, and mustard leaves for the two meals in winter and three in summer. Ram Singh owes 400 rupees plus 36 percent interest, and it would be true to say that his sole possessions are a shirt and a *dhoti.*[3] The first costs five rupees and lasts him four months, the second six rupees and lasts two months.

Jasram, a Jativ, works part time as a temporary laborer, earning one rupee a day. This brings him about twenty rupees a month. He has a buffalo which has not yet begun to give milk. With his wife and three children, one of whom goes to school, he eats only two daily meals consisting of *chapatis,* and mustard leaves when in season.

With the help of a government loan, Jasram has bought a rope-making machine, for which he uses local fibers known as *sann.* This subsidiary means of living can hardly be said to be profitable; the fibers are expensive to buy, considering the very poor returns, and it would clearly be in Jasram's interests if he were to enter into partnership with others in order to reduce the costs, but he refuses to do so.

Amar Singh, a Jativ, works for ten or fifteen days a month for a daily wage of one rupee. His buffalo yields three liters of milk a day; he and his wife and two young children drink some of it, and the remainder he makes into *ghee* and sells for about ten rupees a month. Amar owes 200 rupees at 36 percent interest, a sum which he had to borrow in order to buy food during a lean period.

Chatu, a Jativ, and his wife live alone, their two children having died. In accordance with tradition, he receives cattle carcasses free of charge; he skins these and sells the hides, leaving the flesh and bones to the dogs and birds. He manages to earn between fifteen and twenty rupees a month. For a year he has owed the moneylender Dalip 100 rupees at 36 percent interest. He has no other work.

Manturi is a Muslim who is married with two children. He owns an oil *kolu,* a crusher which is smaller than that used for *gur,* which is driven by a bullock. For three months of the year he extracts oil from mustard seeds; this brings him in about a hundred rupees in wheat

[3] A piece of cloth knotted at the waist and brought up between the legs.

and in cash. For the rest of the year he works in the fields for a wage of one rupee a day.

Maqbul, another Muslim, has a wife and four children. He is a carpenter by trade. He makes and repairs ploughs and other farm implements for about ten to fifteen farmers, and from each of these he receives one maund (37.3 kg.) of grain a year.[4] He works on the land for three months of the year. He hires out his bullock, and he intends to replace his buffalo, which has just died. Until its death he used to earn five rupees a month from the sale of *ghee*. His family lives on *chapatis,* lentils, mustard leaves, and a little milk. Maqbul owes his cousins 100 rupees, interest free. His various means of livelihood make it possible for him to live better than the Jativs described above.

Charan, who is married with four children under twenty-one years of age, is a Dhobi, the laundrymen's caste. He works all the year round and for his services receives 550 kg. of cereal a year. His buffalo yields three or four liters of milk a day. The children drink a little of this; the rest is made into *ghee* and brings in two and a half rupees a week. He had to borrow 100 rupees to pay for the wedding of one of his children. His standard of living comes somewhere between that of Maqbul and the Jativs.

Ram Phal, a Nai, the barbers' caste, lives with his wife and four young children. (Tradition dictates, among the high castes especially, that one should not shave oneself.) Like our Dhobi, Ram Phal receives 550 kg. of cereal a year for his services, which is worth between 200 and 250 rupees at market price. As a sideline he sells fried potatoes and vegetables at fetes. His two elder sons work as peons at the development block. Ram Phal's brother, Bhika, who is a widower, owns a small horse and gathers grass, in this way contributing between five and ten rupees a month to the household income. Our barbers have no cattle, and therefore have to do without milk. They do not owe very much money—only 50 rupees, interest free.

About half a dozen small tradesmen in Khandoï sell matches, *bidis* (cigarettes), cotton goods, sugar, and onions. Tez Singh, a Jat who is married and has two small children, earns as a tradesman between one and two rupees a day, either in ready cash or more often in grain. He has no cattle, and therefore no milk. He has no debts.

Nathu, a Jativ, is a tailor, with two wives [5] and two children. He

---

[4] This is a survival of the tradition that existed before the British came to power, whereby the worker in compensation for his services had a right to a share in the land produce; it is known as the *jajmani* system.

[5] There are still some cases of polygamy. Another Jativ has two wives, so too has a Thakur, a well-to-do landowner, but polygamy is now forbidden by law.

owns a sewing machine and earns a little more than one rupee a day. Since he has no cattle, he rarely drinks milk, and his diet is limited to two meals a day. He is heavily in debt, having borrowed 150 rupees from the government for the purchase of cloth, and 1,250 rupees at 36 percent interest from a moneylender in order to rebuild his house after it was destroyed by fire.

Unemployment and Lack of Manpower

The agricultural workers, who are mainly Jativs, and a large number of artisans complain of lack of work. On the other hand, the medium farmers and those who are rather "well off" do not have always enough manpower. What is the reason for this paradox, which is also found in other regions?

The landless laborers have just cause to feel that their wage of one rupee [6] is totally inadequate. It has scarcely altered during the last ten years, despite the increase in the cost of living. In this connection Jasram's budget is interesting. One day's work costs him a great deal in terms of food, for he needs at least half a liter of milk and 600 to 700 grams of cereal in order to keep up his strength. Sometimes he finds it more economical to stay at home contenting himself with only 400 to 500 grams of cereal and going without milk altogether. Other Jativs confirm this opinion, and only in times of dire extremity will they resign themselves to working for one rupee.

What is the farmers' answer to this? The rate has become fixed at this level, and none of them wants to take the responsibility for raising it. If they do not have enough laborers, they prefer to do extra work themselves. Jats and Brahmins would add that the Jativs are lazy (*sust* in Hindi), working neither willingly nor well, and do not deserve to be better paid. At first this criticism seemed to me merely a sign of caste prejudice, but certain firsthand experiences have shaken that opinion. I needed someone to make a small embankment over the road, which was flooded, so that we could get to Khandoï by car. We arranged with Jasram for four Jativs to do the job at a payment of one rupee each for the three or four hours' work necessary—this being double their usual wage. The interest that I had shown in the Jativs should have given them an additional reason for helping me. The following morning nobody arrived, despite my repeated appeals, and I finally had to do the job myself with the voluntary help of some Brahmins and Jats. The arrangements had of course been made, but the Jativs maintained that there was nobody available that day.

[6] Sometimes a meal of *chapatis* is added to this.

A little later on a *shramdan* was undertaken at Khandoï to improve the road. This is a sort of village work force, to which every able-bodied man is obligated to contribute his labor or else pay two rupees a day. The Jativs and other Harijans were scrupulous in doing the work assigned to them, but only a few were willing to answer my earnest appeal to do additional work for two rupees, which was twice the normal rate.

There are other instances of this inertia. Chatu, interviewed above, told me that he could not work in the field because he did not know how to plough and was afraid of the bullocks.[7] Another eloquent Jativ leader never troubled to give to me the petition for which I asked him, although it was designed to remedy an injustice by which several of his own people would have been injured.[8]

Another circumstance has also to be taken into account. The Jativs have been particularly unsettled by the changing economic and technical structures of the last century. Their traditional livelihood was in leather-work and in addition to this in the past they often used to work as coolies. They would also cut grass and recoat houses with dried mud. The appearance of the modern tanneries dealt them a severe blow; according to the 1911 census, in the course of ten years the number of Chamars (or Jativs) engaged in leather-work decreased by 36.9 percent.[9] A little later, the replacement of the *mot* by the Persian wheel deprived the Chamars of another means of living, that of making and repairing leather water-skins.

What has happened to the Jativs is characteristic of economic changes that took place under the British. The evident progress made in modern methods of production was sufficient to unsettle a number of traditional trades, but at the same time they were not offered any alternative work. Their only recourse was to seek some form of agricultural employment, thereby increasing the agricultural population.

But the economic situation is not the sole explanation for the Jativs' attitudes. One can understand that the extremely poor Jativs feel misused, but a Jativ who owns 3.8 hectares of land has no reason to complain in plaintive tones about his poverty. It is a complex problem, and Brahmins and Jats are too hasty in their criticisms of Jativs. Yet, there is no doubt that in Khandoï the "weaker sections of society," as they are called in India, do not possess the energy and tenacity of the

[7] As I myself know from experience, these gentle-looking animals move their horns in a way that can be very dangerous to those who are not used to them, but is this sufficient justification for Chatu's attitude?

[8] The farmers would have reacted quite differently in similar circumstances.

[9] See Lewis, *Village Life in Northern India*, p. 71.

traditional cultivator castes. Their diet, which is deficient even according to a norm far below our own, prevents them from making the same effort as those belonging to the better nourished high castes.

For centuries the low castes and untouchables have constituted the majority of the landless workers and have lived apart from the high castes. This is particularly true still of the ex-untouchables, who only come into contact with the higher castes on a professional basis. The Jativs seldom stop for long in their parts of the village, and when they approach a group of Brahmins and Jats sitting together on a *char-païs*,[10] they are not offered a seat and will remain squatting on their heels. It was the same when I paid the Jativs a visit. Only on rare occasions did they sit beside me; usually they got out a *charpaï* for me and either stood or squatted around me in a circle.

Such behavior is characteristic of the Jativs' humble attitude, growing out of a traditional sense of inferiority and long years of extreme poverty. A barrier that is both economic and social separates these people from the Brahmins and Jats as well as from the Lodha-Rajputs (Sudras), who, though not a high caste, are superior to the untouchables.

Some Remedies and Conclusions

How can one break down the barrier of extreme poverty, prejudice, and weakness which surrounds and restricts the lives of the Jativs, who number Khandoï's second largest community?

As we have seen, their low standard of living is more an obstacle than a stimulant. The integration of the low castes within the development of the economy represents one of India's most complex tasks, since the decisive factors of will and ingenuity are lacking. It will need a great deal of time to create a spirit of initiative among these men, who have for years led such a miserable existence; nevertheless, some evidence of change is already apparent.

Though for decades their lives have been weighed down, without hope, the Jativs are now beginning to become conscious of the rights guaranteed to them by the Constitution. "There is but one difference between yesterday and today," said Nathu, "we no longer have padlocks on our mouths." A proof of this lies in the fact that many of the Jativs belong to the Republican party, which is in opposition to Congress, and which especially defends their interests. Another new factor is that the government favors the education of the "weaker

[10] A bed made of ropes.

sections of society" by granting scholarships and other advantages. Several Jativ families send their children to school, and, as we have seen, one of them is even at university, reading for a B.A. degree.

These two facts should have a stimulating effect by creating outlets within the tertiary sector; some of the children who will take jobs outside Khandoï will eventually be able to help their families financially.

As I have already pointed out, it would be useless to try to find a solution by the reallocation of land. Since there are no spare plots available, it would be necessary to dispossess the better-off landowners, but the Jativs would obtain much poorer yields, being far less competent and unaccustomed to applying themselves with patience to the kind of work I have described.

Finally, we shall see that the village cooperative farm does not offer a satisfactory solution.

For the immediate future, however, one door is beginning to open: the growth in production cannot fail to bring about an increase in wages. At Unchagaon it is impossible to find a casual laborer for less than 1.50 to 1.75 rupees. The same increase is evident in other parts of the district which are less isolated and more developed than Khandoï.[11]

The situation has changed since my first visit. Between May and June, 1964, owing to poor harvests, the cost of one maund of wheat rose from 24 to 28 or 30 rupees. The farmers of the village have been forced to follow the trend, and the wages of casual laborers have risen to 1.50 and occasionally even to 1.75 rupees.

Progress is being made, since even if prices should fall after better harvests, higher wages would no doubt stay the same; but the Jativs have yet to learn how to benefit from it. My early impressions of the Jativs gave no more encouragement than did my observations after the increase, in August, 1964. The cooperative farm had to engage five temporary Lodhas laborers from another village to help weed the maize, because there was not sufficient labor available on the spot.

This sort of apathy is not generally found among all the Harijan (ex-untouchables). We shall meet examples of much stronger characters among the people in Madras State and in Maharashtra. At Khandoï we have Saggan, a Bhangi, scavenger and sweeper, who belongs to the last rank in the social scale, even lower than that of the Jativs. His sister Prem is strong and artful and never loses an opportunity to make

[11] Along with this there appears to be a reduction in the rates of interest. In the villages around Bulandshahr as well as in those on the main roads, the moneylenders are often satisfied these days with 24 percent.

a little extra money and grain either by working more or by asserting her talent for seeing that her rights are respected.[12] Saggan and his wife live with their daughters-in-law and their children. One of his sons works in Delhi and sends him thirty rupees every month. Our man works sometimes at a *kolu* and sometimes in the fields. He has a small buffalo, and raises pigs which he sells to a military farm. He is one of the few people in the village to keep chickens; these, three in number, lay altogether a dozen eggs a week.[13] Some of these he keeps for the family to eat and the rest he sells. He has no debts and recognizes that his standard of living has improved during the last fifteen years; his diet and clothing bearing witness to this.

The essential factor is that Saggan has no complexes; he talks without emotion and does not complain; in short, he is content with his lot.

What conclusions can be drawn from our observations? Fifty of the 116 families who own land have reasonable, fair living conditions with a margin of savings more or less adequate to increase development. The conditions of about ten families are marginal, and those of the remaining fifty or so provide an inadequate standard of living.

Among the seventy-four landless families there are some—a teacher and his family, for instance—who live rather well. About thirty families just make ends meet by working as artisans as well as temporary laborers. The poorest families, of which there are about forty, have a very hard lot.

Thus in this village, in a comparatively rich and advanced district, we can admit that between 35 and 40 percent of the families manage to attain a fairly satisfactory standard of existence; this they achieve at the price of unremitting labor. Nearly a third of the village lives a poor existence, and the rest fall somewhere in between.

Caste and land, without being absolute criteria, coincide in the main with this division, but the fact that the majority of landowners are Jats does not mean that there are none of this caste among the second and third groups. By the same token, some Lodha-Rajputs as well as a few Khatiks, the lower castes, have managed either to keep up with or to get into the first group.

---

[12] When she worked for our Brahmin neighbors in the morning we often heard the sound of her shrill and demanding voice!

[13] Unlike the Punjab and Maharashtra, poultry farming has made little progress here, where most people are vegetarians. Perhaps the government does not encourage it enough, but the real drawback is the limited urban market for eggs.

11

THE PANCHAYAT AND
LOCAL AFFAIRS

Until 1952 the zamindars wielded very considerable powers in Khandoï. They were responsible for public order and problems of general interest. The panchayats only functioned on a caste basis and seem to have had little influence.

The administration itself dealt only with land taxation and water charges. The patwari, the village accountant in charge of the land records [1] (a hereditary appointment), facilitated the collection of taxes by the zamindars. He resided at Khandoï, unlike the employees of the irrigation department who traveled around in the course of their duties, covering an area or a canal.

Independence and the development plans changed this light organizational structure drastically. The zamindari system was abolished and a much more elaborate administrative set-up was gradually introduced with the aim of stimulating the development of the rural areas.

The Panchayat

The beginnings of village administration in Uttar Pradesh date from 1920, when, to give effect to the Government of India Act of 1919, Uttar Pradesh (then known as United Provinces) passed the United Provinces Panchayat Act. With the approval of the elders, the District Magistrate appointed five to seven persons who formed the panchayat. This development made slow progress: in 1940–1941 the province still had only 4,733 panchayats looking after the interests of ten million inhabitants.[2]

The United Provinces Panchayat Raj Act of 1947, prepared before Independence and passed soon afterward, speeded up the process by enlarging the functions of the panchayats. At Khandoï the panchayat came into being in 1954. Its seventeen members were elected by adults, men and women, bringing together the representatives of the various castes.

[1] The records showed the amount of tax and rent payable by each farmer.
[2] Vijaya Lakshmi Purwar, *Panchayats in Uttar Pradesh* (Lucknow, 1960), p. 71.

The first meeting took place on December 13, 1954, the one called for the 9th having been postponed for lack of a quorum. Thirteen members were present and discussed the following points:

(1) Income and expenditure of the panchayat. Several tax rates were assessed in accordance with the person's occupation.
(2) The improvement of the earth road leading to Unchagaon.
(3) The assistance from the development block.
(4) The repair of the drinking-water wells in the village and the construction of new wells.
(5) The decision to pave the village streets with cemented bricks (possibly with help from the block).
(6) Adult education by means of evening classes.
(7) The obligation on young people to undertake *shramdan* (voluntary work).

The panchayat met six times in 1955 and four times in 1956. Then meetings became less frequent. The minutes reveal one meeting only in 1957 and two in 1958, after which date there are no more entries.

During these four years four drinking-water wells were repaired and one new well out of four that had been decided upon was sunk. A few streets were paved and some street drains improved. Road works were limited to the installation of two big drainpipes at the entrance and exit of the village. Since the road was not raised, they served no useful purpose. One track was widened over a distance of nearly a kilometer. Part of these works was carried out during a week's *shramdan* starting on January 26, 1956, Republic Day.

The minutes mention other discussions, several of which resulted in positive action. The panchayat (July 10, 1955) decided to accept the offer from the block of a radio set, which was in fact subsequently returned as being out of order, and of a metal slide for schoolchildren (received and installed).[3] But after 1955, and especially from 1958 to 1962, the panchayat was dormant. I could find no record covering this period, and no one could remember if one had been kept. The activities of the panchayat were practically nil.

As a result of the Panchayati Raj set in motion by the *Mehta Report* of 1957, Uttar Pradesh passed a law in 1961 establishing panchayats at the block and district levels. One can therefore examine whether the panchayat of the Unchagaon block revived public affairs in Khandoï.

A new record, begun in 1963, mentions a meeting held on November 14, 1962. On January 26, Republic Day, the gaon sabha met in plenary

[3] Reports and other information taken from the *Karyavahiyon ki Pustakon ka Farm, Khandoï* ["Register of the Minutes"].

session, in which all adults [4] took part. India was then suffering from the shock of the events of the autumn, the Himalayan fighting against Chinese troops. Using the blocks as intermediaries, the central government had distributed pamphlets and pictures aimed at arousing patriotic enthusiasm in the countryside. Since several men from Khandoï were at the front with the Jat regiment, the villagers were particularly receptive to the propaganda. The *pradhan* (president) read the proclamation of the state of emergency that had been declared in the face of the Chinese threat. He then proposed the creation of a village volunteer force and a work bank (*shram* bank).[5] Fifty men volunteered for the former. The pradhan proposed that each eligible man should agree to undertake ninety-six hours, that is, twelve days, of *shramdan* per year. The assembly gave the proposal its unanimous approval. Following this there was discussion about road works and the paving of several streets.

The panchayat met a few months later, on April 1. The minutes were not signed and do not mention how many members were present. There was some discussion of a plan for the *kharif*.

At a meeting on July 3 the new president, who had been elected in April, was absent. A committee for the consolidation of holdings was established. The accounts were read. Then it was decided to spend 350 rupees on the paving of a street.

The meeting planned for November 8 did not take place, because the president suddenly had to go to Bulandshahr for a lawsuit. The meeting of the 12th was postponed for lack of a quorum and that of the 20th because of a further visit to Bulandshahr by the president. A meeting eventually took place on December 17 with ten out of seventeen members present. (I was also present.) Discussion on the 1964/65 budget could not proceed because the president and secretary had nothing prepared. There was discussion about paving more streets and improving the road, and it was agreed that the matter should be brought up again at the gaon sabha. Finally the question of electricity was considered. It was suggested that they could now begin to extend to the villages the lines that served the tube-wells. A decision was deferred to a later date, since the pradhan had not made any preliminary study (cost, villagers' interest, etc.) .

Up to the time of my departure (February 19, 1964), no other meeting of the gaon sabha or of the panchayat had taken place.

---

[4] Theoretically of both sexes, but in practice men only. If women were present, they stood at one side. The gaon sabha was supposed to meet once or twice a year, the panchayat administering local affairs between times.

[5] These were general measures passed by all the states.

Here are the results of the decisions taken on January 26, 1963. At the end of the meeting the fifty volunteers performed a few physical exercises for the one and only time—at any rate up to February, 1964. Not one *shramdan* activity took place all year. (The one described below was not initiated by the panchayat.) Finally, the only work carried out was the paving (by paid laborers, not voluntary workers) of some twenty meters of street in front of the house of the retiring president.

The accounts for the financial year 1963/64 were as follows:

Balance from 1962/63...12.93 rs.	Purchase of registers........ 4.11 rs.
April, 1963: Receipts (taxes)..84.34	Secretary's remuneration.....12.00
	Travel expenses for purchase
	of registers............... 3.71 [6]
	19.82 rs.
Oct., 1963: Cash in hand....77.45	Street paving.............60.00
Tax..................00.05	Secretary's remuneration.....17.50
77.50 rs.	77.50 rs.

There was also a sum of 230 rupees on deposit at the post office. I was unable to ascertain why this was not mentioned in the account-book.[7]

The credit balance of the last ten years is small. The panchayat and its members have been quite unaware of the essential economic needs. The facts related confirm what I learned in my talks with the three villagers who have held the office of pradhan. To listen to them, one would think that the objects of the panchayat were to improve the roads, to pave the streets, to supply drinking water, and to encourage education. The *Mehta Report* sought to revive the development blocks by means of a wider general participation by the people channeled by the panchayat. This aim has been neither explained nor understood in Khandoï. Indeed, this state of affairs is made doubly unsatisfactory by the lack of any serious activity. Meetings have been infrequent, and too often, as after the big meeting of January 26, 1963, decisions arrived at have not been put into effect.

The Anatomy of an Election

It seems paradoxical that the panchayat set up in orderly circumstances so little reflects the dynamism of the progressive wing of the electoral body.

Even before Independence the village had been touched by political problems and the influence of Congress. In 1942, after the famous

[6] It is disturbing to see that the travel expenses are nearly as high as the cost of the registers.

[7] *Kosh registar*, Khandoï.

"Quit India" resolution,[8] several of the best farmers demonstrated by setting fire to the canal inspection bungalow several kilometers away. They were imprisoned with other nationalists.

In 1954, when the Unchagaon block was created, Khandoï showed itself very receptive to the approaches of rural leaders. The village took part in big collective works such as the Unchagaon–Jahangirabad road. This was also the time when the panchayat was active. The president, one of the leaders in the 1942 demonstrations, was a good organizer. In 1956 he was replaced by another farmer, a rather color-less man, but he was elected to office again in 1959. In 1962 he was called to sit on the *Kshetr Samiti* (block panchayat). By then, some people had become disappointed with him; some no longer trusted him and others were complaining about various issues. He had one sworn enemy, a cousin, with whom he was in litigation concerning a field. Having grown tired of the one man, some of the villagers took a malicious pleasure in putting up the cousin as his successor!

A second candidate was in the field, a typical progressive farmer. He was an honest man who had no enemies. His only fault was that he was too closely allied to one of the former zamindars whose *kolu* he shared. For this reason a large section of the Jats (his own caste), including the two other ex-zamindars, supported the first candidate, a Vaisya, who finally was successful.

Through the interplay of these two motives, Khandoï succeeded in the remarkable achievement of electing as pradhan a man who was unsuited for this appointment instead of an almost ideal candidate. The man elected had never been a farmer, and had lived with his brother since returning to the village; he was also in poor health. He was, it is true, a former member of the Legislative Assembly at Luck-now, on which he had sat from 1952 to 1957 when he lived in another village, but he had no interest in the office of pradhan or in panchayat affairs. On the contrary, he had no thought in his head except for his lawsuit, which soon became a public joke. In January, 1964, affairs took a bad turn and a dispute degenerated into a brawl between the new pradhan's family and a group of his cousins.[9]

The Community

After the panchayat and its factions, let us consider other aspects of the life of the community.

[8] The Congress party demanded the immediate surrender of power by the British. The latter retorted with all the more firmness that the Japanese were at the gate-ways to India. Nationalists were arrested en masse.

[9] This did not concern the former pradhan but a third branch of the family.

The former zamindars no longer had a real authority in the village, although they still retained a certain prestige and some influence. The two oldest were mainly concerned with managing their holdings. The youngest, who had come from another village to take over his inheritance from his maternal grandfather, was the only one to play a moderately successful part in local politics. He belonged to the Congress party, and sought to become a "leader." At meetings the sole privilege of the zamindars was the rope bed or a chair on which they could sit while the villagers, including the pradhan, took their places on the matting. I often noticed the freedom with which the peasants expressed themselves to their former masters, sometimes even contradicting them.

Were any new forces in evidence? In the whole region the presence of political parties only makes itself felt at the time of elections for Parliament or the Legislative Assembly. At other times hardly any substantial organization exists. In five months Khandoï was visited by one lone politician, the secretary of the district Praja Socialist party. On another occasion a leader of the Republican party spoke at Unchagaon to defend the Harijans, particularly the Jativs.

It is at block and even district level that the direct influence of the parties is exerted: party influence is evident at a lower level only when there happens to be a fairly important politician (or a friend of one) who, as a native of a particular village, still has some local connections and makes use of them.

Through personal ambition or for more devious reasons, a few villagers push themselves forward. Without being necessarily affiliated to any political party, they greet visiting officials, trying to represent themselves as leaders (neta) of the village. In truth, even if their social standing and their activities endow them with sufficient prestige to be in the foreground, they do not amount to much. People do not trust them, often with good reason; in one instance it may be because of some malpractices with an official, in another because of having taken unfair advantage of another villager. Most of the good farmers take little interest in local affairs and intrigues; they are quite fully occupied by work on their farms.

Could this void be filled by social conflicts such as the demands of the Harijans and other landless workers? Their lot is hard, certainly, but they have not been subjected to abuse or even physical violence, as we shall see is sometimes the case in Benares. Furthermore they lack organization, in contrast to the upper castes who, with the Lodha-Rajputs, form a powerful group.

In conclusion, one does not find at Khandoï much awareness of

collective interests or any means of creating or spreading such awareness. The panchayat ought to have taken care of this. One cannot say
that it has succeeded.

Quarrels and Mistrust

Khandoï's society can be bitter and quarrelsome like the countryfolk
in thousands of other villages in all latitudes. The important thing
here is not to establish this fact, but to see its impact on development.

The violent and long-standing struggle between the two cousins, the
pradhan and his successor, is a prime example of how such things can
have important consequences for a village. There are other examples.

When I was in Khandoï, I noted that one of the two diesel pumps
had been broken down since the spring of 1963, at considerable loss to
its owner and the twelve neighbors who bought water from him.
Instead of thirteen well-irrigated hectares producing 1,200 to 1,300
kg/ha of wheat, part of the land had not been sown for the 1963–1964
rabi, and the other part produced but a poor yield, some 700 to 800
kg/ha. Total production was down by at least nine tons, representing a
loss of earnings of 5,000 rupees or more for the farmers concerned. The
loss would have been even greater if the crop had been sugar cane.

The cost of repairing the pump was estimated at 2,000 rupees. The
owner (a joint family holding) had 500 rupees available. He had
obtained a government loan for a similar amount and was awaiting the
sale of his *gur,* at the beginning of 1964, to provide the balance.

The most elementary logic could demonstrate that, instead of losing
a year, the twelve neighbors would do better to share the expense
involved, on condition that they received free use of the well up to the
amount of their credit. Unfortunately, rightly or wrongly, the owner
did not inspire much confidence; there had already been some "incidents." In short, the neighbors were afraid that the owner would not
use the money to repair the pump or would not hold to his part of the
bargain and give them water.

A further example: one peasant gave 120 rupees to another peasant
as his share of the expenses of a well, but then the second peasant
refused to let him have any water. The first man could do nothing; he
was too poor to go to court and he was afraid of the numerous sons of
his adversary.

After the consolidation of holdings, a well which belonged jointly to
three peasants was no longer, as it had been before, at the point where
their plots met, but was now completely in a field belonging to one of
the three. The two other peasants feared that one day the third would

appropriate to himself the exclusive use of the well. They proposed that, in conformity with the limits allowed by the law, the boundaries of the fields should be slightly altered so that each man had access to the well. Only with the greatest difficulty, after lengthy discussions, was I finally able to secure an agreement between the co-owners. In the meantime, whether by chance or by design, some friends of the man benefiting from the well came to make a complaint; one of the other co-owners had tried, if not to violate, at least to assault a girl under the pretext that she had stolen some of his sugar cane!

The expenses of lawsuits, nearly always disputes over land, are another source of waste; instead of being invested in crops, money accumulates at the district court.

A Commonplace Example

Khandoï is not an exceptional case of a divided community; the surrounding villages are proof of this. There is hardly one panchayat that is working at even minimum efficiency. The twelve days of *shramdan* per year and per man agreed upon in January, 1963, have come to naught. In one place the pradhan is incompetent. In another two families of the ex-zamindars prevent any communal action by their violent enmity.

Disputes over water are frequent. A Brahmin in a village three kilometers away interrupted our walk across his fields: he was a co-proprietor with his brother and his cousin of a well whose bucket chain needed replacing (cost 175 rupees). This man and his cousin were prepared to pay their share, but the brother, for some obscure reason, did not want to do anything. The result was that two hectares of wheat were not irrigated in the 1963–1964 *rabi*.

Another owner from the same village had possessed since 1956 a diesel pump which, after giving some trouble, was completely out of action in February, 1962. As in the Khandoï pump affair, the mistrust and misunderstanding of the other villagers prevented him from having it repaired. At the same time the panchayat (one of the few rich ones) spent 5,000 rupees on building a panchayat *ghar* (communal house), which was quite useless, while their lands were badly irrigated.

Elsewhere three brothers, former zamindars, each owned some fifteen hectares, and they had bought a tractor for their common use. After a few years it had become such a bothersome source of argument that they sold it.

The Need for Activators

Every year rains made the earth road leading from Unchagaon impassable at the entrance and exit to the village. I asked why a *shramdan* was not organized to raise the level of the road. A few months later, in connection with the consolidation of holdings, the authorities proposed to reroute the road to the north of the village. It would avoid the areas that were liable to flood, but at the cost of sacrificing a few hectares of fields. I was then approached and asked to intervene to stop this proposed solution. In agreement with the consolidation officer, I called the owners together one evening. The A.C.O.[10] made out his case: instead of rerouting the road, they could keep the existing route by means of some simple terracing works. The meeting ended after confused discussions, without taking any definite decisions.

However, the next day work began. One of the ex-zamindars, Jai Pal Singh, the nephew of Tez Pal, appointed himself site manager. He drew up a list of those who came to work and those who preferred to give two rupees. Each day twenty to thirty persons were working, with picks and baskets. For a distance of 200 meters at the exit and 100 meters at the entrance, the road was raised in the course of three or four weeks.

Maintaining the rate of progress became difficult after a few days. There were "column-dodgers" who had to be fetched and persuaded to come after arguments; there were others who were truly very busy, but at last the work was completed.

The moral is that if the A.C.O. and I had not been there, the work would not have been undertaken. Although the actual part that I played in the operation was small, my presence served as an activator. During the work that followed, my activities were limited to visiting the site and rounding up some waverers.

This example seems to me significant. Left to themselves, with their mutual mistrust and their dissensions, the inhabitants of Khandoï find it difficult to take effective action in their collective interest, in spite of a large reservoir of good will. The panchayat has so far shown itself incapable of arousing the collective spirit, but this position could change. The villagers know where their interests lie and would put their trust in a high official who took on the role of activator. In short, a few expressions of encouragement from outside would be sufficient to set the process in motion from the lower levels upward. The question is, to what extent will the general administration and the development blocks succeed in providing this?

[10] Assistant Consolidation Officer, in charge of the consolidation of holdings.

12

THE UNCHAGAON BLOCK

The Unchagaon block, the first in Bulandshahr, was created in 1954 in the most isolated region of the district. Originally composed of 103 villages which covered an area of 370 square kilometers, it was reduced to 67 (73,000 inhabitants) in 1963 after a reorganization of neighboring blocks.

A main canal, with its branches, several state tube-wells, and the peasants' own wells irrigate 19,133 hectares out of a total acreage of 28,012 hectares (1961). More than a third of this bears double cropping. For the *rabi* the main crops are wheat, covering 4,978 hectares; barley, 1,918 hectares; and barley and peas mixed, 4,420 hectares. For the *kharif* they are maize, 4,936 hectares, and *jowar*, 1,360 hectares. Sugar cane is the dominant crop, with an area of 6,315 hectares. This pattern is clearly similar to that found in Khandoï.

Organization of the Block

The block development officer (B.D.O.) is in charge of both social and economic activities within the block. Several assistants, known as assistant development officers (A.D.O.) are assigned particular sectors: agriculture, cooperative credit, panchayats, animal husbandry, health, village industries, and education. These specialists live at Unchagaon. Finally there are the gram sewaks, or village-level workers, who are generally responsible for liaison between the block and the peasants. The one at Khandoï was responsible for a circle of eleven villages, with a total of 12,578 inhabitants, today reduced by a third; he lives in one of the villages. The block has ten gram sewaks altogether. Five gram sewikas, the women members of the staff, are in charge of social questions—the position of women, child welfare, and so on. Each circle has, in addition, a secretary for the panchayats who keeps the records and organizes meetings.

The district office is run by a staff consisting of a secretary in charge of statistics, known as the progress assistant officer, an accountant, an administrative assistant, and several subordinate employees. All the personnel, from the B.D.O. down, are from another block and often from another district, so that they may be at least partly shielded from local influences. The salary scale provides for an annual increment of a few rupees up to a fixed ceiling:

Office	Monthly Salary	Special Allowances (Added to Salary)
B.D.O.	220–400 rs.	40 rs.
A.D.O.	160–290	40
G.S. and panchayat secretary	80–150	40

The B.D.O. comes from the State Service and has a university degree.[1] The A.D.O.'s have received fairly specialized training: the agronomist has a B.Sc. degree in agriculture, and he has worked for a six months' probationary period before being appointed. The gram sewak holds a certificate of primary, and generally of secondary studies, having followed a two-year training course in one of the institutes in Uttar Pradesh created for this purpose. All these staff officers attend refresher courses from time to time; our B.D.O. was away for three months in 1963–1964 for this reason.

Regulations provide for the B.D.O. to spend fifteen days a month touring the block, ten nights of this period being spent away from home. The gram sewak has to spend twenty days on tour and fifteen nights in various villages of his circle. The B.D.O. has a Jeep at his disposal, but this is the block's only motorized vehicle; his subordinates travel about on bicycles which they themselves have bought and for the use of which they are paid an allowance.

The activities of the block are integrated with the central plan as follows:

Irrigation.—Encouragement is given to *shramdan* in the cleaning and construction of field channels, and credits (either government *taccavi* or cooperative loans) are extended for the sinking of wells and the installation of pumps.

Soil conservation.—There being little serious erosion in the Unchagaon block, only a small amount of work has to be organized.

Modernization of techniques.—This is done principally by demonstrations of, for instance, the Uttar Pradesh method of wheat cultivation, by the distribution of improved seeds, green manure, and chemical fertilizers bought on credit from cooperatives or with government

---

[1] The Indian B.A. comes somewhere between the baccalaureat and the European licence.

loans; by the construction of pits for manure and compost, the use of insecticides, and the introduction of new equipment which is partly subsidized.

Cooperative credit societies.—This means the extension, recruitment of new members, and control of societies created in the villages. The A.D.O. for cooperatives is in charge of supervisors, each of whom is responsible for one or more cooperatives.

Animal husbandry.—Cattle selection and care of animals.

Poultry development.—Encouraging the peasants by demonstrations and loans.

Education.—Building and establishing primary schools, community centers, and youth clubs.

Public health.—Sinking drinking-water wells and installing hand pumps, improving street drainage, building latrines and welfare centers, training midwives, family planning.

Social questions.—Provision of aid to the weaker sections of society, particularly the Harijans, in the form of subsidies for building houses and for employment.

Roads.—Organizing *shramdan* for building metaled roads, with help from the district for the heavy part of the work.

Cottage industries.—Provision of subsidies for buying materials for hand spinning and weaving and provision of sewing machines.

Panchayats.—Supervision of activities in the villages.

Depending on the circumstances, other activities may be introduced, such as a small savings scheme, a village volunteer force, and appeals to the villagers to face the danger from China. (Brochures on the frontier conflict were distributed.)

The block draws up its five-year plan for development and gives a quarterly progress report. Even after certain simplifications, there is still a great deal of red tape and paperwork involved.[2] The gram sewaks prepare the plan for their circles under the same items as for the block. These reports are gathered in by the progress assistant officer who compiles all the statistics; this is a long and tedious task, done without the aid of any machine except a few typewriters.

The plan of Unchagaon follows the usual pattern found in most parts of India, with the exception of a few local variations. The program covers the principal social and economic sectors of rural life. Unchagaon is also the district's pilot block for cooperative farming (see chap. 13), and a chief inspector is attached to it.

[2] The monthly reports became quarterly as from July, 1961.

Normally the B.D.O. holds staff meetings once a fortnight to take bearings, and to give his own instructions, or those of the district. The second staff meeting, which takes place at the end of the month, is the most important, for it is then that each gram sewak makes his report, by which the over-all progress of the block in its different sectors can be judged.

The budget of the block in stage II, that is, after a period of five years, covers little more than staff salaries and allowances.[3] For the 1964/65 financial year these amounted to 48,300 rupees, to which was added a sum of 10,500 rupees earmarked for the repair of the administrative buildings and for several consignments of material, agricultural implements, and equipment for the welfare centers and for animal husbandry.

Targets and Achievements, 1961–1964

The block made a good start in 1954. Being the first in the district, it had the good fortune to possess a staff that was somewhat above average. Several enterprises were undertaken, the most notable of which was the metaled road (12 km.) from Unchagaon to Jahangirabad, to which the villagers contributed the major part of the labor in *shramdan*. The new road has freed the area from its former isolation, especially felt during the monsoon season from the end of July to October; transport conditions have been vastly improved, with less wear and tear on vehicles, and much time saved. Also, a system of cooperative credit societies was established in the block, for the distribution of fertilizers, seeds, and agricultural implements.

The first results, though not spectacular, were encouraging. The block was active, and the B.D.O. made a good impression on the peasants.

Nine years later the picture is no longer quite the same. Lacking documents relating to the second plan, we must concentrate on the third plan, and on the *Quarterly Progress Reports* for 1961 to 1964.[4] The following table shows the yearly targets and the achievements attained.

---

[3] For the first five years (stage I), the total budget was 1,200,000 rupees, or an average of 240,000 rupees a year. For stage II it is 500,000 rupees for five years (see *Third Five Year Plan*, p. 333). At Unchagaon, as in many other blocks, it is often the case that the operating budgets are lower than the estimates because funds are lacking.

[4] The first is in Hindi: *Tisri Panchvarshiya Yojna, Unchagaon.* The *Quarterly Progress Reports,* in English, are presented at the end of each quarter.

Annual Reports at the End of the Fourth Quarter

	1961/62		1962/63		1963/64	
	T	A	T	A	T	A
Masonry wells	90	17	80	10	157	9
Persian wheels	250	25	250	7	176	10
Pumping sets (on canals)	8	2	8	3	18	2
Private tube-wells (with pumps)	5	9	15	2	11	0

T = Targets, A = Achievements.

Loans for Wells and Tube-wells

	Number of Works Sanctioned, Completed and Verified	Number of Works for Which Recovery Was Ordered
1956/57–1960/61	112	33

	Number of Works Sanctioned	Number of Works Completed 3/31/64
1961/62	61	15
1962/63	4	4

These works were carried out by the villagers themselves, with encouragement and advice from the block as well as loans to cover part of the costs.

The situation with regard to chemical fertilizers is hardly better.

Annual Reports (in tons)

	1961/62		1962/63		1963/64	
	T	A	T	A	T	A
Nitrogenous fertilizers	1,042	296.57	1,268	273	882	594.15
Superphosphate	267	85	297	63	243	103

In the third year the gap between targets and achievements decreased somewhat,[5] owing to a fair increase in consumption, but the goals were far from met.

Similar results can be found in other items. Each year 12,445 new acres of wheat should be cultivated according to the Uttar Pradesh method, but 16.9 percent and 9.6 percent were the figures reached in 1961/62 and 1962/63.

[5] The targets for 1963/64 were originally set at 1,763 and 486 tons. They were lowered in 1963, but they were still too high.

Green manure has come up to expectations for some crops other than wheat; on the other hand, we have already seen how badly farm manure is preserved. Now, of the 500 cemented pits planned, only 42 have been built. Progress has not been any better in agricultural implements: the block has supplied only 39 and 130, respectively, of the 2,116 cultivators and 3,610 improved ploughs promised for the first three years.

The cooperative credit societies almost reached their target for the affiliation of new members. In 1964, 45 percent of the families whose livelihood was in agriculture were covered, most of these being either *bhumidars* or *sirdars*. The total amount of short-term loans foreseen for a season nearly equaled the amount of those actually advanced— 1963/64 was in fact a year of progress. The villagers used few medium- and long-term loans, however: the disbursement each year on medium-term loans corresponded to 34, 32, and 13 percent of the amounts planned (these loans were for the purchase of farm implements and bullocks) ; not one rupee was asked for between 1961 and 1964 on long-term loan.

A certain parallel will be noticed between the cooperative credit societies and the results previously mentioned. In 1963 particularly the increase in the sale of fertilizers is linked with the progress of short-term loans. The total absence of long-term loans is only a reflection of the absence of new wells. Loans advanced by the cooperative societies were as follows:

	1961/62	1962/63	1963/64
Short-term	523,000 rs.	755,340 rs.	1,068,545 rs.
Medium-term	25,000	16,972	18,980

In 1963/64 loans from the state (*taccavi*) amounted to 15,500 rupees for irrigation and 87,279 rupees for other productive purposes. (The latter figure coincides with the estimates. The report indicates only the final result for irrigation.)

In the noneconomic sectors for 1961–1963, achievement also fell short of goals: 19 new drinking-water wells out of 27 planned; 132 hand pumps for drinking water out of 348 planned; 11 latrines out of 120 planned; 14 new primary schools out of 17 planned. The plan also included metaled roads, to be built in *shramdam,* but none of the 6.4 km. planned were metaled between 1961 and 1963, and only 14.4 km. of the 80 km. of nonmetaled roads were completed.

The plan projected 45 percent progress in cereals and pulses with a view to reaching a target of 26,830 tons in 1966 as against 17,900 in 1961. By the end of the third year an increase of 30 percent should have been achieved. These estimates were based on standard measures, a sort of scale, or yardstick method, giving the amount of additional yield as follows: [6]

irrigation + 625 kg/ha of cereals and pulses
chemical fertilizers + 1,000 to 1,700 kg/ha
green manure + 379 kg/ha

Other changes followed, generally in the 60 to 100 kg/ha group, owing to different techniques such as the Uttar Pradesh method of growing wheat, sowing in lines, and, plant protection. In fact, having reached a high level in 1960/61, when the weather was considerably better than average, production remained more or less stationary between 1961 and 1963.

In 1963/64 there was a sharp drop, when the *kharif* crops, particularly maize, were hard hit by the exceptionally heavy rainfall in September. Between 30 and 50 percent of the *rabi* was killed by an even more abnormal cold spell. The 1964 *kharif* was scarcely better after further excessive rainfall.[7]

But the reverses caused by nature are only a partial explanation of the lack of progress made by the block. Other factors intervened for which the responsibilities lay sometimes at Unchagaon and sometimes at Bulandshahr or Lucknow. Defects in the planning machinery were evident from the start. The estimated increase of 45 percent for cereals and pulses was much too optimistic (the size of the estimate being due more to initiatives from Bulandshahr or Lucknow than Unchagaon). The real need is for improved irrigation, and at the moment its progress is largely dependent on the farmers own enterprising spirit, and on their ability to sink new wells and install pumps.[8] Today they are waiting for the completion of the consolidation of holdings, which has already been under way more than two years; they are quite understandably reluctant to make heavy improvements on land that may be transferred to another owner. Indeed, the planners themselves should have anticipated this reaction, since the consolidation of holdings was started in the block at the beginning of the third plan.

The targets for fertilizers are no less shaky. Even if the block had been supplied with the quantities estimated—and it is doubtful whether the figure was a reasonable one—the farmers would not have

[6] From Circular No. 2175/XXXV-B from Lucknow, April 15, 1960.

[7] At the time of my departure the final reckoning was not complete, and the figures were still not available.

[8] Another reason for the delay in construction of wells is the lack of cement, which is in short supply throughout India. We shall study this in detail when we come to Maharashtra.

been able to make use of it, given the present conditions of credit. The sums budgeted for this purpose were used at 80 percent or 100 percent according to the years. They correspond to a quantity of fertilizers, which is well below the estimates.

Rural Credit

The conditions on which credit is given, either in the form of a loan from the state (*taccavis*) or from cooperatives, are too restrictive to contribute to an increase in production of 45 percent.[9] The low land taxation, however advantageous otherwise, does not help the farmer in getting credit. The medium-term *taccavis* (five years) or the long-term (about ten years) are calculated in proportion to the rate of tax paid, which works out at thirty times in the case of a *sirdar,* and forty times for a *bhumidar.*[10] With five hectares taxed at 72.32 rupees, someone like Bhola Singh of Khandoï can obtain 2,880 rupees of credit, although the land which serves as guarantee is worth somewhere in the region of 30,000 rupees. It was not until 1964 that the maximum limit became 120 times the rate of tax for a *sirdar* and 150 times that of a *bhumidar.*[11]

The Uttar Pradesh Cooperative Land Mortgage Bank also grants long-term (ten-year) loans. By means of an extremely complicated scale which was somewhat broadened in 1964, the sums about equal those of the medium-term loans.

For short-term loans (between six and twelve months) the cooperatives require security from two people who are members of the society. The sum advanced must not exceed ten times the member's share, with a ceiling of 2,000 rupees for landowners, and 150 for the landless. But this also leaves a narrow working margin with a relatively high interest of 8.75 percent.[12] For medium-term loans (a period of eighteen to thirty-six months) of up to 500 rupees, the security of two members is sufficient. For anything above 500 a mortgage is necessary.

The interest rate is similar for the short-term *taccavis,* and these also require the security of two other persons. The land tax determines the limit of the loan—that is, according to the purpose of the loan, the sum may be from twenty to thirty times the amount of the tax.[13]

---

[9] We shall see other, more favorable terms of credit in Maharashtra.

[10] As we have already seen, a *bhumidar's* taxes are only half as high as a *sirdar's.*

[11] In fact one cannot receive more than two-thirds of the total calculated in this way.

[12] The interest rate was lowered to 8.25 percent in July, 1964.

[13] These calculations and scales are very complicated. For several years now consideration has been given to a way of standardizing rural credit by combining the two types of organizations. Such a revision would, of course, simplify administration.

The procedure for medium- and long-term *taccavis* is a long one. The farmer begins by obtaining a certificate from the lekhpal showing the area of his land. Delays occur, with the official sometimes dragging out the proceedings if he does not receive a bribe. One farmer from a village near Khandoï had to make three journeys on horseback to the land record office six kilometers distant because the lekhpal did not have the time for this formality, which would have taken but a few minutes. When this first condition has at last been fulfilled, the farmer makes his application to the collector, head of the district, who hands it over to his assistant, the district planning officer (D.P.O.), who sends it to the B.D.O. for comments. It then returns to the D.P.O., who gives the final approval. There is no need to stress the delays involved in these circuitous proceedings.

Although the system has been imposed from above, it is the block that is finally responsible for seeing that it is carried out. The cooperative societies and *taccavis* organizations will grant loans for productive purposes only, and to prevent their being used for noneconomic ends, a marriage for instance, they now grant part of the loans in kind.

Half of the Khandoï farmers interviewed expressed more or less acute dissatisfaction with the cooperatives. The dissatisfaction often seems justified. After the harvest the farmers are required to return the loan of improved seeds plus 25 percent more, by weight, as interest. With the help of a bakshish, it may happen that the official responsible will accept poor quality seeds in return, passing them on later to another farmer as improved seeds. Or an illiterate farmer may unknowingly put his fingerprint on a document which states that two bags of fertilizer have been delivered when he has in fact received only one. Another common sort of corruption may occur when the loan expires. On receipt of a bakshish, the official may enter a false repayment of the debt in his books, and several days later he will write out a new loan for the same amount to the same man.

It is extremely difficult to make a stand against the sort of abuses to which, in certain cases, the farmer is a party. In each society the government has provided for a committee which is responsible for controlling the use made of loans and for preventing malpractices. All the members come from the village—certainly a laudable intention—but they are not always carefully chosen.

Corruption could perhaps be halted by the use of severe sanctions, though this is a radical step. All too often, an official who has been on the verge of scandal just manages to avoid the flagrant offense, and he is simply transferred to another district. Having caught red-handed the supervisor of the Khandoï society, I reported the case to the authorities, but despite their diligence they were unable to deal severely with him. These matters lie with the cooperatives' disciplinary committee, which is composed of several eminent people in the district. An intricate network of relationships and favors and exchanges of friendly services served in this case to put down the scandal, with the members of the committee and other politicians preferring to turn a blind eye to the whole affair. It is evident that here the responsibilities lie in the greater part not at Khandoï or at Unchagaon, but at the district level. I heard no complaint against the A.D.O. in charge of cooperatives, but if he lacks support from above, how can he begin to wage war against corruption? He will interfere with his subordinates, the supervisors of the cooperatives, only if there is a formal complaint. The farmers are well aware that their protests will seldom come to anything. "No one listens to us [Koi nahin sunta]," they say when we ask them why they tolerate such a situation.

Nor are these malpractices at all unusual for this area. Some Jativs living at Chhassi, five kilometers from Khandoï, are victims of another supervisor and of a Brahmin from the local committee. A third affair was brought to my notice in the Meerut district, and a fourth in the Bulandshahr block where the abuses had gone so far that several members had left the society.

Despite these shortcomings of the cooperatives, which undermine the farmers' confidence and slow down the progress of the plan, the balance sheet is far from negative. The over-all figures relating to the distribution of credit show a marked improvement, the effects of which are evident at Khandoï. Indeed, in the block the cooperatives have doubled their short-term credits in two years.

Irrigation

Although the delay in the consolidation of holdings has, as we have seen, temporarily slowed the irrigation program, the block has not been energetic in its support of private irrigation. There are the usual delays in issuing loans and in providing cement and electric connection. If the farmer waits for the land consolidation to be finally completed before he takes steps to secure a loan, he is fairly certain of losing a whole season. Once the entire land area has been tentatively allocated,[14] it should be possible to lay the foundations of a new water system. How many peasants need a new well with a Persian wheel, and how many think of installing an electric tube-well? If the gram sewaks

[14] There can be a delay of several months between the time when a person knows the total amount of land allocated to him and the actual act of transfer.

could collect this information early, it would be possible for the block to determine the broad outline of the water utilization program and take the preliminary steps so that later on there would be few delays. Such an idea, however, has apparently not occurred to the B.D.O. and his assistants.

Also, the block could be more scrupulous in its supervision of the use actually made of loans for irrigation. Even allowing for the shortage of cement, it is strange that out of the sixty-one loans advanced in 1961/62, only fifteen works had been completed by March 31, 1964. Most of the work, after the preliminary formalities, ought not to have taken more than a few months. The field channels and state tube-wells depend on the irrigation department rather than on the block, but in these, too, greater progress should be possible (see chap. 14).

How the Block Works

The block should be an extension agent. Its task is to help the peasants to help themselves. Its second role is to ensure the proper working of several economic and social services such as credits, certificates for obtaining cement (B.D.O.), and help for the underprivileged classes. The Unchagaon team seems unable to perform its tasks thoroughly. Apart from the A.D.O. of the cooperatives, who is lively and fairly methodical, it shows little imagination, and sometimes has rather scanty knowledge of its records and basic data.

What are the chief problems, the decisive factors of progress? The immediate answer should be water, credit, fertilizers, and the like; but the replies from the Unchagaon staff are woolly. They are not sufficiently aware of the first priority: production. The wrong orientation of the early years was largely due to an absence of clearly defined priorities.[15]

But it is not the block alone that is at fault. As an example, the 1963/64 plan provided for 230 latrines, despite the failure of the program in two preceding years. (The peasants were unwilling to spend as much as fifteen or twenty rupees for a latrine and preferred to continue to go in the fields.) At the beginning of November, 1963, the B.D.O. discovered that no latrines had been installed since April, and he instructed the gram sewaks each to see that one was built within the month.[16] At the January meeting, no progress was reported, and so the

---

[15] See chap. 4 on the beginnings of community development.

[16] They were all built to the same standard: a piece of cement in the shape of a funnel, a drainpipe, and a slab of cement placed over the pit.

B.D.O. set a target of twenty latrines for February, that is, two per circle. By March 31, only six had been installed. I suggested that the B.D.O. should give up this perfectly useless program, for in order to convince two peasants that they should install latrines the gram sewak would waste at least two or three working days for the sake of what would no doubt be wasted improvements [17]—not to mention the cement, which would have been valuable for irrigation purposes. But the B.D.O.'s reply was: "I cannot give up this point which has been provided for in the district's fixed plan.

Another subject for complaint is the quality of the extension service in agriculture. Often, the farmers know more about agriculture than their instructors, who have been hastily trained in order to keep up with the rapid expansion of community development.

How does one ensure that the service works? Certainly the timetable is not as rigid as it is in the town; the staff does sometimes work on Sundays, and they return home late and tired after a round of visits by Jeep or bicycle. But the office routine is hardly a rigorous one. Officially, the office opens at 10:00 A.M. and closes at 5:00 P.M., with a brief break for lunch, but all too frequently by ten-thirty, or even later, the only people at work are the messenger boys and the old man who sweeps the yard. Is there any wonder then that the block is often slow in answering questions or obeying instructions from Bulandshahr? Similarly, is there any need to ask why the keeping of records leaves much to be desired, and why the statistics on the eventual progress of production in 1962/63 had not been completed by the middle of October, 1963? [18]

For the same reasons, by the beginning of the tenth month of the year, January, 1964, the distribution of subsidies by the block, in the form of free material, had scarcely begun. Out of the 16,081 rupees allocated to agriculture, irrigation, hygiene, and education, only 2,309 rupees had been spent.

Those responsible for the block usually spend the prescribed number of days on their field trips, but they do not spend the required number of nights outside Unchagaon, and all too often their visits are hasty. If they are going to win the peasants' confidence they need to spend more time with them. It is in the evenings, after their work is done, that the peasants will talk at leisure while smoking their hookahs; then is the right time to seek them out and draw them into a discussion of their problems.

[17] The latrine that I had installed near my house in Khandoï was not used after I left.

[18] Remember that the year ended on March 31.

A Gram Sewak's Day

On November 4, 1963, I accompanied the gram sewak on his rounds. We set off on bicycles at 8:30 A.M. for Saujna Rani, a few kilometers away from Khandoï. There we called on two large landowners, each owning fifteen hectares. The G.S. discussed with the first an application for electricity for a proposed tube-well, and he noted several figures concerning the area sown with wheat. He talked privately to the second landowner about a personal matter. At the next village, one kilometer away, we exchanged a few words with a farmer, and we tried to see the pradhan (village president) but found him out. Around one-thirty we returned to Khandoï.

The next morning we met at Safinagar, another village in the neighborhood of Khandoï, at 9:20 A.M. and called on the pradhan. The G.S. gave him some government brochures on the Sino-Indian conflict and told him that he would be at the block office the following day to meet another farmer who was buying a metal plough. We stopped again at the next village, where the pradhan gave us tea. The G.S. took a quick note of the approximate cultivation figures which our host gave him. At the third village, Aurengabad, the pradhan was not in, and we were about to leave when a farmer approached to tell us about the troubles he was having with his tube-well; then another man came to tell us of his quarrel with his brother over a Persian wheel. Ironically, in this village where the irrigation is woefully insufficient, the panchayat intended to spend 5,000 rupees for a new communal house. These problems were serious, and money was being wasted, but our G.S. was in a hurry to get away and he made no attempt either to solve the problems of the two farmers or to persuade the panchayat to use its money for irrigation. "What is the point?" he said. "We have no power, the villagers have little respect for us, and the B.D.O. doesn't have enough prestige. If we interfere in their affairs it will only fall back on us from above. The politicians will become involved and we may be reprimanded by our superiors." We returned to Khandoï at about 2:00 P.M.

On November 29 the gram sewak and I left Khandoï at two in the afternoon to call on the pradhan of Nagla Madaripur. The G.S. took the figures for the *rabi,* our host and several other farmers answering for those who were absent. The next stop was at Narendrapur, where the pradhan wanted to have a depot established for the sale of fertilizers distributed by the block; the G.S. gave him the necessary permit for this. We then stopped at a shoemaker's to offer him a sewing machine for which the government was only asking 150 rupees (its actual value being 450) .[19] At four-thirty we mounted our bicycles and the G.S. went off to Unchagaon to give his report.

What is the net result of all this? A lot of time taken up with traveling, some visits made more for the sake of courtesy than for the purpose of helping the economy, and some administrative tasks completed.

Transport and Communications

The slow way in which the block works is not due simply to the character of the men and the nature of the system; it is also due to the relative isolation of the village and its lack of a speedy means of communication. It is an isolation that one can really appreciate only from experience.

The block is connected by telephone to the Jahangirabad post office, which transmits telegrams and telephone messages from Bulandshahr. The post comes by bus to Jahangirabad, thence by cyclist, each day, to the block. The service works well: newspapers from Delhi arrive on the same day, and a letter from Bulandshahr arrives the day after it is posted. The obstacles exist not between the block and the district, but at the lower, village level. Of course, no one in the villages has a telephone. The mail is delivered once or twice a week from the small towns and from Unchagaon. To be sure of seeing someone in another village, one must send a runner on ahead; otherwise one is apt all too frequently—especially among the relatively well-off landowners—to make the journey only to find them out.

As we have seen, the only motor car for all the sixty-seven villages in Unchagaon is the B.D.O.'s Jeep. The gram sewaks cover a radius of at least five kilometers by bicycle, the A.D.O. a radius of ten to fifteen kilometers. The narrow roads, of powdery earth or sand, are either in ruts longside ditches or, in another season, are muddy and flooded. The heat between April and July and the rains during the following months make traveling difficult and slow.

An Attempt at Appraisement

At the time of my visits to the region, the block was having trouble fulfilling its first mission: that of extension work. As for the second, the functioning of administrative machinery, it has been imperfectly fulfilled, and this is something about which the peasants have com-

[19] This comes under aid to the weaker sections of the society.

plained.[20] Nevertheless, once the machinery had been set up it made the extension of rural credit possible and accelerated the use of chemical fertilizers and improved seeds; certainly these results cannot be overlooked.

These shortcomings seem to me to be within the nature of things and of people. It is absolutely impossible to count on having personnel of high caliber at block and village level. For the most part, the personnel at these levels vary from bad to average, with some mediocre in between. My brief visits to several other blocks in Bulandshahr gave me the impression that Unchagaon is below average.

To sum up, it would be wishful thinking to expect the officials at these levels to show much initiative or imagination. These men lead a much less pleasant life than do the town officials. Many of them live separated from their families because there are no good secondary schools in Unchagaon. The cycle journeys, the low salaries, and the debilitating effect of the climate during the hot months of the year [21] all tend to hamper their productive activity. After observing these men for some time, I can only sympathize with their attitude, which seems to me perfectly normal under the circumstances. Reforming zeal and willingness to sacrifice one's own comforts, including accepting a meager salary and what is often a thankless job, are rare, not ordinary, virtues. Rather than attempt in vain to instill the block with a sense of high purpose,[22] perhaps the government would do better to seek efficient administration by imposing strict discipline.

It would be necessary, first of all, to set up a tight control. It is impossible to expect a greater effort from Unchagaon when the district officers are not even able to visit the block once a month. Second, sanctions should be imposed on any faults in the service or on delays due to serious negligence or to disregard of instructions. Why should these faults be tolerated when it is the peasants who pay for them in the end? Later on, in part 4, I shall comment on these two suggestions again; it is evident that they could not be effected without some difficulty.

[20] We shall return to these complaints in the following chapter and in our conclusions on Uttar Pradesh.

[21] Electricity had just reached Unchagaon, and fans were still rare.

[22] Always a difficult task, for the spirit of initiative is something that is difficult to create, as we shall see in part 4.

13

INNOVATIONS INTRODUCED SINCE 1961

So far we have described the activities of the block as they have developed since it was created. The introduction of the Panchayati Raj and the choice of Unchagaon as pilot-block of the district for the cooperative farms open up new fields of activity.

The Kshetr Samiti

Uttar Pradesh follows the pattern most widely adopted in India [1] and puts at block level the principal authority, the *kshetr samiti*. This is an assembly composed of the village pradhans, a few representatives of cooperative societies, the local elected members of the Uttar Pradesh Legislative Assembly, and any members of the central Parliament who may reside in the block. In Unchagaon, there were 103 pradhans and 17 ex officio members. The samiti elects a president (*pramukh*); in order to minimize political influence, representatives of the provincial or central legislatures are ineligible for this office and for the two vice-presidencies.

The B.D.O. has become a sort of secretary-general of the samiti and its executive agent. He is responsible to the pramukh, but is in turn responsible for the work of his own staff. Each year the pramukh is supposed to reaffirm the B.D.O.'s qualifications.

The samiti discusses the plan of the block and supervises its execution. By law, the samiti is expected to meet at least once every two months,[2] but in Unchagaon only five meetings were held in 1963–1964.

Let us consider the meeting of September 28, 1963, which I attended. Half of the assembly, sixty persons, was present. After approving the minutes of the previous meeting, the assembly asked the president to obtain authority from Bulandshahr for several villages to be declared outside the sugar-mill area,[3] since the factories were too far away for farmers who lacked means of transport.

[1] See chap. 4.

[2] Section 84 of the Uttar Pradesh Kshetr Samitis and Zila Parishad Act, 1960.

[3] In such "mill areas," the farmers are not allowed to make *gur*. They must deliver the sugar cane to the factories.

Following that, it was rather quickly decided that a grant of 23,000 rupees be made for a Harijan housing program, provided they contributed 8,000 rupees themselves. A decision was also taken to establish two new primary schools. One village had not used the grant made for the construction of a house for the schoolmistress, and this sum was available for distribution. Several pradhans put in a claim for it. Eventually a decision was deferred until the next meeting.

Sales of agricultural materials had been proceeding slowly in spite of a 30 percent subsidy offered by the government. One pradhan remarked that the new ploughs were too heavy for the oxen.

The cooperatives were on the agenda. The "tied" loans (part in cash, part in kind) had run into difficulties: it occasionally happened that farmers renounced their share in kind. Also the cooperatives had not been able to dispose of all their seeds. They had had to sell the balance on the market.

Then some pradhans complained of an inequitable distribution of cement, the rationing of which was the responsibility of the B.D.O.

A new messenger for the block was appointed and a petition was prepared seeking the improvement of the Unchagaon postal service. The meeting ended with the preparation of the program marking the anniversary of the birth of Mahatma Gandhi (October 2), which was also the date of the start of community development.

The meeting lasted a little over two hours. The B.D.O. and his assistants presented the items on the agenda, on which the pramukh and the assembly commented. The atmosphere was rather relaxed. None of the really important matters (agricultural equipment, cement rationing, cooperative credits) aroused much interest, but the question of the schoolmistress's house brought animated and prolonged discussion.

The next meeting took place on December 10. The president, for reasons unknown to me, was absent, so the vice-president held the chair. The attendance, as before, was exactly 50 percent.

Several grants were offered for agricultural equipment, for irrigation, for artisans' workshops. The A.D.O.'s explained the procedure to be followed. Then—a separate point—the pradhans were asked to supply a list of old people over sixty-five without means, who would draw ten rupees a month benefit from the state.

The matter of the schoolmistress's house came up again. Three villages were now in the field as claimants, so the acting president proposed to defer a decision again to the next meeting. The problem of cement was also brought up again. The B.D.O. reproached the pradhans for showing favoritism in the advance notifications which they had given him. The block had just received a circular saying that 50 percent of the cement should be reserved for irrigation.

There was some discussion of postal matters and the appointment of a new schoolteacher, and then the B.D.O. broached the idea, which I had suggested to him, of establishing an irrigation scheme for each village, without waiting for the final stage of the consolidation of holdings. The proposal got little response, and the meeting ended soon after, despite a last attempt by one pradhan concerning the schoolmistress's house!

The conclusions that I reached at Khandoï were repeated here: a lack of awareness of the essential factors. The urgent problems—irrigation, cement—received almost no attention. Yet several pradhans were progressive landowners and fairly well off. Good farmers of their own holdings, they seemed little inclined to occupy themselves with public affairs or even to interest themselves therein.

This is the experience over two years. The situation could change one day, for up to now the samiti has had hardly any influence to speak of on the economy of the block. Already showing little enthusiasm for their panchayat, the villagers remain quite indifferent to the samiti except when their own interests are at stake. At Khandoï, forty-three of some sixty farmers questioned expressed their indifference, or even dissatisfaction, toward the panchayats at both levels. Only three of forty artisans and agricultural laborers showed any positive reaction. It can be said, however, that, with all the poor results, at least at Unchagaon the B.D.O. and the pramukh get on well together, which is not the case everywhere (see part 4).

The Panchayati Raj ought, moreover, to speed up the utilization of local taxes levied and used by the villages. In Uttar Pradesh the various taxes of the 1950's have been replaced by a single levy of one-sixteenth of a rupee added to each rupee of land tax. The 1963/64 collection should have brought in 11,135 rupees, to which arrears of 26,522 must be added. The amount actually realized in the whole block was 6,250 rupees, 16.6 percent of the total due for the current year and arrears.

Cooperative Farming

Unchagaon is the pilot-block of the district where ten cooperative farms were to be established. Seven were more or less in action by the end of 1963 and three others were being formed. The Khandoï cooperative was registered on December 23, 1961, with thirty-five members participating. At the outset, would-be "leaders" were again in evidence, seeking prestige and advantage.

The ink on the documents setting up this enterprise was hardly dry when it was rocked by serious disagreements. Nineteen members left within the first year, which is in fact against the law; save in exceptional circumstances, a member cannot leave a cooperative until five years have elapsed. Wishing to avoid trouble, those who remained did not protest the resignations.

The remaining members had at their common disposal 22.12 hectares. Eleven owned lands; five were agricultural laborers. Since the holdings of most of the landowners were large enough to be economic, the aim of the cooperative—to help the very small owners and the workers without land—was in this instance rather wide of the mark.

Under the system, each member retains the ownership of his holdings, but the lands are exploited on a common basis and the cooperative buys up the oxen and equipment of those members who wish to sell them. Profits are shared on a pro rata basis according to the value of the holdings. In addition, members are paid for the work they do on the lands.

The members put 2,250 rupees on deposit and can obtain loans of up to eight times their deposit. The cooperative bank of the district, financed to a large measure by the Reserve Bank and the State of Uttar Pradesh, gives out credits and grants. For the operations of 1963/64, the account books show the following figures:

Construction of a cattle shed and a store (1,250 grant, 3,750 credit)	5,000 rs.
Credits for the purchase of fertilizers, seeds, and equipment	4,000
Credit from the cooperative bank (3,500 of this was to allow members to repay their old debts, 3,300 for the purchase of cattle, and the remainder for labor and purchase of agricultural equipment)	8,000
Credit from the block for purchase of rope-making machinery	1,300
Total	18,300 rs.

Of the total, 4,000 rupees were to be paid back in January–February, 1964, and a further 4,000 in April–May, the balance being spread over five to fifteen years. The 1963/64 operation, the first year when the cooperative was functioning, resulted in an expenditure of 48,869.30 (including the repayment of the 8,000 rupees) and an income of 46,979.97 rupees.

This deficit does not in itself justify the condemnation of the enterprise. After a period of "running-in" and the inevitable unforeseen eventualities of the starting period, the cooperative farm could show itself to be economically viable. For several reasons, however, one cannot be optimistic about its future. The real function of the cooperative should be to exploit the land on a collective basis: the president of the society should organize each day's work with the secretary,[4] and each member or non-member should be paid 1.12 rupees a day. But arguments and disputes become so bitter that the pooling of lands remains little more than theoretical.

As an example, the cooperative did not obtain any chemical fertilizers for the wheat fields for the 1963–1964 harvest. The fear of not having the irrigation necessary to make the fertilizer effective led some members to disapprove the expense, although those whose lands were well watered were in favor of the purchase. A truly cooperative spirit would have resulted in fertilizers being applied only to those lands where there were good prospects of increasing the yield. In the absence of agreement, the cooperative put off a decision and the suitable time for applying fertilizers had soon passed.

Most of the members confessed to me that they were weary of the undertaking. One dispute followed another concerning crop rotation: which lands were going to be planted with sugar cane, and which with wheat? Even if farmers stayed in the cooperative, they still contrived to return to their own individual work.

Other differences arose about the consolidation of holdings. It would have been a logical step for the cooperative to form either one or two large units of land for exploitation. But the law had not laid down any arrangements and the members had so little faith in their enterprise that they refused to work out their own plan. Many were afraid of losing good land in exchange for poorer holdings and thought their chances would be better if the consolidation was decided upon independently of the cooperative.

Is the example of Khandoï exceptional? My visits to two other enterprises in the block led me to similar conclusions, subject to the difference that in these two cooperatives one owner of fifteen hectares played such a dominant part that the operation was quite meaningless. One wonders whether those who interested themselves in the project did not merely want to take advantage of the credits made available thereby.

It is debatable whether the government is following a sound policy in attracting peasants by financial benefits. If the system were to be adopted on a wide scale, it would be impossible for the state funds and

---

[4] A person who keeps the registers and the accounts. His salary is 50 rupees a month. In this case the office was filled by a young Brahmin, the son of one of the members, an honest and conscientious young man.

the cooperative banks to meet the demands for cash—which would amount to some ten billion rupees at the outset if ten million families in India joined the scheme. The government does not want to use compulsion. I do not imply that it should, but it seems to me quite impossible, given this position, to foresee any success for the cooperatives: there are too many farmers who are fiercely opposed to the system. Their common sense leads them to this sort of reasoning: "How can you expect cooperatives to work when two brothers are not even capable of keeping their joint family?" In more than five months in the area, I did not find a single farmer—even among those who belonged to a cooperative—who was really in favor of the system. Not only the large and medium owners, but also numerous small farmers were opposed to it. They had no confidence in it; they were afraid of being tricked and held fast to their independence.

In Unchagaon, one or two lesser difficulties have worked against the success of the system. The post of chief inspector in charge of the program has changed hands so often that no comprehensive works have been possible. One stayed only three months and his successor left after four months. The second man was not exactly bursting with enthusiasm. He visited his cooperatives once a month, or every other month. Between times he could be seen starting his volley-ball game with other officials around four o'clock every afternoon.

A good example should be set from above. From November 2 to 8, 1963, a big meeting of cooperative members was held in Bulandshahr. The Uttar Pradesh Minister of Cooperatives, who came from our area, was present as guest of honor. The president of the Khandoï society received an alarm clock in recognition of his activities (a subtle pointing of a moral, it seemed), and large quantities of delicacies were passed around. But a friend of mine who was a member of the cooperative came back disgusted. "What a waste," he said to me. Instead of these festivities, would it not have been better for the Minister to spend one or two days in examining the operation of one of his cooperatives in detail? [5]

Village Volunteer Force

At the time of the Himalayan fighting between China and India in the autumn of 1962, the government was mobilizing its resources for the defense of the country. In this atmosphere of urgency it decided also to try and turn the patriotic emotions of the people to a more lasting and

[5] The same minister was present at a similar meeting at Jahangirabad on December 6, 1963. He did not go any deeper into the countryside.

productive national solidarity. In this spirit the village volunteer force and the work bank (*shram* bank) were created.

The report of the block for 1963/64 reveals that all the villages accepted the resolution for twelve days of *shramdan* per year. A total of 317,220 working days was promised. In the column reporting the outcome can be read the single word "Nil."

A post of Organizer of the Home Guard and Village Volunteer Force for two blocks was established. Home defense groups were to be raised and given rudimentary military instruction. Apart from the training of a few men at Bulandshahr, nothing was done. The triple aim of the national volunteer force—education, production, and protection—remained a dead letter, confirming at a higher level the inactivity found in Khandoï.

To sum up, the recent innovations in the block aimed at promoting production and encouraging the enthusiasm and participation of the peasants have not so far produced the hoped-for results.

14

THE DISTRICT
OF BULANDSHAHR

One of the chief accomplishments of the British colonial rule of India was the creation of the Indian Civil Service (I.C.S.), the origin of which goes back to the East India Company Charter Act of 1793.[1]

The Old Administrative Framework

The first principle was to make use of a select corps of high officials, well chosen, well trained, well educated, and well paid. The second was to delegate to these men wide responsibilities in the most varied fields and to rely on their initiative. With this underlying idea as the basis, the British administered India by means of a corps of 1,100 to 1,400 higher officials. These men started young (under twenty-five) as assistants to the district head, and went gradually through the various grades of the hierarchy, from the district to the division.[2] In the course of their career they also served in the administration of the provincial capitals and the central government, first at Calcutta and then at Delhi and New Delhi.

The district head (called, according to the region, Collector, District Magistrate, or Deputy Commissioner) was the representative of the government. He looked after law and order and collected taxes. He had, depending on the region and the period, some judicial responsibilities. In addition he had to control the activities of the services that were established during the nineteenth century, particularly after 1850—agriculture, education, communications, health—and he also had to cope with unforeseen or exceptional occurrences such as floods, famines, and banditry. The district contained administrative subdivisions (*tehsils* or *taluks*) whose principal functions were the maintenance of public order and the collection of the land tax. Bulandshahr had four of these. As we have seen, the District Boards made their

[1] See H. H. Dodwell and R. R. Sethi (eds.), *The Cambridge History of India* (Delhi, 1964), VI, 357.
[2] A group of districts.

appearance at the end of the nineteenth century; these were councils which assisted the district head, but without encroaching upon his authority.

To function efficiently, the I.C.S. had to count on obtaining outstanding men of unquestioned integrity, and this condition was fulfilled. From the end of the nineteenth century the doors of the I.C.S. were opened to Indians. In 1929 there were 241 Indians out of a total of 1,122; in 1939, 540 out of 1,299.[3] Immediately before and after Independence, most of the English were replaced.

The hallmark of its founders—integrity and character—was passed smoothly to the Indians; in the difficult times that followed Independence, the worst eventualities were avoided through the I.C.S. (renamed Indian Administrative Service). A reliable and seasoned force was installed, which could face up competently to the new and often overwhelming problems. The services for the district were looked after by the State Civil Service, so far as the important posts were concerned; appointments in the lower grades were made according to needs.

Side by side with the district staff under the collector is the important irrigation department, whose divisions and subdivisions follow the course of the canals or the zones of the state tube-wells, thus splitting up the districts. For example, part of the Bulandshahr system is controlled by the irrigation services installed at Meerut (to the north of the districts) and another part by those at Aligarh (in the southeast). The collector has no effective and direct power over these irrigation divisions which are answerable to Lucknow.

The New Administrative Structure

The Indian nationalists sometimes accuse the I.C.S. of having had a "colonial" nature, its chief functions having been to maintain law and order and to collect taxes. As I have pointed out, the district heads did in fact have to deal time and again with many other problems, and their work frequently had a beneficial effect on the economy;[4] but it must be recognized that their most important task was not development.

With the five-year plans came new responsibilities. Gradually a whole administrative structure was established around the development blocks. Uttar Pradesh adopted the following formula, which is not the same everywhere. The collector is in charge of the district. In

[3] Philip Woodruff, *The Men Who Ruled India* (London, 1963), II, 363.

[4] One should also stress the beneficial effect of the restoration to law and order of the country districts disturbed by all the wars and the banditry of the eighteenth century.

addition to his former responsibilities, he controls the activities of his right-hand man, the District Planning Officer (D.P.O.) ,[5] a new post. The D.P.O. is in charge of a whole service in which we find again the system of the block; he is an all-rounder (with in this case an assistant) assisted by specialists (agriculture, cooperatives, etc.) who have the task of coordinating the programs of the blocks and supervising their execution.

Until the advent of the Panchayati Raj, the D.P.O. was only answerable to the collector. Today he has become the executive agent of the zila parishad, on which the pramukhs (presidents of blocks) sit. The president (adhyaksh) of the new council signs, in conjunction with the collector, the report on the D.P.O.'s annual work performances. This official therefore is dependent on both the collector and the zila parishad.

The collector, the D.P.O., and his assistants are expected to spend a certain amount of time, which varies according to their office, in the field. Following the former British practice, the collector "camps" [6] for part of the winter in different zones of the district, besides making shorter visits during the remainder of the year. The others make visits of varying length to their blocks. Each has a Jeep at his disposal.

Since Independence, the organization of the department of irrigation and electricity has not undergone substantial change. The minister and his staff administer the department,[7] which controls its branches and their subdivisions. The collector still has no authority over the irrigation services in his district.

Activities and Results [8]

The district of Bulandshahr, lying for the most part between the Ganges and the Jumna, measures about 5,000 square kilometers.[9] Its population in 1961 was 1,737,397, an increase of 16 percent over the 1951 census. The overwhelming majority of the population is rural:

[5] He does not belong to the I.A.S. but to the state service, a distinction the importance of which will be seen later.

[6] The collector actually stays often at a rest house, though he sets up his office in large tents erected for the purpose. At times, he does sleep under canvas, but in typically British conditions of comfort in the countryside.

[7] It will be remembered that a department is the provincial equivalent of a ministry.

[8] In addition to my personal notes I have made use of the *Tisri Panchvarshiya Yojna 1961–66* ["Third Five Year Plan"] of the district and the *Quarterly Progress Reports* for the three years 1961–1964.

[9] The figures of the 1961 census and those of the third Bulandshahr plan show a difference of 146 square miles.

1,517,515 persons distributed over 1,318 villages.[10] In 1961 there were 379,360 cultivated hectares, of which 266,000 were irrigated and 165,000 had double cropping. The principal crops for the *rabi* are wheat (84,000 ha.), barley (49,100), and peas (51,200); and for the *kharif, jowar* and *bajra* (49,600) and maize (57,600). Sugar cane, the principal cash crop, covers 69,600 hectares.

The development blocks made their appearance in the district around 1953–1954. At the end of the second plan there were thirteen of them, and six more were established between 1961 and 1963.

In the over-all figures for the district we find the same changes that have occurred at Khandoï. The total irrigated area increased by 30 percent between 1951 and 1961, an appreciable improvement even allowing for some optimism, since not all areas are *adequately* irrigated. The table below is equally revealing about progress in the first and second plans in fertilizers, cooperatives, and social activities.

	1955/56	*1960/61*
Ammonium sulphate	3,790 tons	4,075 tons
Superphosphate used	32 tons	364 tons
Area under green manure	4,384 ha.	27,475 ha.
New plantations	70.8 ha.	1,183 ha.
Number of inoculations	540,000	633,880
Number of hospitals	4	13
Nonmetaled road construction	1,930 km.	1,400 km.
Metaled road construction	16 km.	86 km.
Bridges built	25	53
Primary schools built	21	74
Credit cooperative societies	420 units	766 units
Membership of co-ops	20,511	75,878
Amount of members' deposits	534,000 rs.	1,820,134 rs.
Credit granted by the cooperatives	4,563,916 rs.	8,000,000 rs.

SOURCE: D.P.O.'s office.

It is not possible to state exactly the increase in food grains. Bulandshahr, like the other districts of India, uses the method of crop-cutting samples to determine yields. The latest system consists of laying out a rectangle, then choosing ten circles of one meter radius on each of the diagonals on which the crops are cut and weighed.[11] For wheat, fifty-three samples were taken in 1961 and fifty-six in 1962. The results were sent to Lucknow where the statistical service tabulated the over-all

[10] The exact number is a little more. When the villages are too small, they are grouped into a single panchayat.

[11] The average-yield figure thus obtained is multiplied by the total area under cultivation according to the reports of the lekhpals.

production of Uttar Pradesh. For lack of calculating machines and staff the results for each district are not available.

The only method of measurement (the yardstick method) is the same one that we met with in Unchagaon. It showed in this case an increase of 10 percent between 1951 and 1956 and 30 percent for the subsequent five-year period, when food-grain production reached 309,088 tons. The effective improvement in this second period was actually somewhat less, 1955–1956 being an average year but 1960–1961 a very good year, so far as climatic conditions were concerned.

The Third Plan

The third plan was the subject of a complete document and shows the progress made in planning. In irrigation, the district envisaged only a small number—twenty-six—of new state tube-wells, since the D.P.O. and his assistant wisely chose to work for full utilization of the wells recently sunk rather than to propose the construction of new ones. Private minor irrigation, on the other hand, was encouraged. This was scheduled to comprise 68,000 additional hectares, in contrast to only 3,700 additional hectares in the zone of the state tube-wells, including construction and completion of field channels partly by means of *shramdan*.

Private Minor Irrigation

Yearly Progress

	Targets of the 1961–1966 Plan	1961/62		1962/63		1963/64	
		Targets	Achieve-ments	Targets	Achieve-ments	Targets	Achieve-ments
New wells	9,194	1,481	409	1,318	787	2,854	1,250
Wells repaired	3,403	775	204	616	293	1,031	212
Well borings	11,325	2,812	304	2,405	715	4,544	960
Persian wheels	10,413	2,228	462	1,737	1,000	2,980	1,211
Pumping sets	902	141	73	167	118	302	116
Private electric tube-wells	386	55	43	71	85	81	94

The additional irrigation capacity is estimated in accordance with a fixed formula whereby a new well irrigates 2 ha., a well boring 1.2 ha., a repaired well an additional 1.6 ha.; the installation of a Persian wheel on a well increases the capacity by 1.6 ha.; a pumping set serves 9.6 ha. and a private tube-well 20 ha. In the first two years of the plan the additional land under irrigation was estimated at 10,508 hectares.

Progress can be shown on a different basis, that of credits used and verified (as of March 31, 1964) :

	Credits Sanctioned	Works Completed	Works Verified	Recovery Ordered
1st plan	587	456	456	127
2nd plan	3,970	2,611	2,611	1,359
1961/62	1,781	914	847	512
1962/63	1,198	616	515	15
1963/64	1,468	541	429	—

The budget for the irrigation program as a whole amounted to 36,-074,300 rupees, of which the credits of the state or the sugar mills [12] accounted for 8,270,500 rupees, or a little less than one-fourth. The total credits granted between 1961 and 1964 amounted to 3.8 million rupees.

The consumption of chemical fertilizer has developed as follows:

		Yearly Progress				
		1961/62		1962/63		1963/64
Targets for 1965/66	Targets	Achievements	Targets	Achievements	Targets	Achievements
Ammonium sulphate * (tons)	40,000	14,489	4,929	19,612	5,369	13,560	9,588
Superphosphate † (tons)	13,973	4,900	992	6,900	1,031	4,455	1,802

* Nitrogen content, 20 percent by weight.
† Indicated phosphate content, $\frac{1}{6}$.

For the three years 1961–1964, the construction of new cement pits for manure attained only 14 percent, 20 percent, and 26 percent of the targets. Subsidized purchases of agricultural equipment were even lower: they seldom exceeded 20 percent of the estimate, varying mostly between 5 percent and 15 percent (1961–1963) .

The cooperative societies, on the other hand, fulfilled hopes, increasing in both number and volume. At the end of the third year the number of members was 132,932 (target, 132,900) , and the deposits of the members amounted to three times the estimate, or 4.2 million rupees. Short-term credits were 107 percent, 97 percent, and 81 percent, respectively, of the estimates for the three years. In 1963/64, credits granted came to 18.8 million rupees. Progress with medium- and long-term credits, however, was slow; the former reached 47.6 percent,

[12] The factories grant loans to the producers who furnish them with sugar cane.

20 percent, and 15.6 percent of the annual estimates, the latter virtually nothing. In 1963/64 the short-term state credits (*taccavis*) amounted to 17.3 million rupees for fertilizers and seeds and 50,000 rupees for agricultural equipment.

The education program, too, has kept pace with the plan, and at times has even surpassed it: 238 new primary schools with 12,500 new boy pupils and 3,200 girls have all been achieved in two years.[13]

In public health the installation of hand pumps for drinking water has considerably exceeded the estimate: 2,875 against 1,600. The construction of wells (also for drinking water) has proceeded more slowly and has only reached 30 percent to 50 percent of the targets. Latrine construction has attained about 60 percent, that is, 330 units in two years. Birth control showed no results in 1961 to 1963. During the third year 377 persons had themselves sterilized. As to other methods, no details were given.

The construction of roads and tracks by means of *shramdan* did not fulfill hopes: only 35 kilometers of metaled roadway were completed out of a planned 110 kilometers, and only a fourth—270 kilometers—of the planned nonmetaled roads were completed.

Taxes levied by the panchayats are being paid slowly. In 1963, arrears amounted to a total of 615,813.27 rupees, to which 259,638.32 rupees due for the current year must be added. Some 323,305 rupees were collected during the financial year, but the district wrote off arrears of 152,931.33 rupees.

The over-all results of these three years are appreciably better than those in Unchagaon, which confirms the higher level of at least some of the blocks. Private irrigation has progressed better than in Unchagaon, mainly because in several blocks the consolidation of holdings has been completed and the peasants feel safe in sinking new wells or installing pumps. At the same time, attention must be drawn to abuse of the credit plan for irrigation. Nearly a third of the loans granted in the course of the second plan were diverted to other objects or were canceled before being paid over. Furthermore, over the first three years of the third plan there was a great gap between targets and achievements, except for tube-wells, for which the targets were exceeded in the years 1962–1964.

The increase in fertilizers continued and gained momentum strongly

---

[13] The blocks have been pushing ahead with the construction of new schools, which are subsequently administered by the education department. Between 1947 and 1963 the number of children attending primary schools rose from 20,377 to 109,947 and the number of schoolteachers from 588 to 2,805. See *Shiksha ki pragati par* ["On the Progress of Education"].

in 1963/64, though there was still a wide gap between targets and achievement. In the other economic sectors (except for manure pits) and in social activities, the achievements, without always reaching the goal, attained a satisfactory level.

The district is in a better position than is Unchagaon, but the same defects are evident. Irrigation, chemical fertilizers, improved seeds, new techniques, and improved equipment were supposed to result in an increase of 49 percent in food-grain production in five years.[14] Clearly, so considerable an improvement would require more production-conscious administrative services, a plentiful supply of cement and fertilizers, and a much greater increase in credits than was actually achieved. Since the amounts estimated for short-term loans for seeds and fertilizers were used almost 100 percent, it is evident that there was at least some lack of correlation between the financial estimates and the estimates of fertilizers needed for higher yields.

How can one explain the neglect of the medium- and long-term credit opportunities? Probably the answer lies in procedural delays and the conditions in Uttar Pradesh which restrict credits generally. Most farmers are already so indebted in the short term that they cannot obligate themselves further.

Finally, the planning preparation still needs improvement. The program introduced in 1961 was out of proportion to the material resources available and the administration had not always the talent to improve its efficiency quickly.

How has production progressed since the end of the second plan? Though one must depend on rough estimates, the statistics that I have given are fairly reliable.[15] They show an increase in productive potential. In 1961–1962 climatic conditions were average and production increased. Subsequently a hostile nature canceled out much of man's efforts. After a fairly bad year in 1962–1963, particularly for the *rabi,* real catastrophes ensued. In September, 1963, part of the district was ravaged by quite abnormal floods (Unchagaon escaped, despite heavy rains), and these were followed by a bitterly cold spell in January, 1964. Whereas the previous level had been barely maintained or had

[14] 309,088 tons in 1960/61; 461,400 tons in 1965/66. Improved irrigation was supposed to account for 20 percent of the increase and chemical fertilizers for 40 percent.

[15] For example, the number of wells, sales of fertilizers, etc. The figures for improved seeds, areas under green manure, and line sowing are a different matter. The first of these are by no means always *improved.* The others depend on the grams sewaks, whose statistics are only approximate. Fertilizers, on the other hand, are sold by the cooperatives and the *taccavis* organization, and irrigation works are frequently the object of a credit. For both, the method of evaluation is simple and fairly reliable.

fallen off slightly in 1962–1963, the district as a whole was seriously affected by the bad weather of 1963–1964. In October, 1964, the cereal shortage reached danger point—certainly unusual in a district that normally has an excess of grain and, because of its sugar cane, is fairly rich.

The Budget for the Community Development Program

The financial provisions of the district for community development for the financial year 1964/65 are as follows: [16]

Salaries and allowances of staff	748,700 rupees
Office expenses	47,000
Equipment for agricultural demonstrations	163,000
Equipment for animal husbandry	27,700
Subsidies granted to peasants for minor irrigation	23,400
Campaigns against epidemics	31,000
School buildings and equipment	32,200
Adult education	37,000
Subsidies to craftsmen	43,700
Schoolteachers' salaries (for adult education)	25,600
	1,179,300 rupees

All these expenses are covered by central government funds. In addition, the state of Uttar Pradesh contributes 239,100 rupees as its share of staff salaries, making the total budget 1,418,400 rupees. There are also grants totaling 94,800 rupees to be allocated to peasants for settling their loans or to help with the execution of the public works which they undertake. The grand total (expenditure and grants) amounts to 1,513,200 rupees. This is a long way from the ideal budget, averaging 240,000 rupees a year in stage I and 100,000 rupees in stage II from the sixth year of the block. On the basis of these figures the district should have received almost twice as much as it has.[17]

How the Administration Works

Each month the D.P.O. holds a meeting of all the B.D.O.'s at Buland-shahr. This gives them an opportunity to learn something of the

[16] These are mainly the initial and operating expenses of the blocks. Credits (*taccavis,* cooperatives) are not included. The expenditures for education only cover the activities of the blocks—for example, the construction of schools, for which the state grants a subsidy if the villagers assume responsibility for part of the expenses. The education budget proper is not included in the program of community development.

[17] Similar discrepancies exist in other states.

broader program, to receive their instructions from Lucknow, and to discuss their problems and difficulties. The D.P.O. presides, calling on his assistants as their particular fields are taken up. The agenda for the staff meeting on December 12, 1963, was as follows: (1) statement of sales of seeds for green manure, (2) statement of sales of chemical fertilizers for the cooperatives, (3) total amount of credit (*taccavis*) for chemical fertilizers and insecticides, (4) purchase of cotton, (5) statement of reimbursement (in kind) of improved seeds for last year's *kharif* and *rabi,* (6) arrangements for the storage of improved seeds, (7) progress of recruitment in the cooperatives, (8) the arrears of taxes of the panchayats, (9) farmers' conference, and (10) use of subsidies for the Harijans.

I found no abuse or malpractice in the working of the different wheels of the administrative machinery. The records and documents that passed through my hands were correctly kept. The D.P.O. and his colleagues work with a will. And yet one somehow feels the need for a breath of fresh air.

The main handicap is that the team at Bulandshahr is all but swamped by the daily burden of paperwork. Fortunately, a reduction in the number of reports has simplified the routine somewhat, but there is still a great deal to do. Most of the other eighteen blocks, which are nearly all situated on the main road, are visited more frequently than the one at Unchagaon, but they are still not visited enough. The D.P.O. and the officials in charge of agriculture and of the cooperatives ought to be relieved as much as possible of their clerical duties so that they can be out in the field seeing the peasants, hearing their complaints, and making sure that decisions are implemented down to the village level. Ideally, they should visit all the blocks at least once a month, taking ten days to a fortnight to do so, but the majority of the top officials in Uttar Pradesh consider this impossible under the present system. Moreover, there is now the additional burden of work connected with the zila parishad.

Another handicap is the lack of discipline. How many times has it not been necessary during the monthly staff meetings to remind the B.D.O. to produce such and such a report or to take such and such an action? Instead of imposing penalties, the exhortations are simply repeated after a time.

A third handicap is that in the district there is one man who can assert himself by virtue of his rank, his background, and his employment in the Indian Administrative Service—the collector. At the same time, the one sector that is of prime importance, demanding the greatest skill and the firmest authority, is that of development, and the immediate responsibility for this does not lie with the collector but with the D.P.O., a man of the state service, of less authority. The result is a precarious system in which the collector has his say on development but does not discharge an immediate and direct responsibility.[18] Part of his time is spent on routine tasks which could easily be carried out by any middle-grade subordinate under supervision. As for the D.P.O., he lacks the prestige to deal with the many obstacles in his way. Besides, all too often the intrigues of the politicians are allowed a fairly clear field.

Finally, what of the zila parishad? Since it was only set up in 1964 I have not seen it at work, but there seems to be the same lack of awareness of economic needs and their serious implications. It is not from this side that progress will come in the immediate future.

State Irrigation

Of the 266,000 hectares irrigated in Bulandshahr, privately owned wells account for 94,350. The great majority of lands depend on the canals and the state tube-wells. These are administered by divisions and subdivisions, each having an engineer in charge and an office and itinerant staff who control the canals and collect the irrigation dues. Each state tube-well also has an operator who is responsible for it.

Most of the canals were dug during the second half of the nineteenth century and have more than reached the limit of their capacity, so that frequently their command areas, as at Khandoï, are underirrigated. The task of the department is simply to supervise the correct functioning of the system, and cases of mismanagement are comparatively rare. The following one, however, is worth noting. The small secondary channel to the north of Khandoï has an outlet badly situated on ground that is too high and therefore unirrigable. For years the peasants have been asking that the outlet be shifted fifty to a hundred meters downstream. After countless requests an official finally came from Meerut, the division headquarters, to settle the matter. He indicated that he would gladly give a favorable decision, if he received a bakshish of a hundred rupees. The peasants refused to pay and no more was heard. In November, 1963, I intervened at Bulandshahr, and the D.P.O. forwarded to Meerut a further request by the peasants at Khandoï. A month later, having received no reply, the D.P.O. sent a reminder. In January, taking advantage of other visits I had to make, I went to see the chief engineer, and he promised to look into the affair.

[18] This system deviates from the recommendations of the *Mehta Report;* see chaps. 9 and 26.

But unfortunately he had a heart attack a few weeks later, and nothing had therefore been done when I returned to Khandoï in August, 1964. A mere bagatelle, one might say, but nevertheless several hectares of good land were affected.

The situation regarding the state tube-wells is more disturbing. There are 500 of these, of which the majority use electricity thanks to several new lines of supply. The subsoil water is abundant and shallow, continually being fed by water that seeps through from the canals (which are not lined). Since the risks of waterlogging and salinity are slight, this is an ideal method of irrigation. The water supply is regular, and the cost to the peasants is less than for the more complicated Persian wheels.

The twenty-six new state tube-wells projected for the third plan (1961–1966) were completed before the end of the third year. Each one cost about 75,000 rupees, including labor, materials, and electrical equipment, and the installation of 1,600 meters of lined field channels and 1,600 meters of unlined.[19] This much having been done successfully, administrative failures have prevented maximum benefits from being drawn from them.

Years ago, when cultivation, especially double cropping, was not so intensive, an area of between 320 to 400 hectares (800–1,000 acres) could ordinarily be served by one well, but today, for numerous reasons (see chap. 8), this is no longer possible. The irrigation department has sensibly lowered the command area to 240–280 hectares (600–700 acres), and has used this standard for all new tube-wells since 1961. Most of the old tube-wells, however, have the same command areas as before. It should be noted, too, that even when a state well is unable to serve an entire area, farmers are not permitted to install their own electric tube-wells in the command areas of state tube-wells because of the threat of competing with the state wells. This prohibition was removed only in 1964, but it is still a problem.

Not surprisingly, since the water supply is far short of demand, the operators of the state tube-wells have become important persons. The usual bakshish per watering—whether offered or demanded—varies between 0.25 to 0.50 of a rupee per *bigha kachcha,* or some four to eight rupees per hectare. Influential persons like former zamindars and well-to-do farmers can usually get by without paying, but the poorer peasants are obliged to suffer under the system. Impressed by the complaints from Khandoï, I extended my inquiries in the district; out of eleven operators, only one was honest according to the peasants'

[19] At the outset, the cost was estimated at about 50,000 rupees. The higher figure indicated may well be exceeded during the fourth plan, 1966–1971.

opinions. There may, of course, be exaggerations on the villagers' side, but no doubt a malaise does exist.

An even more serious waste occurs in connection with the field channels. Each tube-well is designed to supply a number of lined channels, usually about 50 cm. wide, with sloping walls 40 cm. deep. When reading the reports of the State Tube-well Division, one often comes across the notation, "tube-well unusable owing to broken channels." The reason for this is simple. The private contractor is issued cement against his government permit to carry out the work. But instead of using it all for the canals, he withholds part of it to sell on the black market; as a result, many field channels are defective because too much sand was mixed in with the cement.

This is all pure fraud, of course. But some of the administrative methods are no more helpful. In 1962 the D.P.O. of Bulandshahr prepared a plan for demonstrations showing how the state tube-wells could be used more effectively. The registers of the division mentioned twenty wells that had worked for less than 2,000 hours [20] a year over three years, and it was thought that the peasants needed to be encouraged to irrigate their holdings. The list of tube-wells was sent to the A.D.O. (agriculture) of the blocks on July 13, 1962, with a request for a report at an early date. The responsible official at Unchagaon forwarded this to his gram sewaks, who sent in their reports on September 2 and 3. Consolidated into a single report, these were dispatched to Bulandshahr on December 6.

The first comment on the above, which does not concern the irrigation department, must be to note the length of time taken to obtain these reports at Unchagaon and to forward them. Since there was no sense of urgency, and since delay carried no penalty, everyone was dilatory, and thus no action on the wells was possible in time for the 1962–1963 *rabi*. The necessary steps should have been taken in late September or October.

The second comment must be: what does the report say about the reasons for the inadequate functioning of the tube-wells? I shall list a few examples:

Tube-well J.B. No. 25. The operator is usually absent. The well had to be re-sunk last year because of defects.

J.B. No. 48. The field channel is broken and has not been repaired yet. Even the main outlet is not working.

J.B. Nos. 88 and 89. The channels must be cemented because the ground is sandy and slightly sloping.

[20] Below this figure the wells do not cover expenses.

J.B. No. 93. Inadequate electricity supply, resulting in a damaged motor; need for lined channels [21] as in 88 and 89.

J.B. No. 92. Needs lined channels.

J.B. No. 91. Needs lined channels.

J.B. No. 90. Needs lined channels.

The B.D.O.'s note in the margin of the report is to the point: "It is not demand for water that is lacking, it is lined field channels. Sufficient evidence of this can be seen in the progress of the private tube-wells, from which the growers buy water at higher prices than those of the state wells."

Several of these defects are rather long-standing and have been reported to Bulandshahr many times. For example, the J.B. 90 was installed in 1960, but the field channels have not been constructed. When an official at last visited the site early in 1964, he said that it would perhaps be necessary to re-site the well in a more favorable position. In December, 1963, the J.B. 86 had been out of action for a month and repairs had only just started. Yet this was the season when water was in great demand. The same well and J.B. 84 had had broken field channels for six months, and a start was only now being made on the necessary repair work.

At Khandoï, the operator was finally transferred to another *tehsil* without any sort of inquiry being made into his conduct despite clear evidence of fraud. With the new operator the situation became even worse. He lived in another village and, in violation of regulations, was often absent from his post. On these occasions he would leave the key with the peasants and let them start up the engine. In the summer there are often sudden power drops, when the pump must be stopped immediately to avoid damage. The first breakdown of this sort occurred in April, 1964. The pump was put back into working order rather quickly, but it stopped again for the same reason. This time repairs dragged on to such an extent that, during the entire hot season in 1964, a number of peasants were able to water their sugar cane only once. They estimated their loss at 50,000 rupees, and this was not an exaggeration. In spite of several requests, up to August 10, 1964,[22] the State Tube-well Division had taken no action whatever.

It is easy enough to criticize these shortcomings, but it must be said in all fairness that some of them, at least, were no doubt unavoidable—particularly those involving delays and lack of communication

[21] The lack of cement-lined channels had already been reported by the block to the Bulandshahr division on April 20, 1961.

[22] The date of the petition sent by the farmers' meeting to the collector. They also reported the bakshishs received by the operator.

over a large area. The point to raise is: could they be reduced, since they have been known for a long time? At this stage two remarks must be made: state tube-wells, which are of such great importance, do not come under the direct control of the officers generally responsible for development at the district level. Second, these defects are found not only in Bulandshahr but in many other districts of Uttar Pradesh.

Before trying to suggest some remedies, let us proceed further in the rural areas.[23]

[23] The agricultural progress from 1964 to 1966 was briefly as follows. The year 1964–1965 had the advantage of favorable weather conditions and as a result there was an appreciable rise in production. Crops in *kharif* were good in 1965. The *rabi* of 1966 would probably be slightly inferior to that of 1965 but nevertheless quite good.

15

THE FUTURE OF KHANDOÏ

Now that we have followed through to district level the village's administrative machinery, the plans, and the way in which they have been put into effect, what conclusions can we make as to the future of a village such as Khandoï—a village in which development has reached the point where the peasants have reacted spontaneously to the idea of material progress, are open to the market economy, and possess fairly sophisticated technical knowledge?

First Hypothesis: The Population Factor

The rate of population growth in Khandoï is on the point of gathering momentum. There is every reason to believe that the 18 percent increase between 1951 and 1961 will become higher. The infant mortality rate is particularly high among the Jativs and others of the poorest groups. Some couples with two or three living children have had as many as seven more who have died, usually at a very early age. This high infant mortality is not confined to the most underprivileged classes, however; well-to-do families also suffer. Tez Pal Singh, the ex-lambardar, lost two of his seven children, and Bhola Singh lost four out of eleven. Another couple in the same economic bracket lost six out of nine.[1]

In my interviews I used to ask the father how many of his children were still alive and how many had died (often at an early age). Out of 94 couples surveyed, there was a total of 309 children alive and 317 dead. The first figure should be fairly accurate, but one could well imagine that, about the dead, there may have been errors by omission or faulty memory; that is why such results should be taken with great

[1] The conditions under which babies are born are precarious. Only rarely is one of the two midwives from Unchagaon present. A Bhangi (of the Harijan caste, scavengers and sweepers) assists at the birth, having learned the rudiments from her sister-in-law, who in turn learned them from her mother. Child care is extremely casual.

care, until there are further and detailed demographic studies (which were not the purpose of my work). Such a high mortality remains, however, startling for an area not particularly unhealthy. Malaria has virtually disappeared during the last few years and there have been no serious epidemics. Also, the drinking water is reasonably good.

What chances of success has propaganda for birth control? A young social worker who is attached to the Unchagaon welfare center tries to encourage the peasants to limit their families. He distributes condoms and vaginal jellies. The men here take little interest in this subject;[2] the women, quite understandably, show a keen interest. (I found an average of six children per couple—three still living—but this is an approximate figure which does not take into account the couples' ages. Some couples, of course, had more than six.) But unless the intrauterine loop, or a similarly effective device, is introduced on a large scale, there seems small chance of any substantial reduction in the birth rate for years to come. It is not easy to change traditional sexual habits, nor can one smooth away all at once a host of practical difficulties. Moreover, birth control propaganda requires a great deal of perseverance and tact. The male social worker does not deal with the women, who want birth control; he ought to have a female assistant. Also, methods that are both efficient and practical must be found: the pill, which appears to be the simplest method, is probably not practicable for India, partly because of its cost, partly because it must be taken regularly to be effective. There may also be secondary effects. Other methods, too, are expensive, or too complicated for peasants to use easily. As for sterilization, it will not be accepted on any wide scale unless there is an effective educational program. The surgical team that stopped at Unchagaon in March, 1964, did not have a single patient.

Faced, therefore, with an acceleration in the rate of population growth—at least for some years—a much greater effort to improve the economic situation is urgently needed.

Second Hypothesis: Opportunities Outside the Village

Today, nearly fifty men earn their living outside Khandoï, sending home the money they have saved to their wives and children who have remained with their parents or other relatives. But the increasing population in India restricts more and more the opportunities for

[2] This is not always the case. Witness the article by Jean-Luc Chambard, "Mariages secondaires et foires aux femmes dans l'Inde centrale," *L'Homme,* I (1961), 2.

work in towns. There are simply more and more people, far in excess of the new jobs created, and the rate of unemployment rises steadily.[3]

Third Hypothesis: Increased Production

Even with a fairly high level of production, it should be possible to achieve still higher yields. But there can be no progress without great improvements in irrigation. The consolidation of holdings will help, of course. For instance, now that their formerly scattered holdings have been exchanged for single large areas, two well-to-do farmers have made application to sink tube-wells, and they intend to sell their surplus water to neighbors. A third has installed an oil tube-well, and a fourth, Nawat Singh, a Lodha farmer, is carrying out an interesting experiment. Before consolidation, Nawat owned two and a half hectares, several plots of which were irrigated. Under the consolidation plan, he exchanged his old lands for unirrigated lands, receiving five hectares, since exchanges are based on the value of the soil. But with typical Lodha spirit, he is proceeding to irrigate his new holdings, and in 1965 he installed an oil tube-well. With the improved water supply, a minimum amount of social cohesion becomes necessary. Mutual aid certainly exists among several families, but not at village level, where disagreements over wells are an expensive luxury. The peasants risk paying dearly for their disputes and mutual distrust: because of a petty quarrel, ten or twenty hectares of land may be either badly irrigated or not irrigated at all; or a quarrel may mean that a silted-up drainage channel stands useless, when, if cleaned, it could irrigate the fields downstream; or heavy legal expenses may occur, sometimes even exceeding the amount of the suit, over a plot of land under litigation.

Obviously, it is difficult to make any forecasts. The gap created by the abolition of the zamindari system has been slow to fill. Men of intelligence are often disinclined to become involved in public affairs, but their contribution would permit the formation of a panchayat worthy of its name.

So far as administration is concerned, Khandoï does not need what one might call the basic philosophy of community development. The problem is not that of propagating new methods (extension), of demonstrating the advantages of green manure and superphosphates, and encouraging the peasants with fine words. Rather, the public

[3] The number of unemployed rose from 5.3 million to over 9 million between 1956 and 1961. At the end of the Third Plan it was around 10 to 12 million. See *Third Five Year Plan*, p. 156; *Fourth Five Year Plan, A Draft Outline*, p. 106; *Overseas Hindustan Times*, May 5, 1966.

services that deal with such practical matters as irrigation, credit, cement, and fertilizers should be made to operate with greater speed and efficiency.

Certan specific things need to be done—such as the revision and limitation of the command area of J.B. 85, perhaps along with the digging of a second state tube-well to irrigate the area that is so inadequately served by the small canal to the north. The serious malpractices involving the operation of J.B. 85 in the summer of 1964 ought never to be repeated, nor should there be any more bakshish for the operator.

The block should devote the whole of its attention to speeding up the credit procedure for irrigation. Ram Singh, a Jat, was quite bewildered by the number of formalities that had to be gone through for a tube-well: a *taccavi* loan, an application for electric connection, a visit to the D.P.O., and to the electric services, and so on and so on. Might it not be possible for the block to act as an intermediary between the farmers and the district administration, thus making all these steps unnecessary? Improvements could also be introduced in credit by ensuring that cooperative credit societies functioned more efficiently and by extending the condition for the provision of credit. Crop loans (see chap. 26) could be of particular interest for very small landholders. Then, once the farmer was sure of his water supply, he could make much more use of chemical fertilizers.

Postscript.—During a new visit in August 1967, I was struck by the fast growth of the economy. No less than eight private tubewells had been installed since 1964. This means that only a very limited acreage is not under irrigation now and that most of the previous shortcomings of the irrigation system have been eliminated. In addition, new varieties of Mexican wheat are being used increasingly and yield an average of 2,000 to 3,000 kg/ha, a figure that can be increased still further.

16

NAHIYAN AND THE BENARES DISTRICT

We are now at the other end of Uttar Pradesh. After a distance of twenty-eight kilometers along the Benares–Jaunpur road, we turn off to Mangari, which is the headquarters of the Pindra block; from there along four kilometers of a rough nonmetaled road, we reach Nahiyan.

The flat landscape is broken by mango trees, pipals, bamboos, and small tanks. The villages are scattered in hamlets containing large farmhouses of puddled clay covered with rounded tiles, and with an inner courtyard. This decentralization of built-up areas is typical of eastern Uttar Pradesh, which is a region that has been less affected than most by the various invasions from the northwest.

The Land and the Men

The pattern of land use is much the same as in the west. Nahiyan covers a total area of 418 hectares broken up as follows:

Arable land	362 ha.
Uncultivated land (56 ha.)	
Tanks	4.4
Roads	1.6
Fallow land	6.4
Fields under litigation	8
Built-up area	15.6
Gardens and orchards	16
New buildings and new gardens	4

These figures are not strictly accurate, since consolidation of holdings had not yet taken place, nor has the map, dating from 1883–1884, been brought up to date in every detail, but they will do for our analysis.

The 1951 census showed a total population of 2,237 (289 families), made up of 1,157 males and 1,080 females. Eighty-seven men and six women knew how to read and write.[1] By 1961 the population had

---

[1] These very low literacy figures are questionable. See *Census of India, 1951, District Census Handbook, U.P., Banaras District.*

increased to 2,500, giving a density of 600 to the square kilometer (for Khandoï the figure is 444) . This was an increase of 11.7 percent, lower than the average rate for Uttar Pradesh (16.5 percent) and also lower than the rate for the district (18.5 percent) .

The old Nahiyan zamindar does not reside in the village. After the agrarian reforms he only kept an orchard, now rather neglected. The four largest landowners, all Thakurs, each own a little more than twelve hectares, which represents a total of 52.5 hectares. The remainder of the land consists of some more or less economic holdings of a few hectares each, and a great number of very small holdings. In all, there are 2,083 plots on 418 hectares of land.[2]

Here the dominant castes so far as land and influence are concerned are mainly Brahmins, Thakurs, and Kayasths, which confirms the relationship between caste and land ownership already noticed in Khandoï. The low castes and especially the Harijans tend usually to be landless or to have very little land.

The Agricultural Calendar and Farming Techniques

The 1962/63 *khasra* or register gives the following figures for cultivated lands:

Rabi

Irrigated land:

Wheat	37.2 ha.
Wheat and barley	25.6
Wheat and gram	2.8
Barley	38.4
Peas and barley	0.4
Peas	50.4
Potatoes	13.6
Total	168.4 ha.

Unirrigated land:

Pulses	31.6 ha.
Peas	0.4
	32.0 ha.
Total for the *rabi*	200.4 ha.
Irrigated land: sugar cane	53.6 ha.

[2] Khandoï: 613 for 276 ha. One shudders to think of the enormous difficulties attendant on the consolidation of holdings when the land is so split up.

Kharif

Unirrigated land:

Jowar and *bajra*	12.8 ha.
Bajra and pulses	4
Early rice	44.8
Normal rice	80.8
Low-quality rice	14.8
Broadcasted rice	40.4
Maize	25.2
Pulses	5.2
Vegetables	2
Fodder	10.4
Total for the *kharif*	240.4 ha.

It should be borne in mind that 131.6 hectares, or 36 percent, of the total arable land of 362 hectares bears double cropping.

These crop figures are typical of the middle Ganges area where, in contrast to the delta, the heavier rainfall makes it possible to grow rice alongside wheat.[3] Sugar cane is a much less important crop than it is in the western part of the province. The peasants take advantage of the more abundant rains and plant most of their crops in the *kharif* and the monsoon period; ordinarily, therefore, irrigation is of less importance than it is elsewhere. Drainage, on the other hand, as we shall see, is often a problem.

Economically, this district is little influenced by the holy city of Benares. Not only is there greater poverty than in the west, but the region is also backward in agricultural techniques, including methods of irrigation. Two state tube-wells were put into operation in May, 1963, commanding an area of 104.8 hectares. The rest of the land has to depend on private wells, none of which is tubed with a pump; they all make use of the old *mot* system, a method which entails the use of single or double equipment in the form of one or two leather bags, each of which is drawn by a pair of bullocks who walk up and down the well ramp. This is hard work for the animals as well as for the man or woman who pulls the bag up to the curbstone, and it is also very slow. Quite a lot of the water falls back into the well and it is necessary to stop more often than with a Persian wheel. Two pairs of bullocks, pulling one bag each, can irrigate 0.10 hectare in a day; a Persian wheel irrigates 0.25 hectare.

Production figures are in general fairly low. Rice, the most important crop in terms of acreage, has a somewhat higher yield than

[3] For eastern Uttar Pradesh, the rainfall is 1,117 mm. in 50 days; for western Uttar Pradesh, 840 mm. in 40 days; see *Census of India, 1951*, I, 15.

elsewhere in the province. For clean or husked rice the peasants give a figure between 700 and 900 kg/ha, as compared with an average of 700 kg/ha for the province.[4] Sugar cane, the second largest crop, is less good, owing partly to the fact that the variety grown is a low-yield local variety, giving somewhere between 2,000 and 3,000 kilograms of *gur* per hectare, as against 5,000 at Khandoï.[5] Also the *kolus* in Nahi-yan are less efficient; many crushers can take only three canes at a time instead of five, and the bullocks are weaker and usually smaller.

Some "large" landowners have adopted the use of improved seeds for wheat, and, with adequate irrigation, their yields have risen to 2,000 kg/ha. Most of the other wheat grown is of rather poor quality, however, and fields are often sparse because of improper germination. When the land is well irrigated, the yield almost equals the average for Khandoï, about 1,200 kg/ha; but when it is not—and this is all too frequently the case—it is only 700–900 kg/ha.[6]

Here, as elsewhere, there is very little grazing land and the cattle are tethered outside the farms. There are few buffaloes, and their diet is inadequate because the fodder yields are extremely poor. (Fodder is cut by hand, with a small knife.) Proportionately, orchards occupy rather a large amount of the total land area—sixteen hectares—but the trees, mostly mangoes, are nearly all too old to bear well.

Some of the land is inevitably not being used to its potential. Poor drainage means that several hectares are wasted each year. One farmer, for example, Kamal Singh, a Thakur, has one good hectare of land which is invariably flooded by the monsoon; no cultivation at all is possible for the *kharif,* and since the water stands on a long time on the sodden soil, the land is hardly usable for the *rabi.*

The soil of this district is alluvial soil, of generally good quality, and if the irrigation were better it could bear heavier double cropping. With better irrigation, too, improved varieties of wheat, which need four waterings a season, could be grown instead of the local varieties which do fairly well with only two. Better irrigation, and a wider use of chemical fertilizers, would also bring about a great increase in the yields of sugar cane; we have already noted the decisive role played by this crop at Khandoï.

[4] *Eastern Economist,* Annual No., Jan. 5, 1962.

[5] Owing to lack of fertilizers and improved seeds, there is no ratoon crop; the canes are pulled up after each harvest.

[6] These figures (for 1964) were taken from the peasants and the block staff and are much higher than the average for the entire district, which was estimated at 560 kg/ha at the start of the third plan (information obtained at Benares). The difference is largely attributable to irrigation, which is more developed here than in many other blocks.

Why do we find in this area so many impediments to increased production—the same sort of conditions, in fact, which are to be found throughout the eastern districts of Uttar Pradesh, Bihar, and vast regions of Bengal?

Lack of irrigation is beyond question the principal handicap. In the west, the land profile has made it possible to construct between the Ganges and the Jumna a close network of canals through which the water naturally flows by force of gravity. In the east, the river beds are frequently below the level of the fields, making this simple form of irrigation impossible. Pumps or pumping stations are necessary, and this is an expensive method which only became popular after the Second World War. Canal irrigation here is fifty years behind the western areas.

After the first attempts at tube-wells (as early as 1929), Sir William Stampe, then chief engineer for irrigation in the United Provinces, launched a project for four hundred state tube-wells, making use of the electricity which had just come to the rural areas of the west (1934–35). In 1939, these watered some 800,000 hectares.[7] The Second World War interrupted plans to extend the network, and these were not initiated until 1946–1947. For most areas, then, the only kind of irrigation has been the *mot*.

The problems of sugar cane are also typical. Most of the *gur* is produced only for home consumption, since a lack of outlets such as large sugar mills and city markets [8] has kept the peasants from pushing this crop. Being a cash crop, it could bring them the capital necessary for modernizing their techniques, for adopting the *rahat* irrigation system, for using more improved seeds and chemical fertilizers, and even, in the case of some of the better-off farmers, for installing a private tube-well.

The situation is aggravated, here as everywhere in India, by the steadily rising population. Between 1921 and 1961 the number of persons in the district increased from 1,314,891 to 2,362,179.[9] Since there are few industries, men have been forced to exist as best they can on their land, which has been more and more fragmented. The cycle of

[7] See L. Dudley Stamp, *Asia* (London, 1959), p. 296, and P.R.A.I., *Report on the Study of Tube-well Irrigation Potential and Its Utilization with Special Reference to Eastern U.P.* (1962), pp. 1, 49.

[8] Such as Delhi, Agra, and the wealthy towns of the Punjab. Out of 330,000 hectares cultivated in the Benares district, only 19,000 are in sugar cane; in Bulandshahr, about 69,100 hectares of improved cane are grown out of a total cultivated area of 379,360 hectares.

[9] *District Census Handbook, U.P., Banaras District, 1951* and *Census of India, 1961, Paper No. 1.*

underdevelopment is depressingly clear: inability to invest in order to produce more, since increasing poverty due to the pressure of population is not compensated by a rise in production.

This analysis would be incomplete without reference to the human factor. In the west, when they talk of a *Purbi* (literally someone from the east, an inhabitant of the middle or lower Ganges), they automatically add the adjective *dhila,* meaning rather unenterprising. One cannot but agree with the epithet. We are a long way from the robust northern castes. In Nahiyan, people do not seem to care very much about their farms—certainly they do not throw themselves energetically into the struggle. When I asked a Brahmin why he had no double cropping on his ten hectares of land, of which 5.6 hectares were irrigated, he replied, "That's our weakness."

The reasons for this attitude can be found, I think, in history and sociology. Northern India, the regions of the Punjab and western Uttar Pradesh, has suffered the disturbances of countless invasions; it has often had to fight and flee, and return to lands sacked by the invader. That kind of martial tradition continued under the British, and the region became renowned for its fine soldiers.

Before the large irrigation networks were constructed, life in the west was harder than in the east. Further down the Ganges, the rainfall is heavier, and man does not have to struggle against both an enemy and the climate; as a result, he may tend to work less hard, and it is a tradition that is difficult to overcome, even with the many pressures of modern India. The dynamism of the west can also be explained in part by the character of the Jats and other high castes who work with their hands. The Jat area begins in the Punjab and ends in the districts immediately to the east of Delhi. Beyond this area, the high castes often observe the taboo on ploughing.[10] Though originally rather flexible, this tradition has gradually become more rigid, and it is observed in a vast number of regions. A Khandoï Brahmin told me that even during a course for cooperative farm secretaries the young Brahmins from the east took zero marks rather than touch the plough.

The practical consequences of this attitude can readily be imagined. Take, for example, a Brahmin joint family.[11] Three brothers, two of

[10] The Laws of Manu reluctantly admit that in cases of necessity a Brahmin may decide to plough (Book IV: 5). Further on (Book X: 83) the rule is more strict: "Sometimes a Brahmin or a Kshatriya . . . must avoid ploughing whenever possible, for this kind of work destroys lively beings and depends on extraneous help, like that of bullocks."

[11] This type of family is not disappearing at the same rate as in the west.

whom are married, with their wives and children form a group of twenty-four, owning eight hectares—quite adequate to support them all. This family has enough manpower among its own members to make it unnecessary to employ anyone except casual laborers at busy periods, but in fact the major part of the work is done by two laborers permanently attached to the household. They are paid five rupees a month each and also are allowed the use of 0.4 hectare of land. Thus the taboo on ploughing means that the Brahmins are losing 120 rupees a year and a tenth of their land.

Take the case of another joint family, that of Bhagavati Prasad, a Kayasth. With twenty-five members, including women and children, three brothers in the prime of life, and grown-up sons, they have a substantial labor force. Altogether they own four hectares of irrigated land. In addition to casual laborers they employ a permanent farm worker who earns two and a half rupees a month and has the use of 0.62 hectare of land.

In both cases, part of the family savings, which should be invested, is used for paying quite superfluous farm workers.

In the past, sharecropping was widespread. Generally the gross product was divided equally, with the landowner bearing hardly any part of the production costs. Today the farmer, *bhumidar,* or *sirdar,* grants part of his land to his farm workers, adding to this a few rupees a month. Sometimes, to prevent legal dispositions, the plot of land changes each year. Under the law abolishing the zamindari system, letting or subletting is forbidden; thus, by virtue of a certain length of time on a plot of land, the farm worker acquires the right to become *sirdar.* For sharecropping, however, subletting is not absolutely forbidden, since sharing the harvest is not considered part of the concept of letting or subletting. Nonetheless, the peasants have thought it wiser to adopt the present system of rotating the land (known as *mafi*), sharecropping having been the object of much criticism and the source of legal altercations.

This example illustrates not only the inadequacy of agrarian reforms [12] but also the difficulty of finding a really effective solution. The *mafi* system is so flexible that it escapes the law; moreover, the farm workers are often reluctant to make complaints for fear of losing their jobs and their plots of land.

The surplus of labor encourages the farm worker to become attached to one landowner, and he becomes tied even more closely by reason of the credit that he obtains from him. Debts accumulate, at

[12] See Baljit Singh, *Next Step in Village India,* p. 22; also see chap. 19.

interest rates of 20 to 36 percent, until the laborer is quite at the mercy of his employer. Inevitably, there are instances of exploitation and occasional grave abuses. Furthermore, the work of these undernourished, badly paid laborers is of poor quality, since they take no interest in looking after land that does not belong to them—a second loss for the landowner.

Conditions and Standard of Living

Kamla Prasad Singh, a Thakur, is a comfortably off farmer, interested in new techniques, with land covering an area of fifteen hectares. His three brothers are co-owners but they work outside the village—one as a barrister at Benares, the second as director of a small factory in the Holy City, the third as an agricultural assistant at the University of Agra. The families of all three brothers, totaling seventeen, live together at Nahiyan.

Our landowner has profited from instruction given by the block: he uses chemical fertilizers, and two-thirds of his land is irrigated and bears double cropping. His cattle consists of six bullocks, a buffalo (yielding eight liters of milk a day), and two cows (between seven and eight liters a day). The family has no debts, and it is well nourished on cereals, pulses, milk, and occasionally mutton.

Kamla carefully supervises the work of his five permanent laborers, each of whom has the tenure of 0.25 hectare and is paid four rupees a month together with a little food. When their wives work, they earn seven and a half rupees a month, and also some food.[13] Kamla Prasad manages very well, thanks to an extensive area of land and the earnings of his brothers, who are well employed.

Mata Prasad, a Brahmin, lives with his two brothers, who, like him, are married. The joint family consists of six adults and ten children. It owns 4.25 hectares, for which it employs casual laborers who cost them about fifteen rupees a month and a little food. They own three bullocks and a cow (yielding one liter of milk a day). The entire family eats two meals a day—cereals, pulses, a few potatoes, very occasionally some tomatoes (bought), and sometimes *gur*. The small supply of milk is given to the children.

The debts of the joint family amount to 2,000 rupees; they borrowed 800 rupees to buy bullocks, and 1,200 rupees to pay for the marriage of

---

[13] In this region, women who are Harijans, or who belong to a low caste, work more in the fields than they do in the west.

the youngest brother. They just about manage, but they save almost nothing. They do not have enough money to buy fertilizers.

Kamlaya Dubey, a Brahmin, has a household composed of his wife, three young children, and a married son and his wife. He owns two and a half hectares, all irrigated, and two bullocks. He buys a little milk for his children, but the adults eat only cereals and pulses.

Kamlaya does very little of the work himself. Instead, he employs casual laborers whom he pays at a rate of one rupee a day, in addition to a little food. He is 300 rupees in debt, 200 of which he borrowed to buy the bullocks. Kamlaya's lot has been but little improved in the past fifteen years. Unlike the Khandoï Brahmins who own the same amount of land, he finds it difficult to make ends meet.

Ram Sarup presents quite a different picture. He and his brother own 6.25 hectares, and there are altogether nine people in their two households. There is no doubt about the improvement in Sarup's standard of living: his rate of production is rising, and he uses the recommended amounts of chemical fertilizer. He and his brother now own two pairs of bullocks, three cows, and a buffalo. They have no debts. Why are they so successful, while the Brahmins and Takurs who own the same amount of land complain of their lot?

Ram Sarup is a Kurmi, a Sudra caste of farmers which does not have the taboos of the high castes. He and his brother work very hard on their fields, only occasionally hiring daily laborers. They can therefore save and invest, and they devote much greater care and attention to their farming than would a badly paid laborer.

For the small landowners, whatever their caste, life is hard. They cannot make ends meet, and their standard of living remains stagnant, or perhaps in some cases declines.

Gaurisankar Ram, a Kurmi, has a wife and four children. He owns 0.75 hectare, part of which is under double cropping, and he has two bullocks. His family drinks no milk, but makes do with cereals, lentils, a little sugar-cane juice in season, and occasionally some goat's meat. He does not know the exact amount of his debts: "Many," he says, "something like 2,000 rupees borrowed from various landowners at a rate of 25 percent interest." From time to time, Gaurisankar earns one rupee a day, without food, as a casual farm worker.

Pitam, a Chamar, ex-untouchable, is a widower; he lives with his married son and his wife and three children, and his daughter. He owns one-half of a hectare, on which he grows vegetables, cereals, and sugar cane. He has two small bullocks and a heifer. He consumes all he produces, and spends his occasional earnings on food: these amount to half a rupee and a meal each day from various landowners. His debts amount to 1,000 rupees; these were incurred for his son's marriage, his wife's funeral, and for food, with the interest rate varying from 24 to 36 percent according to the moneylenders.

Dewan, a Chamar, has a household consisting of his wife, three children, and a married son and his wife. As a farm worker attached to a Thakur, he has the use of 0.25 hectare of land. He does not own a bullock, but the landlord lends him his together with his plough in return for which he has a right to the straw and fodder. On his field Dewan grows maize in the *kharif* and wheat in the *rabi*. He also receives from his employer four rupees a month and one meal a day. His wife, who works about four days a month for the same Thakur, receives half a rupee and her meals. Dewan owns a cow, which has a daily yield of half a liter of milk—all for the children. Only occasionally does the family eat more than one meal a day. It owes 150 rupees to its employer.

Let us take a look at our last Chamar, Bulli, who, with his wife and four young children, is in a state of almost complete destitution. He has neither land nor cattle, and he owes 200 rupees which he borrowed for his daughter's marriage and for buying food. Once or twice a day he eats *chapatis,* some chilies, and occasionally some potatoes. He does not know how many days he works on an average. His daily earnings (when he gets work) amount to one rupee, and his wife earns about half a rupee. He is a tragic figure, weighed down with poverty, just managing to survive, and with scant hope of ever escaping his lot.

Debts

Here, too, credit is obtained from three sources: the state *(taccavis)*, cooperative societies, and private moneylenders charging very high interests of 25 to 36 percent. As we have seen, the practice of an employer granting loans to his farm workers is more common than at Khandoï.

Out of seven medium landowners (those owning between two and six hectares), four have on an average a debt of 350 rupees, most of which is on loan from the cooperative for the purchase of bullocks and fertilizers. The other three have a total debt of 6,500 rupees. The difference is due mainly to the cost of marriages and other prestige expenses demanded by custom. Most of these loans have come from private moneylenders.

It is the same with farm workers, small landowners, and artisans: six families have an average debt of 250 rupees which they have incurred mainly to meet the cost of survival—in other words, for buying food. Another group owes 2,000 rupees; this is a large Chamar community of forty people (two families) who together own one hectare. Each family has a debt of 1,000 rupees, about half of which went for marriages and funerals, the remainder being used for day-to-day subsistence. Another Chamar who owns 0.75 hectare owes 2,000 rupees for the same reasons.

The burden of sumptuary expenditure seems to be heavier than at Khandoï, with even more unfortunate consequences on a lower standard of living. A medium landowner can easily spend 5,000 rupees on a wedding,[14] and a Chamar, whether a farm worker or a small landowner, cannot get by for less than 500–800 rupees.

Impressions of Bitterness

It is difficult to measure extreme poverty in terms of statistics. It has to be seen and described by those who bear it: "Poverty does not leave the poor," a Chamar said to me. It is painful to see the dejection that overwhelms those at the bottom of the social scale. Their poverty puts them at the mercy of their masters, who sometimes resort to physical violence. Hardly had I settled into Nahiyan when three Bhars (Sudra caste) came to ask for my help. Their Brahmin neighbors had beaten them with sticks and cut open their scalps in a quarrel involving two square meters of land that were under litigation for right-of-way. The Brahmins had also pulled up the thicket of bamboos belonging to the Bhars.

Even if many of the medium farmers make use of hired labor, which is even more poorly paid than at Khandoï, this must not allow us to think that they live any better than medium farmers at Khandoï; on the contrary, they are generally worse off, though owning three or four hectares, since they have smaller crop yields and higher labor costs than farmers who work their own land.

Communism and the Panchayat

At Khandoï, in over five months, I heard the word Communism uttered only once by a dissatisfied peasant. In the Pindra block several panchayats are overwhelmingly Communist, and a Communist candidate was elected to the U.P. Legislative Assembly in 1962.

[14] At the time of my departure from Khandoï, a Brahmin (owning 3.3 ha.) was making preparations for his daughter's wedding which was going to cost him 3,000 rupees.

The strength of the Communists in Nahiyan is easily explained by conditions in the area, where there is a growing conflict between those who have their land ploughed for them and those who do it themselves and are slowly improving their standard of living. The many Harijans (more than 600 at Nahiyan) are in obvious sympathy with the latter, although they are too poor to play a really active role.

What is the real influence of the Communist party? At Ghaghri, a village near Nahiyan, where twelve of the thirteen members of the panchayat are party members, the pradhan reveals a profound ignorance of the doctrine. He believes that communism originated in Calcutta, and he knows nothing whatever about Marx, Lenin, and Stalin. He only knows M.L.A. Adil, for whom he voted in 1962. The pradhan complains of the inefficiency of the panchayat, whose meetings are often adjourned for want of a quorum, and whose disputes make any form of *shramdan* impossible. The thirty members of the C.P. who live in the village never hold meetings; they only come together at block or district level.

In another village I met a charming and intelligent young man, a Kurmi, who was said to be one of the heads of the local party. He had a rather sketchy acquaintance with Marxist–Leninist doctrine, following the Russian line (March, 1964), though many Indian Communist adhere to the more rigid Chinese line. He believed that there should be no attempt to use violence to overthrow the government, that it should be done democratically, through elections. Like all the farmers, this young man was deeply religious; every morning he bowed before Krishna. "India is above all a religious country," he said, "and it is quite wrong to maintain that communism is incompatible with religion."

What this young man seeks is an end to corruption and abuse. He tries to help the peasants to use better techniques, and whenever possible he takes part in Communist party demonstrations in the towns or attends meetings which are held once a fortnight at *tehsil* level.

In Nahiyan the panchayat is obstructed by caste antagonism. At the 1961 elections a Thakur and a Kurmi opposed each other for the office of pradhan; the Kurmi won, and the Thakur contested the election. The case passed from one tribunal to another and is still before the Allahabad court. Meanwhile another Kurmi has been provisionally appointed to carry out the duties of pradhan. The few meetings that are held accomplish little. The two Kurmis in question are not members of the C.P., but they are very sympathetic to it: "The Party cares about the poor, the M.L.A. Adil is very competent, and so on." They have heard of the names of Stalin and Khrushchev, but that is as far as their knowledge goes.

The Pindra Block

The Pindra block was created on July 1, 1957. It is composed of 192 villages grouped into 108 panchayats; the total population is 103,180.[15] The area cultivated covers 17,500 hectares; 4,000 hectares are not arable, and there are 466 hectares of fallow land. A little more than half the cultivated land—9,300 hectares—is irrigated, or is supposed to be, since irrigation is often inadequate. About one-fourth of the land—4,200 hectares—is double cropped.

The development plan is much the same as for the Bulandshahr district. Gradually, by encouraging irrigation, the use of fertilizers, and rural credit, it is achieving results. As we have seen, some peasants have been able to take advantage of the system, but inevitably the over-all rate of progress is slow.

The minor, private irrigation program produced the following results up to December 31, 1963:

No. of Loans Granted		*Works Completed*	*Loans Withdrawn Because Work Not Carried Out*
2nd five-year plan	81	47	34
1961/62	55	3	4
1962/63	20	0	0

The heavy decline is largely due to lack of cement and to the peasants' incompetence.

The administration of the block is considerably smoother than at Unchagaon. The B.D.O. is a former member of the Etawah pilot scheme, and his assistant for agriculture is a bright, intelligent man who knows what he is doing. The running of the office is disciplined: the staff is at work at the proper time (ten o'clock), and the records are clear and well kept. The gram sewak responsible for Nahiyan is not up to the standard of the block staff, however.

Despite the fairly high quality of the staff, their achievements are not impressive. The B.D.O. and his colleagues do not hide the fact that their work is made very difficult by the attitude of the high castes and the extreme poverty of the region: how can they boost private irrigation when the farmers have such a narrow margin of savings, and how

[15] 1961 census; between 1951 and 1961 there was an increase of 11 percent.

can they perfect drainage systems when the people concerned are not ready to cooperate? [16]

In the cooperative societies, the rise in credits extended has been accompanied by the same sort of problems found in Unchagaon, including bakshish and delays in payments. The cooperative farms are by and large strongly disapproved by the peasants, and no particular effort has been made in this direction.

Finally, the village panchayats, Communist or otherwise, which have become more widespread since 1949, have not produced the hoped-for results.

On the noneconomic side we must note the establishment of two welfare centers and the existence (as of December, 1963) of sixty-five primary schools, nine lower-grade, and four higher-grade secondary schools.[17]

The Kshetr Samiti

The president of the kshetr samiti is a Thakur who owns about fifteen hectares. His desire for economic progress is unquestionable and he looks after his land with great care. He seems to get on well with the B.D.O. and takes a closer interest in the business of the block than does his colleague at Unchagaon. Even so, the samiti does not work with the greatest of speed. It met in August, 1963, but the November meeting was deferred for want of a quorum, and it was not until March 8, 1964, that a meeting was held, with 60 percent of the members present. I attended the meeting and observed with interest. It began on time, with the first business being a lengthy discussion on the taxes levied by the panchayats. In 1963, 7,000 rupees were collected, leaving arrears of 20,000 rupees. Several pradhans proposed that these should be written off and that they should start again from scratch. Those whose villages had paid up naturally opposed this, and so for the sake of peace and quiet the arrears were allowed to stand.

On the matter of the program for subsidized cottage industries, it had been proposed to set up a workshop, but the president of the village concerned had not prepared his report and a decision was deferred until the next meeting. Plans for a new welfare center were adopted without much discussion. Last on the agenda came the problem of cement, on which the B.D.O. provided details.

The meeting was livelier than those at Unchagaon, partly because

[16] The cases of dispute or mistrust are similar to those at Khandoï.

[17] For a complete set of figures for the block, see the *Quarterly Progress Reports, Pindra Block*, for 1961–1964.

the president evidenced a certain amount of authority as well as an idealism (at least in words), which was quite sharply rejected by a group of his colleagues. When, on the subject of the panchayats' arrears, he appealed to their better nature, talking of *"Prem, mahabat!* [Love, love!]" someone declared that only under compulsion would the tax be paid.

The infrequency of the meetings was my first indication of how little influence the kshetr samiti had. My conversations with several pradhans led me to conclusions similar to those I had reached in Unchagaon. One looks in vain for priority to be given to any sort of economic activities; there is merely a weak pricking of conscience, and either complete lack of directives, or a bad example. When I reproached a pradhan for building a house for the panchayat [18] he retorted, "And what about all the administrative buildings and those of the Legislative Assembly in Lucknow?"

The District of Benares

The total area of the Benares district is 5,030 square kilometers. In 1961 there were 330,000 hectares under cultivation, of which 113,000 had double cropping and 147,000 were irrigated more or less adequately. The main crops are rice, 120,000 hectares; wheat, 25,000 hectares; and barley, 40,000 hectares. Sugar cane, which is the chief source of income (for the better-off farmers it can be rice), covers an area of only 19,000 hectares.

The organization of development is identical to that of the Bulandshahr district. I shall therefore not go into it in detail again but shall confine myself to the basic features only. Here, as in Bulandshahr, there is a notable lack of harmony between the means available and the targets; in the course of the three first years of the third plan, achievements fell far short of the envisaged increase of 40 or 50 percent for food products and the 500 percent leap forward forecast in the consumption of chemical fertilizers. In irrigation, however, appreciable differences between the two districts are evident—one further striking proof of the great disparity between them. Bulandshahr can confidently launch a much larger program of private irrigation, in terms of the number of wells or borings: 386 tube-wells were envisaged, for example—a target on the way to being achieved—as against only three in Benares.

For reasons already given, the peasants in the Benares district often

[18] A subsidy of 1,000 rupees was provided by the block, and 1,500 more were collected in the village.

lack the minimum basis of savings, and this situation is again evident in the amount of cooperative credit, which is at least 25 percent greater in Bulandshahr.

Taking into account the poverty of the peasants and the limited possibilities, one must acknowledge that the state is making a real effort to improve irrigation and halt the backwardness of the eastern regions. The construction of state tube-wells, not begun until after Independence, reached a figure of 299 units for the district in 1962–1963. The third plan envisaged the installation of 100 new wells of this type (Bulandshahr, 26 units).

There was a similar rate of progress in the medium and large irrigation works; these are mostly reservoirs to catch the water on the northern slopes of the Vindhyas and canals from the Ganges and other rivers. At the beginning of the first plan only 15,300 hectares were irrigated in this way, but in 1961, ten years later, 80,000 hectares were reached. The third plan envisaged yet another increase of 11,000 hectares.

These projects are encouraging, though it will of course take time for them to reach their full economic value. I shall return to this in the following chapter when I discuss state tube-wells and shall merely pause here to mention medium and major irrigation. The changeover from the *mot* system to a larger hydraulic set-up is a complicated procedure. The distribution of water, the maintenance of canals, the construction of field channels (a job carried out by the peasants) are all operations requiring efficient organization. Also the persons concerned need to familiarize themselves with the system, and to carry out their responsibilities without becoming involved in too many disputes. It is equally important for *rabi* crops to be encouraged, for they are less common here than in the west.[19] But all these changes take time, particularly in an area where the peasants are not very enterprising.

The Administration and the Politicians

Benares is the chief city of both the district and the division,[20] which is actually a group of districts. The political atmosphere in Benares seems to be more tense than at Bulandshahr. The high officials are

[19] A brochure published by the Benares Irrigation Division expresses these problems very well: *Sinchai ki Samasya* ["The Irrigation Problem"]. I have taken the figures for major and medium irrigation from it. Those for the state tube-wells were given to me orally in Benares.

[20] At its head is the division commissioner whose duties are more to coordinate than actually to carry out plans. This latter duty is first and foremost that of the collector and his assistants.

often competent men, but this does not make their means of action any less restricted. The Panchayati Raj has opened up here a particularly fertile field for the factions which were already in some evidence before.

Irregularities are not lacking, both in the cooperatives and in the irrigation program. Hardly had the operators of two state tube-wells arrived in Nahiyan when they started asking for bakshish as a matter of course. And what can be done when a member of the Legislative Assembly manages by questionable tactics to see that a tube-well is sunk in his constituency? The M.L.A. would then be ill-placed to defend his constituents against the operator's abuses.

The Future

We have seen what complex reasons there are for the very slow progress of the Benares region. Even the most talented of men cannot work miracles, and here conditions are such that it is difficult even to make a rapid start; there is not the same spearhead to be found as there is among the resolute and already more advanced peasants in the west. But if the immediate future promises no striking increase in production, one can perhaps reasonably expect the peasants to participate more and more in the programs for irrigation and rural credit.[21] As we have seen at Nahiyan, the region is not totally stagnant, even if there is no driving force. It will take many years to eradicate the worst marks of poverty. For this reason one might question the tendency in Lucknow to want to make a particular effort in eastern Uttar Pradesh. In short and medium term, the economic return on investments will be less than in the west; also, without neglecting the eastern districts, the desire to eliminate the economic disparity as quickly as possible seems to be rather a hazardous one.

[21] In 1967 I was in North Bihar, where the socio-economic and psychological conditions are rather similar to eastern U.P. It was encouraging to see more medium farmers begin to invest in irrigation, chemical fertilizers and high yield varieties.

17

THE DIFFICULTIES
OF UTTAR PRADESH

The facts obtained in the districts of Bulandshahr and Benares, the information gathered in other regions visited more rapidly, and the contacts made at Lucknow enable us now to revert to the general problems of the state and to summarize these as a whole.

The Third Five-Year Plan

The third Uttar Pradesh plan maintained the sensible agricultural orientation of the two previous ones:

Public Sector	Amount Invested (in rupees)	Percent of Total
Agricultural programs	880,700,000	17.54
Cooperatives, community development, panchayats	666,200,000	13.26
Major and medium irrigation	517,100,000	
Flood controls	57,500,000	33.02
Power	1,083,600,000	
Industries and mines	214,900,000	4.28
Transport and communications	308,600,000	6.15
Social services	1,248,500,000	24.85
Miscellaneous	45,400,000	0.90
Total	5,022,500,000	100.00

SOURCE: Uttar Pradesh, *Third Five Year Plan*, I, 29.

This distribution of investments was intended to produce a rise of 35 percent in food-grain production. Five years later, cereals and pulses were scheduled to reach 18.3 million tons, an increase which would represent three times the gains made during the second plan. Progress is calculated on the basis of a bench mark of 13.54 million tons for 1960/61 instead of the actual but exceptional figure of 14.15 million (pp. 36, 37).

The report on the third plan at once reveals its anxiety. Uttar Pradesh is made responsible for 19 percent of the total agricultural increase of India, but at the same time it is allotted for major and medium irrigation schemes only 9 percent of the total for India, and 14.6 percent of the funds estimated for the agricultural program. In order to remedy this "inadequate share," the report says (pp. 17–18) : "It is important that the State administration and the democratic bodies at the village, block and district levels approach the third plan with faith, courage, confidence and enthusiasm." In other words, political and administrative factors must make up for the inadequacy of financial provisions.

The 4.74 million tons of extra food grains were to be obtained by the following means:

Major and medium irrigation (state)	208,000 tons
Minor irrigation (state tube-wells and private irrigation)	518,740
Soil conservation	54,790
Dry farming	100,000
Soil improvement	6,760
Improved seeds	310,200
Chemical fertilizers	1,208,040
Farm manure and composts	420,480
Green manure	918,500
Improved techniques	400,000
Double cropping	600,820
Total	4,746,330 tons

The same yardsticks were applied to the whole of the state, without taking soil conditions into account. When applied to the districts of the plains, where soil conditions are fairly homogeneous, the order of importance may be allowed to be reasonable. The essential items are chemical fertilizers, irrigation, green manure, and composts, not to mention double cropping which is made possible by irrigation.[1] The priority given in irrigation to minor works is noteworthy. This general scheme of development seems reasonable. What are less so are the program's size and method of execution.

Progress per sector is scheduled as follows (pp. 87–88) :

	1960/61	1965/66	1961–1966
	(millions of ha.)	(millions of ha.)	Percent of Increase
(I) Area in cereals and pulses	18.68	21.0	12.1
Area in sugar cane	1.1	1.2	6.76
Area in other food grains	0.36	0.48	31.24
Area in double cropping	4.74	6.94	46.29
Area irrigated, state	4.18	4.98	19.14
Area irrigated, private	2.74	3.53	28.91

[1] The table shows the gains relating to the change from rain-fed crops to irrigated farming as well as the introduction of second crops.

	(tons)	(tons)	
(II) Nitrogenous fertilizer used*	200,000	990,000	395.
Phosphatic fertilizers used *	60,000	300,000	400.

	(millions of ha.)	(millions of ha.)	
Area under green manure	0.26	3.6	1,285.
Composts	—	—	46.88

	(millions of ha.)	(millions of ha.)	
(III) Japanese method of rice cultivation	0.4	1.92	380.
U.P. method of wheat cultivation	0.6	1.3	120.
Other techniques	1.1	3.9	250.
Soil conservation	0.05	0.4	750.
Dry farming	—	1.6	
Improved seeds	7.6	11.7	54.21
(IV) Number of development blocks	506	899	77.67

* In terms of ammonium sulphate and superphosphate.

The report on the plan shows us how these figures were derived: "A comprehensive programme for preparing village and block production plans was chalked out in the State in April 1960. The targets for various items were discussed and adopted in gaon sabha meetings by the village people themselves; village level workers, panchayat secretaries, village teachers and cooperative supervisors providing the necessary guidance. They were then consolidated into block plans. . . . The draft district plans were then prepared by consolidating block plans." The total of these plans was adjusted and partially modified in Lucknow.[2]

The circular (No. 2175 XXXV B) of April 15, 1960, sent by the development commissioner to all collectors was explicit. The general orientation of the plan was decided at Lucknow: "The objective of the third plan," the circular announced, "is to increase the production of foodgrains by about 50%."[3] The laying down of an increase of this order induced the districts to conform to it, as we have seen in two detailed cases.

In practice the role of the village assemblies, the block, and the district is much more modest than would appear from the text. The bulk of the work to be undertaken is prepared by the staff of the block on the general instruction of the district. I did not see in Uttar Pradesh

[2] Uttar Pradesh, *Third Five Year Plan*, I, 86–92.
[3] Initial target, subsequently reduced in several districts.

any real village plan (which does not of course mean that none exists). It is more a question of collecting, often in a rather arbitrary manner, figures relating to new wells, fertilizers, cooperatives, and so on.

In addition to the blocks, one must pick out the programs that depend on the departments in Lucknow and their branches in the districts: irrigation (apart from minor private irrigation), soil conservation, certain cooperatives for the marketing of agricultural products, the main activities in the field of education, and the like. Finally there are major projects, notably in irrigation, which depend directly on Lucknow.

The total capital devoted to agriculture amounts to 2,121.6 million rupees (p. 88):

Agricultural development	333.9 millions of rupees
Minor private irrigation	330.9
Soil conservation	40.9
Other programs	176
Community development	516.7
Panchayats	41.1
Cooperatives	108.4
State irrigation and flood control	574.6

To this investment and outlay must be added 600 million rupees annually for short-term cooperative credits, 100 million for medium-term credits, and 100 million for long-term credits. The total should rise from 300 million in 1960/61 to 800 million in 1965/66: this was to cover 75 percent of the farming families (*bhumidars, sirdars*) and 55 percent of the rural population.

The planners worked to a tight budget. The expenditure on community development, to come up to the standards laid down, would have had to amount to 650 million (p. 131), meaning that certain of the social activities would need to be cut back.

Credits (*taccavis*) for minor irrigation were limited to 243.2 million, although demand was estimated at 380 million. The districts and blocks would have to manage to bring about "necessary adjustments of annual budgets" (p. 147). (These are included in the 330 millions in the table above.)

The *shramdan* is another source of capital formation. The plan is based on the following hypothesis: "It was agreed in the conference of planning officers that it should be possible for every family in the village to contribute at least 72 hours of work freely in the form of voluntary labour for works of common benefit" (from the circular of April 15, 1960).

Appreciation of the Position

The plan depended on the following factors: (1) the attitude of the peasants and their opportunities to invest in agriculture; (2) the real cost of progress, or in other words the correlation between the budgeted expenditure and possible achievements; (3) the organization of this expansion. Notwithstanding the factors unknown in 1960–1961, it is difficult to understand how the government of Uttar Pradesh could arrive at or accept this 35 percent increase in production in five years. Given the almost perfect execution of points 2 and 3, one has still to take into account the behavior of the farmers. Entrepreneurship and a minimum of savings are certainly not confined to the four western districts. Several parts of Rohilkand (central U.P.) are definitely progressing. In the *terai,* one comes across colonies of new settlers (often refugees from Pakistan) who are doing very well, and even in other districts there are progressive areas. One must, however, admit that in many districts the prevailing social, economic, and psychological conditions of the people would seem to make such an increase highly unlikely.

In considering points 2 and 3, let us examine again the tables given earlier in this chapter. The increase planned in area (from new land, irrigation, double cropping) seemed reasonable—the goals varying between 10 percent and 30 percent apart from a 46 percent increase in double crops. This should have provided 1.3 million of the extra 4.7 million tons of cereals and pulses. The increases for fertilizers and new techniques, on the other hand, are astonishingly high. Was it reasonable to think that production could be increased so much in so short a time, and to expect that the peasants could be persuaded to accept all these changes? [4]

These increases of 100 to 200 percent, in some cases even 400 percent or more, presupposed, to quote the plan, "a supreme effort of organisation" (p. 87). But it is doubtful whether human nature and the general conditions of Uttar Pradesh justified such a vague optimism.

The future inevitably had some uncertainties: for example, the correlation between the budgeted expenditure and the practical results, and the inflationary pressures which became ever stronger after the start of the third plan. On the other hand, a few estimates were known to be too low (*taccavis,* community development), and there were some errors in calculation (we shall see some examples of this in irrigation). One also had to reckon on some waste in the use of rural

[4] Such a rapid multiplication of the blocks carried a strong risk of damaging their efficiency.

credits (cooperatives and *taccavis*), a general phenomenon the extent of which, as we noted at Khandoï, can be rather sizable. In brief, the plan started on April 1, 1961, with a number of imponderables.

The 1961–1964 Results

The results of the plan in districts as different as Bulandshahr and Benares are disappointing. They reflect the general weaknesses that are felt at state level. In November, 1964, delays became more and more evident: "Particularly slow is the progress of the plan in Assam, Bihar, Gujrat, Madhya Pradesh and Uttar Pradesh." Official sources give as the main explanation the insufficient increase in minor irrigation and fertilizers.[5] In Uttar Pradesh production steadily declined: 14.15 million tons (cereals, pulses) in 1960/61; 13.9 million tons in 1961/62 (target, 14.4 million); [6] less than 13.2 million in 1962/63 (target, 15.3 million). It decreased even more in the third year of the plan. On the other hand, it reached 15.2 million tons in 1964/65.[7]

Let us start with the programs carried out within the block framework. Minor private irrigation, which is scheduled to extend from 700,000 to 800,000 hectares (almost as much as the state works) has progressed as follows:

	1961/62		1962/63	
	Achieve-ment	Percent of Target Reached	Achieve-ment	Percent of Target Reached
Minor Private Irrigation				
New masonry wells	21,587	47.8	29,105	49.3
Repair of old wells	12,750	55.7	17,521	59.5
Boring	9,209	37.3	14,415	47.6
New Persian wheels	12,600	47.2	19,090	56.6
Pumping sets	1,620	65	2,356	66
New tube-wells	1,369	97.4	1,855	78.3
Small dams	7,979	50.8	19,130	83.9

SOURCE: *Annual Review of Development Activities* (Uttar Pradesh) for 1961–1962 and 1962–1963.

Progress is evident but, except in the case of pumped tube-wells, achievements are rather a long way short of the estimates. State credits were used up 98–100 percent.

[5] *Overseas Hindustan Times,* Nov. 26, 1964.

[6] Moderate increase for 1961–1962 because of the exceptionally good crops of 1960–1961.

[7] See Uttar Pradesh, *Third Five Year Plan (Progress Report), 1962–63,* p. 8; *Times of India,* Nov. 29, 1963; *Overseas Hindustan Times,* May 27, 1965.

	No. of Loans Granted	No. of Works Completed	No. of Loans Withdrawn
1956–1961 (2nd plan)	109,110	62,684	20,268
1961–1963	132,152	29,685	2,858

There was a 20 percent loss over 1956–1961 (which may yet be greater) and slowness of execution. Minor irrigation projects should take only a few months, but two years after the end of the second plan some 30,000 credits granted between 1956 and 1961 had not been utilized or had been spent for other purposes. One can well understand that "the situation continues to be alarming" and that the collectors themselves are asked "to keep an eye on this project." [8] (The main responsibility lies with the district planning officer.)

On the question of *shramdan* for the construction of small field channels, drainage, and reservoirs, the successes of the order of 80 percent, 100 percent, or sometimes even more claimed by the plan seem to me debatable. Both at Benares and Bulandshahr, the figures provided by the blocks and districts did not accord with my observations in the field. Yet I did not have the impression that these two districts were especially backward in this matter.

The following table shows the progress in measures aimed at soil improvement:

	1961/62		1962/63	
	Target	Achievement	Target	Achievement
Nitrogenous chemical fertilizers (tons)	276,212	157,191	387,786	209,271
Phosphatic chemical fertilizers (tons)	90,683	26,456	126,614	33,104
Cemented manure pits (units)	—	123,683	183,566	109,485
Area under green manure (million ha.)	1.43	0.64	1.86	0.80

The expansion of green manure represents 44 percent of the estimate; new techniques (Japanese for rice, Uttar Pradesh for wheat) attained 60–80 percent. The program of improved seed reached about 50 percent. We should not rely too much on these statistics, however, since they are so difficult to establish.

In the sector of cooperative credits, the number of new members exceeded the targets by several percent. The volume of credits was as follows:

[8] *Annual Review of Development Activities*, 1962–1963, pp. 2, 4.

	1961/62		1962/63	
	Target	Achievement	Target	Achievement
Type of Loan	(millions of rupees)		(millions of rupees)	
Short-term	360	360	420	366
Medium-term	20	10	40	12.8
Long-term	20	1.4	10	4.14

SOURCE: *Progress Report, 1962–63*, p. 60.

On the subject of the panchayats, the *Annual Report* notes (1962–63, p. 65) that the village councils met too seldom; they did not adhere to the rule for a monthly meeting. In 1962/63 the taxes levied by the village panchayats amounted to 10.3 million rupees, which represents 35 percent of the estimated levy and arrears. These arrears had reached 20.7 million.

These general results of the plan correspond to those obtained in the blocks and districts visited. The relation between the funds provided and the physical results was not satisfactory; in private irrigation and in use of chemical fertilizers the vast majority of the credits (cooperatives and *taccavis*) produced effective results of only some 40 to 60 percent of expectations.

This does not explain everything, however. Production still ought to have risen—admittedly at a rate below that estimated—instead of falling between 1961 and 1964. But at that stage the weather reversed itself; from very favorable in 1960–1961 it subsequently became rather adverse, particularly in 1963–1964.[9]

State Irrigation

Major and medium projects (canals, dams) irrigated 3.08 million hectares in 1960/61. The works undertaken over ten years are still far from reaching 100 percent of the target (*Third Plan,* p. 140) : for 1951–1961, the additional potential was set at 800,000 hectares, but only 592,000 hectares of that were utilized.

In order to avoid the fault so often criticized—as we have seen— Uttar Pradesh devoted more than half its estimated expenditure (total 517 million rupees) to completing works in progress. Of the new works, three-fourths were sited in the eastern districts. The program as a whole was to extend over a further 400,000 hectares. Since these works are spread over several years, it is too early to evaluate the results.

[9] Then very favorable in 1964–1965 and passable in 1965–1966.

Minor state irrigation, involving less delay, is easier to analyze. Indeed, the state tube-wells could be called the vital weapon for the future. Much use is already being made of the great Himalayan rivers; the smaller rivers descending the northern slopes of the Vindhyas have a variable and limited flow, dependent solely on the monsoons. The subsoil water in the plains is often abundant, however, and tube-wells are successful. In 1960/61, minor state irrigation covered 1.1 million hectares—an increase of 686,000 hectares in ten years. This figure refers to the area effectively irrigated, but the installations constructed could serve up to 1.33 million hectares. This gap is high for such rather simple works.

Although the plan does not give separate figures for the areas irrigated by state tube-wells, small reservoirs, and field channels, the tube-wells absorbed more than two-thirds of the expenditure (a total of 200 million rupees for the five years).[10] The entire program was to irrigate an extra 400,000 hectares by 1966. Some 1,500 new wells were to be constructed. As the plan proceeded, 149 wells were constructed in 1961–1962 (225.8 percent of the target) and 243 were constructed in 1962–1963 (96 percent of the target). The additional network of cemented field channels depending on these wells exceeded the target by 37 percent in the first year and reached 67.9 percent of the target in 1962/63.[11] These wells were in addition to the 6,181 that existed in July, 1961.[12]

It is one thing to construct but another to make them work. The facts that I have reported correspond with the general studies on the state tube-wells. In its fifth report the Public Account Committee of Uttar Pradesh says with brutal frankness: "While presenting the scheme of State tubewells, the irrigation department had estimated that every tubewell would give a net income of Rs. 2,000 a year on an average, that the economic position of the people in the areas of tubewells would improve. . . . In the opinion of the committee none of these aims has been fulfilled satisfactorily." Financial estimates often prove false; three projects for 1,615 wells needed eight years for completion, and the additional costs amounted to 39 million rupees. Technical weaknesses could have been avoided at the time of boring and pump installation. In addition, the numerous defective field chan-

10 Uttar Pradesh, *Third Five Year Plan,* pp. 144, 145.

11 *Annual Review,* 1961–1962, p. 2, and 1962–1963, p. 3.

12 P.R.A.I, *Study of Tube-well Irrigation Potential and Its Utilisation with Special Reference to Eastern U.P.,* p. 1. According to another report, *Progress Report, 1962–63,* p. 47, the number of wells completed in 1962/63 was 363.

nels [13] seriously slow down effective irrigation. Altogether, these weaknesses in carrying out the program mean a net loss of 20 million rupees a year to the treasury of Uttar Pradesh. In another report [14] the same committee complained of the slowness of the authorities in supplying exact figures on the number of wells constructed and their cost: "It is indeed surprising that the various departments are not yet able to tally the figures regarding the actual number of tubewells constructed. This indicates an extremely sorry state of affairs in the disbursement of money for development purposes."

The responsibilities of the peasants and the authorities should be laid down. Several reports, including the one previously quoted of the Planning Research and Action Institute in Lucknow, show that the demand for water is not the same everywhere. In the west, state tube-wells rarely lose money for lack of customers, since the peasants there have long been used to this type of irrigation, and they generally have the means to pay water fees. In the east, where the program started at least ten years later, the peasants, who are poorer and less enterprising, have been rather slow to change their habits. As we saw at Nahiyan for wheat growing, not only must they become used to paying for the abundant water of the state tube-wells instead of using the *mot*, but also they must understand that they should buy improved seeds. Since there are small tanks or ponds in the wet eastern area, the state tube-wells have not been so attractive, especially since they must be paid for. Also, many peasants are still prejudiced, through sheer ignorance, against such techniques as annual double cropping, regular and controlled irrigation, and chemical fertilizers.

Additional liabilities of the administration are mechanical or electrical breakdowns: in 1959–1960 the inquiry conducted by the P.R.A.I. by sample survey showed an average of 324 hours' stoppage per well in the east. The bakshishs that have to be paid to the operator and other officials are another discouraging element, especially if the peasants are very poor. Delays in the completion of field channels have their effect on the working of the wells. They are more frequent in the east, where the program is of more recent origin.

These different factors explain why in the east a state tube-well only works for 1,526 hours yearly against an estimate of 3,017, as compared with 3,730 hours against an estimate of 4,312 in the west. In the first case the rate of use is 50 percent, in the second 86.5 percent. But to

[13] The reasons were given in chap. 14. For statistics and quotations, see *Overseas Hindustan Times*, Sept. 24, 1964.
[14] As quoted in *The Hindu*, Apr. 28, 1964.

cover its operating expenses a well must work at least 2,300 hours a year.[15] A final factor to be reckoned with is the loss of water owing to noncemented channels—sometimes as much as 25 to 30 percent—or to leaks in badly cemented channels.

The command area of a state tube-well is the subject of justified criticism at all levels, from that of a village such as Khandoï to that of the state. At the time of the P.R.A.I. inquiry (1960–1961), the engineers of the irrigation department were keeping to 1,000 acres (400 ha.) in the east and 900 acres (360 ha.) in the west (p. 12), despite the desire of the peasants for smaller areas, which we saw to be well-founded. Shortly after this inquiry the department lowered the limits to 600–700 acres (240–280 ha.) for the western districts and 750–900 acres (300–360 ha.) for the rest of the state,[16] though for the west, at least, this was still too large.

Would it not be more suitable to start by fixing realistic and effective standards of agricultural expansion, instead of establishing a loose network of state tube-wells providing inadequate irrigation? As another study emphasizes, "this state of affairs not only increases the cost of irrigation, but also affects the interests of the cultivators adversely, since the government policy is neither to give any loan nor even to allow other facilities like electric power for private tubewells in the command area of a State tubewell." [17]

The same report (pp. 145, 166) mentions numerous field channels in Uttar Pradesh which do not have the statutory length (1,600–3,200 meters cemented, 3,200 meters merely dug, work which is the responsibility of the irrigation department). This echoes the complaints about the bad state of a number of channels (p. 146).

Coordination and Subordination in the Administration

What has "the supreme effort of organisation" demanded by the plan produced? One of the criticisms frequently aired related to the lack of coordination or even understanding between the departments responsible for development. Several official chains of command have been established: the department of community development, to which are subordinated the district planning officers (D.P.O.), to whom the B.D.O.'s (block development officers) and gram sewaks are responsible;

---

[15] P.R.A.I., *Study of Tube-well Irrigation Potential*, pp. 7, 50.

[16] A conversation was reported to me (August, 1964) between an important farmer and a high official of the irrigation department who refused any further reduction.

[17] Programme Evaluation Organisation, *Study of the Problems of Minor Irrigation*, p. 166. It will be recalled that this last ruling has been relaxed since then (1964).

the technical departments, for agriculture, sugar cane, veterinary service, and so on, represented by technicians in the districts and blocks; and finally the cooperative movement, which is subject to the department of cooperation, and the organization of cooperative banks and rural credit societies.

Under these conditions the D.P.O.'s and B.D.O.'s do not have full control over their technical services. There is a dual responsibility, which hinders the smooth working of the services, the strict carrying out of orders, and the application of firm disciplinary measures, the need for which we have seen. The problem is particularly serious with regard to the cooperatives. The *U.P. State Government Audit Report* laid before the Legislative Assembly of Lucknow on August 17, 1964, recounts numerous weaknesses. The Uttar Pradesh Co-operation Federation has become heavily in debt in circumstances which give rise to some "misgivings." Besides, twenty-nine societies responsible for the sale of agricultural products have left unused more than 1.07 million rupees since June 30, 1962, owing to an insufficient volume of activity. Lack of use has also kept twenty cooperative silos established between 1958 and 1962 from even covering their operating expenses.[18]

At the start of 1964 an important rearrangement of the administration took place. The post of development commissioner was abolished. The government created a post of agricultural production commissioner responsible for the coordination of the main services. Under his supervision are the secretaries of the departments of agriculture, minor private irrigation, sugar cane and veterinary services, cooperatives, and community development. He in turn is responsible to the agriculture subcommittee established within the cabinet and bringing together the interested ministers. It is in many ways a good arrangement, but the state department of irrigation, which is one of the principal agents of expansion, still remains outside the scheme, and dissension within the cabinet, as we shall see, often hampers effective coordination.

The idea of one man in sole charge of the entire development of a district, which is gradually gaining adherents in New Delhi, has not yet been accepted, nor is it easy to implement. It would encounter some serious technical difficulties. The system of irrigation canals, for example, which covers several districts, cannot logically be administered by each separate district independently. On the other hand, why should not district divisions of state tube-wells be established? The electricity services, hitherto attached to the irrigation department, could also be integrated under this new arrangement. The reorganization of these two services within the district could speed progress. One strong man,

18 *Times of India,* Aug. 18, 1964.

endowed with wide powers, would be needed. The collector seems destined for this task.

Corruption

Corruption is not, of course, a new phenomenon in India—there is much evidence of the abuses of minor officials and police during the British period. One I.C.S. member of many years' standing told me how, on his tours of the villages, he always made a point of settling himself in full view of everyone so that all the peasants could speak to him directly without having to pay a minor official for the privilege. In *Behind Mud Walls, 1930–1960,* William and Charlotte Wiser recount all the malpractices committed in the villages of Uttar Pradesh before Independence. "There is no one to advise us honestly or to help us escape from fraudulent men," the peasants said." [19] In recent years, the expansion and the complication of all the apparatus of development—the blocks, cooperatives, and irrigation services in which men abound who are inevitably badly paid and possess wide powers for augmenting their personal budget—have multiplied the opportunities for corruption, with the help of politicians whose influence steadily increases.

There is no need for us to shout about scandals. Nineteenth-century Europe did not develop in an atmosphere of irreproachable integrity. Nor is corruption always an obstacle to development: the Punjab experienced a remarkable expansion under Pratap Singh Kairon, a chief minister who had to resign following serious abuses. What is involved here is corruption that is coupled with incompetence, or, by being a steady and slow drain, is a real deterrent to economic progress. The bland official who receives his rake-off during the consolidation of holdings is not a danger to the economy. But the contractor who makes irrigation channels with poor cement, the state tube-well operator who refuses to dispense water unless he receives bakshish, the cooperative supervisor who, because of his corrupt practices, turns the peasants against the rural credit system, the official who drags out the necessary formalities when dealing with a request for electricity connection—these men hold back development and deserve to be hounded relentlessly.

The Administration and the Politicians

For many years the political situation has not allowed the efficiency and the integrity which are entrenched in the Indian Administrative

[19] *Behind Mud Walls, 1930–1960* (Berkeley and Los Angeles, 1963) , p. 124.

Service to be utilized to the full.[20] Although not all the politicians of Uttar Pradesh are of the stock described below, one must clearly see under what sort of conditions planning and administration are working, and why I.A.S. cadres find it so difficult to fight against abuses, waste, and corruption.

Suppose that a collector wants to take the initiative for a general cleaning-up of his district. Some member of the cooperative committee or of the zila parishad will perhaps find it to his advantage to suppress the exposure of scandals in his branch; some politician will want to draw a veil over the malpractices at a state tube-well which he has used his influence to have sited in his own constituency; others, because of some caste ramifications, will want to obstruct any action to avoid unwelcome disclosures. In the end the politicians will have the troublesome collector transferred.

To act effectively the administration needs to feel itself supported by the cabinet at Lucknow, but the latter has been so racked with dissensions since the departure of Pandit Pant in 1954 that it is at the mercy of political intrigues. The administration is usually subordinated to the short-term interests of the local leaders.

Let us follow the course of the government during recent years. In August, 1963, the Congress launched the Kamaraj plan,[21] the aim of which was to revitalize the party, which was experiencing a growing erosion of its power. Several ministers of the central government and states were asked to resign in order to take up militant activities in the ranks of the party. Although they would not admit to it, the Indian government would also benefit by getting rid of politicians who could not count on the votes of their own party. The Chief Minister of Uttar Pradesh, C. B. Gupta, was one of these. For a long time his clan had been engaged in a fierce struggle, within the local Congress party, with the followers of Mr. Tripathi, splitting both the cabinet and the party machine by this clash of interests and caste (Gupta is Vaisya, Tripathi Brahmin).[22]

When Gupta had been removed, a replacement had to be found; this took over a month and a half. Eventually, after much difficulty, Mrs. Sucheta Kripalani formed a cabinet, one-third being Tripathi's supporters, including himself, and two-thirds his opponents or noncommitted. As the *Times of India* remarked in an editorial of October

[20] Cases of corruption in the corps may perhaps exist but I have not heard any complaints about its conduct or its good intentions.

[21] From the name of the then chief minister of Madras who on this occasion became president of the All India Congress party.

[22] Caste was by no means the only factor in the dispute: certain Brahmins supported Gupta, and some Vaisyas were found in the Tripathi clan.

14, 1963, "During this entire period there has been no administration worth the name, at the ministerial level, in the country's most populous State."

This governmental formula showed itself so inefficient that two months later Tripathi, who held the important portfolio of finance, offered his resignation. He withdrew it shortly afterward, while another source of trouble arose, the postponement of the elections to the Uttar Pradesh Congress committee which had been scheduled for January, 1964.

On May 11, 1964, Tripathi again offered his resignation in order to canvass for the post of party president in the state. C. B. Gupta, the other candidate, obtained the majority by a few votes at the elections on May 12. The defeated side disputed the good faith of the procedure and demanded a recount. In the end, after a fruitless attempt at mediation by the central committee in Delhi, President Kamaraj agreed to the Tripathi group's request. The votes of the May 12 election were counted again on August 9 and gave a three-vote majority to Tripathi. How Tripathi had looked after his finance portfolio in the meantime—for Mrs. Kripalani had not accepted his resignation—I should be very interested to know.[23] When she had to accept it, she found herself again paralyzed by the rival factions in choosing a successor and finally had to take on the responsibility of finance herself, despite her already heavy responsibilities. In February, 1965, Mrs. Kripalani found another solution: while still supervising the finances herself, she passed over the administration of them to the minister of education, who nevertheless did not become the minister of finance in title and in fact.[24]

Is it possible, in the midst of intrigues of this sort, to look after public affairs? The *Statesman* commented (Jan. 28, 1964) : "Obviously, political interests weigh more with State leaders than the development of the State. Probably, as party men they cannot think otherwise even if it involves decline in agricultural production from year to year." This diffusion of power also prevented a real integration of the departments concerned with agricultural development. Integration was only found at the level of civil servants because, as the *Statesman* adds: "Politically it is unthinkable that any chief minister could hand over these two departments (agriculture and community development) to a single minister, making him more powerful than any other colleague. . . . Political exigencies, therefore, dictated that fragmentation of de-

[23] See *The Hindu,* May 16 and 22, 1964; *Hindustan Times,* July 24, 1964; *Times of India,* Aug. 10, 1964.
[24] *The Statesman, Overseas Weekly,* Feb. 6, 1965.

partments should continue." Let me add that the minister of agriculture, the author of this proposal, was apparently not very closely acquainted with his colleague of the community development ministry.

The spectacle of the Legislative Assembly is hardly more edifying: neither Congress nor the opposition parties appear to be much aware of the essential needs of the economy. One minister was accused in a debate of sheltering bandits and two others were attacked for nepotism.[25] At the end of 1962, taking advantage of the state of emergency proclaimed after the fighting between India and China, the Assembly voted an additional 25 percent on land tax. This was a wise measure, completely justified. A year later the same parliamentarians rescinded the decision. The government even received the congratulations of the Praja Socialist party (P.S.P.).[26] Clearly, the move was designed simply to retain popularity with the people.

Such an unhealthy condition of the executive and legislative could not fail to affect the administration. The creation of the post of agricultural commissioner put an end to the intrigues of certain high officials, but the press drew attention to other cases, in which civil servants brought influence to bear from their connections in the cabinet or Assembly. It was found necessary to send out a circular reminding officials that the rules of the service forbade them to make use of political connections in the exercise of their duties.[27]

Instances of this sort are, as I have pointed out, unusual in the corps of the I.A.S., which is usually honest and at odds with the politicians. We may find cynicism and disappointment in the high official in his fifties, enthusiasm in the young collector who has not yet met with too much opposition, and the initiative taken by a young man in his first post shaken by political intrigues.

These examples illustrate a great waste of talent. With a stronger and more united cabinet, the top administration would be sure to produce better results, feeling itself stimulated and supported.

1964–1967

After taking over in the autumn of 1963, Mrs. Kripalani did her best to improve the political situation. She does not belong at all to the same category of politicians as Gupta and Tripathi, and she tried to remove the defects mentioned above, either by backing honest civil

[25] See *Hindustan Times*, Feb. 25, 1964; *Northern India Patrika*, Feb. 26, 1964.
[26] *Times of India*, Dec. 11, 1963.
[27] *Hindustan Times*, Jan. 28, 1964.

servants or by supporting members of the Legislative Assembly who were sincerely dedicated to the public interest. In certain cases the latter could have more influence against the sheer opportunists and troublemakers, but the feuds of the Gupta and Tripathi groups remained as tense as before, Tripathi being the U.P. Congress party president, while Gupta had the majority support in the Assembly. In addition to these discords, there were grave incidents in several universities, some of which deteriorated into serious riots in the autumn of 1966. It is obvious that troubles of this sort are likely to cost the politicians dear. As they pursue their intrigues, in the countryside the saying goes: *"Koi nahin sunta* [Nobody pays any attention]." The losses of the Congress party at the general elections of 1967 were a clear outgrowth of the situation. Despite losing the majority in the Legislative Assembly, the Congress party managed to set up the state cabinet, but a coalition of the opposition parties brought it down after a few weeks. The leader of the new coalition cabinet is a shrewd and able politician, Charan Singh (ex-Congress member of the state cabinet for several years), but will he be able to keep together such a mixed team of ministers, ranging from Communists to members of the extreme right Jan Sangh and including various shades in between?

Inevitably, the political malaise affects the administrative shortcomings already described. The latest *Audit Report* available is no less severe than the previous ones quoted above: "Defalcation of Government funds has registered a disturbing rise. . . . In finalising these cases, government took as much as 10 years for 121 cases involving 660,000 rupees." Auditors have brought to light other irregularities in the working of the cooperatives in which the directors nominated by the government are frequently absent from meetings of the board. Other defects are found in flood-protection works. The Chitauni Bund was originally estimated to cost 227,000 rupees; now it seems likely to reach 19 million, if full protection is really achieved.[28]

The economic development situation is less gloomy. Growing attention is being given to minor private irrigation and to state tube-wells. Some of the defects mentioned above have been reduced, and the rate of construction of tube-wells has been speeded up. During the third plan 1,600 state tube-wells and 21,545 private tube-wells have been completed, which is no mean achievement. Particularly striking is the progress of the private tube-wells. The intensive cultivation program of wheat and paddy is gaining momentum in 1966–1967; fifty additional blocks should be affected. Recent experiments with the

[28] See *Hindu Weekly Review*, Nov. 7, 1966.

seeds of Mexican varieties of wheat have been encouraging, with yields obtained of up to 6,000 kg/ha. In 1966–1967, the government envisages distributing 10,000 tons of improved varieties of wheat.[29] During a brief visit to Bulandshahr district and Khandoï in August 1967, I could see how Mexican wheat was becoming popular due to its remarkable yields. Yet there was a rather serious bottleneck on the supply side of chemical fertilizers.

In 1964–1965 the efforts made and exceptionally generous natural conditions allowed food-grain production to reach 15.2 million tons.[30] In 1965–1966 Uttar Pradesh was on the whole spared the extremely severe drought which affected the Deccan and several coastal regions in Andhra and Madras so drastically. Though figures are still unobtainable, it is likely that production was able to maintain the 1964/65 level—still well below the target of 18.3 million tons, however.

At the same time, this improvement has been upset at the start of the Fourth Plan by the severe drought of 1966–1967, which caused such ravages in Uttar Pradesh and Bihar. In Uttar Pradesh forty-one of the fifty-four districts were affected—75,000 villages and 60 million people. Though the districts of Himalaya and the west were spared, the southeastern part of the province is in grave danger: in September, 1966, rainfall there was only 51 mm.—far below the seasonal normal of 179 mm.[31] In these circumstances, a considerable drop in production must be expected in 1966–1967. This will increase the deficit in food grains, which in the last few years was from 700,000 to 900,000 rupees.[32]

[29] *Overseas Hindustan Times,* Sept. 22, 1966.
[30] *Ibid.,* May 27, 1965.
[31] *Ibid.,* Oct. 20, 1966.
[32] *Ibid.,* Oct. 22, 1966.

PART III

Madras and Maharashtra

18

THE STATE OF MADRAS

Now, after having had a look at the vast and populous state of Uttar Pradesh, beset with problems in both politics and development, we turn to an environment that is notably different geographically, economically, and socially. Madras has rightly been called one of the model states of India.

The Political Situation and Administration

The Congress party was not only the majority party here until 1967, but—and this is the essential point—it was homogeneous. One did not find in the Madras press or in private conversation the constant disputes between the different factions which are characteristic of Lucknow. This stability had its effect in the districts, where the government could ensure that administration proceeded smoothly and the organization that it set up was fully utilized.

The only important element of dissent to the general harmony was the Dravida Munnetra Kazhagam (D.M.K.), a Dravidian autonomist movement which is opposed, sometimes violently, to the politics of northern India and to the Brahmins and a few other high castes.[1] The Brahmins are numerous in Madras and have retained great influence there, the caste divisions being particularly marked. In the 1962 Legislative Assembly the D.M.K. had 50 seats as against the 138 seats of the Congress party and those of several minor parties including the Communists (two seats).[2] It was thus a power to be reckoned with. Occasionally it provoked demonstrations and incidents, but it did not actually interfere with the planning process and administration.

Population and Resources

Before Independence, Madras comprised a much greater area than today, including part of what is now Andhra Pradesh (separated in

[1] Rightly or wrongly, the Brahmins are considered to have come originally from the north, hence the hostility of the Dravidians, who inhabited the southern peninsula long before the arrival of the Aryans.

[2] *Madras State Administration Report, 1962*, p. 4.

1953) and several districts that were yielded to Mysore and Kerala in 1956. As a result of these cessions it now consists of a homogeneous group of Tamils,[3] an able and enterprising people with a rich and noble past who, in the nineteenth and early twentieth centuries provided numerous emigrants to Asia, Africa, and as far as the West Indies and British Guiana. They mostly worked on plantations and in commerce.

In 1961 the state had 33.7 million inhabitants, living in an area of 128,847 square kilometers. The rate of population increase is the lowest in India apart from Kashmir. During the decade 1951–1961, the increase was only 11.8 percent,[4] a continuance of the trend seen in previous censuses: 1921–1931, an increase of 8.25 percent; 1931–1941, an increase of 11.91 percent; 1941–1951, an increase of 14.66 percent. (The higher figure for 1941–1951 was due largely to the return of Tamils who left Southeast Asia following the Japanese invasion.) Overseas emigration has completely ceased. On the other hand, many Tamils have taken up residence in other Indian states (2–3 percent of the population between 1951 and 1961), so that the actual rate of increase may be between 1.38 percent and 1.48 percent per year. Even with this adjustment, the rate remains well below the national average of 2.15 percent.[5] This phenomenon, as strange as it is exceptional, deserves serious investigation. The statistics that we have established in the village of Kila Ulur only confirm the fact without explaining it in a satisfactory way.

Despite the low rate of population increase, there is still an imbalance between population and resources. The average density is 260 persons per square kilometer; at the same time, though agriculture has reached a fairly high level of production, the scope for development is limited.

The mineral resources are somewhat less indifferent than in Uttar Pradesh: the deposits of lignite and iron ore [6] might justify the establishment of a steel works, but they are much inferior to the iron and coal of the northeast corner of the Deccan. The consumer goods industries and the tertiary sector are much more advanced. Madras has

[3] Tamil is one of the principal Dravidian languages. These changes formed part of the rearrangement of states on a linguistic basis. The only acquisition to Madras was of a small territory at the tip of the peninsula, a Tamil area hitherto belonging to Kerala.

[4] *Census of India, 1961, Paper No. 1,* pp. 32, 365.

[5] Information supplied by P. K. Nambiar, Superintendent of the Census, Madras, in April, 1964.

[6] Ore from the Salem district of inferior quality, containing 35 percent iron. About double this grade is found in northeast Deccan.

been a well-developed area for more than two centuries, and it follows
Calcutta and Bombay as one of the great commercial centers of India.
It also possesses a number of manufacturing industries, which have
expanded since 1947. As a result one finds active and well-educated
upper and middle classes, particularly among the higher castes well
known for their culture and lively minds. They provide India with a
number of efficient high officials: "The State has had a 'leader' position
in the training and supply of technical and skilled personnel even to
the rest of India." [7] The urban population is 26.7 percent of the total
population, and the rate of literacy is 31.4 percent.[8] In 1956 the
primary sector absorbed 6 million people, the secondary sector 1.11
million, and the tertiary sector 2.24 million, a division not so unequal
as in Uttar Pradesh or in India as a whole, and a reflection of an
economy already fairly diversified.[9]

The Five-Year Plans

The total outlay (including the first operating expenses of the new
projects) has risen with each new five-year plan.

Public Sector (millions of rupees)

	1st Plan *	2nd Plan *	3rd Plan †
Agriculture		168	369.8
Community development and cooperatives	96.7	152.3	251.8
Irrigation	201.5	170	274.2
Power	302.8	787.8	1,001.9
Industries (large and small)	15.3	138.5	235.1
Roads and tourism	27	53.8	112.5
Education	38.2	137.3	321.6
Health	64.2	143.5	215
House construction	12.9	48	70
Social services	45.2	52.5	51.1
Miscellaneous	—	10.1	5.9
Total	803.8	1,861.8	2,908.9

SOURCE: Madras State, *Third Five Year Plan*, p. 11.
* Actual expenditures.
† Estimated expenditures.

Loans and grants from New Delhi cover 1,900 million of the third
plan, the remainder being provided from local resources (p. 12).

[7] *Techno-economic Survey of Madras*, (1960), p. vi.
[8] *Census of India, 1961*, p. 341.
[9] *Techno-economic Survey of Madras*, p. 5.

These figures relate only to the state plan; they do not include projects financed and directed by the central government—which are mainly concerned with industry and include a steel works at Salem, lignite mines at Neyveli, and a power station at Neyveli.[10]

The general orientation of planning is less uniform than in Uttar Pradesh. For one thing, agriculture plays a less dominant role in the economy of Madras, and education is more strongly encouraged. The industrial investment financed by the state is directed essentially to the small rural and cottage industries in the form of loans and grants.

The investments of private industrial firms are not indicated. The plan merely points out the great increase in the authorized capital of companies, which has risen from 452.6 million rupees between 1951 and 1956 to 1,840 million between 1956 and 1961 (p. 84). The number of newly registered companies has risen from 586 during the first plan to 796 during the second plan.

Agriculture

At the start of the first plan, Madras State had a deficit in food grains (cereal and pulses); ten years later it had a surplus of 300,000 tons. Production had risen from 3.8 million tons in 1951 to 4.4 million in 1956 and 5.3 million in 1961. The over-all increase was of the order of 30 percent. In the same period, irrigation was extended to 136,800 hectares with improvements to 108,000 hectares that had formerly been inadequately irrigated. Deliveries of improved seed were sufficient to sow most of the rice fields and 45 percent of the millet in 1961. Supplies of fertilizers amounted to 100,000 tons of ammonium sulphate—about a quarter of the total requirement. As for the credit of the cooperatives, this rose from 60 million rupees in 1955/56 to 257 million at the end of the second plan. The great majority of villages now have cooperative societies.[11]

Of the 5.4 million hectares devoted to food grains in 1960/61, rice accounted for nearly half (2.5 million); the remainder consisted of various types of millet and pulses. There is practically no wheat. Expansion has been primarily in the areas put to rice: in 1950/51 there were 1.7 million hectares with an average of 1,150 kg/ha (clean or husked rice); in 1960/61 the area had increased to 2.48 million hectares, with an average of 1,430 kg/ha. Areas and yields of other crops rose as much as 10 to 15 percent: *cholam* (a species of millet), 790 kg/ha, and *cumbu* (another millet), 540 kg/ha in 1960/61.

[10] See chap. 23 of *Third Five Year Plan* (Madras, 1961).

[11] For the statistics of these two paragraphs, see *ibid.*, pp. 2, 4–6.

The state has two important cash crops—groundnuts and cotton—which occupy 25 percent of the cultivated area, that is, 1.8 million hectares, a higher proportion than in Uttar Pradesh or India as a whole. In 1960/61 there were 860,000 hectares in groundnuts and 390,000 hectares in cotton. The former represents an increase of about 20 percent (both in area cultivated and average yield) in ten years, the latter a little more than this.[12]

Taking account of variations due to nature (a million tons plus or minus), the *Third Plan* (pp. 20–21) projected an increase of 31.2 percent in food grains (i.e., 1.65 million tons), broken down as follows into specific areas:

Major and medium irrigation	94,000 tons
Minor irrigation	197,000
Chemical fertilizers	618,000
Farm manure	371,000
Improved seed	136,000
Soil protection	66,000
Japanese method of rice cultivation	172,000

Much was to depend on fertilizers—40 percent of the expected increase. Irrigation, on the other hand, accounted for less than 20 percent, a low figure which needs explanation.

Soils and Water Utilization

In Madras, soil formation and water resources are much more varied than in the plains of Uttar Pradesh. The flat coastal zone is alluvial soil of recent origin, which in these fertile regions is irrigated by the rivers flowing down from the plateau—the Cauvery and, further south, the waters of Lake Periyar, which have been diverted to the east by means of a canal dug by the British. Of the 2.4 million hectares of land that are irrigated, 840,000 are watered by state canals. The Tamil peasants also make great use of tanks, which are natural basins in low-lying areas reinforced by earthen dikes or bunds. The rains collect in the tanks and can be channeled out. In certain regions tanks occupy up to one-third of the total surface,[13] and altogether they irrigate some 920,000 hectares. Private wells, some temporary and some permanent, irrigate 560,000 hectares.[14]

[12] For all these figures, see Madras State, *Basic Agricultural Statistics* (1963). These represent gross areas, including double crops.

[13] P. Gourou, *L'Asie* (Paris, 1953), p. 427.

[14] For irrigation figures, see *Basic Agricultural Statistics,* p. 34.

The plateau areas, where the soil is often poor and eroded, are not very well suited to agriculture. The subsoil water is frequently too deep for use except by pumping, and the rainfall is less plentiful than in the coastal areas. In the latter, it varies between 1,000 and 1,400 mm., but in the interior and certain districts in the extreme south, it is less than 1,000 mm. Owing to these geographical and climatic differences, there have long been wide discrepancies between the development of the district of Tanjore and that of several regions in the interior.

Irrigated land represents 40 percent of the total area under cultivation; 20 percent produces more than one crop annually—both percentages being better than the average for India in general and for Uttar Pradesh.[15] The additional potential that remains to be irrigated is limited both by the relatively high level already reached and by the scantiness of water resources. Since tanks are already numerous and the canals are reaching—or have reached—the limit of their capacity, Madras must use its ingenuity to find new ways of getting water. One possibility is to catch the water from other rivers in the neighboring states of Mysore and Andhra, which have larger reserves. Negotiations have already been concluded with Kerala for the Parambikulam–Aliyar project, which will irrigate 96,000 hectares in the district of Coimbatore; a hydroelectric station of 180,000 kilowatts will also be constructed.[16] It is doubtful, however, whether other projects of this sort can be worked out, partly because of the enormous costs, partly also because there is no strong spirit of cooperation among the states involved. Several medium-sized projects which are underway indicate that the maximum investment has been reached: the cost per hectare irrigated is more than double the average attained by other states, that is, 1,160 rupees per acre (0.4 hectare), compared with 500 in general.[17]

Much can be done, however, in the way of improving the existing systems. As we shall see in the district of Tanjore, large quantities of water are wasted because of inadequate maintenance of the canals. And many of the tanks, which serve 40 percent of the area under cultivation, are partly silted up and therefore reduced in capacity.

In tube-wells, which are so important in Uttar Pradesh, Madras made a late start, the first wells not having been sunk until after Independence. They are also less efficient here, since the subsoil water on

[15] *Techno-economic Survey of Madras*, pp. 72, 75.
[16] Madras State, *Third Five Year Plan, Mid-Term Review* (1964), p. 44.
[17] These figures are slightly out of date. They would be higher today. See *Techno-economic Survey*, p. 84.

the plateau is often very deep, and more scarce than in the Ganges basin. The output of a tube-well is often only a third or a quarter as much as that of Uttar Pradesh wells.[18] In the canal zones, on the other hand, there is more water, at a shallower level, and the potential for pumping sets or tube-wells is substantial.

Progress of the Third Plan

With legitimate pride, the Madras planners write in their *Mid-Term Review* of 1964 that "Madras is among the few States in India where there has been no default in the fulfillment of the plan" (p. 6). An impartial source, relying on the statistics of the Planning Commission at New Delhi, is no less positive: "Only three States, Punjab, Madras and Andhra will reach three-fourths of the targets of the plan set for the first four years, or even a little more." [19] Using the yardstick method as in Uttar Pradesh, the administration estimates that between 1961 and 1964 the additional potential developed represents a gain of 866,000 tons, or 50 percent of the final target.

What are the first results in irrigation? If it is too early to speak of major and medium projects spread over several years, progress in minor irrigation, the main key to expansion, can be more easily determined. Projects estimated at 80 million rupees are underway for the rebuilding of the tanks belonging to the state and the small canals deriving from one source in the hills. At the end of the third year, 65 million had been spent and a supplementary budget of 30 million drawn up to extend the program. Other programs benefit private irrigation works. The maximum credit for digging a well has risen from 1,000 to 2,000 rupees, of which a quarter need not be refunded. In addition, 37,500 new wells are proposed, at an estimated total cost of 37.5 million rupees (10 million from the special fund created during the second plan and the remainder from the block development funds). On these, the *Mid-Term Review* notes merely that the 10 million credit has already been exceeded and that additional funds are required to continue the program. The plan also envisages 2,000 wells with a pipe of baked clay laid in position at the bottom of the well. By 1963, 726 had been completed.

With the extension of the electric power system to the rural areas, the installation of pumps has spread rapidly, so that about 23,000 pumping sets are being installed each year. These are simple but efficient arrangements—small motors set up near an open well which

[18] *Ibid.* p. 85.
[19] *Overseas Hindustan Times,* Nov. 26, 1964.

can irrigate several hectares. By the end of the third plan, the majority of villages were to have electricity and a total of 200,000 pumps were to have been installed. Finally, after the 41 tube-wells of the second plan, 150 are envisaged in the period 1961–1966. These are of the same type as those used by the peasants in Bulandshahr, capable of irrigating about forty hectares.[20]

Madras also has a number of state seed farms, which produce strains of improved seed. These are being developed more or less according to schedule: of the 210 rice farms to be established in the five-year period, 200 were opened between 1961 and 1963. The *Mid-Term Review* notes, however, without giving any details, that improved seed for millet is behind schedule.

Progress in fertilizers has been slower: even during the second plan, which had a fairly low target, annual deliveries to the peasants were far from met: 100,000 tons of ammonium sulphate as compared with a target of 175,000 tons. The target of the third plan is much more ambitious: 580,000 tons of ammonium sulphate (400,000 tons for food grains, the rest for cash crops) . Phosphate and potash fertilzers are to be increased, respectively, from 60,000 tons to 320,000 tons and from 12,000 tons to 90,000 tons.[21] The total amount of ammonium sulphate used has been less than the estimates: 1960/61, 114,000 tons; 1961/62, 166,000 tons; 1962/63, 242,000 tons; 1963/64, 300,000 tons (estimate) . The shortfall is, however, less than in Uttar Pradesh.

Green manure shows a satisfactory increase: 74,0000 additional hectares by the third year, against 120,000 foreseen by the end of the plan.

The protection of plants against pests receives more attention and—most important—greater allotments than in Uttar Pradesh. Insecticides are sold at a quarter of their cost for cereal crops and at half-cost for cash crops; sprayers are distributed free. As a result, the area of rice fields treated rose from 300,000 hectares in 1961 to 850,000 hectares in 1964, which is three-quarters of the target for 1965/66. The package program has been launched in the district of Tanjore, and it has carried all the more weight by reason of the relatively small size of the state (twelve districts and the municipality of Madras) . In Uttar Pradesh, even if the package program of Aligarh had been fulfilled 100 percent (and this was not the case) , it would have had no significant effect on the fifty-three other districts which make up that vast state.

The progress of the cooperatives continues: the number of affiliated members of credit cooperative societies is expected to rise from 2.83

[20] These wells are of smaller diameter and power than the state tube-wells of Uttar Pradesh. See *Mid-Term Review*, p. 55.

[21] Madras, *Third Five Year Plan*, p. 26.

million to 3.87 million (85 percent of the rural families). The credit provided should almost double in reaching 500 million rupees. Actual achievement in the first three years has been in accord with the plan.[22] The state of Madras helps to improve credit conditions by contributing a share of the capital of the State Co-operative Bank. It also supports the cooperative marketing of agricultural products.

In sum, although the *Mid-Term Review* is less detailed than the reports of Uttar Pradesh, one cannot doubt the satisfactory progress of the plan, which in every respect shows only limited gaps between targets and achievements. As we have seen, political stability within the ruling party and good administration are partly responsible for these excellent results; but there are other contributing factors.

First of all, by reason of its size, the state of Madras can be administered much more easily than can the unwieldy Uttar Pradesh. The administrative services are less numerous, which simplifies part of the problems of coordination: the secretary of the Ministry of Finance also acts as development commissioner. Also, the economy is more diversified than in Uttar Pradesh. The cities of Madras and, more recently, Coimbatore are industrial and commercial centers which ensure the state of a steady and sizable revenue and represent "poles of development." Finally, mention should again be made of the character of the Tamils and the active elites which they provide.

The Panchayati Raj

The tendency to set up or re-form local authorities started in Madras State, as it did elsewhere, well before Independence, and in 1950 an important step was taken: the Madras Village Panchayats Act, which increased the powers of the village councils and gave a spur to their establishment where they did not exist. Eight years later the Madras Panchayats Act of 1958 introduced the reforms recommended by the *Mehta Report* (see chap. 4). The Act was put into effect in 1960, and a period of two years was set for its adoption throughout almost the entire state.

As in Uttar Pradesh, the system has three levels: village, block, and district, with resources concentrated at the middle level. The arrangement and coordination of the various powers and responsibilities is better than in the past: the B.D.O. (now called the Panchayat Union Commissioner) is the executive agent of the Panchayat Union Council which brings together the village respresentatives—one delegate from

[22] *Mid-Term Review,* chap. 7.

each panchayat. A program has been drawn up for the allocation of funds put aside for community development as well as those originating from the Ministry of Agriculture, the Ministry of Education, and so on. "The resources available from the community development allotment have thus been effectively integrated with the general developmental plan of the State. The staff in the field will no longer be confused about the sources of various allocations whether from community development funds or not." [23] The situation has been well and truly clarified and can be grasped at a glance from a few simple documents.

The projected five-year expenditure is 1,420 million rupees, or an average of about 3.8 million rupees for each block. This schematic budget, as it is called, does not include certain initial costs and some expenses connected with loans programs.[24] The funds are to come from several sources: government grants, taxes levied by the villages or the Panchayat Union Councils, and additional villager taxes giving the right to matching grants ranging from 75 percent to 150 percent.[25]

The first results have been encouraging; the block councils have voted an additional tax (local cess surcharge) corresponding (on average) to 30 percent of the land revenue.[26] However, to take a decision is one thing; to put it into effect is more difficult. We shall see that in the district of Tanjore there were quite substantial shortfalls and large tax arrears. Nevertheless, some progress has been made, as is shown by the matching state grants. These have risen from 3.7 million rupees in 1961/62 to 9 million in 1963/64.[27]

The schematic budget for the five years shows the following main divisions:

Funds used by village panchayats	370 million rupees
Funds used by Panchayat Union Councils (round figure)	1,000
Funds used by town panchayats	50
Total	1,420 million rupees

The detailed breakdown of the allocations for the villages is not given, apart from 150 million (village work grant). For the Union councils, the breakdown is as follows:

[23] Madras, *Third Five Year Plan*, p. 61.
[24] Madras Rural Development and Local Administration Department, *Demand No. XXVI*, 1961–1962, p. 12. This is one of a number of special reports.
[25] *Demand No. XXIII*, 1964–1965, p. 2.
[26] *Ibid.*, p. 2.
[27] *Ibid.*, p. 3.

General funds	231.5 million rupees
Education	655
Agricultural production	115
	1,001.5 million rupees

The planning can be fairly flexible, and if necessary the general funds can subsidize expenditures in sections where money is insufficient. The principal beneficiary has been education: in the Union's allocation, education has received about 100 million additional rupees, to which was added an appreciable amount of the 370 million of the funds used by the village panchayats. (The village work grant is chiefly used for drinking-water wells, roads, and schoolhouses.) Education thus absorbs more than 50 percent of total expenditure, against less than 10 percent for agricultural production.[28] One must of course not forget that, through other channels (irrigation, credit societies, etc.) the state is investing large additional amounts into agriculture, but it must be made clear that the Panchayati Raj is not strikingly production-oriented.

Madras has always been in advance of most of the other states in the field of education: the percentage of children from six to eleven attending primary school increased from 57.4 percent in 1950–1951 to 77 percent ten years later. The present plan envisages a further increase to at least 90 percent.[29] Three-quarters of the money allocated to education is devoted to this aim.

The greater part of the education budget goes for teachers' salaries. Many new teachers are hired each year, at an average annual salary of 1,100 rupees; each teacher has from forty to forty-five pupils. Free midday lunches for all pupils cost another 60 million. The expenditure on schoolhouses cannot be given exactly, since it includes a voluntary contribution by the villagers; we shall see an example of this in Kila Ulur. The government has also begun to provide preschool education for children from two to five years old: 730 kindergartens were functioning in 1963–1964,[30] with aid from the American organization CARE.

The educational program is indeed meeting with great success: between 1961 and 1963, the increase in the number of pupils at school exceeded the estimates, with nearly 900,000 new enrollments.[31] As one special report says: "One of the major development activities which

[28] Madras, *Third Five Year Plan*, p. 123.
[29] *Demand No. XXIII*, 1963–1964, p. 4. Nationwide, 42 percent of the children aged six to eleven attended school in 1950–1951, and 62.7 percent in 1960–1961.
[30] *Ibid.*, p. 4.
[31] *Ibid.*, p. 3.

Panchayat Unions have undertaken is the universalisation of elementary education." [32] I should go further and say that this program supersedes all the others, since it receives more than 50 percent of the projected expenditure.

Since we shall have to deal with a similar problem in Maharashtra, I shall make only two comments here. First, the Panchayati Raj established as its initial objective the reactivating of the development blocks and the stimulating of production (see chap. 4) ; in Madras, however, a vast extension of school education has been put ahead of the main task, notwithstanding the specific preamble to the Act of 1958: "Whereas it is necessary in the national interest that the production of food should be increased progressively . . . and that the growth of population should be brought under control . . . Be it enacted . . . as follows." [33] The second point is that Madras has not been averse to spending money for refinements of the program—some of them, like school lunches, rather a luxury. Humanitarian principles could certainly justify free lunches for the very poor, but this would be difficult to put into practice. In any case, the establishment of kindergartens at state expense is, I think, a quite excessive innovation which even western Europe did not make general until after 1945.[34]

Under the heading of production there are several activities: minor irrigation works no longer come under the Revenue Department, but under the Panchayat Unions. Grants are made for the maintenance and repair of tanks and canals associated with them amounting to 20 million rupees.[35] A sum of 75 million (200,000 rupees per block) is allocated to other purposes, including fertilizers, green manures, and insecticides for the tree plantations belonging to the village panchayats. The villages, or individuals, receive financial aid in ratio to their own contributions.[36]

The panchayats also have a duty to encourage birth control. Special grants (of twenty rupees) are made as a kind of reward to encourage men and women to have themselves sterilized. (No results were reported by 1964.) Another activity of the panchayats in the state of Madras, as in the rest of the country, has presumably been the formation of village volunteer forces, but the annual reports show little in

[32] *Demand No. XXIII,* 1964–1965, p. 3.

[33] *The Madras Panchayats Act, 1958,* p. 1.

[34] I dwell on these two points, since they are good illustrations of an attitude to which I shall return: the scarcity of money is so often quite forgotten and definite priorities omitted.

[35] *Demand No. XXVI,* 1961–1962, p. 27.

[36] See *General Order No 664,* Aug. 16, 1960.

the way of concrete results, and I found no evidence of the existence of such forces in the districts of Tanjore or Coimbatore.

Restraint and Realism

Good administration has for a long time been the rule in Madras, and it was therefore especially desirable that its structure should not be drastically altered by the innovations introduced after Independence. In adopting the Village Panchayats Act of 1950, the legislators particularly avoided making the administrative apparatus unwieldy. Instead of creating panchayat secretaries, the *munsif,* or village tax collector, was made responsible. On the whole, Madras was only moderately enthusiastic about the new program, and it kept certain administrative safeguards which are unknown in many of the other states. The collector is ex officio president of the District Development Council, which means that he can exercise a certain amount of control.[37] Also the law envisages several measures that are intended to prevent abuse. The government of Madras is well aware that discontent and differences of opinion are often aggravated and exploited by the politicians, and it has managed not to leave them too wide a field for their activities. The result, as we shall see in Tanjore, has been an administration reasonably free to go about its work in a steady and efficient manner.

The Position of the District of Tanjore

Before studying the district of Tanjore, one should understand the important place it occupies. It is a rich area, the state's bowl of rice as it were, where both irrigation and rice cultivation have reached a higher than average level. Most of the soil is alluvial, and part of it has only been intensively developed since 1935.[38] It accounts for nearly a quarter of the total rice production in the state. Nonetheless, the high density of the rural population and certain unusual sociological features place this district within the average for the state, with an estimated annual revenue per head of 230 rupees in 1955/56. Seven districts were below it, two were on the same level, and two—Coimbatore and the Nilgiris— along with the municipality of Madras, were above. Tea plantations

[37] Unlike many other states, Madras conforms to the recommendation made by the *Mehta Report* (I, 128).

[38] Eighty-four percent of the area irrigated is under cultivation, 25 percent yielding more than one crop annually. See Intensive Agricultural Programme, *Report 1961–63,* p. 87.

account for the high level of the Nilgiris (543 rupees per head). In Coimbatore (297 rupees per head), it is man who has triumphed over rather adverse natural conditions, such as poor soil which is difficult to irrigate, and who has in addition industrialized the region. Coimbatore is particularly dynamic and its expansion is shooting ahead rapidly.

1964–1966

The last two years of the plan were characterized by an uneven rate of production: a rise, based on the 1960/61 figures, of at least 10 to 20 percent in 1964/65, and then a decline following the drought. Because of its good irrigation system, Madras suffered much less from the dry spell than Maharashtra, for example, but even so production may have fallen by about 15 percent.[39]

The gravity of the situation only served to render more urgent the need for measures in favor of agriculture, for, regardless of natural calamities, it is precisely in this sector that the weakness of the Panchayati Raj, to which I have already referred, is revealed. In 1966 the Chief Minister of Madras, Mr. M. Bhaktavatsalam, made a candid assessment of the situation: "The Panchayat Unions gave all their attention to more visual development work like the laying of roads and construction of school buildings," despite the fact that the Madras Panchayat Act of 1958 laid the main emphasis on agricultural production.[40] The Chief Minister failed to add, however, that such a result was inevitable, based as it was on the schematic budget drawn up by the government services.

The agricultural program was given new strength with the addition of funds specifically allotted to irrigation. In July, 1966, a special allotment of 20 million rupees was put aside for sinking new wells and for completing the well program already underway.[41] This measure was but one in a series which expanded the original minor irrigation budget for 1965/66 from 40.5 million rupees to 73 million. With this impetus, the total number of pumping sets should have reached a figure of 253,000 units, well above the original target of 200,000 envisaged for the end of the third plan. Some of them are electrified;[42] others use fuel. As we shall see later in studying Tanjore, more definite action also seems to have been taken with regard to new high-yield varieties of rice.

[39] *Hindu Weekly Review*, Nov. 7, 1966.
[40] See *The Hindu*, Feb. 17, 1966.
[41] *Hindu Weekly Review*, July 25, 1966.
[42] *Overseas Hindustan Times*, Mar. 10, 1966.

The extension of the package program under the name of the Intensive Agricultural Area Programme (I.A.A.P.) [43] has made it possible to reach part of the Chingleput district which, with 320,000 hectares of rice fields, is the state's second largest agricultural district, although its average yield for rice is appreciably below that of Tanjore (about 1,250 kg/ha as against 1,500 kg/ha in Tanjore in 1959/60).[44]

So far as the efficiency of the development blocks is concerned, there is clearer recognition than in the past of the need for a close check on the work of the village-level workers. Again, we find the question of coordinating the different services within the district. Specifically—and I shall return to this point in chapter 25—the district officer needs to exercise much stricter control.[45]

Given a not too hostile nature, the general effect of these measures and of the care being taken should be a definite strengthening of the agricultural program in Madras.

The 1967 General Election

After all that has been said about the healthy political and administrative situation in Madras, the collapse of Congress in the 1967 elections needs some comment.

The Dravida Munnetra Kazhagam won more than half the seats in the Legislative Assembly: 138 out of 222; the Congress party got only 49 seats (in 1962 the figures were almost exactly the reverse), the third group being the Swatantra party (20), followed by the Communists (11) and a few minor parties. Do these results mean that my analysis at the beginning of this chapter misrepresented the real situation?

As I mentioned, the D.M.K. had for some years shown considerable strength, but being in the opposition it did not hinder too much the work of the ruling party. The latter was not torn by the feuds and factions so typical of Uttar Pradesh, and because of its strength and unity the administration could operate with efficiency and the whole process of economic planning went smoothly.

The fall of Congress in Madras is a good example of the way in which sociopolitical and psychological factors may be more important to public opinion than economic achievements. In Uttar Pradesh, the Congress party can boast of only limited success throughout the first

---

[43] A program launched in 1964—not to be confused with the Intensive Agricultural District Programme (I.A.D.P.) or the package program. The basic principles are similar but it has fewer resources at its disposal.

[44] *Hindu Weekly Review,* July 26, 1966.

[45] *Ibid.*

three five-year plans, yet it avoided a major defeat in 1967. It has, no doubt, lost its majority in the Legislative Assembly, but it has retained 198 seats out of 425. It is followed by the Jan Sangh (97 seats) and several smaller parties. In Madras, Congress has been notably successful, and yet it lost.

The victory of the D.M.K. was mainly a result of the linguistic issue and anti-Hindi agitation. In 1965, serious language riots occurred and there were even several instances of self-immolation among the supporters of English as well as supporters of local languages. Since then, a shaky compromise has eased the tension, but the issue is still not resolved.

The important question is, what are the prospects of economic development under the D.M.K.? Unfortunately, a clear answer is impossible because the party does not appear to have a very clear-cut social and economic program. It is in favor of the nationalization of road transport and the abolition of horse races, among other things. It has also suggested reopening the touchy issue of land reform, and advocates lowering the ceiling on landholdings from about thirty acres (12 hectares) to half as much. Such an aim well accords with its policy of supporting the lower castes and the Harijans, but it remains to be seen whether the reform can be carried out. The D.M.K. will also insist upon greater autonomy of the states.

19

KILA ULUR

The village of Kila Ulur is situated in the new Cauvery delta, a region developed after the completion of the canals of the Cauvery Mettur Project (C.M.P.) in 1935. Fifteen kilometers southeast of Tanjore we leave the district's main road and cut across footpaths for one and a half kilometers to the village, which can also be reached by a detour of a few kilometers along a very bad road.

The flat landscape of paddy fields is bordered on the horizon by casuarina woods, with a few coconut palms, bamboos, and banana trees surrounding the houses. These are of a much lighter construction than those in the north, with walls of mud or bamboo and plaited palms, and palm roofs.

The Population and the Land

The region of Kila Ulur has always been poor, incapable of supporting a large population. For many decades its size was kept at a minimum by emigration. In the half-century between 1901 and 1951 the population scarcely altered—from 1,310 to 1,444.[1] Since 1951 the increase has been somewhat more rapid—a growth of 9 percent (11.8 percent for the state), to a total of 1,574 inhabitants in the 1961 census. This was a density of 262 inhabitants per square kilometer.

Kila Ulur is made up of several hamlets, each containing members of a single caste. The largest is that of the Kallars, the next is the Ambalakkarars, and the third the Harijans; to the south of the fields there is another group of dwellings, known as Paruthiapparkoïl, on *inam* land, that is, land owned by the local temple.[2] Being on a slight incline, it is out of reach of the irrigation channels and therefore unsuitable for rice crops. Casuarinas grow there mainly.

---

[1] *Descriptive Memoir of Kila Ulur, Resettlement Fasli 1333 (1924–25)*. The other figures were given to me in Tanjore.

[2] Religious foundations were exempt from tax until the Inam Assessment Act of 1956.

The last land revenue settlement took place in 1924. The land was then divided as follows: [3]

Inam land	141 ha.
Perambokes (communal land) and dwelling areas	49
Unoccupied land	31
"Wet" land	58
"Dry" land	309
Total area	588 ha.

The term "wet," as used by the Madras administration, refers to land irrigated by the state or by village tanks. "Dry" land includes the fields that are privately irrigated by the peasants. At Kila Ulur there are few wells and these are mostly small. In 1924 there were only 103 hectares of paddy or rice land; 160 hectares were in groundnuts, and the remaining land was planted with various types of low-grade millet common to the south known as *cholam, cumbu,* and *ragi.*

The situation was radically altered by the Cauvery Mettur Project. Apart from the *inam* land, which remained unchanged, the 447 hectares belonging to Kila Ulur itself can now be broken down as follows:

Area irrigated by the C.M.P.	323.4 ha.
Area irrigated by private wells	3.5
Unirrigated area	36.2
Area occupied by dwellings, communal land, tanks, and casuarina woods	83.8

Paddy fields—some 300 hectares—have practically eliminated other crops. Groundnuts now cover only four hectares, and *ragi* and coconut plantations each cover about the same. Rice has become both the basic food and the principal source of ready cash; a large part of it is sold in the commercial market. At first, one is struck by the fact that despite the extent of irrigated land, double cropping is done only on 70 hectares, that is, 20 percent of the total area cultivated. We shall see later on the particular reasons for this situation.

In the state of Madras, most land is owned on the *rayatwari* system whereby the peasant actually owns the land and pays tax directly to the state. This is the system practiced in Kila Ulur. The complexity of the land records [4] and lack of time prevented me from making a detailed analysis of land distribution as I had done at Khandoï, but I was able to draw up the following tabulation on the basis of figures given by the

[3] *Descriptive Memoir of Kila Ulur;* dated February 4, 1924.
[4] In Uttar Pradesh there were two records; here there are several.

peasants. The absence of large landowners is even more evident than in the Uttar Pradesh villages:

Less than 0.4 ha.	70 holdings
0.4–2 ha.	100
2–4 ha.	35
4–6 ha.	15

There are no high castes in Kila Ulur.[5] The dominant group, the Kallars, belongs to the Sudra category. The Kallars (the word means thief in Tamil) are traditionally noted for their uproariousness, and for centuries war and brigandage constituted their main activity. Now they have become peaceful farmers.[6] The Ambalakkarars, another type of Sudra, are slightly inferior to the Kallars in social and economic status. The lowest are, of course, the Harijans, and here, as elsewhere, they have the least amount of land.

The 1951 census divided up the population as follows: [7]

Cultivator-owners	672
Peasants in the main cultivating land that does not belong to them	125
Landless laborers	410
Noncultivating owners	2

These statistics, confirmed by my own observations, show that share-cropping is of small importance here, but this is far from being the case in the district as a whole.

In addition to the men occupied in agriculture, there are three families of artisans (a jeweler, a blacksmith, and a carpenter), two families of barbers, and four laundrymen. Two others have a shop where they serve tea and coffee.[8]

The Agricultural Calendar and the Crops

The agricultural year begins toward the end of June when the water from the C.M.P. reaches the delta. There are three rice crops: *kuruvai*, from the end of June to September, 105 days' growing season (90 under water) ; *thaladi*, from the end of October to February, 105 days'

---

[5] Except for a few special cases, I shall omit consideration of the *inam* land of Paruthiapparkoïl owned by Brahmins.

[6] Professor Louis Dumont's book about the Kallars of the Madura region, *Une Sous-caste de L'Inde du Sud,* is of particular interest.

[7] These figures include dependents such as wives, children, and old people.

[8] Coffee often replaces tea in southern India.

growing season (90 under water) ; and *samba,* August to January, 180 days' growing season (120 under water). For the first two crops the layer of water must measure 10 cm. and for the third crop, which has a longer period of maturation, hence a greater need for water, 15 cm. Irrigation is indispensable to the *kuruvai* and the *samba.* The *thaladi* needs less, since it has the benefit of the monsoon from the northeast in October, November, and December.[9]

In June the ploughing and preparation of the seed beds begins. The fields are flooded, then ploughed, and the soil is leveled with a plank. These operations are repeated six or seven times, the last two just before the paddy is transplanted; this happens twenty or thirty days after sowing in a nursery.

It takes three ploughs six hours to plough 0.4 hectare. The peasants help one another or work on their own, as the case may be. Transplanting requires a lot of manpower: about fifteen persons, including many women, can complete 0.4 hectare in a day. Then the paddy must be weeded. This is a painstaking task, which really ought to be done two or three times in a season, but most farmers, lacking the money for laborers, have to get by with one weeding. The job requires between ten and twenty-five persons to do 0.4 hectare in a day. For the same reason the Japanese method of line transplanting is not employed, for two additional laborers would be needed to hold the string.

About three-quarters of the paddy fields have *samba* crops; on the other quarter, the *thaladi* generally succeeds the *kuruvai.* The farming schedule is thus a heavy one up to February and March, but the following months are slack. The C.M.P. sluices are closed and the canals are dry. Cultivation is possible only where the peasants themselves own wells. (The tanks have not yet dried up, but they are intended for pisciculture rather than for irrigation.)

Since the subsoil water is four or five meters deep, it is possible to sink temporary wells along in February and March, but these are closed in June and July when the rice is planted, so as not to waste any space. The temporary wells irrigate *ragi* (millet) and groundnuts. They are operated by hand with a pulley and a stone in counterbalance drawing the water into a pail which is emptied into the channels. Two men, working in shifts, can lightly irrigate 0.4 hectare a day. Altogether, about ten hectares are irrigated in this way.

In this rather heavily wooded area, where there are nearly thirty

[9] The monsoon from the southwest from June to October is stopped by the Malabar Ghats and has only a slight effect on the southeastern part of the peninsula, though it does replenish the Cauvery and its tributaries. The C.M.P. Lake Stanley can open its sluices from mid-June in order to refill the canals.

hectares of casuarinas, the peasants do not have to burn cow dung for fuel and can use it to fertilize their land. They also grow green manure (*kulunji*) which they plant after the rice harvest—it is, indeed, one of the traditional crops—and chemical fertilizers are widely used, even by those who own less than one hectare.

With subsidies from the development block, the panchayat has acquired a sprayer and insecticides. It takes four rupees' worth of powder and four to five hours' work to cover 0.4 hectare, and, according to the gram sewak, this treatment is in common use.

What are the yields? As we shall see at district level, they vary a good deal depending on good and bad years. At Kila Ulur the average paddy harvest yields 2,000 kg/ha. Some peasants obtain 2,800 kg. and a "large" landowner (4 ha.) sometimes manages 4,000 kg/ha by using plenty of irrigation, improved seeds, and the proper application of chemical fertilizer. (For clean rice the figures are 1,350, 1,850, and 2,700 kg/ha.) The average yields are thus much higher than the average for the whole of India (900 kg/ha during the period of 1956/57 to 1960/61) and a little higher than the Madras average.[10]

Yields for *ragi* and groundnuts are good, owing to the intensive cultivation of small, well-irrigated plots. The *ragi* harvest yields 1,400 kg/ha, and the yield for shelled groundnuts is 575 kg/ha. For the state, the average yields for these crops are considerably less: 1,000 and 360 kg/ha.[11]

The Effects of the Package Program

It would be a little naïve to expect an agricultural revolution in six years, and so far the package program launched in April, 1960, as part of the Third Plan (see chap. 4) has brought no radical changes. There have been the inevitable delays in putting the new program into practice, and of course there are too few qualified personnel for the large number of villages. Nevertheless, there are several indications that Kila Ulur is gradually entering upon a third epoch in its history. As a poor village surrounded by scantily irrigated fields, it only began to have access to the market economy with the arrival of the C.M.P. canals. It is now passing through a phase of increasingly intensive agriculture.

As we shall see, the principal weapons of the program are credit, chemical fertilizers, and a greater concentration of extension services

[10] See *Eastern Economist*, Annual No., 1962, p. 107, and *Basic Agricultural Statistics*, Madras, p. 10.

[11] *Basic Agricultural Statistics*, pp. 13, 25.

than is usual in other blocks. We shall study at district level the progress made in the organization of rural credit. But first, let us take a look at the local cooperative (multipurpose society No. T. 815). It is a comparatively old society, founded in 1936, but under the influence of the program it has widened its activities. Between 1960 and 1963, the number of members almost doubled, from 127 to 250; so, too, did the amount of credit extended in short- and medium-term loans. From 24,000 rupees in 1960, credit rose to 46,000 rupees in 1963—38,000 in short term, 8,000 in medium term. The gram sewak, a capable man, helps the peasants to estimate their agricultural needs—seeds, fertilizers, and farm implements, for the purchase of which they are entitled to loans from the society.

Although the Orathanad block, to which Kila Ulur belongs, dates from 1957, it has only been since 1960 and the start of the intensive program that it has had any particular influence on the farmers. I questioned a number of farmers on this subject and found that most of them had started using chemical fertilizers in 1960 or so. Most of them were satisfied with the results and with the system for obtaining credit. Six farmers had seen their paddy production increase by 100 to 160 kg/ha; another had only recorded a slight increase. One man was dissatisfied, but his low yield was the crop of 1962, a year when heavy rainfall nullified the effects of the fertilizer. These landowners possessed between one and four hectares. Three other peasants I talked to had only a half or three-quarters of a hectare of land each. They were so poor that they did not have even the minimum of savings to join the cooperative in order to obtain credit, nor perhaps were they as energetic as the others.

Irrigation

The secondary canal of Paruthekotaï runs about 500 meters to the west of Kila Ulur. Four small tertiary canals issue from it. The water takes ten days to come down from Lake Stanley to the delta. The sluices are opened around the twentieth of June and preparation of the soil commences at the end of the month. The schedule is tight. If the rains in October and November come too early, the *kuruvai* harvest is caught and can be seriously damaged. The *samba* runs another risk in that should the rice growth be delayed, even more water would be needed in January at the very time when the lake's reserves are getting low. The sluices are finally closed at the end of January or the beginning of February.

Ideally, irrigation should start by early or mid-June, but it is precisely at this time that the monsoon from the southwest falls on the Ghats and the Malabar, and it takes some weeks before Lake Stanley is filled. Since the lake cannot be replenished any earlier in the season, the time lag is probably unavoidable, unless the capacity of the lake could in some way be enlarged.

A second problem of the irrigation system is that there is frequently too little water, now that there is more intensive cultivation. Part of the trouble is due to the heavy losses of water percolating into the soil from the unlined canals. Besides, the canals silt up and the flow is uneven. Although the Paruthekotaï canal is cleaned every three or four years by the Department of Public Works,[12] in May, 1964, I measured a thirty-centimeter layer of alluvium. Unfortunately, desilting the canal is not enough: the tributaries should be desilted also, and this would be a complicated undertaking, for too much time has been allowed to pass since the last cleaning operations.

The peasants make no secret of their dissatisfaction. The Department of Public Works, which is responsible for the main works, seldom sends a man out to inspect, and the local panchayat only concerns itself with the field channels. Some uncertainty seems to exist in the division of labor and responsibilities.

These weather and water conditions explain why there is little double cropping despite a high rate of irrigation. By dint of hard work and ingenuity, the peasants manage to fit in their three rice harvests between June and February. But from February to June, most of the land is idle. If there were more wells, more *ragi* and groundnuts could be grown. The intensive program is contemplating the distribution of pumps in areas with electricity, but it will be an uphill task, because many farmers may be reluctant to make this investment for a few short-term crops as a supplement to rice watered by the state canals. Nevertheless, it is in this direction that a new possibility for intensifying crops will be found.

The Standard of Living

A. Pichaya Thevar is a Kallar, forty years old. His household consists of his wife, his three children, and his two widowed sisters. He is a "large" landowner, with four irrigated hectares—1.2 hectares growing *kuruvai* then *thaladi*, and 2.8 in *samba*. In addition, he has 0.12 hectare of coconut trees, banana trees, and mangoes. His cattle consists of seven bullocks and three cows (yielding a total of two liters of milk a day). He also has a hen and nine chickens.

[12] Responsible for state irrigation.

He has no debts and his standard of living is rising. He has sold poor land and bought better. Like the other Kallars, he works with his hands and only employs farm workers in busy periods (ploughing, transplanting, weeding, and harvesting). Sometimes he and the other peasants help one another.

Pichaya Thevar produces about 11,000 kg. of paddy a year. He sells more than half—6,700 kg.—and consumes the rest, except for some 1,100 kg. which he uses to pay his harvesters. The farm workers whom he employs for other purposes generally receive one rupee a day. Paddy is the only source of ready money. It brings in between 2,400 and 2,900 rupees a year, at a market price somewhere between 20 and 26 rupees for a 56-kilo bag (February, 1964). The price is usually lowest at harvest time.

The family eats three meals a day, all composed of rice [13] mixed with copra oil and a few chilies. Once a week they eat meat, either mutton or goat,[14] and twice a month they have fish, both bought at the bazaar in the next village on the main road. Some vegetables, a little milk, and bananas in season complete their daily diet, and on special occasions they may also have eggs.

Tholappa Thevar, another Kallar, thirty-five, who has been married five years, lives with his wife and small daughter. He owns 1.6 hectares of irrigated land, of which 0.6 has a *kuruvai* crop followed by *thaladi*, and one hectare has a *samba* crop. He applies the amounts of chemical fertilizer recommended by the block, and his three harvests yield 5,600 kg. of paddy. He sells three-fifths of this for about 1,200 rupees.

For a year now, Tholappa has grown *ragi* between February and May. He has sunk a well which irrigates 0.4 hectare, and he has a yield of 560 kg. which he sells for 240 rupees. Two coconut trees (50 coconuts a year) shade his house from the sun and shelter his stock—two pairs of bullocks and a heifer. Three hens, each of which lays an egg every other day, also scratch about there. His diet is similar to that of our "large" landowner.

Tholappa has borrowed 300 rupees, on medium-term credit, from the cooperative for the purchase of a cart and bullocks, and 450 rupees, on short-term credit, for chemical fertilizers. He still owes 1,750 rupees at 24 percent interest to a dealer who bought his paddy.[15] This sum of

[13] Breakfast often consists of cold rice left over from the evening meal of the previous day.

[14] A meal of meat (for the entire family—1.5 kg. of mutton) costs 1.5 rupees, and a meal of fish one rupee.

[15] There is no moneylender at Kila Ulur. It is usually the rice dealers who lend money to their clients.

money has enabled him to enlarge his house and cover some sumptuary expenses.

Thalappa is content with his lot, yet eager to take advantage of advice from the block and raise his income so far as possible on his small plot. He is enterprising and hard-working and successful within the limits of his circumstances. Nor is he an isolated case. Samaiya Arsuthiar, a Kallar, manages quite as well with 1.2 hectares of land and a larger family—he has two wives (the first did not bear him a child) and two daughters.

Another Kallar, Swaminathan Malusuthi, aged fifty, lives with his wife, and his twenty-year-old son and daughter of seventeen, both of whom are unmarried. The family manages with 0.8 hectare of irrigated land, half of which bears two crops of rice. After satisfying their own needs, they can sell 560 kg. of paddy for between 200 and 260 rupees.

This family has neither coconut nor banana trees. In addition to their two bullocks, they keep ten hens and sell the eggs, which average one per hen every other day. The father and son work mainly on their own land; the mother works for other peasants in the transplanting season in late June, and earns about sixty rupees a year.

The family diet consists mainly of rice and a small amount of meat twice a month. They drink no milk, since they have no cow, and they buy fruit only occasionally. During the fishing season in April and May they eat a little fish. Swaminathan has borrowed 200 rupees from the cooperative to buy fertilizer and 100 rupees at 26 percent interest from a rice dealer in a nearby town to buy his bullocks.

This father and son are obviously less well-off than the other Kallars I have described, yet they complain little and think that their lot is improving slightly. They are pleased with their chemical fertilizer which has helped to increase their production. The father is quite old now and has lost some of his resilience, but the son is lively and energetic.

Samudram Ambalakkarar, forty-five, is married and has three children between three and ten years old. He owns only 0.2 hectare of land, from which he gets 560 kg. of paddy. For four or five months of the year he works for other farmers, ploughing, transplanting, weeding, and harvesting, usually for wages of one rupee a day. His wife does likewise. He owns no cattle, but he has two hens, which lay one egg each every other day; half of these he sells. He also makes a little money by selling some of the coconuts from their four trees, each of which bears fifty coconuts a year. The family diet consists of rice, a little *ragi,* and some fish or meat once a month.

Samudram is certainly interested in the intensive program, but he has too little land to take part in it. He subsists, but makes no progress. He is heavily in debt: 1,000 rupees at 26 percent which he borrowed five years ago from a rice dealer.

Dharumaiyan, an Ambalakkarar of twenty-five, has been married for two years and has no children yet. He does not own any land. In May, when the tank near Kila Ulur is emptied,[16] he works as a fisherman, at a rate of one and a half rupees a day and the equivalent of a quarter of a rupee in fish. During the next five months he works in the rice fields of a nearby landowner. For this he receives fifteen rupees a month in addition to his food. His wife helps elsewhere with planting out, weeding, and harvesting, and earns one rupee a day (one and a half rupees at harvest time.)

Dharumaiyan spends the first fortnight of November with another employer, helping with the *kuruvai* harvest and threshing. Then he goes to help with the *samba* harvest which occupies him until the beginning of February. In the slack months from February to May, he takes on other manual labor such as road building and canal repairing. He has no debts. He eats a meal of rice three times a day, and in May he has fish. When he has a few coppers to spare he buys meat. His standard of living is static, but he seldom complains. He tries to get as much work as possible and makes a good impression.

Let us take a look at the Harijans of the Paraiyar caste.[17] Their hamlet seems much poorer than the one inhabited by the Kallars, although it is clean and attractive with its thatched roofs under the coconut palms. It really amounts to a work force for the paddy fields—only a few possess a little land. But their way of life seemed to me less wretched than that of the Nahiyan Chamars. They have more work, at daily wages of one or two rupees, and they are well treated. Many of the wives, too, go out to work.

In slack periods the whole hamlet makes mats. They buy the fiber in the region, then they dye and weave it. In one day, one person can make by hand one mat measuring one meter by two. After deducting production costs, a family can earn between fifty and a hundred rupees a year in this way. One might well say that this is an absurdly low sum, and yet it is perhaps this small additional working margin that enables these Harijans to achieve a living standard which, although very frugal, is almost acceptable.[18]

[16] At first, while the tank is gradually emptying, the fish are caught by hand; nets are used when there is hardly any water left.

[17] Whence comes the term Pariah, the principal caste of untouchables in Madras.

[18] By acceptable I mean an existence where material cares are not so great that they eliminate every satisfaction but that of survival.

In answer to my questions they replied that their lives had scarcely improved materially during the last fifteen years. On the other hand, their social status has risen as a result of the abolition of untouchability. Here, as in every other village, the castes have not disappeared overnight. The Kallars do not eat with the Harijans, and there is of course no intermarriage, but the worst of the abuses have disappeared: the Kallars' temple is now open to all by right as well as in practice, and the Harijans go there once or twice a month. They can bathe and wash in the Kallars' tank, and they have a drinking-water well. They have also been given several hectares of communal land to cultivate. In the past, the Harijans were not allowed to stop in the Kallar's hamlet but had to go through it barefoot, and they were not allowed access to the tea shop. These prohibitions no longer exist. When a Harijan travels within the district he is sure of being allowed on a bus where even a Brahmin will not mind sitting beside him. In education, too, the Harijans are making progress. None of the adults is literate, but a number of children go to the village school, and I met one young girl who was attending high school.

At Kila Ulur living conditions differ in several respects from those in our two Uttar Pradesh villages. The crucial element is rice, which allows a family to subsist, and even progress, with less than two hectares of land, which I have already mentioned as the minimum for the north (double cropping not included). Here a family manages to make do with 1.6 hectares (four acres). An economy based on rice cultivation needs to have either a very efficient system of cooperative production—as difficult to achieve here as it is elsewhere in India—or quite a high labor force of agricultural workers, since even those who own as little as one hectare cannot manage without some help. This means that there is work for the landless, though not all the year. Rice is, of course, the staple of the diet, but even so the diet in Kila Ulur is a little more varied than in the north, where, apart from sugar cane, cereals, and pulses, there are really only milk and mangoes in season to supplement the daily fare. Here no one is a vegetarian, and they can eat meat, fish, and eggs; and nature can offer other foods which are seldom found in the middle basin of the Ganges: coconuts and bananas make a considerable contribution which it is difficult to assess in figures.[19]

Although they are not as lively and hard-working as the Khandoï farmers, the Kallars are certainly more industrious than the inhabit-

[19] This is even more noticeable in Java and to a certain extent in East Pakistan, where these "extras" often enable the people to avoid the most overwhelming forms of poverty despite the extremely high density of the population.

ants of eastern Uttar Pradesh. The surroundings are favorable to the intensive program, and they are stimulated by the idea of economic progress.

Not the least of the differences is the size of families. In Kila Ulur they are generally much smaller than in the north, and many parents have only a few children. These were my observations, and they seemed to be confirmed by the slow growth of population in the state. It is a subject worthy of deeper study.

A last but by no means trivial difference is sumptuary expenditure, which in Kila Ulur, for weddings especially, is less than in Uttar Pradesh. A Harijan will limit himself to about 100 rupees (some Nahiyan Chamars spend as much as 800 rupees) and a Kallar owning two hectares will get away with about 1,000 rupees.

The Panchayat

Evidence gathered from records of the reports and from conversations point to the fact that the panchayat, set up in 1956, is really functioning. Meetings have been held much more frequently than at Khandoï, especially since 1960.

The president, a Kallar, who owns two hectares, told me of the aims and activities of the panchayat. As a result of its decisions roads have been improved and three culverts built; two drinking-water wells have been sunk; a library and a new school have been built; and the village will soon have electricity. As elsewhere in the vicinity, the panchayat has been responsible for planting a hundred coconut trees on common land. (The village volunteer force, however, though it has fifty members, exists only on paper.)

Instead of one single tax, as in Uttar Pradesh, the state of Madras levies several: seven rupees per house, and three for each bullock cart. Their collection is not easy. In 1962/63, only 209.43 rupees were collected of an assessed 603; in 1963/64, out of the same assessment (603), only 17.30 rupees were collected. Part of the trouble that year was no doubt due to the change of *munsif* (tax collector at village level) just before the end of the financial year, his successor arriving too late to collect the tax. The panchayat also receives a part of the land revenue, called local cess, which is collected from the village by the Land Revenue Department. The sum collected amounts to about 700 rupees.

If the program is much more positive than at Khandoï and Nahiyan, the members of the panchayat do not consider production to be of top priority. They are less concerned with the problem of cleaning secondary canals and irrigation channels than they are with building the school or, at the moment, bringing electricity to the village. Their outlook has been little changed by the introduction of the Panchayati Raj, the purpose of which should be, according to the president of Kila Ulur, the construction of roads, of drinking-water wells, libraries, and school buildings. The planting of coconut trees or the improvement of pisciculture come later.

The School

The great effort put into improving education by the state of Madras can be seen in material form at Kila Ulur. For about thirty years school was held in a house rented for ten rupees a month. In February, 1964, the new schoolhouse, belonging to the village, was officially opened. It cost 7,100 rupees, half of which was provided by the Kila Ulur panchayat and the panchayat union (at block level) and the rest by the government. There are two teachers and ninety pupils.

The schoolhouse is of brick faced with cement inside as well as outside, with a roof made of double tiling and six windows with wooden shutters outside. It is not pretentious, yet it could have been built more cheaply: by going without cement facing inside, they would have saved 250 rupees and, more importantly, a third of the quota of a product in short supply throughout the country. Probably, too, the shutters (120 rupees) were not indispensable, and the roof could have been of simpler construction.

Schoolbooks and other materials cost about twenty-five rupees per pupil a year. These are free to the Harijans. For five years now the schoolchildren have received a free midday meal composed mainly of rice; this costs 0.28 rupee per child, half of which is met by the government and the rest by local donations. In addition to their meal they have a large glass of milk, made from powdered milk contributed by the United States.

Electrification of the Village

The state is in the process of laying a line that will provide Kila Ulur with electricity. This measure is certainly worthwhile for rural areas with irrigation pumps, but the timing for electrification of the villages themselves would appear to be questionable, since in Madras, as in the other states, there is still a shortage of power. Moreover, the thirty-three lamp posts assigned for street lighting are made of cement and, without including the installation of the line, cost 120 rupees apiece (a new diversion of cement for unproductive purposes) .

"Why do you want electricity?" I asked a group of Kallars.

"After the streets are lighted there will be fewer burglaries at night, and we shall no longer run the risk of being bitten by snakes."

More than 2,000 miles away, the Khandoï peasants had given me exactly the same reply! The use of electricity in workshops is not envisaged for the moment at least. The electrification of the villages is partly a political move, not an unfamiliar phenomenon in a democratic country. The peasants want to have lighting as well as the townfolk, and if the government refused it would risk losing votes.

Kila Ulur and the Tanjore District

Kila Ulur is less representative of the district as a whole than Khandoï is of Bulandshahr or Nahiyan of Benares. The predominance of the Kallar caste, which is a feature of several villages in the new delta, gives way to the Brahmins in the principal zones of the district, especially in the old delta, around the great temples of Chidambaram and Kombakonam. Here the Brahmins own most of the land. Like the Brahmins in the northeast, they do not cultivate it themselves, and there is widespread sharecropping and a system of fixed rent or renting by oral agreement.

The Fair Rent Act of 1956 sought to guarantee to the sharecropping farmer 60 percent of the gross product instead of the usual 50 percent, but witnesses are unanimous in saying that this allocation is not respected. As a study made in 1947 has already revealed: "In spite of this inadequate return the tenants do not give up the tenancy. The main reason for this is that they have nothing else to do. Due to over-pressures of population and the absence of facilities . . . for other occupations people have necessarily to accept tenancy under even unfavorable conditions." [20] Thus even under the new Act the peasant seldom complains or takes advantage of his legal rights. Rent charges, which have a tendency to rise, are also a burden. Finally the oral tenancy and subtenancy agreements leave tenants in danger of sudden eviction, an apparently common occurrence.[21]

These different forms of tenancy—especially the first and the third—represent serious obstacles to development, since the man who cultivates the land, and has borne all or nearly all the expenses, can

[20] Report of the Special Officer on Land Tenures in the Ryotwari Areas of the Madras Province, p. 58.

[21] Intensive Agricultural District Programme (I.A.D.P.) , Report, 1961–63, p. 78.

scarcely be inclined to make any extra effort when half the profit will go to someone who has done nothing at all. It is not surprising, then, that the intensive program is particularly effective among the cultivator-owners of the Kallar type. Elsewhere in the district, among the sharecropping farmers and tenants who cultivate nearly half the land, the response has been only halfhearted. This difference also explains to a large extent why the program is making better progress in the district of West Godavari (Andhra), another large rice-growing area which is widely irrigated and where nearly 95 percent of the land is cultivated by the landowners themselves.[22]

It is obvious that one solution could be agrarian reforms—but how would they be carried out? By what criterion should these Brahmin landowners be deprived of their few hectares? Despite the current hostility felt by many Tamils toward the highest caste, the Brahmins' influence has not declined to such an extent as to allow the local Congress to accept such radical measures, and it remains to be seen how the new D.M.K. government is going to tackle that problem.

It is difficult to see how, in the near future, the beliefs and practices of the Brahmins can be altered, or how a good reason can be found for dispossessing these noncultivating owners who quite often are by no means landlords.

[22] *The Hindu,* Apr. 30, 1964.

20

THE INTENSIVE PROGRAM IN THE DISTRICT OF TANJORE

Before tackling the intensive program at the district level, it is interesting to observe its implementation in one of the blocks and see how it is organized.

The Orathanad Block

The Orathanad block, of which Kila Ulur is part, was formed in 1957. Three years later it started benefiting from the intensive program begun in April, 1960, and the Union of Panchayats of 1961. The block consists of sixty-three villages and 113,352 inhabitants (1961); the population increase was of the order of 10 percent between 1951 and 1961. In its fourth year the program involved thirty-eight villages whose total cultivated areas amounted to 3,260 hectares for *kuruvai,* 3,250 for *thaladi,* and 12,950 for *samba.* Irrigated lands totaled 1,250 hectares for groundnuts, 320 for *ragi,* and 150 for maize.

The program is centered essentially on agriculture. The staff establishment is more generous than in the usual blocks. The B.D.O. has two agricultural A.D.O.'s and two cooperative A.D.O.'s instead of just one for each sector. Each agricultural A.D.O. is responsible for a depot of fertilizers and equipment. In principle, each block should contain twenty gram sewaks; so far the target has been only half-met. Nevertheless, in 1964 the gram sewak of Kila Ulur was responsible for five villages, which is less than the average in non-package areas.

An important place is reserved for the production plans for cultivation. The gram sewak makes out a standard form for each farmer, stating the cultivated areas, the types of improved seed, the requirements in chemical fertilizers and manure, the additional equipment foreseen, and the insecticides needed. In this way the farmers are encouraged to apply improved techniques while at the same time the gram sewak can determine the amount of credit that the cooperative should advance. This very heavy paperwork is accomplished mainly in the slack season. The Kila Ulur gram sewak, for example, completed

580 forms between 1960 and 1964. At block level the number had reached 6,529 at the end of 1963/64.

For each block the agricultural A.D.O.'s prepare ten other much more detailed production plans, listing a complete inventory of all the production factors, their respective cost, and the results obtained. The main object in this case is to pinpoint the range of the program by examining very closely this particularly complex problem of input-output in a rural economy. The staff being more numerous in this block than elsewhere, demonstrations are also more frequent. There were 225 in 1963–1964. Ninety of these explained the use of all the improved techniques (tools, seeds, fertilizers, insecticides); the others were mainly concerned with fertilizers.

The cooperative sector was reinforced: the forty-two societies which serve the thirty-eight villages operate to a large extent on the basis of the production plans. The credit conditions imposed on the peasants were broadened and relaxed.

	1960/61	1963/64
Number of villages covered by the program	14	38
Short-term credits	468,708 rs.	1,213,495 rs.
Medium-term credits	57,800 rs.	519,085 rs.

Repayment was gratifying: for short-term credits the uncovered balances were 15,700 rupees in 1960/61 and only 3,140 in 1962/63.

Another aspect of the program dealt with a problem that exists even in Western countries: the marketing of agricultural products under conditions favorable to the growers. In Madras as elsewhere in India, there is a wide gap between prices prevailing at the time of the harvest and later, and it was to offset the disadvantages of the system that the Orathanad Marketing Society was established, in January, 1962. It buys rice from the growers at harvest time, at market prices, and sells it several months later at the prevailing rate. Half the profit is returned to the grower.

The use of chemical fertilizers has shown a very clear expansion:

	1960/61	1961/62	1962/63	1963/64
Total consumption				
Ammonium sulphate	376 tons	707	851	1,442
Superphosphate	256	963	1,308	2,786
Consumption per acre (0.4 ha.)				
Ammonium sulphate	21.7 kg.	27.0	29.0	33.0
Superphosphate	14.2	39.8	45.0	62.0

In insecticides and equipment, as well, there has been progress. Deliveries of insecticides rose from 7 to 35 tons in four years. In the same period 150 sprayers were acquired by the villages. Equipment was improved with the purchase by the farmers of new ploughs and more than 300 tools for the preparation of soil and weeding (1960–1964).

As we shall see, these data are all together a good reflection of the general development of the program in the district of Tanjore.

The Budget of the Block

It is interesting to see in a detailed case how the general pattern of the plan's budget operated (see chap. 18). The total expenditure for 1961–1966 was to be 6.04 million rupees. This figure, well above the average of 3.8 million, is explained by the size of the block and its situation in a rich area where land revenue is accordingly higher. The planned expenditures by the Union of Panchayats were these: general expenses, 2.51 million; education, 3.0 million; and production, 0.53 million. (It will be remembered from chapter 18 that the funds allocated for education are supplemented by funds from the general expenses and by part of the village panchayats' expenses.) The 539,000 rupees to be invested in production included 200,000 rupees for grants (purchase of agricultural equipment by peasants, coconut tree plantations for the villages, and so on) and 337,000 rupees for the maintenance and development of small irrigation works (tanks) executed under the control of the Union.

The balance sheets for 1961/62 and 1962/63 reveal that the sums provided by the state (coming from grants or land tax or surtax) were used more or less according to the estimates. On the other hand, local taxes collected by the village panchayats gave a poor return, as shown by the figures for the house tax:

House Tax	1961/62	1962/63
Amount to be collected	46,047.50 rs.	35,556.70 rs.
Arrears	38,159.21	45,928.99
Amount collected	38,277.72	28,584.22

Tax delinquencies of this amount are not unusual. Even in a stable and well-managed state like Madras, it is difficult to collect local taxes, apparently because the village authorities are not sufficiently respected or are badly organized for the job.[1]

[1] All the figures for the intensive program come from the *Intensive Agricultural District Programme, Orathanad,* a mimeographed document, and information provided by the block administration.

The Union of Panchayats

The Union of Panchayats of Orathanad block seems to be fairly active. It meets usually once a month, and the discussions are numerous and varied.[2] The meeting of February 12, 1963, for example, was devoted to fifty-one items; eleven of these concerned production—grants for composts, pisciculture, aviculture—and forty related to such matters as school equipment, the selection of teachers, and the social position of women. The meeting of April 30, 1964, included on the agenda ten questions of production—composts, rice mills, soil analysis, animal husbandry, and so on—and thirty-eight others, ranging from the social position of women, the construction of schools and dispensaries, school equipment, and a theatrical performance, to the sponsoring of baby contest in which the best-looking would receive a prize. There is one similarity to Kila Ulur: the council operates and takes its job seriously, but production is not its main concern.[3]

The Program at District Level

Despite serious sociological obstacles, mainly having to do with the Brahmins, there is no doubt that the program is generating some economic progress. At the end of the fourth year it covered 957 villages, representing 276,000 hectares out of a total cultivated area of 574,000 hectares in the district (total population, 3.24 million; density per square kilometer, 335 inhabitants). At the start of 1966, all the thirty-six blocks of the district were covered, representing 1,750 villages. The advances in specific items were considerable: [4]

[2] The minutes of the meetings were translated for me from Tamil.

[3] A short visit to the Thondamutur block in the district of Coimbatore led me to the same conclusions. The president of the Union was alert and intelligent and took his work seriously, but instead of concentrating on production, and especially on irrigation, he seemed most proud of the new administrative building constructed at a cost of 70,000 rupees and, more recently a theater.

[4] These statistics relate only to the area of the program. See *Brief Note on the Work Done Under the I.A.D.P., Thanjavur District* and *Note on the Co-operative Part of the I.A.D.P., Thanjavur,* a mimeographed document. In fertilizers, the gap between the quantities required according to the cultivation plans and actual deliveries has gradually decreased. In 1963/64, deliveries of superphosphate exceeded the estimates by 2,600 tons. On the other hand, requirements of ammonium sulphate had been estimated at 17,377 tons.

	1960/61	1963/64
Consumption of ammonium sulphate	5,660 tons	13,198 tons
Consumption of superphosphate	4,360 tons	18,684 tons
Consumption of insecticides	271 tons	1,146 tons
Number of improved ploughs delivered	2,806	7,904
Number of production plans	36,683	105,437
Improved seeds used	759 tons	4,628 tons
Demonstrations	514	3,509
Cooperative membership	76,153	206,856

The cooperative membership represents an increase from 56 percent to 89 percent of the rural population. Short- and medium-term credits rose similarly, from 2.5 to 14.6 million rupees. In 1964/65 the amount of short-term loans only was 15 million. Most of the increase was a result of the more generous conditions granted the peasants. Each co-op member can borrow up to ten times the amount of his share (not merely eight as elsewhere). Up to 1,000 rupees the loan must be guaranteed by the personal security of another member. Above this and up to a maximum of 5,000 rupees a mortgage is required based on the value of the land (another provision more favorable than in Uttar Pradesh). The tenants can borrow a maximum of 250 rupees (previously 50) with the security of another member. Interest rates are lower than in Uttar Pradesh; 7.2 percent for short-term credits and 8.4 percent for medium-term.[5] Part of the credit is granted in kind. One further liberalization, and at the same time a welcome administrative simplification, is that all the credits are provided by the two central cooperative banks of the district.[6] The *taccavis* (state credits) have been abolished.

The cooperative societies responsible for the sale of rice have been particularly active since 1961–1962, and in one year the volume of their purchases and sales almost doubled, to reach 8,100 tons.[7] Another field of progress, especially since 1964, has been in the use of new high-yield varieties; in 1966 these were grown on 80,000 hectares. As a result, yields have increased as much as 100 percent, as shown by certain rice fields at the time of the *kuruvai* harvest in 1966.[8]

Rice Yields

There being now comparatively little new land that can be brought under cultivation, the struggle to increase food production must de-

---

[5] Moneylenders in the district (often rice dealers as well) demand up to 30 percent or 40 percent interest. For the credit, see *Brief Note*.

[6] These banks cover the societies at village level.

[7] I.A.D.P., *Report, 1961–63*, p. 79.

[8] See *Hindu Weekly Review*, Nov. 7, 1966.

pend first and foremost on the obtaining of higher yields per hectare from the areas already being cultivated. The program included a detailed study of the factors involved. Unpredictable climatic conditions make it impossible to chart a precise graph of production, but the data collected are nonetheless useful and are more reliable than the usual statistics.

In 1959/60 the average yield in the district for clean rice was 1,500 kg/ha, a figure above the state average (1,430 kg/ha). The yields in the area of the program were 4 percent above those of the rest of the district in 1960/61 and 18.3 percent above in 1961/62. Within the program itself, there was an advance of 26 percent between 1960/61 and 1961/62, mainly because of particularly favorable weather conditions; but in 1962/63 a decline was evident:

Clean Rice Yield (kg/ha)

Season	1960/61	1961/62	1962/63	1963/64
Kuruvai	1,620	1,670	1,740	1,700
Samba	1,510	1,760	1,520	1,640
Thaladi	1,440	1,700	1,440	1,375

SOURCE: I.A.D.P., *Report, 1961–63*, p. 5, and personal letter from Tanjore, April 5, 1965.

Samba covers 68 percent of the rice fields, the others each 16 percent.

In the fifth year of the program (1964/65) the annual average for clean rice of the three harvests within the area of the program was 1,750 kg/ha. The following year, because of the exceptional drought, production dropped about 15 percent. The rice surplus of the district was thus reduced, and prices rose sharply in 1966.

Another study[9] analyzes the cost of progress by taking sixty-eight farmers and their rice fields in *kuruvai* and *thaladi* (1961/62). It divides them into three categories:

	Yields per Ha. (paddy)	Equivalent in Rice (approx.)
1st category	3,780 kg.	2,500 kg.
2nd category	2,900	1,850
3rd category	2,230	1,450

The quantities of manure in the three categories varied little, but there were appreciable differences in the application of chemical fertilizers: the doses giving the best results were 170 kg. of ammonium

[9] Robert W. Herdt, "The Effect of Purchased Inputs on Paddy Yields of Selected Cultivators in Thanjavur District, 1961–62," *Indian Journal of Agricultural Economics*, No. 3–4, December, 1964.

sulphate and 170 kg. of superphosphate per hectare. The maximum yields involved expenditure of 100 rupees per hectare, 15 for insecticides and 85 for chemical fertilizers.

The other imputs cannot be easily isolated. To try and convert into monetary terms such items as manure and the wages in kind of agricultural workers is risky. Furthermore, the character of the peasants and their attitude to work and organization of course vary greatly, so that there is finally a "very limited relationship between total expenditure and profit." [10]

The Organization of the Intensive Program

The inauguration of the intensive program was accompanied by an organization markedly superior to that of the usual block. A Joint Director of Agriculture with an assistant directs all the technical activities at the district level. He has under his command an agronomist, an insecticide specialist, a seed specialist, and an agricultural engineer. The cooperatives are controlled by a Deputy Registrar, two assistants, and five inspectors. A statistician and a research officer complete the staff at district level.

Organizational structure is, of course, less important than the quality of the personnel. The main officials appeared to be competent and energetic. The Joint Director of Agriculture understood his task and held to the policy of the program, which emphasized production. He was a man with a practical mind; rather than sit in his office in Tanjore, he preferred to get into the field.

The one serious weakness of the program is irrigation, which depends almost solely on the Public Works Department.[11] As we saw at Kila Ulur, the maintenance of the field channels leaves much to be desired, and water is in some places sorely needed. Drainage is another problem, particularly in the old delta. The Public Works Department Office at Tanjore is divided into three divisions for irrigation administration. It seems to function efficiently, but perhaps somewhat less vigorously than the program itself. It must be admitted, however, that it would be extremely difficult to put the irrigation services directly under the control of the program. Indeed, it would mean a veritable revolution, the details of which will be seen later in part 4. Short of that, a closer coordination would be clearly desirable.

Although the program can take no action for the maintenance of the canals, it does have a free hand in minor private irrigation. In May,

[10] *Ibid.*

[11] I.A.D.P., *Report, 1961–62*, p. 77. This concerns the canals of Cauvery.

1964, a first project for the sale of 1,000 pumps to the peasants was prepared; with a diesel engine these cost 2,000 rupees, with an electric one 1,000 rupees, plus an additional 2,000 rupees for the improvement of the well (cementing). The irrigable area per well is 1.2 to 2 hectares. After a few months only, the program had received 2,000 requests; credits covered the total cost of the operation, repayable in twenty years at 5.5 or 6 percent annual interest.[12] The program entered the implementation phase in 1965. In two years 3,000 pumping sets and small tube-wells were set up, out of which, unfortunately, 1,000 remain still idle for want of power. The 2,000 that are working have allowed many farmers to start their nurseries before the Mettur reservoir is full—a great advantage, since the crop cycle is very tight. Also, several farmers have begun growing crops like cotton or *cholam* in the dry season.[13]

The District Management

As we have seen, the collector holds a more important position in the state of Madras than in Uttar Pradesh, partly because of better organization. One of the sub-officers relieves him of the secondary tasks and routine administration, and he has two other assistants who are each responsible for the development of one part of the district. Under these conditions, the collector has the time to direct the broad program instead of occupying himself with minor matters. He is directly responsible for the blocks that have not yet been covered by the program, and he supervises the program's activities by coordinating the various services. The collector at Tanjore is exceptionally well qualified. Like the best young Indians, he has a direct, informal approach, and he keeps in close touch with agricultural development by going frequently on tour.

The Cost of the Program

Thanks to the Ford Foundation, whose report in 1959 first recommended a program of this sort, the intensive program has had ample funds and technical aid. The budget of the first seven districts (cooperative credit not included) is 77.7 million rupees for five years. Of this, the Ford Foundation is to provide 44 million, the central govenment 6 million, and the states 27.7 million.[14] These funds are for the salaries

[12] Information provided by the Joint Director of Agriculture, May, 1964.
[13] See *The Hindu*, July 29, 1967.
[14] I.A.D.P., *Report, 1961–63*, pp. 44–46.

of extra staff, the training of personnel, research and laboratory equipment, vehicles, the construction of depots, and the like.

In the Tanjore district the budget for the total program is 15 million rupees. An examination of the accounts shows delays in the early years: 326,000 rupees spent in 1960/61 against 3.2 million in 1964/65. Of this last sum, 1.8 million was for salaries of additional staff. The second highest item was transport, 790,000 rupees.[15] Additional funds are contributed by the cooperatives, an arrangement made possible by the increase and extension of credit as a result of higher operating funds advanced by the Reserve Bank. Between 1959/60 and 1961/62, the increase in the seven districts was of the order of nearly 60 percent, or a total of 161 million rupees.[16] Tanjore exceeded this rate of increase.

At the moment, it seems impossible to hazard any generalizations about such a program for the whole of India. It would be enormously costly. If the Ford Foundation contribution were extended to 300 districts (330 in all India), 1,800 million rupees would be needed for a five-year period. The increase in credits would entail nearly 2,700 million rupees in two years.[17] The budget could be reduced somewhat, under the headings of staff and transport, without seriously hampering the effectiveness of the program, which certainly is not dependent on the multiplication of gram sewaks and other cadres. The *Report, 1961–63* (p. 214) observes that even in the seven districts, the often limited ability of personnel had slowed down progress. The men who really count are those in charge in the higher ranks, like the deputy director of agriculture in Tanjore and the collector. The reduction in staff would in turn reduce the number of vehicles needed. The district of Tanjore has received thirty-five since the start of the program. Nor does every district, like Tanjore, need a fleet of twenty-six tractors. There is much room for improvement within present circumstances without switching immediately to mechanized farming.

Appreciable reductions in credits seem difficult to achieve; I have given sufficient examples to show the close relationship between fertilizers and the peasants' financial requirements. By tightening the link between credits and production, the program could reduce the wasting of funds on nonproductive expenses.

To sum up, these seem to be the essential requirements for a sound and workable program: (1) A few really able men in charge of the

[15] Extract from the accounts, seen at Tanjore.

[16] I.A.D.P., *Report, 1961–63*, p. 35.

[17] Another problem is chemical fertilizers. Of the funds given by the Ford Foundation, $5,700,000 were used for direct imports of fertilizers in the first two years. The return from sales subsequently covered part of the salaries of extra staff (*Report*, p. 46).

districts; (2) a comparatively healthy political climate, in which politicians do not interfere too much with the civil servants; (3) a hard-working peasantry, particularly at the middle level.

At Tanjore the first two conditions are being fulfilled, the third only partially, particularly in the old Brahmin-dominated delta. Nevertheless, the first results have been encouraging. In Madhya Pradesh (Raipur), Bihar (Shahabad), and Uttar Pradesh (Aligarh), where the average peasant may be disinclined to work hard in the fields and political conditions are unfavorable, the obstacles are difficult to overcome, even by a competent staff.

Postscript.—A very important innovation was introduced in 1967. Samba paddy was replaced by two successive shorter crops of a high yield variety called ADT 27. At the same time, credit allocations were increased from 30 million rupees in 1966/67 to 60 million in 1967/68.[18]

[18] Statesman, Aug. 8, 1967.

21

MAHARASHTRA

In 1956, at the time of the reshaping of the Indian Union on a linguistic basis, the state of Bombay handed over to Mysore several districts speaking Kannara (a Dravidian language) and received in exchange the region of Nagpur known as Vidarbha, where Marathi is spoken. This region had been part of Madhya Pradesh and Hyderabad. The extremely bitter demands of the Gujaratis and the Marathis finally brought a further partition in 1960, when a new state of Gujarat, with its capital at Ahmedabad, was created. What was left of Bombay was given the name of Maharashtra.

This state, in its present form, possesses some distinctive characteristics. Out of a total population of 39.5 million,[1] 27.9 percent live in towns, a figure considerably above the all-India average of 18 percent. It has two large cities—Bombay and, since Independence, Poona, both of which are large industrial and commercial centers. Twenty percent of the whole of India's industrial production and manpower (not including artisans) as well as 20 percent of its commercial activity are concentrated in Maharashtra, and 40 percent of its sea-borne trade passes through Bombay, the state's only port.[2]

But although Maharashtra is rich in industry, commerce, and banking, it is very poor in agriculture, which only provides one-third of its income as against 46 percent at national level. Much of the soil is mediocre, irrigation is limited, and high-yield crops are grown less generally than in Uttar Pradesh or Madras. There has been appreciable progress in recent years, but the output of food grains is still insufficient to meet the needs, and several regions frequently become scarcity areas.

In terms both of its total area—304,000 square kilometers—and of its population, Maharashtra is the third largest state in the Union, but the average population density is below the national average—only

[1] *Census of India, 1961, Paper No. 1,* 1962, p. lxvi.
[2] For the figures in this paragraph, see Maharashtra State, *Third Five Year Plan,* pp. 5–7.

130 to the square kilometer as compared with 143 nationally. This low density is changing, however. Between 1951 and 1961, the population of Maharashtra increased by 23.6 percent, though the national increase was 21.5 percent.[3]

Like Madras, Maharashtra has the well-deserved reputation of being governed by capable men. The present Chief Minister, V. P. Naik, is a man of practical mind who has little time for demagogic slogans and is not afraid to act firmly.[4] The political situation is relatively calm, and Congress has reunited following the turmoils of partition in 1960. The administration, too, is exceptionally good, in consequence of a century or more of development and because of the presence of a particularly large intelligentsia.

The First Two Plans

The changes which on two occasions have altered the boundaries of the state make it difficult to give an accurate assessment of the economic growth. The following statistics are, as the *Third Five Year Plan* cautions, based on "rather rough estimates" (p. 19). Investments in the public sector during the second plan amounted to 2,160 million rupees: [5]

Agriculture and community development	658.2 million rs.
Irrigation and power	671.2
Industries and mines	57.9
Transport and communications	198.2
Social services (education, health)	542.8
Scientific research and miscellaneous	31.8
Total	2,160.1 million rs.

Income per individual increased from 348 rupees in 1951 to 418 in 1961, as opposed to 330 for the whole of India in 1961.

The report (p. 22) also gives figures of investments in the private sector. For the second plan they amounted to 5,720 million:

[3] For these figures, See *Census, 1961*, p. xii, and *Basic and Current Agricultural Statistics of Maharashtra State*, p. 1. The rate of increase is, however, less than it is in Madhya Pradesh and Rajasthan.

[4] A certain amount of pluck was needed to relax the prohibition of alcoholic beverages imposed for so many years; prohibition is an expensive luxury of very questionable value.

[5] Maharashtra, *Third Five Year Plan*, p. 20. These figures refer to the state's plan, public sector only.

Agriculture and community development	810 million rs.
Industries and mines	2,210
Irrigation and power	100
Transport and communications	130
Social services	1,620
Stocks	850
Total	5,720 million rs.

Investments of this size are not extraordinary in a state in which the secondary and tertiary sectors started from a relatively high level just after Independence and where the rate of private savings was already rather high.

Agriculture has progressed as follows (p. 23) :

	1951/52 (millions of ha.)	1960/61 (millions of ha.)
Total area cultivated (including double cropping)	17.1	18.4
Area with double cropping	0.54	0.92
Area irrigated	0.94	1.17

Production in food grains increased from 3.88 million tons in 1950/51 to 7.23 million ten years later, This increase looks doubtful even if explained by the fact that weather conditions at the beginning of the period were poor and ten years later were exceptionally good.

Our earlier investigations have been in areas where wheat and rice, or rice alone, are the principal crops; we now find ourselves in a region, typical of the Deccan, where varieties of millet represent more than two-thirds of the total food grains, rice less than a fifth, and pulses and wheat a similar proportion (*Third Plan*, p. 124). By the end of the second plan the state showed an annual deficit of nearly two million tons in cereals and pulses.

In education, progress has been considerable. The literacy rate for the population as a whole rose from 21 to 29.7 percent in the decade 1951–1961, and among children aged six to eleven it reached the high rate of 73.3 percent (the figure for India as a whole is 61.1 percent) .[6]

The Third Plan

The third plan followed more or less the same lines as its predecessors, with the state leaving the principal role in the industrial sector to

[6] *Ibid.*, p. 29. All these figures are very approximate.

private enterprise so that it could concentrate on agriculture, infrastructure, and social services.

	Expenditures Public Sector (millions of rs.)	Percent of Total
Agricultural program	623.4	15.98
Community development and cooperation	391.6	10.04
Irrigation	690.6 ⎫ 1,520	38.95
Power	829.4 ⎭	
Industries and mines	155.3	3.98
Social services	860.9	22.06
Transport and communications	344.8	8.84
Miscellaneous	6.0	0.15
Total	3,902.0	100.00

Maharashtra provided 2,200 million rupees of the total budget and the central government 1,700 million (p. 15).

Food-grain production under the third plan was expected to increase by 28 percent, or some 1.77 million tons, which would have reduced the deficit in food grains to one million tons. For the principal commercial crops—cotton, groundnuts, and sugar cane, which occupy a little less than a quarter of the area under cultivation—comparable increases were envisioned: for cotton, 27 percent over the 1.5 million bales produced in 1960/61; for groundnuts, 39 percent (1.1 million tons); and for *gur,* 44 percent (1.2 million tons).[7]

In the agricultural program the main items are soil conservation, 197 million rupees; minor irrigation, 158 million; and production, 127.3 million (p. 154). Insufficient and often irregular rainfall in all but the coastal areas makes the need for irrigation particularly acute. By the end of the second plan only 6.24 percent of the area under cultivation (5.45 percent in 1951) was being irrigated. The maximum limit appears in the long term (after three more five-year plans) to be between 20 and 22 percent, that is, between 3.6 and 4 million hectares. Various methods of irrigation are used:[8]

Large and medium state irrigation (canals, tanks)	240,000 ha.
Minor private irrigation (canals, deviation of streams)	251,000
Pumping sets (private)	39,000
Wells (private)	634,000
Total	1,164,000 ha.

[7] *Ibid.,* p. 124; *Basic and Current Agricultural Statistics,* p. 19.
[8] *Third Plan,* p. 35.

The third plan envisaged an additional 760,000 hectares of irrigated land, 247,000 of which would be irrigated by large and medium projects (the majority having been started between 1956 and 1961). Minor irrigation was to reach 513,000 hectares: 270,000 by wells, and the rest by *bandhara,* as at Eksal. This expansion meant that no less than 11,000 private pumps would have to be installed along the banks of the rivers. In addition, 64,000 new wells were to be sunk, 32,000 repaired, and 21,000 supplied with motor pumps. The total cost of this program was estimated at 50 million rupees, which was to be covered in the form of subsidies (grants) included in the plan, in addition to 160 million rupees' worth of credit provided by the Co-operative Land Development Bank.[9]

The struggle against erosion should save or improve 1.4 million hectares, using several different methods of control as explained in the following chapters.

For fertilizers, the report on the plan estimated the need at two and a half tons of manure for every unirrigated hectare and twelve tons for every irrigated hectare, but there is only enough cattle dung for half this amount. An effort is being made to boost the growth of green manure and to teach farmers better conservation methods for cattle dung.

In 1960/61 the consumption of chemical fertilizers amounted to 20,000 tons of nitrogen (N), 8,840 tons of phosphate (P_2O_5), and 5,000 tons of potash (K_2O).[10] By the end of the third plan requirements were estimated at 136,000, 63,000 and 30,000 tons, respectively, in order that the estimated increase of 28 percent in cereals and pulses might be attained, as well as the targets for cash crops. We are familiar by now with this kind of leap forward in the consumption of chemical fertilizers. Other improvements were also envisaged in the way of farm implements, mechanized cultivation, insecticides, and the like.

Short-term credit for the peasants was estimated at 1,520 million rupees a year. In 1960/61 the cooperatives extended credit of 373 million rupees, and the third plan estimated an increase to 900 million, to be at the disposal of 71 percent of the farmers (38 percent in 1960/61). Medium-term credit was to be doubled, to 100 million a year, and long-term credit was to increase tenfold, to 500 million.

[9] *Ibid.,* p. 37. As the plan proceeded, these targets were set still higher: 47,000 private pumps, 96,000 new wells, and an additional 720,000 hectares for minor irrigation.

[10] In terms of nitrogen content, etc.

Other programs were outlined for the areas of cattle raising, dairying, poultry farming, and pisciculture.

Education and the Social Services

The third plan aimed to introduce free, compulsory primary education in the first five classes of the primary schools (children between six and eleven). Later it was hoped to expand the program to the three upper classes. Secondary education has also become more widespread; so too has university education. A separate place is reserved for technical education. Within the framework of the social services, general education absorbs 238 million rupees. Primary education alone is allotted 134.5 million, including 38.5 million for the normal expansion of free compulsory primary education, 70 million for the generalization of free compulsory primary education, and 17 million for teacher training. Secondary education receives 53.8 million, universities 33 million. Then come several other items: bureau of textbooks, promotion of physical education, school libraries, museums, state board for literature and culture, and so on, which altogether amount to 16.7 million. Technical education, a separate item, is allotted an additional 67.2 million, mainly for colleges of engineering.[11]

Other investments in the social services devote 125 million to health and the training of medical staff, 138 million to the supply of drinking water, and 136 million to house building and slum clearance.

The First Realizations of the Third Plan [12]

It has been difficult for the plan to keep to the timetable. In the first three years only 50.8 percent of all the investments were spent. There is particular evidence of delay in the first two years following natural calamities, the state of emergency declared at the time of the border fighting with China, and the consequent slowing down in certain economic sectors. Moreover, the organization of development on such a large scale proved to be more difficult than had been foreseen.

Agricultural production marked time with 6.35 million tons of cereal and pulses produced in 1961/62, 6.22 million in 1962/63, and an estimated 6.77 million in 1963/64. These figures, even for the third year, are below the exceptional level of 1960/61 (7.23 million), and

---

[11] For these figures, see Maharashtra, *Third Five Year Plan*, pp. 155, 200–209.
[12] See *Annual Plan for 1964–65*, pp. 20–22, 29, 31, 34, 51, 3, 16.

they barely exceed the annual average for the second plan, 1956–1961 (6.46 million).

In commercial crops, results were somewhat better, especially in sugar cane, which had an increase of about 20 percent. Cotton production increased by 4–5 percent, but production of groundnuts declined.

The discrepancy between the final targets and the actual results of the first three years was marked:

	Target for 1965/66	Result in 1963/64
Delivery of improved seeds	99,000 tons	22,000 tons
Ammonium sulphate	675,000 tons	231,000 tons
Area of green manure	36,000 ha.	16,000 ha.
Soil conservation programs	2 million ha.	0.8 million ha.
New wells	96,000 units	46,000 units
Pumps	47,000 units	21,500 units
Potential additional irrigation (minor works)	720,000 ha.	336,000 ha.

Cooperative credit, which had been set at 1,000 million rupees for 1965/66 (short and medium term), had only reached 380 million in 1963/64, and in 1964 the ultimate target was lowered to 700 million.

Other changes took place during the last two years. It seemed necessary to increase the total size of the plan from 3,900 to 4,183 million rupees. Certain projects, notably education, proved to be more expensive than had been anticipated, and the agricultural sector had to be reinforced, particularly soil conservation and minor irrigation. Altogether the agricultural program should have benefited from extra grants amounting to 80 million rupees, and general education by about 150 million.

In spite of these measures, it appeared already in 1964 that the completion of the agricultural plan would be very doubtful. The gap is particularly wide in the case of chemical fertilizers, and it is not much less noticeable in the case of irrigation and soil conservation. Disregarding the organization of these programs, where are the peasants to find the necessary credit? Not only are the cooperatives behind schedule but their ultimate target has been reduced by 30 percent. How is this situation to be improved and its problems solved?

Another difficulty was that the plan increased the subsidies for minor irrigation by about 50 percent, even though—as I was told in the government secretariat in Bombay—it had no assurance that New Delhi would increase its quota of cement. There is a trend now toward decontrol (see chap. 26).

A New Form of Panchayati Raj

The disputes between the Gujaratis and the Marathis and the consequent prospect of seeing the state of Bombay split in two have delayed
the introduction of the Panchayati Raj. The new state was not in a
position to tackle the problem until 1960, when, in its wisdom, it
began by making a detailed study taking into account experiences
elsewhere as well as local conditions.[13]

Administrative decentralization did not come about ex nihilo. In
the different parts of the new state a tendency in this direction became
evident in the last third of the nineteenth century with the creation of
district boards. Laws affecting village panchayats were passed during
the period 1920–1935, and the powers of the panchayats were reinforced in the state of Bombay in 1939, in the Central Provinces
(Nagpur) in 1946, and in Hyderabad in 1951. The reshaping of the
state in 1956 entailed the unification of these laws by means of the
Bombay Village Panchayats Act of 1958. Then, with the Maharashtra
Zila Parishads and Panchayat Samitis Act of 1961, which went into
effect in May, 1962, there occurred a large-scale revamping of local
government and of development.

In Maharashtra, the center of gravity of the system is not, as in
most other states, at block level; rather, it is at district level, and, many
projects concerned with economic development, education, and health
are undertaken by the block and the district together, with the latter
often providing most of the money. I have stressed the importance of
development operations being carried out by especially qualified
officials. Now, as the *Report* observes (pp. 74–75) : "The district body
is the best operative unit of local administration as it alone will be
capable of providing the requisite resources, necessary administrative
and technical personnel and equipment required for a properly coordinated development of the district. . . . It would be imperative to
establish a strong executive body at the district level." My observations
in Uttar Pradesh confirmed the lack of "necessary calibre" (p. 74)
among block officials.

The zila parishad in Maharashtra therefore found itself invested
with heavy tasks. To it fell the responsibility for the whole of the
sector dealing with local development, that is to say, projects exclusively affecting the district. As to irrigation, the Public Works Department kept most of its responsibilities. In addition to the economic
program, the zila parishad took charge of social activities, education,

[13] *Report of the Committee on Democratic Decentralisation*, 1961.

and health. Out of the 944.3 million rupees allocated to the plan for the financial year 1964/65, some 129.6 million were given to the zila parishads.[14]

Although the general practice is for the council to be elected indirectly, in Maharashtra the majority of the members are chosen by direct elections.[15] Only a few, including the presidents of the block councils and the president of the District Land Mortgage Bank, are ex officio members of the council. With a membership of between forty and sixty, the zila parishad is not in a position to deal with the administration of day-to-day affairs. The president, acting with the members of the three main committees, is responsible for seeing that the decisions taken by the council are carried out. Without being a "full-time official" as the *Report* proposes (p. 86), under the law (Art. 46) "the president shall devote sufficient time to the duties of his office." This article is also extended to apply to the three presidents of the commissions. These four people are entitled to a salary in addition to several advantages about which I shall speak when dealing with Satara.

The administrative machinery is completed by a reorganization of the administration proper. All services in charge of local development are grouped under the direction of the chief executive officer (C.E.O.), who is a member of the Indian Administrative Service nominated by the government. By attending meetings and maintaining contact with the people, he ensures that there is liaison between the administration and the zila parishad. The C.E.O. has the same rank as the collector and might well have performed these duties elsewhere. The collector has retained his former functions (law and order) and is concerned with development projects undertaken by the state (state projects) in his district. His particular responsibility is the creation of industries (p. 101). In this way two high officials share the principal social and economic activities, with the C.E.O. taking the larger part.

The first change at block level took place in 1953. In a laudable effort to simplify the administration the government decided to amalgamate the blocks so as to correspond to the existing *taluks;*[16] this organization has been maintained in all but a few cases.

The plan of the zila parishad is repeated at block level except that the panchayat samiti is less a council with broad powers than it is an

[14] *Annual Plan for 1964–65,* p. 3 (public sector only).

[15] The president of the zila parishad must be an elected member (Art. 42 of the Act).

[16] A subdivision of the district, equivalent to a *tehsil* in Uttar Pradesh. Since the *taluk* is larger than a standard block, it has the right to more staff and funds than the standard block.

extension of the zila parishad. The method of election is the same, and, as in the zila parishad, the president and vice-president devote most of their time to public affairs; the B.D.O. is the secretary of the samiti as well as executive officer.

The 1958 Act had invested the *talathi* (village accountant in charge of land records) with the additional responsibility of secretaryship of the village panchayat. To this the *Report* proposed the addition of a third activity: that of gram sewak. In this way there would be one official for each village instead of several in charge of one single activity for a circle of villages. The *Report* states candidly (p. 117): "The present-day gram sewak who is expected to spend 80 per cent of his time on agriculture is not of much use to the agriculturist due to his limited knowledge of agriculture."

The new legislation also tackled a problem common to the whole of India, that of rural taxation. After noting that the current land tax represented only 1.5 percent of the net product (p. 129), the *Report* proposed that the zila parishads impose a surtax which would entitle them to an additional subsidy or matching grant from the state. The proposal was adopted, and between 1962 and 1964, twenty-two out of twenty-five districts increased the land tax. The increased revenue amounted to 18.3 million rupees and produced a matching grant of 17.1 million rupees.[17]

1964–1966

After a relatively satisfactory production in 1964/65, Maharashtra of all Indian states was the hardest hit by the drought in the summer of 1965. Natural conditions such as soil, often of very poor quality, and inadequate irrigation made the state particularly vulnerable to the lack of rain. In this respect, the conditions of a village such as Eksal are certainly not the worst one has met. There are many villages even more dependent on rainfall which saw their harvests, never abundant, almost totally ruined by the long dry spell. Nineteen of the twenty-five districts, with a population of 12.4 million spread over 15,000 villages, were affected by the drought. According to official estimates, there was a drop in production of 46 percent.[18]

Despite this catastrophe, Maharashtra succeeded in avoiding famine, and no cases of death due to starvation were reported. At the same time, in Orissa, where the drop in production was 23 percent—only half as much as in Maharashtra—the food distribution system tempo-

[17] *Outline of Activities, 1963–64 and 1964–65,* p. 107.
[18] *Overseas Hindustan Times,* Mar. 3, 1966.

rarily collapsed in six districts and some cases of death due to starvation were officially admitted. Maharashtra's success in weathering the crisis can be attributed in part to supplies of American wheat, but one must also point out the efficiency with which the wheat was distributed by government officials in the state. Starting in the summer of 1965, the Maharashtra government set up fair-price shops in the drought-stricken regions, so that people could buy cereals at reasonable prices. Nearly 1.2 million tons of wheat and millet have been distributed in this way. The system also acts as a curb on inflation of prices of cereals released on the open market and discourages hoarding by grain merchants. In addition, one must mention that Maharashtra has for many years been fairly experienced in the matter of procurement and distribution of food grains.

Following the practice of the British in similar emergencies, authorities have undertaken relief works to provide employment; some 550,000 people have so far been put to work. In addition, 7,500 tons of food grains have been allotted by the central government for free distribution among the old, the infirm, and the children. The state government has also been given 8,000 tons of powdered milk. Rationing—admittedly not easy to regulate—has been introduced in the cities of Bombay, Poona, Nagpur, and Sholapur.

Another urgent problem has been the shortage of drinking water. In some areas wells have been deepened, but in others it has been necessary to organize distributions of water by every possible means from water carts to camels and bullock carts.[19]

Despite the prolonged unfavorable weather, renewed efforts are being made to stimulate production. Campaigns are underway to speed up the progress of minor irrigation, the sale of fertilizers, and the improvement of high-yield varieties of rice and millet. For the first year of the fourth plan (1966/67) 500 million out of a total of 1,200 million rupees (public sector) have been assigned to agriculture and irrigation; this is a higher proportion than for the third plan.[20]

In Maharashtra, unlike Madras and Uttar Pradesh, Congress was victorious in the 1967 elections. Since they still have the backing of an absolute majority, Chief Minister Naik and his cabinet should be able to pursue their efforts under relatively stable political conditions.

[19] For all these measures, see Government of India, Ministry of Food, Agriculture, Community Development, and Co-operation, *Review of the Scarcity Situation and Measures Taken to Meet It* (1966).
[20] See *Hindu Weekly Review*, Apr. 18, 1966.

22

EKSAL

The village of Eksal gives one a clear picture of peninsular India, and it is representative of the hinterland that stretches beyond Bombay and the Ghats, a vast area of plains, eroded plateaus, and flat hills, where the rivers are often dry and the crops are generally poor.

The built-up area of the village of Eksal is situated on a second-class metaled road a few kilometers from the small market town of Koregaon, to which it is linked by a bus service. Satara, the chief town of the district of the same name, is thirty kilometers distant.

Population and Land

The population rate of growth exceeds even the high average of Maharashtra: the number of inhabitants increased from 907 in 1951 to 1,173 ten years later, an increase of 28.2 percent for the period.[1] This is a density of 175 inhabitants per square kilometer, a relatively low figure in comparison with the swarming millions of the Ganges or Cauvery areas, but too high for the poor soil of the region. Of a total area of 672 hectares, cultivated land accounts for 606 hectares, of which 92 are irrigated and 33.6 have double cropping. Roads, paths, and the railway occupy 8 hectares, the built-up area 6.8 hectares, and area unfit for cultivation (watercourses, rocks), 49.2 hectares. In other words, a fairly high proportion of the land is unusable. Nor is all the usable land good farming land. Half the total area consists of fairly good soil, although not of the quality of the alluvial plains. But 232 hectares are mediocre soil, and 96.8 hectares are extremely poor soil, on slopes furrowed by erosion or gently sloping plateaus which bear only sparse crops. Furthermore, if there is insufficient rain, some 40 to 70 hectares cannot be cultivated at all.[2]

How is the land divided? It is not possible to be as precise as one would wish from the data given in the censuses and land records or

---

[1] The high rate of increase is apparently due to lower infant mortality, which is noticeably less than in Khandoï, though for reasons that are not clear; social and economic conditions and sanitation do not seem to be vastly superior.

[2] In many regions of Maharashtra the soil is even poorer than it is in Eksal.

from the study of Eksal that was made by the Koregaon block in 1959. For each land holding, the quality of the soil, which is far less homogeneous than in the villages we have studied heretofore, would have to be taken into consideration.

The 606 cultivated hectares (with the qualifications just made) are divided into nearly 200 holdings. To have enough to live on as well as some savings, about 0.8 irrigated hectare and three nonirrigated hectares are necessary. One-fifth of the landowning families are above this level, occupying about 160 hectares. At the other extreme, between seventy and eighty families live at barely subsistence level, occupying between them less than 100 hectares. Slightly more than 300 hectares are shared between eighty and ninety farmers. The census of 1951 showed twenty-one landless agricultural workers and their dependents, and more than 800 landowners (and their dependents), the rest being artisans, servants, petty traders, and so on. This is a fairly accurate reflection of the situation; men without any land are rare in Eksal.

The Marathas [3] are the dominant caste, comprising about 80 percent of the population; because of their socioeconomic level and past history they can be likened to the Kshatriya group. The Marathas saw their star in the ascendancy in the second half of the seventeenth century at the time when Sivaji's soldiers from the mountains swept down on the massive Mogul armies. Until they submitted to the British at the beginning of the nineteenth century, their military and political role was one of great influence in the Deccan and even in the Delhi area. They are a martial people, who recall the Jats; they do not mind working on the land and in addition they supply military contingents of a high standard.

There is only one important Brahmin landowner. Most of the Harijans are Mahars, a poor group with very little land, but of a quite different stamp from the Chamars of the Ganges basin. There are also some forty people called Nandiwalas. The Nandiwalas were nomads for centuries until they finally settled on some land given to them by the village. Artisans, potters, and merchants, they speak Telugu (the principal language of Andhra). They live more or less on the fringes of Eksal. Finally, there are about fifty Muslims, most of them landowners.

Land Tenure

Before Independence, a large part of what was then Maharashtra had the *rayatwari* system, as in Kila Ulur, under which the state levied the

[3] By this term I denote the caste; the word Marathi can indicate both the language and a person who comes from Maharashtra.

tax direct on the farmer. The state was theoretically the owner, but the farmer did in fact have certain rights in respect of his property. The system was a more healthy one than the zamindari system, but it was complicated by the proliferation of contracts for letting, subletting, and sharecropping. In 1948 the Bombay Tenancy and Agricultural Lands Act was passed as a means of protecting tenants and sharecroppers while at the same time giving them an opportunity to obtain property rights over the land they cultivated. Several amendments strengthened the provisions of the Act without, however, eliminating all the abuses. As in Madras, the trouble is not with the law, but with the long-entrenched injustices which custom still tolerates in violation of the law. One wonders, among other things, how well an amendment that gives the sharecropper five-sixths of the gross product is being observed when he used to receive only half.

The acuteness of this problem varies. In the districts of Thana, Kolaba, and Kolhapur, 45 to 50 percent of the land is cultivated by tenants, whereas in Sholapur and Khandesh, for example, the percentage drops to 17–22 percent. In Satara it is even lower—less than 15 percent.[4] In Eksal sharecropping is of little importance. It is practiced only on a few small pieces of land owned by a man who works in Bombay.

The Agricultural Calendar and the Harvests

The monsoon proper does not arrive until the second half of June, but the early rains that come at the end of May or in early June allow work to commence on preparing the *kharif,* which is by far the most important harvest. Irrigation is too limited to allow a large *rabi.* The peasants plough the soil once or twice, then level it and make it friable with a blade *(kulan)* drawn by oxen. This operation is repeated four times before the sowing, which is done in June or July. The month of August is taken up with hoeing and weeding. The harvests and the preparation of the *rabi* take place from the end of September to November. During December and January the sugar cane, which has a growing period of eleven to thirteen months, is cut and planted. The harvesting of the *rabi* crops is done about March, and this is followed in April and May by vegetables and fruits.

The land records reveal strikingly that the *kharif* area has tended to increase and the *rabi* to decrease. In the 1952/53 season, there were 400 hectares of *kharif* and 170 of *rabi;* eleven years later, in 1963/64, there were 500 hectares of *kharif* and 70 of *rabi.* The decrease of the *rabi* has

[4] See V. M. Dandekar and G. J. Khudanpur, *Working of Bombay Tenancy Act 1948* (Poona, 1957), pp. 28, 189.

been mainly due to a reduction in *jowar,* one of the two chief food grains of the region; but there has been only a slight increase in *jowar* in *kharif.* The increase of *kharif* area results from the expansion of other crops, including one—grapes—that is indeed an innovation.

Jowar and *bajra,* the principle food grains, occupy more than half the land for the two harvests, *jowar* being sown in both seasons, *bajra* in *kharif* only. Yields vary greatly, according to the soil. Between 330 and 460 kg/ha is usual for *jowar,* but *bajra* seldom exceeds 270 kg/ha. (State averages in 1955/56 were 380 and 230 kg/ha, respectively.) [5] Not enough is grown to feed the village. Fortunately, however, the losses can be offset by other, richer crops.

One of these is sugar cane, a traditional crop for the region but grown on a greater scale in the last ten to fifteen years. From 3 hectares in 1952/53, it increased to 11.2 hectares in 1963/64. Whereas formerly the yields scarcely exceeded domestic requirements, today the crop is in part a commercial one, and efforts are being made to expand. The peasants use specially selected plants, make the *gur* on the spot, and sell part of it. As at Khandoï, there is a first harvest and then a ratoon crop. The sugar cane is well tended and is always grown on irrigated land. Good farmers irrigate three or four times a month; they spread manure, nitrogen and phosphate fertilizers, and groundnut cakes. The result is a yield averaging 6,500 kg/ha of *gur,*[6] which can be sold at 70–80 rupees per 100 kilos at harvest time or later on at somewhere between 90 and 115 rupees.

Groundnuts today occupy 25 percent more space than in 1952–1953. Improved seed has given encouraging results. The groundnuts are sold unshelled at 60 rupees per 100 kilos after the harvest, and for 85–90 rupees six months later. The cultivation of potatoes, chilies, and vegetables has also increased and made available other sources of ready money. The area given over to potatoes has risen from 5.3 to 31.2 hectares. The yield is 6,000 kg/ha, sold at 10–24 rupees for 37 kilos. Chilies bring in 700 rupees net per hectare.

To these traditional crops which have been improved has been added a new one—grapes, which occupy 2.5 hectares. Fresh grapes are sold at Koregaon or Satara, and go from there to Bombay. The net profit is considerable because they bring in approximately 12,000 rupees per hectare.

Manure and chemical fertilizers are used for all these crops, which are grown principally by farmers owning five to ten hectares; chemical

---

[5] Arakeri *et al, Soil Management in India,* pp. 330, 336.
[6] The 1955/56 average for the state of Bombay was 6,400 kg/ha; see *ibid.,* p. 358.

fertilizers have been used particularly since the creation of the Koregaon block in 1957.

Irrigation

There is only one part of the good land in Eksal that is easily irrigated.
This is an area lying at the bottom of a broad and undulating valley
that stretches along at the foot of a hill immediately below a sloping
plateau where the soil is of mediocre quality. Two or three small dams
(*bandhara*) deflect the water from the watercourse during the rainy
season and allow several hectares to be irrigated, although the flow has
hitherto been very limited.

The irrigation methods bringing in the greatest profit are the wells.
The traditional method recalls the *mot* of Nahiyan, but is more
efficient. There is the same pulling by oxen, but the leather water
scoop has been replaced by a metal pail with a movable base which
opens when it goes into the water and closes when the container is full.
The pail, pulled by the oxen on the curb of the well, empties automatically into the channel. Only one pair of oxen and one man are needed
to irrigate 0.4 hectare in two or three days. Each well supplies an area
of one or two hectares. There are twenty-seven masonry wells and
seventeen without an inner lining.

The contours of the landscape make well construction more difficult
and costly than in the alluvial plains. Not only is the subsoil water at a
considerable depth, of eight to ten meters, but, more important, one
strikes rock fairly soon. It takes twenty-five men at least six weeks,
sometimes three months, to dig a well seven meters in diameter and ten
meters deep. This brings the cost of a well to a high sum. Labor
amounts to 1,500–3,000 rupees (two rupees per man per day), and to
this must be added the cost of cement (about 1,100 rupees) and the
wages of the masons. Two masons are needed; they are paid six rupees
a day and work for several weeks.

During the last ten years there has been a tendency to replace the
mot with a diesel pump adjacent to the well. Such a pump costs 3,000
rupees, and daily fuel oil and maintenance come to six or seven
rupees. At present, there are ten of these wells, each irrigating 1.2
hectares in a day.

Because of the scarcity of the subsoil water, there is a limit to the
expansion of irrigation. Until March, the pumps can operate for eight
to ten hours a day, but after that until the rainy season—that is,
during the hottest time—water is so scarce that the pumps can operate
only two hours a day. When I arrived in Eksal at the beginning of

June, the sugar cane was beginning to turn yellow and some of the vegetables were withering. Several wells of the *mot* type are quite dry from February–March onward.

Erosion

The plateau lying to the west of the village of Eksal is severely eroded. Although the slope is slight, the topsoil is easily washed away in violent rainstorms, so that in many places bare rock is exposed.[7] In an effort to combat the steady erosion, some peasants have erected bunds a meter high. These gradually give way, and every ten years they must be remade. For the system to be really effective, there should be a bund every thirty meters or so.

Different Standards of Living

Ramachandra Ganapati Bhosle (a Maratha)[8] provides an example of remarkable success. Starting with only 0.4 hectare, he is now the most important landowner in Eksal, with fifteen hectares. He is sixty years old and keeps a close watch on his crops. Two of his sons who are married help him; the other four sons are either at school or at the University of Poona. His four daughters are married. Almost one-third of his land is irrigated by three wells, each of these being provided with a diesel pump. Ramachandra grows the usual crops of the region. In *kharif* (none irrigated) he has *jowar*, 1.6 hectares; fodder, 3.2 hectares; and *bajra*, 1.6 hectares. In *rabi* (irrigated) he has 1.6 hectares of *jowar*. He also has 1.6 hectares in groundnuts. But because of his irrigation system, he can also grow some crops that yield a high profit: 1.6 hectares of sugar cane, 2 hectares of grapes (a crop which he introduced to Eksal), 1.6 hectares of vegetables, 1.2 hectares of chilies, and 0.4 hectare of potatoes.

Most of the time Ramachandra employs thirty agricultural workers, such as landless peasants or very small proprietors, to whom he pays two rupees a day each. He has three pairs of oxen, and he is the owner of the village's power-driven grain mill. He even has an automobile. It is twenty-five years old, but it enables him to deliver his produce to Satara.

---

[7] Erosion is caused more by the violence of the rain than by the amount. In the region, this washing away can erode 120 to 250 tons of soil per hectare in one year. See *A Manual of Soil Conservation* (Department of Agriculture, Poona, 1956).

[8] Bhosle is the name of a Maratha subcaste. Where there is no indication to the contrary, the other peasants in Eksal belong also to this group.

This dynamic man has managed to break the vicious circle of misery and want, enlarging his holding little by little by hard work, methodically extending irrigation on small patches of good land.

Hanumant Genu Bhosle owns 3.6 hectares with his brother. They are both married, and the two families total thirteen persons. They manage to make ends meet thanks to one-third of their land being irrigated, which makes it possible to grow sugar cane and bananas in addition to the usual crops. Hanumant has also recently added 0.1 hectare of grapes. For the rest, he grows 2 hectares of *jowar* for *kharif* and 0.6 for *rabi,* as well as 0.4 of groundnuts. The family just manages to cover its cereal needs from its own produce and buys only 40–80 kilos of rice each year.

Livestock consists of three oxen, two cows (each producing 1.5 liters of milk a day), one female buffalo (one liter a day), and two small buffaloes. Only the children drink milk regularly. Near the stable I also saw two chickens.

Hanumant's standard of living is slightly improving. He and his family are better fed now than they used to be. They have three meals a day, including *chapatis* made of *jowar,* some vegetables, and, once a month, some meat. Hanumant has no debts.

For Hanumant the breakthrough to a better existence came about in the same way as it did for Ramachandra. Fifteen years ago, Hanumant only produced sugar cane for his own domestic purposes. Today he has improved his yields thanks to better irrigation and chemical fertilizers. After this first step forward, he made a second when he planted some grapes.

Shivram Ramachandra Bhosle lives with his wife, his four young children, his daughter-in-law, and her baby. His land covers 2.4 hectares, of which 0.6 hectare is irrigated a little. He can hardly grow anything for the *rabi* because the water supply of the wells is insufficient. He grows mainly *jowar* and *bajra,* and a few groundnuts. This is not enough cereal to feed his family, and so he has to buy approximately 400 kilos of *jowar* every year and 40 kilos of rice, at a total cost of 330 rupees.

He has no oxen of his own, and hires some from a friend for 100 rupees a year; he has neither buffaloes nor cows, but he has two goats which yield together half a liter of milk a day. Shivram borrowed 1,400 rupees, interest-free, from friends for the marriages of a daughter and a son, and 900 rupees from the block for a well.

Despite these liabilities and the limited chance for maneuver, Shivram does manage to make ends meet. Even if he has not been able to improve his crops, he has taken advantage of another outlet that is popular in the area and has put his eldest son to work in a spinning mill in Bombay. Out of a monthly salary of 125 rupees, the son saves 300 rupees in a year to send to his father. Shivram's second son (not yet married) is a soldier who can put by 400 rupees a year out of his monthly pay of 60 rupees.

Govin Pandurang Sawan is a Harijan (Mahar) who lives with his wife and four young children. He has 0.8 hectare, part of which is good irrigated land. He grows more than half his crops for the *kharif* (*jowar* and groundnuts) and grows a little wheat for the *rabi,* thanks to a well. His total cereal yield, 400 kilos, is only a third of his needs and he has to buy more than 800 kilos a year.

To make ends meet, Govin works eight months of the year for Ramachandra Ganapati; this brings him 500 rupees (two rupees a day). Furthermore, he is in the process of finding another source of revenue; following his employer's example, he has planted 0.1 hectare in grapes.

Govin has not quite extricated himself from his state of precarious existence, but he is close to doing so. He already owns one bullock, a heifer, two chickens, and a goat. His family eats twice a day: *jowar,* some vegetables, meat once a month, and occasionally an egg. The goat's milk is kept for the children. He borrowed 250 rupees from the cooperative seven years ago to dig his well.

Calm and intelligent, Govin is one further example of a man—this time at the foot of the social ladder—who does not need to be prodded toward making progress. Moreover, the Mahars form a community noted for its energy.

Another Mahar, Maruti Aba, has had less success. He lives with his wife and two young children on 0.6 hectare, but he lets his land for 40 rupees a year to a farmer owning 2.8 hectares. He earns 50 rupees a month as a roadmender. He just about manages to make ends meet, but his standard of living remains stationary.

The only important Brahmin in the village owns ten hectares, half of which is on the slopes of the plateau. He ought to build anti-erosion bunds as his neighbor Jaganath Dada Bhosle, a Maratha, has done, in order to check the washing-away of the soil and to raise the level of the subsoil water.[9] The well on his land would not dry up so quickly and he could grow a *rabi* on at least two hectares. This is exactly what Jaganath has been able to do. But the Brahmin leaves his land to be looked after by sharecroppers, without bothering to push production.

[9] This is a very important aspect of the struggle against erosion. The subsoil water tends to rise, as experiments made in several districts, including Coimbatore (Madras), have shown.

In spite of more or less hostile natural conditions, a good number of the peasants in Eksal are making progress and have found out how to make the best of their land. Their farming methods are praiseworthy, except for the way their manure is kept. In this fairly wooded region fuel is more easily found than in the great plains, so that it is possible to use most of the cattle dung from the fields for fertilizer. But the dung is piled up in crude pits, carelessly and without protection, as I found in other villages.

One characteristic of the region is employment outside the village. Out of a total 200 families, 125 men have found work outside, four-fifths in Bombay or Poona in industry, the others in the army. Their savings allow their families to live, even if they have no land. This outside employment, certainly more common here than in many other regions of India, compensates for the poorness of the soil. It is characteristic of Satara and of other districts of Maharashtra.

Indebtedness

My inquiry into indebtedness covered twelve farmers. Ten were in debt for a total sum of 22,250 rupees, of which 11,850 rupees had been provided by the Eksal cooperative society or the Co-operative and Mortgage Bank (mortgage credit) and 10,400 rupees by private individuals. A large part of the loans for production is destined for construction of wells and purchase of chemical fertilizers. Marriages are responsible for most of the debts owed to private individuals. They seem to spend more money on marriages than in Kila Ulur. One Maratha who owned only two hectares spent 1,500 rupees on his daughter's marriage.

Private credit is obtained from friends, often interest-free, or from third parties who take a piece of land as security, the produce from the land taking the place of interest. In general, 0.2 hectare of average land is worth 500 rupees of credit.

The Panchayat

As at Kila Ulur, the panchayat is in existence and working.[10] Meetings are held every one or two months. Our Brahmin, the first *sarpanch* (president), was replaced in 1961 when the village elected Ramachandra, whose strong personality has had quite an influence on public affairs.

[10] Thanks to an interpreter, I was able to analyze the minutes (*Masik Panchayat Tarau Pustak*).

The panchayat has improved the roads, some of which are paved with bricks; and a stream which had caused flooding has been canalized. Several oil street lamps have been installed to light the roads. Drinking-water wells have been improved. Since 1960 there has been more method in the panchayat activities. At this time the Third Five-Year Plan was being prepared. Measures envisaged to stimulate "development from below" have affected a village like Eksal: on August 6, 1960, the plenary session of adults (gaon sabha) adopted the plan proposed by the panchayat:

First year: construction of a *samaj mandir* (a building to serve as a public meetinghouse and library).

Second year: purchase of sprayers to fight malaria and protect the crops.

Third year: construction of a panchayat office and road repairs.

Fourth year: purchase by the panchayat of an iron plough (130 rupees) which would be hired out to the peasants.

Fifth year: completion of work on the school and construction of latrines.

By June, 1964, the plan had been partly realized: sprayers had been purchased, the panchayat office built,[11] roads repaired, and the schoolhouse almost finished. The *samaj mandir* and the latrines were still outstanding.

The panchayat draws its revenue from local taxes (on houses and business), from fines that it imposes, from its share of the land revenue (see chap. 23), from grants from the block, and from local voluntary contributions.

With the arrival of a new *talathi* in 1963, to be in charge of the land records (and secretary of the panchayat and gram sewak), the accumulated backlog of uncollected local taxes could be dealt with. In 1963/64, he collected 1,096 rupees, of which 450 were due for the current year and 646 were arrears.

By way of example, let me quote the budget of 1963/64: in credit there was the surplus left from the previous budget, that is, 1,416 rupees, plus 450 rupees of local tax on houses, 1,150 land tax (levied by the state and handed over to the village), a gift of 500 rupees for the schoolhouse, and several small items, making a total of 3,696 rupees. Expenditure was estimated at 2,810 rupees. I quote a few examples: office equipment and peon wages, 180 rupees; oil for street lighting, 210 rupees; drugs to be distributed, 50 rupees; purchase of a

[11] Cost 3,378 rupees, half paid by the block, the remainder by voluntary contributions.

radio set, 500 rupees; expenditure for building the school, 1,000 rupees.

In liaison with the panchayat, the *talathi* had been preparing since 1962 an annual plan for the village's requirements in seeds, fertilizers, agricultural tools, and so on. This voluminous document [12] has no fewer than sixteen separate columns.

The School

The Eksal primary school, established in 1924, has provided free compulsory education since 1956. The number of children actually attending school rose from 78 boys and 25 girls in 1956 to 181 and 74 in 1960 and 200 and 105 in June, 1964. Children start school at the age of six and continue through seven classes. Attendance is not, perhaps, very regular. According to my study of the teachers' daily attendance records, taking the random days of January 9 and 15 and June 18, 1964, a fourth of the children were absent. Variations were slight among the three days, and the teachers confirmed that a figure of this order was common in the region. [13]

The annual examinations (April, 1964) gave the following results for the first six classes: pupils enrolled, 281; present at examination, 241; passed examination, 219. The syllabus contains the usual primary school subjects. From the fifth form on they have an hour of English and an hour of Hindi every week. The staff consists of a headmaster and seven teachers. The teaching level is mediocre. Children in the higher classes whom I interviewed in Hindi were lively, but their knowledge was often slight.

The cost of compulsory primary education is high. A schoolhouse had to be constructed (19,000 rupees), because the temple where school had formerly been held was too small, as were the annex buildings. Before 1956 one headmaster and two teachers sufficed. The five newcomers represent a total annual expenditure on salaries of 7,200 rupees.

Choice of Priorities and the Panchayat

The peasants have taken the right road toward improving their crops and have in addition benefited from a more generous cooperative

[12] "Gram Panchayat Eksal Yethil Sheti Utpadan Arakha."

[13] In the case of unexplained or unjustified absence, the headmaster writes a letter to the parents reminding them that primary education is obligatory. If this brings no result, as frequently happens, the headmaster has no power to impose a penalty.

credit than in Uttar Pradesh (cf. chap. 23). The Eksal cooperative society, which was created in 1954, has grown steadily, from 88 members in 1959 to 169 in 1964; [14] this includes the great majority of landowners. A special program for pumps has been launched in the district, and in the Eksal society twenty members have applied for credit, with more certain to follow.

In spite of the peasants' determination and the potential progress attainable, agricultural expansion is severely limited by the nature of the soil and the climate: absolutely constant irrigation on low land will always remain difficult. As for the plateau, general anti-erosion measures would increase its worth, though they could never bring it the fertility of really good land.

The safety valves which Bombay, the army, and on occasion the police force represent are very likely not going to open any wider; indeed, the people of Eksal will be able to count themselves fortunate if the safety valves do not tend to close up. Under these conditions an increase in production is indisputably essential yet at the same time limited in its scope. It would therefore seem correct to observe a strict sense of priorities. In this connection, it is worth mentioning that the Eksal panchayat, though functioning in a praiseworthy manner, is not oriented toward economic growth. Problems of education and hygiene and works of social interest receive more attention than irrigation, fertilizers, and soil conservation. The effort that was to be made in carrying out a village plan has not been very encouraging. At Eksal, the work has not even kept up to date on paper, let alone in fact.

Most importantly, the village ought to launch a determined effort to protect all the high land by anti-erosion bunds. No one seems to have thought of doing this because it is difficult to reconcile the often opposing interests of the peasants, nor are the villagers really aware of the necessity for priority in agriculture.

The education program should be viewed in its local context; by postponing for, say, at least five years, the expansion that was begun in 1956, they could have saved the 19,000 rupees spent on the schoolhouse and the 36,000 rupees spent on the new teachers' salaries. In my view it would seem better to have devoted those 55,000 rupees to productive aims, mainly irrigation and the fight against erosion, leaving primary education to be made general at some future date.

One last fact—a positive one—and this is that the administrative organization has been properly set up. The *talathi* of Eksal combines the jobs of land registrar and secretary of the panchayat and the

---

[14] Unfortunately the cooperative was faced with a particularly awkward situation in that the secretary had vanished with part of the money.

gram sewak. This permanent organization seems preferable to the way things are done in Uttar Pradesh.

In order to draw up a more careful analysis of the repercussions of the panchayats on development, I made brief visits to other villages.

Tadwale, South Koregaon

The village of Tadwale is in the same block as Eksal. It has a population of 2,500, including 190 men who work outside. The cultivated area is 800 hectares, 65 of which are irrigated by wells or by diverting the river (bandhara).

The panchayat has been functioning since 1952, with the same president, a man who fought with the Indian army in the difficult Burma campaign against the Japanese and who now owns sixteen hectares of land, two of them irrigated. He is an example of an enterprising Maratha par excellence, and his influence has been decisive in keeping the village together. His panchayat has approximately 6,000 rupees at its disposal in annual revenue. In addition to the 20 percent surtax on the land tax, it has voted an additional surtax which gives it the right to a matching grant.

In 1954 a system of wide, clean roads was laid out, supplied with lined channels for discharging water and waste matter. Then a samaj mandir was built at a cost of 8,000 rupees, half of which came from a grant from the block, the remainder from voluntary contributions. It consisted of a room for meetings and two rooms for the panchayat office. After this a school costing 21,000 rupees was built and finally a house for the panchayat, the samaj mandir having proved inadequate. The new building for the panchayat cost 27,500 rupees, half of this sum coming from the panchayat, the remainder from grants made by the zila parishad. The luxury of the building is somewhat astonishing. It has two stories, with floors of fine stone slabs and walls of handsome polished tiles; there is a bathroom with shower and WC. Eventually the new building will house a welfare center along with the panchayat offices.

Other works have been more productive. Village teams are improving the track that leads to Koregaon and have already completed three kilometers. In September, 1963, in the context of a program to which I shall refer again later, the panchayat decided to build a bandhara. This was to consist of a dike 33 meters long by 2 meters wide and 3 meters deep to dam the village's watercourse. Two sluices were to be fitted for drainage. The purpose was to retain the water during the rainy season and to irrigate twenty hectares during the rabi.

I visited the site in June, 1964. The embankment was three-quarters finished, but the sluices had not been fitted. Because of lack of cement the work had stopped and would not be completed before the monsoon, which was imminent. Normally an undertaking of this nature can be completed in two or three months. This will in fact have taken more than a year, probably not even in time for the 1964–1965 *rabi*. Three-quarters of the financing of the project (total cost, 10,000 rupees) was assured by interested parties, owners of fields, and so on (long-term credit, ten years at 4.5 percent) and the remaining quarter by a state grant.

Two lessons are implicit in the work of this panchayat, which on the whole is fairly efficient in comparison with others: (1) The most urgent tasks are carried out last instead of first. (2) The delay in the delivery of cement for the *bandhara* prevented twenty hectares of good land from being utilized. Slightly more than a third of the cement used for the panchayat house would have sufficed for the *bandhara*.

Lhasurne

Lhasurne is another village in the Koregaon block. Out of 1,975 inhabitants, 200 men work in Bombay or Satara or are in the army. The cultivated area is 800 hectares, of which 160 are irrigated. The panchayat, which was created in 1952, is presided over by a farmer owning twenty hectares, a man of the same enterprising character as the *sarpanch* of Tadwale.

Here the panchayat has begun with the essential thing, a *bandhara* on the river Vasua five kilometers outside the village, which will irrigate 140 hectares at Lhasurne. This important work had to have the support of the Department of Public Works, which is in charge of irrigation. The panchayat agreed with the department that the 150 growers concerned would undertake to dig the canal if the department built the dam. By the end of 1957 the dam was completed, a substantial delay for a fifty-meter-long wall. Meanwhile the peasants had begun to dig the canal but had found the work far more arduous than had been anticipated. One meter below the surface they encountered laterite and rock. At the end of 1957 the panchayat asked the department for help. There were three more years of discussion, which resulted in an agreement that the village would undertake two kilometers and the department three. In 1961, the peasants had at last begun to obtain a little water to irrigate 40 hectares, but the panchayat did not foresee the full completion of the project and irrigation of 140 hectares until the 1964–1965 *rabi*.

The cost of these operations was 100,000 rupees, of which 28,000 were for the dam, the rest for the canals. The Department of Public Works paid for the dam and for two-thirds of the canal, and the villagers paid the rest. Meanwhile the panchayat had begun to build a school (27,000 rupees). It has not yet considered a building for the panchayat, being content to hire a house for 45 rupees a month.

Two remarks: the panchayat tackled a task which was beyond its own powers; as for the Department of Public Works, one can only point out its slowness. This example shows at the same time the limitations of "development from below" and the need for better coordination between the administration and the village panchayat.

Saswad

The village of Saswad is in the Phaltan block, which even under normal conditions is classified as a "scarcity area." The soil, of an exceptionally poor quality, is quite exhausted, but the 2,620 inhabitants have 2,000 more or less cultivated hectares, of which 180 are irrigated.

Here also the panchayat dates from 1952. It meets regularly—the minutes show meetings nearly every month—and it completed as its first project a schoolhouse costing 16,000 rupees. The next project was a system of water supply, including wells with pumps and distribution of the water by metal pipes and taps at several points in the village. The installation cost 25,000 rupees, of which half came from Saswad and the other half from the zila parishad.[15]

This expenditure was certainly no luxury. Till then, the water had often been so bad that it weakened the peasants physically and demoralized them mentally. The panchayat has renovated the access road to the village, and electricity was introduced in April, 1964. There are twenty street lamps, and "well-to-do" people have electricity in their houses. Thirty-five peasants have requested credit for the purchase of electric pumps.

[15] A special effort in this direction has been made in Maharashtra, particularly at Satara.

23

THE SATARA DISTRICT

The district of Satara [1] is divided into eleven *taluks,* each one consisting of an enlarged block of development. The whole area covers 10,344 square kilometers, a higher figure than in districts previously visited. Between 1951 and 1961 the population increased by 21 percent. This is slightly lower than the average rate for the state, probably because of emigration from the district. The density per square kilometer amounts to 140 inhabitants, and the total population is 1,400,000. [2]

The area does not constitute a homogeneous whole; the western zone with the eastern slopes of the Ghats behind it has a yearly rainfall of 3,200 mm., which means that rice can be grown there. The central area (Eksal), with a rainfall of 650 mm., is mainly a *jowar*-growing area. The eastern part is even drier: barely more than 450 mm. of rain. The only possible crop is *bajra,* and even this is grown with great difficulty, since the periods of drought are often severe. [3]

Before the Zila Parishad Act

Because the soil in several areas of the district is of very poor quality, there is a limit to the expansion of cultivated land. On the other hand, irrigation and its corollary, double cropping, are increasing:

	1955/56	1960/61
Unirrigated area	616,000 ha.	602,000 ha.
Irrigated area	57,000	70,800
Total area cultivated	673,000 ha.	672,800 ha.
Area under double cropping	49,000 ha.	77,000 ha.

Irrigated land represents 11 percent of the total area cultivated, and the land under double cropping is 12 percent. Here, as elsewhere, there

[1] Given the new administrative structure of Maharashtra, it seems more logical to deal with the district first before taking the Koregaon block.

[2] *Census of India, 1961,* pp. 32–33.

[3] For this paragraph, see Satara Zila Parishad, *Satara Agricultural Programme, 1963–64,* p. 1.

are several methods of irrigation. State canals and dams account for 25,200 hectares, private canals for 16,100 hectares, and private wells for 30,800 hectares. The limited role of irrigation by the Public Works Department will be noted.

In 1960/61, the principal food grains were *jowar* (202,000 ha.), *bajra* (150,000 ha.), and pulses (48,000 ha.). Cultivation of rice did not exceed 25,000 hectares, and of wheat, 13,000. Cash crops were groundnuts (68,000 ha.), sugar cane (9,600 ha.), and—of limited importance—vegetables, including potatoes (8,000 ha.).[4]

Along with irrigation, the cooperative system was being extended, and this stimulated the consumption of chemical fertilizers; 627 tons of nitrogen fertilizers in 1955/56, and 2,009 tons in 1960/61.[5]

Before the introduction of the zila parishad, the collector who was head of the district would delegate some of his powers to two assistants; one was the district project officer, who was concerned with development and whose duties were similar to those of the district planning officer in Uttar Pradesh, and the other was responsible for the village panchayats. Both of them belonged to the state service, not to the Indian Administrative Service.[6]

The Organization of the Zila Parishad

The zila parishad was set up in May, 1962. It was composed of sixty-three members, fifty-four of whom were elected by universal suffrage. The first meeting took place on August 12, 1962; three further meetings were held that year, and five more in 1963.

Recognizing the importance of its duties, the zila parishad wisely divided itself into several committees, which can meet as frequently as necessary in order to administer day-to-day affairs (such as standing committees, finance, agriculture, education, health, public works, and cooperatives). The committee for agriculture (ten members) was constituted on September 11, 1962. According to the minutes, it met regularly once a month. The president and vice-president are elected by all the members of the zila parishad; the former is also president of the standing committee, and the latter is president of two of the other committees. The four other committees are presided over by two members elected by the zila parishad. The president of the zila parishad receives a salary of 500 rupees a month, and the three committee

[4] For all these figures, see Satara Zila Parishad, *Master Note on Progress Report, 1963–64.*

[5] *Note on the Agricultural Activities in Satara District from 1955–56 to 1961–62,* p. 58.

[6] Satara Zila Parishad, *Annual Administration Report, 1962–63,* p. 33.

presidents receive 300. They are entitled to free accommodation and other benefits which I shall mention later. They have an office at their disposal in Satara.

Although the members of the zila parishad look after the general administration, it is the chief executive officer (C.E.O.) who is responsible for seeing that they are carried out efficiently. The C.E.O. is assisted in this work by a large staff, each of whom deals with different services.

To try to gain some idea of the activities of the zila parishad, let us take a look at its accounts for the 1963/64 financial year:

Members' fees, allowances, and other perquisites	236,208 rs.
Administrative staff's salaries and other expenses	1,391,187
Education, teaching staff's salaries, scholarships	11,718,104
Health (hospitals, staff, public hygiene)	681,417
Agriculture (loans, subsidies, agricultural competitions)	366,299
Animal husbandry and poultry	198,770
Community development	1,640,100
Public works (district roads, bridges)	3,016,736

With a few other minor items, the total comes to 21.6 million, which covers running expenses and investments of a more permanent nature. Agricultural credit is not included in these figures.

Assets amount to 21.8 million rupees. The basic land tax (which has not been revaluated since the 1920's), brings in 2.5 million rupees, to which are added two surtaxes.[7] The first, averaging 19 percent, was voted by the village panchayats after the 1958 Act; the second, of 40 percent, was adopted by the zila parishad, making a total of 4 million. Irrigation dues have been raised by 19 percent, bringing in payments amounting to 1.2 million. Taxes on houses and businesses, fines, secondary school entrance fees, and certain hospital fees paid by patients represent altogether a total of some 100,000 rupees. About 15 million rupees, in the form of state subsidies, complete the budget. Part of these funds are remitted to the development blocks.

The Agricultural Development Program

The production of food grains was estimated at 296,400 tons in 1960/61, of which 239,000 tons were in *jowar* and *bajra*. Satara antici-

[7] The Land Revenue Administration, which is the responsibility of the collector, levies tax and surtaxes.

pated a jump of 31 percent, that is, an increase of 92,000 tons in five years. A scale similar to that of U.P. is used. State irrigation was due to progress by 4,800 hectares, producing an additional 4,000 tons, and private irrigation by 40,000 hectares, or 28,000 tons. Chemical fertilizers with deliveries of 9,000 tons in 1965/66 were due to produce 15,000 additional tons of cereals and pulses, and improved seeds 20,800 tons. Soil conservation would ensure 10,000 tons and dry farming 11,000 tons. Finally, there were the minor improvements: compost, green manure, farm machinery, and the beginning of the intensive program.[8]

How did the plan look at the end of the third year? The zila parishad saw itself entrusted with the construction and administration of works irrigating less than 100 hectares (particularly *bandharas*), which until then had been dealt with by the Department of Public Works. This department retained the administration of large and medium projects. At the beginning of the third plan ten small *bandharas* were under construction and six were about to be put in hand, making a total irrigated area of 690 hectares. Six were completed in the first two years of the plan and none was constructed in 1963/64. They should all have been finished by 1964/65. The main cause of the delay was lack of cement. Later on, it often happened that the use of the *bandharas* was deferred because the field channels had not been finished (see chap. 22 and *Agricultural Programme 1963–64, List No. 4*).

The zila parishad administration studied eighty-six new projects, of which only thirty proved to be workable under the prevailing natural conditions.

The progress of private irrigation was as follows:

	1961–1966 Targets	1961–1964 Results
New wells	5,000	1,365
Pumping sets	5,000	977

(The targets were increased in 1964. At first they were estimated at 3,000 units under each heading.) For the irrigation works, these were the pertinent data:

Cost of sinking one well	2,500–5,000 rs.
Cost of an oil engine	3,000–3,500 rs.
Cost of an electric engine	2,000 rs.
Command area for one pump	2 to 3 ha.

A crash program was launched in January, 1963, and, thanks to the collaboration established between the C.E.O. and the Land Develop-

[8] Satara Zila Parishad, *Annual Administration Report, 1963–64.*

ment Bank, credit procedure was simplified. In one month nearly 10 million rupees were advanced to the peasants for the sinking of 1,746 wells and the purchase of 632 pumps, but complete utilization of these funds was unfortunately delayed because of lack of cement and, in some cases, lack of electricity.

Motivated by the intensive program (as in Tanjore), the authorities made a special effort in areas where the rainfall was heavy and/or where irrigation was already well advanced. Out of the 40,000 hectares forecast for 1961–1964, 87 percent have so far been covered; 10,000 of these are paddy fields, 1,200 are wheat, and the rest are *jowar* and *bajra*.

The consumption of chemical fertilizers should have reached 9,000 tons by 1965/66, but the figures for the first three years are still far below this target: [9]

	1960/61	1961/62	1962/63	1963/64
Ammonium sulphate (tons)	2,009	2,473	2,060	3,745
Superphosphate (tons)	—	1,007	944	1,000

Other campaigns, such as the protection of groundnuts, were also launched. In normal times losses due to pests can amount to as much as 25 percent of the harvest, but credits and deliveries of pesticides have protected 6,400 hectares in 134 villages, increasing output by 20 percent. One campaign improved mango trees by grafting, and another intensified grape cultivation, the results of which we have already seen in Eksal.

All these operations are of undeniable benefit; they are proof of imaginative thinking and are typical of a realistic appreciation of needs and possibilities.

The Place of Education

The zila parishad's balance sheet for 1963/64 shows very clearly what an important place education occupies in the budget: it takes up a little more than half, that is, 11.7 million out of 21.6 million.

There is rather a long history behind the expansion of this sector. In 1927 the government of Bombay began to encourage the establishment of primary schools in rural areas. Twenty years later, immediately after Independence, the program of free compulsory primary education in rural areas began, and it is now affecting nearly all the villages.

[9] See *Master Note, 1963–64*, and *Agricultural Programme, 1963–64* (annexes).

	1955/56	*1963/64*
Number of schools	not available	1,481
Number of teachers	3,053	5,554
Number of pupils	149,934	240,000 (est.)

At secondary school level, education is free only for pupils whose parents earn less than 100 rupees a month, and the question of raising the limit to 150 rupees is under review. But the fees paid by the parents are too low to meet the whole of the cost of the schools. Each term the pupils pay between three and seven rupees in school fees; in addition, they spend 25 rupees a year on schoolbooks and other materials. The secondary school that I visited in Satara had 1,538 pupils, 10 percent of whom were villagers. School fees covered a little more than a third of the annual expenses, and the government provided the rest in the form of grants. (It was, as is often the case in India, a private school.)

I questioned the top class (the eleventh), which consisted of sixteen-year-olds. More often than not their knowledge proved to be rather thin: nearly half the pupils, for instance, did not know that rice was India's principal cereal crop, and more than half thought that the capture of Delhi by the Muslims took place in the eighth century (some four hundred years too early). Out of twenty-two schoolchildren, only six thought that agriculture was at this time the decisive factor in India's economy. Their standard of knowledge was similar to that of the Eksal primary school. The increased number of pupils was not matched by an improvement in the quality of the teaching; on the contrary—as many educators maintain—the standards tended to be lower.

Might it not have been wiser to have held back educational progress a little? If, between 1955 and 1964, they had limited themselves to 1,500 additional teachers instead of 2,500, they could have saved at least 1.2 million rupees a year. They could also have slowed down the rate of school construction and in that way saved cement for other uses in agriculture. It can certainly be argued that four or five badly educated children are no substitute for one or two really well educated persons. However, as we shall see in the following chapter, the problem is much more complex than it appears to be here, and it cannot be confined simply to the allocation of capital.

The Cooperative Credit

The organization of cooperative credit at district level is not the direct concern of the zila parishad, but it is linked to it in its transactions.

The Satara District Central Co-operative Bank gives financial support to the village societies by granting short-term credit, and to its branches in the *taluks* by medium-term loans. For some years now the Land Development Bank has been the mortgage bank, responsible for long-term credit, absorbing *taccavis* credit now abolished. This administrative simplification which many states still lack has had good results. Moreover, it has eliminated a good many of the abuses and malpractices to which the *talathis* and other officials in charge of the *taccavis* proceedings were subject.

The interest rate for short- and medium-term loans is 7.5 percent; the money is advanced to the peasants provided that two members of the cooperative stand security. The maximum amount of short-term credit is ten times the member's share. Short-term loans must be repaid within a period of six to eighteen months, and medium-term loans between three to five years. Part of the credit (between 35 and 50 percent) for short-term loans is granted in kind in the form of fertilizers or improved seeds.

At the beginning of the plan short-term credit rapidly increased, jumping from 12 to 18.5 million. This was apparently the limit, however, under conditions prevailing at that time, for in 1963/64 the District Co-operative Bank advanced 25.8 million, of which only 18.2 million were used. Not only had the peasants reached the limit of their capacities in the present stage of their development at least, but there were long delays in the repayment of short-term loans. The amounts outstanding increased from 14 million rupees for the 1960/61 financial year to 23 million three years later.

Long-term credit (for wells, engines, and soil conservation) is extended at varying interest rates, from 4.5 percent to 5.5 percent, depending on the sort of project for which it is granted. A quarter of the credit is converted into nonrepayable subsidies on condition that it does not exceed 500 rupees for a well and 800 rupees for a pump. It is worked out in the following way: the value of the well, or pump, is added to the land tax and multiplied by 300. Half of the total amount represents the maximum limit of credit. Certainly the ideal would have been to take the value of the land itself rather than a multiple of the tax, but the latter is already rather high, amounting to 180 until 1963. The volume of long-term credit increased from 4.8 million rupees in 1960/61 to nearly 7 million in 1963/64.

As we have already seen at Eksal, the efficiency of the primary societies is not without defects; further abuses were revealed to me in Satara. If these negative aspects are not new to us after what we have seen in Uttar Pradesh, we must also look at the improvements, which are far from common everywhere. The first important change has been the broadening of credit, with conditions that are a good deal more generous than in Uttar Pradesh. The second change—simplifying the procedure and reducing delays in obtaining credit—has been no less successful. In addition, and most importantly, there has been excellent synchronization of transactions between the services of the C.E.O. and those of the cooperatives.[10]

Soil Conservation

In Maharashtra, where soil erosion has long been a serious problem, soil conservation goes back to 1942, when the Bombay Land Improvement Scheme Act was passed. In 1958 the Act was amended to widen the powers of the Soil Conservation Department. Certain conservation projects in Eksal are undertaken within the framework of the zila parishad, but most of the activities are the responsibility of the Soil Conservation Department, which has divisions throughout the state. The Satara division covers the entire district as well as the northeast part of the adjacent district of Poona.

Operations are spread over areas of between twenty and eighty hectares where anti-erosion bunds and terraces are constructed. The program is drawn up by agreement with the landowner in question, and the department carries out the works, which are financed by the peasants with the aid of a 4.5 percent loan from the Land Development Bank, to be repaid in fifteen annual installments. The state also meets a quarter of the costs in the form of subsidies.

After a slow beginning, the program gained momentum with the third plan: the subdivisions operating in the Satara district gave me the following figures:

Area Protected	1961/62	1962/63	1963/64
By anti-erosion bunds	2,400 ha.	8,800 ha.	10,000 ha.
By terraces	—	150	600

To take an example, let us look at the village of Mandve (Khatav *taluk*), a treeless, hilly area where infrequent but hard rains year after year have washed away the soil. Of the 1,120 hectares under cultivation, 280 have now been protected from erosion. In one month an

[10] The credit statistics were given to me by the two Satara banks.

area of 80 hectares can be properly rebuilt with bunds, on which sisal is planted to hold down the soil. It takes twenty-five men one day to set up bunds over an area of 0.4 hectare, and such a project employs a total of fifty to a hundred men. After the bunds have been completed, the landowners level their own plots and are responsible for the maintenance of the bunds.

This example together with many others that I observed while touring the district confirms the upward trend shown in the statistics. But I could not help wondering if, in addition to the efforts made by the department, the panchayats could not be given more encouragement to undertake similar projects, perhaps on a smaller scale. Soil conservation needs to become a kind of obsession, and it should certainly be one of the prior concerns: on the one hand there is only a narrow margin of potential progress, given the limited scope for irrigation, and on the other hand the areas threatened continue to expand. Since conservation measures enrich the soil, preserve the humidity, and make the subsoil water rise, one cannot lay too much stress on the need for placing conservation projects at the center of agricultural strategy in areas where erosion is severe.

The Cement Problem

In every part of India I visited, I heard a chorus of complaints about the shortage of cement. The recurrence of the problem prompted me to take a close look at it as it affected Maharashtra. The shortage became acute around 1960, near the end of the Second Five-Year Plan, and it was accentuated by the state of emergency declared at the end of 1962, which brought an increase in military expenditure, armament factories, public works in border areas, and so on.

According to information given to me in Bombay, Maharashtra received scarcely more than half the cement it needed.[11] Owing to the acuteness of the shortage, priorities had to be set up, and, as I learned, one-fourth of all the cement available in the districts was reserved for irrigation. On the operational level in Satara, the situation reflected the shortage. The collector received a certain quantity, which he distributed for houses and the like, but he got less than half of what he hoped for. Of the 2,700 tons promised for 1963/64, only 1,200 were delivered. The zila parishad's quotas, similarly, were not fulfilled:

[11] The proportion received could be even less than half. With some exceptions, the state reserved the right to distribute cement produced in the private sector, but this arrangement was changed at the end of 1965.

Date	Amount of Cement Requested (tons)	Amount Committed (tons)	Amount Received (tons)
2nd term, 1963	1,444	629	486.50
3rd term, 1963	1,017	528	528
4th term, 1963	1,313	480	189
1st term, 1964	1,090	396	396
Total	4,864	2,033	1,599.50

The difference between the amount requested and the quantity granted had already become a source of difficulty, but even more worrying was the difference between the amount promised and that actually supplied. It is clear that the problem was more than just a shortage of cement, that there were defects in the distribution system also. For example, in June, the beginning of the monsoon season, Satara received a quota of cement that should have arrived several months earlier, since the rain made it impossible for it to be used between June and October.

Another disturbing factor is that those responsible for cement in the district do not seem to think in terms of reserving 25 percent for irrigation. Neither in Satara nor in the Koregaon block could I obtain any precise indication of the way in which this valuable product was allocated. Roads and buildings absorbed most of it. We shall look later at some examples of the buildings that have used large quantities of cement, including the zila parishad administrative buildings and the cooperative bank. Let me just mention here the bus stations belonging to the public transport companies, the cement shelters at bus stops in many of the villages, and the new district schools which for the period 1961–1966 came to at least fifty new buildings having a total of 352 rooms. Finally we must include the panchayat houses, ten of which the Koregaon block hopes to have in the villages, not to mention its own house which is scheduled for construction. Given these conditions, is there any wonder at the perpetual bottlenecks which impede the construction of even minor irrigation works?

Another problem is added to this shortage and lack of priorities in deciding which works should be carried out, and that is the absence of any synchronization between rural credit and the distribution of cement. Far too often when a peasant receives a loan for a well he cannot be sure of receiving at the same time the bags of cement that he needs. One solution to this state of affairs would be to allot a quota of cement to the Land Development Banks in the district, which would allow them to create a new form of tied credit (partly in cash and partly in kind). It is, I think, an experiment worth trying.

One should not overemphasize the technocratic annoyance at this constant diversion of cement to nonproductive ends. In every country in the world shortsighted political interests far too often impede any sound administration of public affairs. The ideal solution does not exist in practice; it is simply a question of trying to limit losses. This is why the question of cement, its production, importation, distribution, and apportionment, should be given priority at every level of administration from New Delhi down to the last development block.

The Zila Parishad and Development

My conversations with the president of the zila parishad, as well as conversations with various committees, my reading of the minutes of the meetings, and the observations I made at village and block level, all led to the same conclusion—that development, particularly in the field of agriculture, is not the zila parishad's main preoccupation. The members who dominate the zila parishad and set the tune are generally landowners with between ten and twenty hectares belonging often to the Maratha caste. They are successful farmers, who are attracted to district government by political considerations. Thus their primary concern is simply to maneuver affairs in such a way as to ensure their own re-election; they are far from being wholeheartedly dedicated to the improvement of agriculture.

The taste for power also develops appetites, not uncommon among officeholders, for luxuries. Not content with a salary, traveling allowance, and free accommodation provided under the Act, the presidents persuaded the zila parishad to furnish them with private automobiles, the Jeep station wagon which they originally shared in common not being elegant enough for persons in their position. These four automobiles cost 68,000 rupees and were paid for by public money. By paying a small fee of 60 rupees a month, the presidents can have free use of these automobiles. And Satara is not an exceptional case. I was given examples of at least three other districts where the same abuses had occurred.[12]

Political considerations also result in expenditures on a broader scale that are unwise, to say the least. A typical example is the use made of the surtax on the land tax and the matching grants arising therefrom. It would have been logical to invest them in projects yielding high profits, but the zila parishad did quite the opposite;

---

[12] An added point is that, although the automobiles are certainly more comfortable in the village, they are not good on the poor roads in the countryside, so when the presidents go on tour they requisition the B.D.O.'s Jeep.

hoping to please the electorate, it dispersed the funds among as many villages and works as possible. Instead of being methodical and constructing good roads which would not be destroyed each monsoon, they were tempted to make a lot of minor roads which would not last for more than one or two years.

The administration was not able to stop all this waste, but it proposed capital expenditure on a project which, though of secondary value, was at least durable—namely, a group of buildings to house all the zila parishad offices, which until then had been scattered about the town of Satara. The estimated cost was one million rupees, and it would require 2,000 tons of cement. But this project, the lesser of two evils, did not get past block level, where the members of the samitis had launched all sorts of minor projects to please the electorate. At the same time, the board of the Co-operative District Bank started construction on a building several stories high, costing 500,000 rupees, to house its own offices.

What is the behavior of the administration? Despite Maharashtra's political stability, its role is sometimes difficult, and there are differences of opinion between the zila parishad and the C.E.O. Many times a C.E.O. has been transferred in order to avoid further dissension. At the beginning of this system of administration in May, 1962, it was anticipated that the C.E.O. would remain for three or more years in the same post, but within two years, out of twenty-five of the state's rural districts, only four, including Satara, still had the same C.E.O.

The Direction of Operations

If the members of the zila parishad do not constitute a driving force so far as development is concerned, with the C.E.O. it is another matter. This man, scarcely thirty years old, has a quick and incisive mind. He knows his job thoroughly and has the ability to distinguish the essential points from those of secondary importance. In common with other civil servants, he has to cope with a heavy mass of red tape, but despite this he manages to go regularly into the field to see that projects are being carried out and to visit the blocks and villages. His relationship with the peasants is straightforward and direct. In two years he has succeeded in starting an undeniable movement in the rural areas, examples of which we have seen in agriculture and in rural credit.

This system of leadership represents distinct progress over that in Uttar Pradesh. But the personality and attributes of the C.E.O. cannot make up for every weakness. In the first place, the C.E.O. has too many tasks of minor importance such as the paperwork which takes up a good deal of his time. Second, his assistants are not all well qualified. The two senior assistants are able men, but other officials tend to have limited talent and ability. It is surprising, for example, that an important official of the Co-operative Credit Society should be unable to describe in detail the procedure necessary for obtaining a medium-term loan, or that a school director should not have a thorough knowledge of his school's teaching program.

In other words, though one cannot expect miracles from one man of strong calibre at the head of each district, as Satara well shows, much is gained from the influence of a strong personality. The C.E.O. could do even more with an organization whose responsibilities were better distributed, thus enabling him to concentrate on a few points crucial to development such as agriculture, irrigation, soil conservation, and cement distribution. I shall make no mention here of rural credit where, at the moment, liaison seems to be quite good.

The Koregaon Block

The Koregaon block,[13] to which Eksal belongs, was created in 1960. It consists of seventy-six villages with 138,838 inhabitants (1961). More than half—87,033—work on the land; 81,724 of these are cultivator-owners, 3,825 are agricultural workers and their families, and 1,484 are sharecroppers and tenants.

Coinciding with the *taluk* of the same name, the Koregaon block corresponds to two standard blocks, and therefore has a budget and a staff twice that of the ordinary block. Owing to insufficient subsidies, however, out of the estimated expenditures of 2.4 million rupees for the first five years, only 954,411 rupees had been spent after three and a half years. (Nearly 100 percent of the money received was actually spent.) The block can be rated as fair for its activities and for the results it achieves, and the B.D.O. and his colleagues perform their duties conscientiously.

The panchayat samiti is in a way comparable to the zila parishad. It meets every month to discuss the development program and to decide how to allocate funds. According to the minutes, economic questions figure prominently—as they should—in their deliberations. In the irrigation program, in 1963/64, 249 loans were granted for wells and 168 for pumps. Just how many of these works were completed during 1963/64, however, I am not certain. All too often, it seemed, the loans

[13] See *A Note on Development Activities of Panchayat Samiti Koregaon,* Apr. 30, 1964.

could not be used as planned because of lack of cement, or, occasionally, of electricity.

Chemical fertilizers have made erratic progress; after a decline in 1962/63, they made a steep rise in 1963/64. Other projects have been approved, including the establishment of new plantations of mango trees and coconut trees as well as some afforestation programs.

Credit trends are similar to those of the district. The peasants have reached the limit of their capacities, and the membership of primary societies has stayed almost constant for several years; there were 14,762 members in 1962/63, representing 77 percent of the farming population. Short-term credit reached an apparent ceiling of 1.4 million rupees a year, and the return of arrears began to make progress with the appointment of a new official with specific responsibilities for this problem.

The panchayat samiti cannot be accused of carelessness, or even inefficiency, but here, too, the general trend is not sufficiently directed toward production; this was no new phenomenon to me by the time I had reached the end of my tour. Not only did the block receive only part of the funds to which it was entitled, but it used the funds much more for social ends than for economic ones. Of the 2.4 million rupees estimated for the five years, 680,000 should have been allocated to irrigation, but in fact only one-sixth of this amount was used for this purpose. For other items the differences are rather less.

Finally, I should point out that Koregaon is distinctive in that it is one of the pilot blocks of the district, in which rural projects are being carried out with the dual purpose of stimulating the economy and restricting unemployment. For the year 1963/64 a subsidy of 200,000 rupees was utilized, 80,000 of which were for roads and 120,000 for *bandharas.*[14]

Some Final Observations

The combination of geographical factors and economic forces has endowed Maharashtra with its own special character. It has few natural resources, and, like many other parts of the Deccan, the soil is more often than not of poor quality. On the other hand, the industrial and commercial centers of Bombay and Poona have an important compensatory effect, for they absorb part of the manpower which agriculture could not support.

[14] This comes under the rural works program; see Government of India, *Third Five Year Plan,* p. 165.

Despite the undeniable progress made during the last fifteen years or so, a certain number of questions still remain unanswered.

The first is of a political nature. Even in a state that quickly regained its political stability after the creation of Gujarat in 1960, local politicians sometimes seem unable to realize what their long-term interests are, and therefore what the priorities for development should be. Certainly, the administration has better support from the government than is the case in Uttar Pradesh, but what is the answer to the transfer of twenty-one out of twenty-five C.E.O.'s in less than two years? This important link in the chain of development is still far too weak. At least five of these transfers were due to disputes between the C.E.O. and the zila parishad. Others were part of a more general weakness (to which I shall return in chap. 25) that lies in the administrative set-up. This malaise affects not only the C.E.O.'s but also other civil servants, in Maharashtra and elsewhere. One report says that "Out of 70 officers interviewed 34 had not been in their district more than a year. Ten out of these 34 had been in the district less than two months." [15] Such a turnover cannot but have shaken the smooth working of the administration.

The second question touches on planning organization: here, certain weaknesses could be overcome, such as, for example, the contradiction between higher production targets and the fall in cooperative credit, or between the extension of the irrigation program and the availability of cement. One must also remember the rather serious shortcomings in the progress of rural cooperative credit, despite the achievements recorded. The heavy arrears of primary societies as well as the delays are found in other districts. In its report for 1964/65, the Maharashtra Public Accounts Committee complains of these defects and also mentions cases of misappropriation of funds owing to inadequate finance or political party factions.[16] In the field of minor irrigation the delays mentioned in Satara district represent a more or less general situation if one is to believe the Estimates Committee of the Maharashtra Legislature. In some cases a period of ten to fifteen years elapsed before some of the schemes could be completed.[17]

The third question concerns the Panchayati Raj. Maharashtra is notable for its use of an original policy demanding positive measures. However, at the present stage it does not seem to be achieving results that are much better than those in a state like Madras.

These weaknesses could well disappear as time goes on. During the

[15] See J. K. Lele, *Local Government in India* (Ithaca, N.Y., 1966), p. 31.
[16] *Hindu Weekly Review,* Oct. 24, 1966.
[17] *Ibid.,* May 16, 1966.

long period of linguistic turmoils between 1956 and 1960, Maharashtra was often in a state of disorder and production was necessarily a secondary consideration. But if the present Chief Minister, V. P. Naik, continues to assert himself (he has been in power since the end of 1963), considerable progress could be made. There are many able administrators at state as well as district level in the I.A.S., and the peasants, on whom much depends, are mostly hard-working and conscientious. To complete the triangle, it is the local politicians who need to pull their weight more fully.

PART IV

An Attempt at Synthesis

24

PEASANTS, PROGRESS, AND EDUCATION

We have looked at the details. Now let us proceed to some more general observations. The basic feature of India's rural areas which I described in the preface by the expression *"solve et coagula"* has been apparent in a sufficient number of examples to show the diversity of currents running through the rural population. The enormous complexity of their development also helps to show the futility of any attempt at generalization. Whether we like it or not, agricultural expansion cannot be confined to one or two set patterns.

I shall try to center my attempt to arrive at a synthesis around the factors that seem to me to be decisive: (1) the peasants' attitude to development; (2) the organization of development from the three points of view of the peasants, the administration, and the politicians; (3) the agricultural policy within the national planning process.

The Social and Economic Conditions of Progress

The peasants' adhesion to a process of growth is dependent on three basic elements: the minimum economic holding, an enterprising spirit, and caste, which is linked to the first two. The interrelation of the three elements does not, of course, follow a uniform pattern but creates various broad categories of situations.

By a minimum economic holding, I mean a minimum amount of land that ensures a working margin over and above subsistence level. This small saving makes it possible to invest money in irrigation, fertilizers, and seeds, and, in time, in better equipment. Cooperative credit or *taccavi* will extend the formation of capital by helping it to move around more easily.

The size of holdings is closely linked with caste, since in most villages the upper castes usually own most of the land or at least a sizable part; but economic holdings and caste are not enough to set the process in motion. There must also be what I have called the enterprising spirit, best exemplified by the medium farmers of Khandoï and some of the Eksal Marathas. When this spirit is lacking, the mere possession of an economic holding rarely ensures a substantial rise in output, as Nahiyan well proves. There, the upper castes, which hold the bulk of the acreage, are slow-moving and entrenched in their taboos. An enterprising spirit without a minimum economic holding can, however, help a man to achieve better results. The Paraiyars of Kila Ulur do not live too badly thanks to the small profit they make on their mats. The Eksal Mahar who plants grapes on his thousand square meters will find himself in the same process of development as Saggan, the Khandoï Bhangi who has no land but much vitality.

The rank of the caste is by no means an absolute criterion. The Lodha-Rajputs of Khandoï and some Nahiyan Kurmis belong to the Sudra category, but this does not prevent them from making progress. The same applies to Harijans like our Mahar or our Banghi mentioned above. But if a peasant has neither the land, the energy, nor the social status, then his handicap is too great. We have seen examples of this among the Jativs and Chamars of the Ganges basin, where the underdevelopment is of such tragic proportions that it will take years to overcome.

To sum up, it may happen that a particularly strong enterprising spirit, which is often closely linked to caste, will compensate for a low caste status and lack of a minimum economic holding.

Obviously, with so many variations, one cannot easily determine how many peasants, with or without land, have broken through or are in the process of breaking through the "wall of poverty." We shall see in chapter 26 and in the appendix how the rural population is distributed; three-quarters of the families are either landless or come below the two-hectare level. Although a great many of them live under extremely hard conditions, examples of which we have seen, not all are reduced to the last extremity, and fortunately in the rice-growing areas a man can live on one and a half hectares.

Would it be relatively near the truth to suggest that a third of the families in rural areas possess the minimum necessary for existence with a small savings margin, while the remaining two-thirds hover between the bitter lot of the Nahiyan Chamars and a meager frugality? Only greater research into rural areas could produce an answer to the question. Allowing for their inevitable uncertainty, I suggest that the estimates of food consumption do not differ greatly from my tentative assumption. According to Dr. P. V. Sukhatme, a quarter of the total population of India suffers from undernutrition, and half has more or less enough food in quantity, though the diet is unbalanced (malnutrition) .[1]

If the future of the medium, dynamic peasants is more or less assured, particularly if it is sustained by a vigorous agricultural policy (see chap. 26), what can be said of the very small landowners, the farm workers, and the rural artisans? There is every reason to suppose that the general movement of the economy will in the end have a beneficial effect on these "weaker sections of the society." We have seen an example of this in the comparison of the moneylenders' rates of interest and the wages of casual laborers in a village such as Khandoï and in the more advanced regions of Bulandshahr. Also with a rise in production will come the possibility of creating more opportunities for work in villages such as Kila Ulur, where today the average peasant does not have enough money to hire extra workers to help him in the line transplanting of paddy.

I have serious reservations about the size of the educational program, as I shall explain later, but educational progress in the lower castes offers one more outlet, a narrow one perhaps, but certainly not negligible, for it means that some young people will manage to find work outside the village.

Neither is industrialization without influence on the situation. Large-scale industry will not do much to relieve the existing rural densities, since the rate of population growth remains high, but it should maintain a current which, in the long term, could increase the flow of money to the village as more and more workers leave their families to take jobs in town. Small-scale industries may also offer an outlet. It is certainly difficult to start them in comparatively isolated villages like Khandoï, where even a nail is a rare item, but the prospects are better in larger, roadside villages and small towns, as can be seen in the Punjab.

None of these forecasts can be made with any certainty, but if in the immediate and medium term the prospects of a noticeable progress for many sections of the population are limited, it does not necessarily follow that their future should be without hope *ad eternum*.

Social Change and Education

It would be tempting to conclude from these observations that social change is a prerequisite to development and should be the primary

[1] "The Food and Nutrition Situation in India," *Indian Journal of Agricultural Economics*, XVII, No. 2 (1962), 22, 28.

target of any planning policy. Professor H. W. Singer says in this connection: "In providing the initial resources for the better health, better education, better nutrition, better housing, greater social security, etc., which are the keys to growth, we must make people aware of the possibilities of improving the quality of life . . . The raising of the level of the people's life is both the objective of development, and also its instrument." [2] This argument might have a certain effect on the Chamars and even on the high castes who are still not sufficiently active, but where are these "initial resources" to be found in a country like India? Professor Singer's opinion is typical of a wide current of thought in the West and in a large number of countries of the Third World. It leads to propositions that are difficult to understand.

The history of world economy shows that development depends on one elementary determining principle before anything else: increased production. Side by side with, or after this, comes social progress. In what part of the world have they ever been able to afford the luxury of raising the standard of living before any substantial increase has been made in production? In other words, is there any one country where social progress has *preceded,* or even occurred simultaneously with, economic progress? [3] Such a process is even more impossible in the underdeveloped countries where limited resources contrast with the high rate of population growth.

Another view, somewhat simpler than Professor Singer's, holds that rapid mass education is a prerequisite to economic growth. It is such a view that has brought the programs of free compulsory education in Maharashtra and Madras. This view is so natural to Westerners, or to highly Westernized Orientals, that it is necessary to go back to its origins in order to show how invalid it may be as the solution for present-day India. Especially since the nineteenth century, Western culture has considered the ability to read and write the great criterion for knowledge and development, and it has had a more or less conscious contempt for oral culture, and, by implication, for countries in which that is the prevailing culture. More and more, this view is being accepted in the Third World as well. As the Bombay planners write, "Provision of adequate facilities for education at all stages, especially

[2] H. W. Singer, *Problems of Social Development* (Geneva, 1965).

[3] This is one of the contradictions facing the Third World. Scarcity of capital could lead to ruthless exploitation of labor, as it did in nineteenth-century Europe. But people's attitudes have so altered that they would oppose such exploitation today even in countries having rigid political systems. Concessions of a social nature are indispensable, but sometimes they run the risk of going too far.

in rural areas where ignorance and illiteracy are rampant . . . is therefore one of the main objectives of planning." [4] But what about the scores of illiterate (so-called "uneducated") makers of history? Akbar, one of the greatest emperors of India, did not know how to read and write!

What can be learned from facts? According to Mary Jean Bowman and C. Arnold Anderson: "That education is one of the few sure roads to economic progress has become a contemporary creed. Yet evidence remains slim and confused, and while human-resource development should and must receive increasing attention, there are dangers in too simple a faith. It can lead to misplaced efforts and destructive frustrations in countries that can ill afford either." [5] It is not the need for education that is in question, but merely the dimensions of the policy. Granted that the opening of schools and universities is indispensable, it is also true to say that we should not delude ourselves over the economic consequences of extending education to everyone at once.

My first point is that, as Europe has shown, vigorous development is perfectly compatible with a relatively high proportion of illiteracy. In Great Britain it was not until 1880, after a century of tremendous progress, that primary schooling became compulsory and free, and on the Continent this innovation only dates from the end of the nineteenth or the beginning of the twentieth century. Another example to bear out this point, this time *a contrario,* can be found in the Philippines, where the rate of literacy had already risen to 50 percent of the population by 1935, and between 1946 and 1961 reached a level of 64 percent.[6] Although it is not negligible, there is nothing spectacular about the Archipelago's economic progress as compared with other countries in Southeast Asia where education is less widespread.

New and persuasive proof of this contention is the attitude of a large number of illiterate peasants, some of whom I have quoted in this book, who have shown themselves to be perfectly open to progress and to modern agricultural techniques. I do not deny the existence of taboos, reticence, and mistrust, yet those who accuse the Indian peasantry of superstition and ignorance often reveal their own ignorance in so doing.

[4] Maharashtra State, *Third Five Year Plan,* p. 82.

[5] In C. Geertz (ed.), *Old Societies and New States* (New York, 1963), pp. 247–248.

[6] G. Willoquet, *Histoire des Philippines* (Paris, 1961), p. 122, and *Five Year Integrated Socio-economic Program for the Philippines,* p. 124, a program presented on January 22, 1962, to the Philippine Congress.

To sum up, lack of general education available to all does not impede progress.[7] Indeed, I should go further and say that general education does not automatically guarantee faster economic progress. It would be naïve to suppose that a Brahmin, simply by attending school, would be persuaded to abandon caste custom and put his hand to the plough. School in fact might well strengthen his prejudices against manual work.

My second point refers to the quality of teaching. If education becomes widespread too quickly its standards are almost certain to be debased. Hardly one educator in India at this time would argue with this all too evident truth, which exists at secondary as well as at university level. The Vice-Chancellor of the University of Bombay has complained vigorously of this problem,[8] and Mr. Chagla, the then Minister for Education, described the secondary school examinations in which half the candidates failed as "a national calamity and a tremendous waste." [9] The serious riots that took place in several universities in 1966 were not without connection with this problem. The low level of education was one reason for agitation, and it was exploited by politicians of one sort or another and troublemakers. The University of Calcutta was practically unable to function between early October and early December, 1966, because of the continuous picketing of students at its gates, and on December 8 it was officially closed. And in Lucknow, the university was closed for the months of October and November because of student unrest.[10]

We have seen in detail in Maharashtra what advantages there could be in a less ambitious timetable for educational progress. By slowing down the construction of primary schools and by being less lavish in the materials used in them, money could have been saved for diversion to agriculture, and cement could have been put aside for other purposes.

Other Indian states would be well advised not to hurry themselves in this field of development. Yet, the draft outline of the Fourth Plan aims to enroll 92.2 percent of the children in the six-to-eleven age group (there were 78.5 percent in 1965/66). Government authorities are, in fact, prompted by another reason quite apart from a belief in education, though they are somewhat reluctant to admit it. There is no doubt that the rural population is insistent in its demands for the

[7] See T. W. Schultz, *Transforming Traditional Agriculture* (New Haven, Conn., 1964), which skillfully shows the need for education in rural areas, at the same time pointing out its limitations.

[8] *Times of India,* July 1, 1964.

[9] *Ibid.,* Dec. 1, 1963.

[10] *Overseas Hindustan Times,* Dec. 8, 1966.

terms of the Constitution, specifically Article 45, to be put into effect. Article 45 reads: "The State shall endeavour to provide within a period of ten years from the commencement of this Constitution, for free and compulsory education for all children until they complete the age of fourteen years." This rather unrealistic promise (the ten-year period expired in 1960) stems from a mixture of complaisance toward the electors and genuinely good intentions, including the desire to eliminate caste differences. Traditionally, the Brahmins have had the advantage of a much better education than other castes, and as a result they have long played a prominent role in administration and government, whether Hindu, Muslim, or British. Today they still hold a number of very high positions quite out of proportion to their low numbers.

Traditional Values and Development

There is a wealth of superficial literature trying to persuade us that the traditional Hindu is opposed to the idea of economic progress. Apart from the taboos that stem from social rather than spiritual causes, the Hindu is supposed to show little interest in the material things of this world. Totally absorbed on a higher spiritual plane, he is said to attach scarcely any value to human existence, regarding self-denial as all important. Now this way of thinking is indeed a very real one, as it was at the height of the Moissac and Chartres period, but in India, as with the Middle Ages in Europe, it does not apply to everyone. Alongside the deeply religious, the hermits, the great metaphysicians, and the sages who have renounced the world, the majority of Hindus are guided by three concepts: the idea of *dharma* (allegiance to spiritual traditions), by what is known as *artha,* material interest and profit, and by *kama,* or pleasure. The second concept explains the rise, long ago, of the Indian economy and commerce.

The wretchedness and poverty of today have little to do with religious beliefs but are the result of demographic, sociopolitical, and economic factors.[11] It is clear that even during India's period of intensive development following the granting of independence, spiritual traditions and economic progress have existed side by side. This can be said especially of the rural areas. The dynamic peasants of Khandoï are no less religious and faithful to their rites and beliefs than are the peasants of Nahiyan; religion is not the determining factor.

Nor is this compatibility likely to vanish quickly as India pro-

[11] See my book, *L'Inde—Economie et population* (Geneva, 1955).

gresses; it will continue for a long time. Certainly, the partial modernization of techniques, the use of irrigation and of chemical fertilizers do not in any way undermine spiritual and religious values.[12] It will only be in some very distant future when the standard of living is so high and the economy fully mechanized and modernized that these values will be gradually undermined as they have been in Europe. Even in industry, where the traditional way of life has undergone more drastic changes than in agriculture, the worker of today can remain perfectly faithful to his religious rites and work well at the same time.

Finally, what of the caste system? First of all, despite the attempts of the legislators, we must not be led into believing that it will disappear overnight. What is more, according to some anthropologists, like M. N. Srinivas, the system may tend to become more firmly entrenched in certain sectors at least of social and economic life. The least that one can say is that this fundamental feature of Indian society will remain in being for quite a long time.[13] Some superficial observers feel that the system represents a major obstacle to development. But, in fact, in the field of agriculture the effects vary a great deal. When the dominant castes (who, as we have seen, own the major part of the land) have a pronounced inclination for agriculture, the system helps to promote progress. We have seen examples of this at Khandoï. At the same time, in other places such as Nahiyan, the system can just as easily retard development.

Let Us Not Complicate the Issues

Finally, I wonder why so many economists and sociologists seek to complicate problems that are not simple in the first place. Two facts are particularly evident from the picture of rural life I have presented: either social change is not indispensable, the peasants being quite capable of taking part in the development process without much change in their mentality, or it is necessary, but impossible to intro-

---

[12] The reader will probably challenge me with the respect accorded to cows. On this point, it is true, traditions do hamper development rather considerably, for the slaughter of this animal would give the people an immediate source of food and would facilitate the selection, feeding, and milking of cattle. These taboos will die hard and we must adapt ourselves to them, as other countries have had to adapt themselves to their prejudices. In China, for example, the Communist regime has not yet really attacked the problem of the graves, which take up a considerable amount of arable land. Instead of ploughing the graves outright, they are tactfully trying to encourage cremation and, on a small scale, are having the graves moved to areas of land unfit for cultivation.

[13] See in this connection the excellent book by Louis Dumont, *Homo hierachicus, essai sur le système des castes* (Paris, 1967), pp. 284–301.

duce with any speed. It would in fact require a violent revolution, which is another unrealistic hypothesis in the short as well as perhaps the medium term. The political forces in power do not desire it, and the Communists are too weak and divided to win, despite local successes like Kerala. Given these conditions, I cannot quite see how this idea can throw any light on the situation. For me the question is not whether or not we shall know in thirty years' time if the Brahmins and Thakurs of Nahiyan will do the ploughing themselves, but whether we can at least find a starting-off point very soon.

I shall probably be reproached for concentrating my argument too much on the immediate present without taking account of long-term phenomena. It would be permissible, for example, to think in terms of a policy of long-term development, without caring too much about present difficulties. This is an acceptable attitude for an economy that is already fairly well established, but it does not work in a country whose fortunes are as precarious as India's. Before any long-term view is taken, India must solve the immediate and urgent problems that exist in certain rural areas. There will be time later to think about other, more subtle ideas than those dealt with in this book. The situation could be summed up by the metaphor of a man drowning. Only one action is possible—to jump into the water and save him. After that we can worry about giving him food and warm clothes and helping him on his way to a happier life.

Where, then, are the answers for India?

Let us begin by admitting three assumptions that have been stressed in many ways in this book. (1) There is a scarcity of cadres whose training and talent are proportioned to the magnitude of the tasks. (2) There is a scarcity of capital. (3) The difficulties and obstacles in the way far exceed those in the West, or in Japan and the Soviet Union during their early stages of growth.

The first two assumptions are so evident that I should not bother repeating them were they not so frequently forgotten. The third is less evident. Historically, the balance between population and resources in India began to be in jeopardy under the British regime, when population trebled without being accompanied by an equivalent increase in production. In recent years, the rate of its population growth has quickened. India is faced with a problem of far greater enormity than faced advanced nations during their periods of industrial development.[14] Since 1951 the annual rate of population growth in India has

[14] There is a great need for careful research into population growth at village level. It would be useful to be able to explain the differences described in the rates of growth by infant mortality and birth rate as well as the apparently very high

been double that of Japan during the period 1890–1910.[15] Under these conditions any rise in per capita income is slow, unemployment increases, and a great deal of capital expenditure is necessary on education and housing.

Proceeding from these three assumptions, let us try to make two firm rules derived from the art of war and political wisdom: (1) to organize agricultural development by concentrating resources in terms of men and capital on the decisive points; (2) to ensure that it is done by taking as one's maxim the "art of the possible."

---

mortality observed in Khandoï. One point that is clear, however, is the quite ridiculous nature of the assumptions so often made concerning Indian sexuality, namely, that couples are unusually active for want of other distractions! I have the impression, however, that the opposite is true at least in some villages visited, where sexual intercourse is practiced rather less frequently than in more developed countries.

[15] Even between 1910 and 1940 the Japanese rates did not exceed 1.5 percent a year. See A. Okasaki, *L'Histoire du Japon* (Paris, 1958), p. 56.

25

THE BASIC TRIANGLE

Let us try to introduce the principles that we have just arrived at into the triangle made up of the peasants, the administration, and the politicians, and at the same time look for the factors that could eventually speed up development.

The Intelligentsia and the Rural Population

Although part of the peasantry is gradually becoming more receptive to the processes of a modern economy, the intelligentsia,[1] from whom the administrators and politicians are recruited, is tending to lose touch with the rural population. This is a fairly general phenomenon in underdeveloped countries.

Let us consider first of all the politicians holding ministerial responsibilities and the high officials—in brief, those responsible for agricultural policy. Many of these men who are now over fifty were born in a village or small township, and have had, in their youth at any rate, some contact with rural society. On the other hand, their children have generally been born in the towns and have grown away from their origins. A number of young Indians have thus become as much a foreigner in the villages as a Westerner. Being without firsthand experiences, they tend to indulge in abstract analyses of the peasants' needs.

Even ministers and high officials do not always find time to feel the pulse of the countryside, or they do so in an imperceptive way. I was talking to a minister of the central government about the abuses indicated at Khandoï. "What do you expect?" he replied. "When I go to a village I am surrounded by a veritable screen of people of some sort of official capacity who keep me from seeing what is really going on." Another minister announces that he will visit a district, and a program and a report on local problems are prepared for him. He

---

[1] I use this term in a very broad sense; it denotes not merely the elite but also many officials of lesser status and politicians whose education does not go beyond secondary level.

spends less than a day there and confines himself to conversations in the district town.

With his innate understanding, the late Prime Minister Shashtri recognized the blindness of this lack of contact: "We have waited for long. It is time we go to the villages ourselves. So far as I am concerned, I propose to go without pomp . . . to a village and stay there for three or four days and get in real touch with the people. Once in a year or twice this should not be difficult for us." [2] At the moment it is difficult to know whether this idea has been translated into fact. It runs counter to long-established customs. I know several important men who would be in no way discouraged by the mean conditions of life in a village,[3] but the organization of their work is such that they have no proper time to go into the field. Like any other country in the world, India is subjugated to the tyranny of office and paperwork, which are apt to be even more onerous there than elsewhere.[4]

Besides Shashtri's proposition, other measures are being directed at re-establishing contact between the peasants and the authorities. I mentioned (chap. 2) groups of inspectors sent by the Planning Commission into the states. The Programme Evaluation Organization, attached to the Planning Commission with an autonomous statute, also fulfills this function. These steps are no doubt useful, but Shashtri's idea would be by far the most effective remedy.

This lack of contact is also found in foreign experts and advisers. Some of them, for example the Ford Foundation, are undeniably efficient and are in touch with the realities of the countryside, but with the best will in the world they often have too few opportunities of leaving Delhi except for quick visits to rural areas. Others quite simply prefer the comfort of their air-conditioned offices to field work, another characteristic not uncommon with foreign experts in many underdeveloped countries.

Finally, another factor that widens the gulf between decision-making and the implementation of the decisions is the tendency of planners to deal mostly with large problems without taking into account all the practical details. The opinion of the men on the spot no longer seems to have the same influence as under the British. As Professor N. V. Sovani has remarked: "A district collector was listened

---

[2] *Indian Express*, June 26, 1964.

[3] It must be admitted that others are less charmed by the rustic surroundings.

[4] As long ago as the seventeenth century, when the emperor Aurangzeb was traveling around, the caravan of state archives and documents that accompanied him consisted of eighty camels, thirty elephants, and twenty bullock carts. See Niccolao Manucci, *Memoirs of the Moghul Court* (London [1950–1960?]) , p. 56.

to with the greatest respect in higher echelons and in turn those in higher echelons were persons with considerable district experience. Something of this has disappeared during the last two decades and there is no channel today through which there can be a feedback of local experience at higher levels in the planning process." [5]

Politics and Administration at State Level

To display their full capabilities, high officials (collector, C.E.O., etc.) need to be supported. Without giving them carte blanche—since this could lead to abuse—they require a minimum guarantee of support to protect them from the maneuverings of local politicians. In such a changing field, rigid precepts are impossible and there is no ideal solution. There will always be conflicts, but the problem is to try to reduce their negative impact on development.

In the extreme case of Uttar Pradesh, the primary responsibility is in Lucknow. The dissensions within the Congress party inhibit any effective administrative reform and therefore any substantial speeding-up of development. Without a minimum of political cohesion, it will be impossible to give back to the administration the bite which the schemings of the politicians at all levels have been blunting. In the case of Maharashtra, political cohesion has not ipso facto eliminated the conflicts between "vested interests" and the administration. The latter does have the benefit of some support from Bombay, however, despite some difficulties. Finally, in the state of Madras the situation seems still more stable, and complaints by the administration about politicians were, I learned, comparatively rare.

The Political Parties at District Level

The political parties, not realizing the importance of the rural areas, do not turn their attentions to the farmers much except at election time. Prestige, intrigue, and the manipulation of power are far more important in their eyes than development, an attitude that finally cost the Congress party dear in the 1967 elections. There is no doubt that the political parties could, if they chose, play an important part by supporting the administration, by trying to make the peasants understand the sometimes unpopular but necessary measures that are taken, and by really lending their support to the execution of the plans. They could form rural cadres devoted to agriculture and in general give a

[5] N. V. Sovani, "Planning and Planners in India," *Indian Economic Journal*, January–March, 1966, p. 484.

lead in rural affairs.[6] This separation of political life and rural problems is not confined to the Congress party. Other parties also show a
lack of imagination and operational shortcomings. The Republican
party, which claims to be the defender of the Harijans, could be more
militant, and the same can be said of the Communist party of the
Benares district, whose members do not even provide a quorum at the
meetings of the panchayats which they completely dominate.

It can well be understood that in these conditions the reactions of
the peasants to political parties vary from indifference to cynicism or
contempt.[7] The heavy losses of the Congress party in the 1967 elections
are clearly not unconnected with this fact.

This limited political activity in the rural areas comes not only from
lack of interest but also from lack of organization, another implementation task which is by no means easy. The acceleration of economic
growth will not therefore arise quickly from this source.

Local Politics, the Panchayati Raj, and the Administration

Can it be hoped that the administrative decentralization inspired by
the *Mehta Report* will stimulate production in the near future? The
direct participation of the masses and their representatives is essential
for speeding up the economic movement. They will know how to
defend their own interests much better than officials. This is one of the
reasons why community development had, at the time of the report,
achieved only a limited success. It was imposed from above whereas it
should have been started from below.

This line of thought is behind the Panchayati Raj, the first results of
which we have seen: either the system works badly, or else it operates
worthily but has little to do with development except for a few
positive items such as the increase in local taxes and land revenue in
states like Madras or Maharashtra, the planting of coconut trees, or the
purchase of sprayers.

Unfortunately, the new councils seem to represent just so many
additional opportunities for the local politicians.[8] The development in

---

[6] In 1964 the report of a committee of the Congress party, presided over by
Mr. U. N. Dhebar, proposed the training of cadres in the rural areas, but so far
this proposal has not been implemented. See *The Hindu,* May 19, 1964.

[7] Regarding the meeting of the Congress party at Bhubaneshwar (1964), at
which there had been much talk of socialism, Jayaprakash Narayan remarked:
"All those fine words had hardly any relevance to the people in the villages; 82%
of the people of this country are more or less left out of it all." *Seminar on
Fundamental Problems of Panchayati Raj* (New Delhi, 1964), p. 35.

[8] See particularly the periodical *Seminar,* September, 1963.

Bihar is typical: the electors at village and block level brought in some new blood in the shape of energetic young men. This delighted New Delhi, but the Bihar government took a different view. Though it was powerless to call off the elections, it got its veteran politicians to enter the fray so as at least to obtain a majority in the zila parishads. The local Congress even lifted the rule forbidding members of the Legislative Assembly to stand for a district seat.[9]

S. K. Dey, as Minister for Community Development and Panchayati Raj, recognized with his usual frankness that factions were hampering the efficient working of the system and that local leaders were using it as a springboard for their personal ambitions.[10] In April, 1964, at the time of the debates in the Lok Sabha on this subject, a number of M.P.'s did not conceal their concern at the rivalries between political groups and castes which were tearing apart many panchayats.[11]

In addition to struggles within the panchayats, it is not unusual to find misunderstandings between administration and panchayats, with equally negative results as in the case of some transfers of C.E.O.'s in Maharashtra. The danger is latent at all levels, as was admitted at a regional conference on the Panchayati Raj held at Hyderabad (capital of Andhra) at the end of 1964. Relations between block presidents and B.D.O.'s are often strained and this adversely affects the efficient functioning of the service.[12] Two years later G. P. Jain repeated this comment forcibly: "Clashes immediately began between the elected representatives and the block staff. . . . As a result useless favourites were pampered and hard working dissidents pulled up. Lack of initiative took hold of the blocks." [13]

While recognizing that the system has until now had very little effect on development, its defenders rightly point out that the experiment is still too recent to be condemned out of hand. In the course of time it is quite possible that the old political hacks, who count prestige and personal advantage as more desirable than efficiency, will be replaced by young dynamic personalities. In any case, all the wrongs are not on one side. The members of the I.A.S. do not perhaps always display the utmost tact and understanding when dealing with members of the

[9] This rule was adopted in several states at the instance of New Delhi in order to avert the domination of the Panchayati Raj by political interests; see *Hindustan Times Overseas Weekly,* Dec. 17, 1964. The local members of Parliament or of the Legislative Assembly are usually permitted to take part in the discussions but not to hold the office of president or vice-president.

[10] See, among others, *Hindustan Times,* Mar. 5, 1964.

[11] *Ibid.,* Apr. 11, 1964.

[12] *Hindu Weekly Review,* Dec. 7, 1964.

[13] G. P. Jain, "Devaluation of the B.D.O.," *Kurukshetra,* Annual No., Oct. 2, 1966.

samitis and zila parishads, for they see only the evil aspects of mean rivalries. In Maharashtra it can happen, albeit only rarely, that the mainstay of the zila parishad is not the C.E.O. but, very clearly, the president of the zila parishad, as is the case in the Akola district. I was also told that members of the I.A.S. sometimes displayed an excess of youthful impetuosity, which could be the cause of friction.

To sum up, it is no use engaging in conjectures about whether or not there should be a Panchayati Raj. Like it or not, it exists and the clock cannot be put back. On the other hand, it is important to assess its value for the future. I should not rule out the possibility that it may bear fruit in the long term in the field of agricultural production, and there are some encouraging signs such as progress on the fiscal side. In the short term, however, almost universal experience shows that it provides neither a solution nor even a short cut toward a faster rate of development.[14]

Collective and Individual Interests

How has it been possible to trace areas where the panchayats have been working and where they have not? According to Professor D. R. Gadgil,[15] the successful ones are in the areas such as Madras and Maharashtra where the *rayatwari* system had been in force for a very long time. The important intermediary, the zamindar, did not exist. The peasant used to pay his taxes direct to the state and had therefore long been in the habit of taking an interest in local affairs, so he had been somewhat prepared for the establishment of a panchayat. In Uttar Pradesh the zamindar was in fact, and to a certain extent by law, responsible for local affairs, the peasants having very little voice in them. The disappearance of the system left a void that has been slow to fill, especially in villages divided by factions.

Second, why do the panchayats, when they are operating, have so little concern for agricultural production? At the outset the introduction of the Panchayati Raj was not accompanied by any real propaganda in this direction, and when it happened that the members who set the pace in the panchayats were, in the main, comparatively well-off peasants, whose agricultural exploitation was going well or fairly well, it naturally followed that they would not worry much about production. They still seem more interested in playing a part, displaying their

[14] Since writing these comments at the beginning of 1966, I have not met with any evidence of a definite and rapid improvement.

[15] Professor Gadgil became vice-chairman of the Planning Commission in September, 1967.

prestige, or merely concerning themselves with the general interests of the community.

To these two reasons must be added a third more important one. By definition, a panchayat must give its attention to the interests of the *community*. But production is organized on an *individual* or *family* basis. To find the point of contact between the interests of the community and those of individuals is a delicate problem. It is easy to obtain unanimous support in a village for a school, a panchayat building, or drinking-water wells because these things benefit everyone.[16] But a *bandhara* for irrigation interests only ten or twenty farmers, as does a program for erosion control or drainage channels.

To try to settle in the name of public interest problems that concern only one section of the community is nearly similar to seeking to square the circle. It will be argued that these productive works do not assist merely the immediate beneficiaries, that they set in motion a whole economic movement which eventually affects a large number of agricultural workers, giving them higher wages and so on. This is true enough, but such reasoning is rather too abstract for a poor landless peasant to follow. His benefits will not be immediate, but will come about as the result of a number of intermediate steps.

Even in so small a matter as making a road in *shramdan*, this difficulty arises, and the Jativs of Khandoï do not hide their skepticism. What advantage is a metaled road to an agricultural laborer or a smallholder of a few hundred square meters? The man who owns a cart and oxen, and has *gur* and wheat to transport, is quite willing to take up a pick and help to improve the road. But a wretched laborer is not likely to work with the same kind of enthusiasm even when he is being paid.

These perfectly reasonable reactions can be overcome if the village is sufficiently homogeneous, if its president carries great authority, or if an agent outside the village community creates unity. But these conditions are very often not fulfilled.

The Administration: Its Responsibilities and Capabilities

If it appears doubtful whether the political parties or Panchayati Raj are really fit to speed up development, one can be more hopeful about the initiative of the administration, provided certain modifications are introduced.

It is comparatively easy to draw up the broad outline of a plan in

---

[16] The wells, it may be added, are supposed to be free to all castes, but this is not always the case.

the offices in Delhi or Bombay. The formula is more or less the same everywhere: water, fertilizers, credit, and so on. It is in the implementation of the plans at district level that the difficulties arise, and there is too great a tendency to underestimate them. A *good* B.D.O. or a *good* gram sewak requires qualities of character, ability, and imagination that one very rarely finds at this level in the hierarchy.

When I arrived at Khandoï in September, 1963, I considered that I had a certain experience of development behind me. Yet I needed at least several weeks to get rid of a priori ideas and find the technical solutions compatible with existing psychological and sociological conditions. One is also apt to forget the thankless nature of the work of local officials. I described this in detail for the Unchagaon block, and it varies very little in other regions. How can one demand a spirit of sacrifice, or at the least a maximum effort, from poorly paid men, often of little talent, who will derive no immediate personal benefit from this effort?

The government is seeking to eliminate these defects through salaries and promotion, but in any case it has only limited room to maneuver. Salaries already account for a considerable proportion of the budgets of the blocks. It does not seem possible to find any suitable formulas to establish the desirable competition.

Let us turn to the knowledge of the personnel of middle or lower rank. Here again we must beware of fine-looking charts and tables describing the operations of a block. Everything works splendidly with men of high quality, but such men are few and far between. A number of times I have come across a B.D.O. or an A.D.O. for agriculture who did not know the approximate cultivated and irrigated areas of his block. Nor is it unusual at district level to catch the specialist in this typical gesture: when asked for a more or less precise answer to a question, he presses a bell to ask his subordinate for the figures or facts. Maharashtra has recognized these weaknesses clearly by ceasing to require from gram sewaks really effective agricultural knowledge.

This problem has been the subject of ever more animated discussions, as G. P. Jain mentioned in the article previously cited, "Devaluation of the B.D.O." The government of Madhya Pradesh, for example, has "jettisoned the B.D.O. as undesirable functionary and elevated the A.D.O. (agriculture) to the post of coordination officer to do what the B.D.O. did in addition to extension work."

All these questions were brought up again at the Conference of the State Ministers for Community Development and Panchayati Raj in October, 1966. The criticisms were so serious that some persons thought about abandoning the program of community development.

The conference decided that these institutions "should be revitalised." As the *Overseas Hindustan Times* wrote on October 20, 1966: "This should be done by raising extension services to higher levels of skill and knowledge, concentrating on efforts to bring the entire community within a minimum framework of development."

This is all very good, but how is it going to be carried out, when India (like most other developing countries) finds itself faced with a contradiction that has not really been taken into account in the agricultural policy? The middle and lower grades do not have the ability to cope with their jobs, and this situation is bound to continue for many years despite the efforts being made to remedy it.[17] It is impossible to surmount this contradiction entirely, but it could at least be lessened if the responsibilities of the collector were modified and if discipline were enforced. The working of the administration lacks strictness and one encounters too many instances in which slackness and casual disregard of inefficiencies have repercussions on development. It would certainly seem that much improvement could be made simply by enforcing regulations already in existence—certainly without introducing any sort of dictatorial or arbitrary regime. If, for example, an official of a block or of the irrigation service knew that he risked losing his job if he did not submit his report by the required date or if he did not at once carry out an important instruction, some of the defects would disappear. The same should apply in case of corruption or the many other abuses, to the great relief of the peasants, for it is they who are the real victims of administrative shortcomings.

It would not be easy to tighten discipline. Certain politicians and high officials know how to show their authority—like the collector who during the war imposed six months' imprisonment and a fine of 500 rupees on a merchant who violated the price ceiling by a few rupees—but there are others who tend to be almost too tolerant of their fellows. They will cover things up, shut their eyes, or arrange to transfer the person to blame in order to avoid any unpleasantness. Sometimes, too, the necessities of local politics will lead them to suppress the matter.[18]

---

[17] The trend is accentuated by the rapid establishment of development blocks, which in eleven years (1952–1963) have extended over practically the whole of India.

[18] In this connection it should be emphasized that the Panchayati Raj regulations are not uniform all over the country. It may happen that, so far as disciplinary measures and annual reports on officials' activities are concerned, responsibilities are shared between the collector and the president of the zila parishad. Such a situation is bound to hinder the implementation of a stricter discipline and firm leadership in planning.

The Direction of Operations in the District

The efficient working of a district depends on the personality of the man in office and how the administration is organized. We have examined three systems. In Uttar Pradesh the collector delegates the execution of a great part of development to the district planning officer, who usually does not belong to the I.A.S. In Madras the collector looks after the direction of operations himself without this intermediary. In Maharashtra two officials of the I.A.S. of equal rank share the responsibility.

The first system seems very inconvenient.[19] The collector remains tied to the routine of his office, while his subordinate, who has not the rank, nor the prestige, nor the training, is responsible for the implementation of the most important and difficult development tasks.

I should be much less categorical about the other two systems. The Madras system has the advantage of forming a solid entity. The collector delegates several routine tasks to his assistants in order to devote more time to development. The question remains whether one man can really keep a close eye on operations or whether his responsibilities need to be shared, as in Maharashtra. This last formula, it will be recalled, is directly linked to the particular pattern adopted for the Panchayati Raj. It is therefore difficult to transpose into another system.

In fact I have the impression that a collector with one or two good assistants could manage.[20] And it is perfectly possible to find such assistants, despite what I have said about the weakness of the middle grades. The first two aides to the C.E.O. at Satara, for example, have carried out their functions in a most satisfactory way. In Uttar Pradesh, the D.P.O.'s may not be in a good position to direct the community development of a district, but many of them would make good assistants for a collector, the latter being directly and primarily responsible for the conduct of operations.

---

[19] The *Mehta Report* (p. 40) contained this recommendation: "The district collector should be provided with a whole time additional collector to relieve him of the general administrative duties, so that he can himself, as far as possible, function and be designated as the district development officer."

[20] The ideal would be to have also a capable agronomist for each district. It would be necessary to upgrade such a post (rank and salary) at the district level, while making more widespread efforts to improve the teaching of agronomy, as the agricultural universities of Ludhiana (Punjab) and Pantnagar (Uttar Pradesh) have undertaken to do.

A certain analogy exists between the conduct of an army and the operations of agricultural development in the Third World. What is needed is an organization that works and a leader full of drive who can concentrate on the essentials, in this case development, while confining himself to supervising secondary and routine jobs delegated to subordinates. The head of the district must be as often as possible "in the front line," that is to say, in the villages and blocks. It is by personally supervising the work of the subordinate ranks that he will speed up the rate at which the administrative machine works and improve contact with the peasantry.

Under this system the collector would have firm control of the decisive factors of progress, so that the main inputs necessary to agricultural growth would reach the farmer. This choice could perhaps lower the productivity of the other services, but the concentration of forces on the essential points is one of the things that will enable the rate of agricultural growth to be accelerated.

As they may be applied, such ideas will face up to two obstacles: the familiar attitude of the politicians, and the way in which the administration is organized. It would seem particularly desirable to put an end to the haphazard and frequent transferring of officials from one post to another.[21] A certain minimum of continuity is essential for the efficient operation of public affairs, and the examples referred to in Maharashtra are, alas, by no means exceptional.

Another problem is that the irrigation department is everywhere a sort of private domain from which the C.E.O. and the collector are shut out apart from some consultation. Such a fact was very clearly admitted by Mr. C. Subramaniam, then Minister for Food and Agriculture, when, referring to irrigation engineers, he commented: "They have been an empire by themselves. They confine their interest to the constuction of irrigation works . . . Meanwhile cultivation practices have undergone a change." [22] If, where canals are concerned, it is difficult to put the irrigation services under the control of a single district (since the canals usually serve several), the tube-wells, which are an important weapon in the fight for production, ought to come directly under the district head.[23] With the assistance of his technical aides, he

[21] See, among others, the *Times of India,* Nov. 11, 1963: "Transfers for Political and/or Administrative Reasons."

[22] *Kurukshetra,* Oct. 2, 1966, p. 37. This accords with my observations, as I have noted earlier.

[23] The Uttar Pradesh authorities, aware of this problem, began in 1965 to put the state tube-wells under the B.D.O. in some experimental blocks. I wonder nevertheless whether the *direct* control of the collector would not be preferable.

could re-establish the strict discipline formerly imposed by Sir William Stampe in the first state tube-wells of Uttar Pradesh.[24]

The present organization of the cooperatives also deserves some attention. The cooperative banks receive part of their funds from the Reserve Bank which they pay over to the scores of village societies or lend directly on long-term credit. We have seen that it is very difficult for the collector to intervene with the firmness desirable. Would it not be possible to review the position of this organization?

The blocks are, of course, already integrated into the district hierarchy; all that matters is to tighten the bonds by frequent control and a policy of personal attention.

To sum up, the basic idea is to have in each district a man directly responsible for *all* the principal activities connected with agriculture. On a countrywide scale this would mean about three hundred high officials of top quality who can be found easily. By their authority and ability they would at least partly make up for the deficiencies of their subordinates.

These observations and suggestions partly coincide with the *Report of the Working Group on Inter-departmental and Institutional Co-ordination for Agricultural Production* of 1963, the moving spirit behind which was D. P. Singh, a particularly well-qualified man who was both member and secretary of the group. The report says: "Unsatisfactory administrative and organisational arrangements was, by far, the most important single factor responsible for inadequate progress in the sphere of agricultural production." The coordination of services must be tightened up at state level, and the measures that we saw in Uttar Pradesh had this in view. In the districts the report proposes the setting up of a committee presided over by the collector or C.E.O., on which would sit the heads of the various services affecting agricultural production. An enforcing of discipline is also proposed, the personnel of the blocks being threatened with dismissal in the event of bad reports for three consecutive years.

The strengthening of coordination between the principal technical services affecting agriculture is a need which, though long recognized, has progressed slowly. Three years after the Working Group's report, the Fourth Plan returned to the subject. In the meantime certain steps had been taken; in the central government the ministry of community development, Panchayati Raj, and cooperation had been incorporated into the Ministry of Agriculture. Agricultural subcommittees presided

[24] One of Sir William's former Indian subordinates told me how during an inspection tour he had an operator sacked because his pump was not properly lubricated.

over by the chief minister have been created in several states. At district level the plan recommends the creation of a full-time agricultural officer responsible for coordination: "He should act as lieutenant of the district officer, who should have overall charge for co-ordination . . . including irrigation." [25]

The inclusion of irrigation in this program is welcome, but I wonder whether this system does not run the risk of having defects similar to those brought to light in Uttar Pradesh. More than coordination is needed: the collector of another I.A.S. official of equivalent rank should assume this heavy responsibility *directly*.

The application of the ideas outlined above would not establish a perfect system, but it would at least represent a step forward.

The I.A.S.: Advantages and Risks

The regular recruitment for the Indian Administrative Service has gradually expanded since Independence until in 1962 there were a hundred or so candidates, mostly chosen by competitive examination.[26] There is also a possibility of promotion from the state service. Out of the 2,147 members of the I.A.S. in 1961, 550 had entered the service by this means.

It seems an excellent system. The principle of a select corps of high officials is an essential condition in a country where the middle and lower grades cannot reach an adequate standard. We have seen just what a man in high office can achieve by his inspiring example, integrity, and intelligence. Nevertheless, like any mandarin system, the I.A.S. is not without its faults. Officials of other services sometimes complain strongly of the tendency of I.A.S. members to despise the provincial technical or general personnel. Proud of belonging to this corps of the elite, proud also of their education, their place in society, and of course their salaries, they appear disdainful or at least unfriendly. My own observations do not support these complaints, which are not untinged with jealousy. Yet such cases may sometimes occur.

More serious from the development standpoint is another grievance.

[25] *Fourth Five-Year Plan.*

[26] See *Report on Indian and State Administrative Services and Problems of District Administration* (1962), p. 10. With the aim of widening the field of recruitment, Harijans and aborigines are entitled to 12 percent and 5 percent, respectively, of the posts regardless of their ranking in the examinations. These provisions could adversely affect the smooth running of the service. Although one may have reservations about the part played by the high castes in some rural areas, it must be stressed that their qualities are ably demonstrated in the management of public affairs. Many brilliant members of the I.A.S. are Brahmins or Kshatriyas.

According to Ralph Braibanti, the I.A.S. personnel have their eye particularly on the posts in the central administration in Delhi, the state capitals, or the industries of the public sector. Hugh Tinker goes still further and quotes a young official as saying: " 'Frankly I do not like to spend a night in a village. I have nothing to say to the villagers, nor have they to me.' The same official added with a remarkable self confidence: 'I am trained to find out all I need to know in one day.' " [27]

It is true that the old days so well described by Philip Woodruff [28] are gone. Today collectors no longer have a free hand and politicians may obstruct them in their tasks. Methods have changed, too. The unhurried traveling round, the camps on the outskirts of the villages where the peasants used to come in the evening to find the collector, the early-morning rides between the fields of sugar cane—all that has changed. It is true, also, that flying visits by Jeep are not the best means of establishing real contact with the rural scene. But one must adapt oneself; it is as pointless to mourn the passing of the old type of collector as it is to lament the disappearance of squadrons of hussars and dragoons! However, when that has been said, there still remains the great problem which Braibanti and Tinker have raised—namely, that of contact between the collector and the peasants. Without disputing the statements of these writers, I wonder whether their findings would apply generally, since my observations of several I.A.S. members have led to much better conclusions. Nevertheless the danger of lack of contact exists. It is indeed inherent in the system, as observations in other countries have shown.[29]

To develop the practical sense of officials-to-be, a further probationary period of ten to twenty months follows the year spent at the National Academy of Administration. The *Report on Indian and State Administrative Services* (p. 17) recommends that, in this second period of training, the trainees should spend three months as assistants to a B.D.O. This proposal seems inadequate, for the lack of contact is seen even between the staff of a block and village. I suggested to the Home Minister in 1964 that each trainee should be sent to a village for at least three months.[30] His mission would be simply to observe, to prepare a report on the progress attainable, and to help the peasants as

[27] In R. Braibanti and J. J. Spencer (eds.), *Administration and Economic Development in India* (Durham, N.C., 1963), pp. 63, 122. These remarks confirm mine at the start of this chapter.

[28] *The Men Who Ruled India.*

[29] A former high French official spoke to me of the lack of practical sense in the young and brilliant cadres coming out of the National School of Administration.

[30] On further reflection, I feel that this period is too short; it would be better to think in terms of six months.

he came to understand their needs. Thus at the start of his career each official would have the opportunity to learn to know the often complex mechanisms of a village and to make use of his practical sense.

As a result of these slight alterations to their training, the members of this *corps d'élite* could represent an important asset; it is essential that the maximum benefit be obtained from it. This conclusion is not going to be shared by everyone in India, and that is why one last point should be clarified. The I.C.S. of the old days has in some instances left bitterness in men who were nationalist leaders before Independence. Such a feeling is perfectly understandable, but, today, it is both wrong and unfair to associate more or less the I.C.S. or I.A.S. officers with the colonial rule, and, hence, to distrust them. First of all, many of the old I.C.S. officers have been of great help in building an independent state since the departure of the British. Second, how can a young I.A.S. officer who was ten or fifteen years old in 1947 be suspected of a colonial mentality? If this is true twenty years after the end of the British Raj, then what has been done in India in the meanwhile?

The "art of the possible," the sense of priorities and concentration on essentials: let us now transpose these themes to the level of planning and agricultural development policy.

26

THE ART OF THE POSSIBLE

During the last fifteen years a distinct impetus has been given to India's rural areas. Development has been uneven, but there is nothing at all unusual about this as I was able to observe when I was there. Some of the districts are stagnant, others are in a state of "ferment," while a third group has become fully engaged in the process of economic growth.

Among the dynamic areas are for instance the whole of the northwest from the Punjab up to and including western Uttar Pradesh, the rice and coastal districts of Andhra, and certain districts of Gujarat. At the other extreme are the isolated zones of the Deccan which are often populated by aborigines. The coastal part of Orissa, most of the middle and lower Ganges, and parts of the Deccan fluctuate between semistagnation and a slow movement toward agricultural development. Soil conditions and irrigation are not the sole determining factors, for, as the case studies show, much is dependent upon the extent to which the dominant castes possess a vocation for agriculture. It is strange how this aspect of Indian society is neglected or sometimes completely overlooked in the plans drawn up by the government and in so many works devoted to Indian development. It is small wonder that agriculture lends itself to so many false or oversimplified judgments both outside and even inside India, yet it should be obvious that the same amount of investment will not produce the same return in, say, a Jat milieu as it would in a Thakur one.[1]

The Problem of Statistics

Climatic conditions are another cause for variations; here they occur in time rather than in space.[2] After a disastrous beginning, the decade

[1] So far as official documents are concerned, I am well aware that for political reasons it might be difficult to put too much emphasis on the role of castes in agriculture, but it would help if more use could be made of the concept of dominant castes and its implications.

[2] See the very interesting article by S. R. Sen, "Growth and Instability in Indian Agriculture," a technical address delivered at the Twentieth Conference of the

1951–1961 was relatively favorable, with really serious calamities occurring only in 1957–1958. The Third Plan, however, was inflicted with the worst possible bad luck, with three rather mediocre years, one very good year, and a last one that was really catastrophic. To make matters worse, the following year, 1966–1967, was also quite bad.

The speculations of grain traders and farmers have been another source of confusion. In 1964–1965, India had to import 6.75 million tons of grain in order to compensate for requirements that were in fact likely to be below this figure.[3]

More recently, yet another source of confusion has appeared. Was the figure of 72.5 million tons of food grain for 1965/66 a true one? On his return from a study mission in India, Professor Daniel Thorner revealed some disturbing facts about Andhra. According to him, the statistics were deliberately falsified in order to avoid having to surrender the rice surplus for 1965–1966. (It is fair to add that the surplus was less than in the previous year.) Other surplus states may have done the same, and deficit states may have artificially increased their deficits in order to be sure of receiving the necessary minimum. "On the all India scale," adds Professor Thorner, "I found fundamental reservations . . . about the credibility of the global estimates of foodgrain production issued by the Ministry of Agriculture."[4] Being far from India at the moment, I am unable to endorse or to reject Professor Thorner's observations, but they are perhaps plausible.

In addition to all this there are the basic facts outlined in chapter 3. The crop-cutting sample method only gives rough indications; the samples are sometimes questionable, as are the exact dimensions of the areas sown for each crop.[5] An examination of the land records is revealing. The columns giving the names of the farmers and the size of the fields are well kept, but this is not true of those showing the crop grown in each plot. The only consolation is that the actual situation is perhaps better than the official statistics show!

There is a similar uncertainty in working out forecasts, the same method being employed from New Delhi down to the development blocks. Schematic tables show that the irrigation of X hectares will

---

Indian Society of Agricultural Statistics, January, 1967. The author analyzes the impact of the weather and makes a classification of districts according to the danger of drought.

[3] See Dick Wilson, "Must India Starve?" *Far Eastern Economic Review*, Feb. 18, 1965.

[4] Daniel Thorner, "Coastal Andhra: Towards an Affluent Society," *Economic and Political Review*, Annual No., February, 1967.

[5] The samples give the yield per hectare which is then applied to the whole of the area devoted to each crop according to the regions. The areas in question come from reports furnished by the land record officials.

bring about a Y increase in output, similarly for fertilizers, seeds, and soil conservation. The total sum of these entries gives us the final target. As Professor M. L. Dantwala observes: "A comparison of these estimates and the actual performance during the first and second plan period would indicate the utter undependability of such estimates." [6] In fact it seems almost impossible to specify the contribution toward improvement that is made by each factor, given their interdependence and, what is an even greater obstacle, the variations of nature from one year to the next.

Is this method successful? Would it not be possible to envisage a form of planning that is less precise on paper but more realistic so far as the land itself is concerned? It would mean deciding on possible investments for each large sector: irrigation, cement, fertilizers, soil conservation, and seeds, without placing too much insistence on forecasting the exact results. There are, after all, a good many countries that have reached an advanced state of development without making forecasts of their economic growth.

This relief from statistics would have the advantage of freeing men for more essential duties. For example, instead of preparing a report on the hypothetical progress of production in such and such a block, the person responsible for statistics could begin by planning the distribution of cement. (I tried in vain to get some clear information on this subject in Koregaon, Satara.) He could keep a closer watch on the sale of fertilizers and seeds, giving the higher authorities sufficient warning when the stocks ran low. The same official could keep strict control over the state tube-wells, making sure that they functioned properly and got the necessary repairs.

This method would surely be better than relying on village plans, which, as experience has shown, do not seem to be very conclusive. Under present conditions there seems to be a tendency to overestimate the capacities of the gram sewaks and the villagers. One runs the risk of having either no plan or false statistics. This is one of the reasons why a simpler method could be sought. At district and state level it would be possible by one and the same action to release officials from this statistical work for other, more essential duties. And this brings me back again to the principle of concentration.

Basic Achievements and Shortcomings

Although it is not possible to have a precise idea of production, the basic trend is fairly clear. There is no doubt that during the decade

---

[6] *India's Food Problem* (Bombay, 1961).

1951–1961 the over-all tendency was to increase and to exceed the rate of population growth. (For 1951–1961 official statistics give the rate of population increase as 2.15 percent and the rise in production as 3.3 percent per year. Mellor and Lele give 2.45 percent for the latter.) Later on, while admitting on the basis of 1964/65 figures that a potential of nearly 90 million tons has been created—that is, an increase of 10 percent over 1960/61—production has been overtaken by population, which between 1961 and 1966 increased by about 12 or 13 percent. More and more imports have been needed to overcome the deficit.

Having said that, however, the target for the Third Plan, without really favorable weather conditions, was clearly very ambitious (+32 percent for cereals and pulses). We have seen in detail how the budgeted sums have been calculated at the lowest possible rate and how the forecasts for chemical fertilizers have not come up to expectations. Nor have requirements for rural credit always been met, resulting in considerable delays even in the construction of minor irrigation works.

There are several factors involved: first of all the amount of capital required and its proper use. The necessary amount of capital has not been secured in all cases, as we have seen with reference to block financial allocations. As for its use, we have noted various shortcomings which teach us a lesson that is applicable to India and to most of the developing countries alike: to organize the proper use of capital is at least as difficult as finding it, if not more so.

In addition, there are the general conceptions of planning, to which we shall return later.

Finally, what of the successive waves of community development, of panchayats and cooperatives? They have not contributed very much to reinforcing the general line of progress, but to what extent have they been a hindrance? I do not share the opinion of a foreign expert who after a fleeting look at Indian agriculture wrote in a confidential report that community development is a real obstacle to increased production. I should merely state that these measures have not lived up to all the original hopes.[7]

The Most Serious Trial Since Independence

Before reverting to economic problems, some word must be said of the political situation, where increasing difficulties have occurred, at the

---

[7] See, in this connection, the extremely detailed analysis made by J. P. Bhattacharje: "Agriculture Extension, Inputs and Outputs and Community Development," *Economic Weekly*, February, 1965.

very time when the growth of the economy has slowed down considerably.

The armed conflicts with China in 1962 and with Pakistan in 1965 brought about an almost fourfold increase in military expenditures; in 1960/61 the defense budget amounted to 2.8 billion rupees, whereas in the last few years it has been more than 9 billion.[8] It seems hardly necessary to point out that this is a very heavy drain on resources.

Internal politics have also been affected by events of no less importance. There has been a succession of premiers: Jawaharlal Nehru died in May, 1964; he was succeeded by Lal Bahadur Shastri, and when Shastri died in January, 1966, at Tashkent, Mrs. Indira Gandhi became Prime Minister. In the meantime dissensions within the Congress party increased and the opposition parties became stronger. In 1966 there was a particularly large number of cases of violations of law and order. Apart from student agitation, there were the cow riots in Delhi as well as demonstrations to get a steel works established in Vizakhaptnam. It seemed as if any pretext was used to create difficulties for the government: the Hindus' attachment to traditional values as well as the desire for economic advantages demanded in a highly questionable but distinctly modern fashion! In addition to the political factors, discontent was heightened by a more and more difficult economic situation and by the growing increase in the cost of living. The 1967 elections saw the Congress party defeated in several states. In the central parliament, however, it managed to retain an absolute majority and was thus able to form the government.

We have already noted (at the end of chap. 18) that the verdict of the electorate is in many respects paradoxical. In any case it is far from being linked exclusively to economic questions. A new situation has therefore been created which will not make the process of economic planning any easier. We have seen what a big part the states play in elaborating and implementing the plans, especially where agriculture is concerned. It may be difficult to find a formula that will satisfy, for instance, the Communists in power in Kerala as well as the right-wing Swatantra party in Orissa. Moreover, we must expect an unstable situation in several states given the coalition cabinets which include

[8] See *Overseas Hindustan Times,* Mar. 30 and Apr. 6, 1967: the 1967/68 budget envisages 9.7 billion rupees for defense. For 1966/67 the figure was 9.4 billion (spent). To deal with India's foreign policy would be outside the scope of this book. Nevertheless one question at least must be asked: are the roads leading toward better relations between India and Pakistan, as well as India and China, totally blocked? The answer depends, of course, not only on India but on all the countries involved; but the question must be stressed since, as S. M. writes in the *Hindustan Times* of April 6, 1967: "Defence expenditures of the present scale can only come at the expense of economic development."

members of the Jan Sangh (extreme right) as well as Communists of both camps, pro-Peking and pro-Moscow.

What, under these conditions, will be the fate of the Fourth Plan, the draft outline of which (August, 1966) had not been adopted by parliament before the elections?

Another conflict that is gradually crystallizing is the one between the dogmatists and those who take a more pragmatic view. The latter are more interested in the implementation of the plan and its concrete achievements than in fine political slogans empty of any content. A clear example of this conflict was given at the beginning of 1966. As we shall see, the production of chemical fertilizers particularly is behind schedule. Faced with the danger of famine, the government is making a greater effort and has authorized the private sector to establish new plants in collaboration with foreign capital. However, in the name of the "socialist pattern of society," members of the Congress party have accused the government of having sold out the country to capitalist interests.[9] In other words, let us stick to our principles no matter if the peasants perish as a result! The disturbing fact about this attitude is that these dogmatists will certainly be the last to pay the price while many poor farmers may die of starvation in the meantime.

The result of this conflict between, on the one hand, shortsighted or intriguing politicians who know little of economic realities, and, on the other, men endowed with a minimum of understanding is of utmost importance. If the former camp becomes any stronger, India's economic future will be seriously endangered and the country will find itself restricted to the old methods of the 1950's. If, on the other hand, the tendency toward pragmatism increases, then the practical measures taken will come to complete fruition.

Before the elections I had the feeling that, without losing the whole of their influence, the dogmatists and others of an unrealistic frame of mind were losing ground. The agricultural policy of a man like Subramaniam seemed to be particular proof of this. Now that the elections are over it is more difficult to make up one's mind. In any case the dogmatic current remains pretty strong.

The Global Process of Planning

After more than fifteen years of planning some very important lessons can be learned not only for India but for other developing countries as well.

In the first place, a general observation springs to mind and in this

[9] See "All India Congress Party session at Jaipur," *Times of India*, Feb. 13, 1966.

connection I can do no better than quote Professor Sovani: "Indian economic thought has a built in anti-laissez-faire tradition. . . . We adopted nearly full scale economic planning shortly after independence, and, in our excitement we did not pause to consider whether the Indian conditions and traditions were sufficiently suitable for such planning. . . . As a consequence we very considerably underestimated the difficulties of planning. . . . Instead of treating economic planning as the art of the possible in the given environment, we have, it seems, believed that planning does the impossible immediately." [10] If these observations appear to be valid for the general economy, they are no less so when applied to agriculture. By sheer coincidence (very encouraging for me!) Professor Sovani has also reminded us of this idea, so often forgotten, of the art of the possible in development.

When considering the hard facts of the case, to what extent are the principles of planning gradually moving nearer to the art of the possible? The draft outline of the Fourth Plan gives a clear picture of the rather ambiguous situation described above in which a pragmatic attitude and rather unrealistic ideas come into conflict. Sound and concrete steps are proposed, while at the same time the temptation of the impossible has by no means disappeared; this means a glaring contrast between very positive measures and dangerously optimistic assumptions.

The first question that is debatable, and has led to some lively controversies both within and without India, is the size of the plan. Total outlays should double (public and private sector) to reach 237.5 billion rupees, of which 213.5 billion are investments proper. But are the economy and the administration in a position to absorb such a mass of capital and channel it adequately? Would it not have been wiser to have envisaged a period of consolidation in order to strengthen an economy that has been badly shaken in the last five years? Besides, instead of starting certain new projects in several industries, would it not be better first to make maximum use of existing industries, at a time when several factories are not working at full capacity?

The second question refers to the distribution of investments. One cannot but welcome the trend already noticed in the Third Plan to pay more attention to agriculture, and it is a point that is even more emphasized in the Fourth Plan; yet I wonder whether the reorientation is deep enough? The first task of the Fourth Plan reads as follows (p. 16): "For ensuring the achievement of self reliance as early as

[10] "Planning and Planners in India."

possible, highest priority will be given to all such schemes of agricultural and industrial production as are designed to promote exports and replace imports." Does this mean a first and drastic priority for agriculture and industries supporting agriculture? [11] This is not absolutely certain since the *Draft Outline* adds (p. 43) that the total provision for agriculture "including projects of direct benefit to agriculture . . . in other sectors" will be over 50 billion rupees, double that of the Third Plan. Since the Fourth Plan itself is double the size of the Third, there does not appear to be a drastic reorientation of the main priorities. This point becomes even more evident when comparing outlays and investments in industries and mining: they have been increased by 130 percent, whereas in agriculture and irrigation the increase is 100 percent.

As to agricultural targets, it is assumed that, from a potential of 90 million tons of food grains by the end of the Third Plan, production should reach 120 million tons in 1971. Very high targets are also envisaged for cash crops:

	Base Level, 1965/66	Target for 1970/71
Sugar cane (*gur*)	11 million tons	13.5
Oil seeds	7.5 million tons	10.7
Cotton	6.3 million bales (of 180 kg.)	8.6

SOURCE: *Fourth Five Year Plan, A Draft Outline,* p. 184.

Heavy increases in inputs are needed to achieve such targets; this means a big challenge for the industries concerned, which might have been made easier had there been a relaxation of effort in the field of heavy industry. The production of chemical fertilizers (in terms of N and P_2O_5) should have reached 1.2 million tons in 1965/66; in fact, they have only achieved 344,000 tons (*Draft Outline,* p. 291). The Fourth Plan sets a target of 3 million tons, but even if we disregard the most recent delays which took place in 1966/67 in completing various projects, such a target does not seem feasible.

So far as cement is concerned, the situation is not basically different. From 10.8 million tons in 1965/66, production is expected to rise to 20 million tons. On the other hand, prospects are more promising in the power-driven pumps industry. The Third Plan exceeded its

[11] The Chinese have gradually evolved a kind of model which could equally apply to India and other developing countries: first comes agriculture, then industries supporting agriculture, and only after these two comes heavy industry.

targets by 50,000 units, to reach the figure of 200,000 in 1965/66. The amount should double by 1970/71 (p. 291) .[12]

To sum up, although undeniable importance has been placed on agriculture and on certain industries which supply it with inputs, it is doubtful whether the targets assigned to agriculture and the industries directly supporting it can be reached in view of the very heavy commitments in other sectors.[13] Besides, even if all the inputs were available, could one *organize* their sound use on such a large scale and within so short a time? Finally, would the farmers be able to absorb them? For these reasons one would doubt the assumption that by 1971 it should be possible to dispense with American grain surplus—unless nature is exceptionally generous for several years.[14]

Public Sector Versus Private Sector

Any economic policy is judged on the basis of its results. Clearly the principle of the socialist pattern of society has not been an answer to

[12] In their agricultural policy the Chinese have in the '60's given as much impetus as possible to several inputs, particularly pumps and pumping sets, about which we find repeated references in the Chinese press. There are no data available in this respect but the following table is an attempt to indicate the progress of chemical fertilizers (in terms of N and P_2O_5). There is not much difference, it should be noted, in the net cultivated areas of the two countries.

	Output (tons)	Imports (tons)
1957	170,000	260,000
1964	800,000	200,000

Sources: A. Eckstein, *Communist China's Economic Growth and Foreign Trade* (New York: McGraw-Hill, 1966) , p. 70, and *Far Eastern Economic Review*, Nov. 12, 1965.

[13] Fixed investment outlay in organized industries and mines:

Manufacturing industries (metals and machinery)	28.3 billion rs.
Fertilizers and pesticides	4.93
Intermediate goods	9.50
Consumer goods	7.22
Miscellaneous	2.6
Mining	9.9
Total	61.93

(private sector, 26.50 billion; public sector, 35.43 billion)
Source: *Fourth Plan, A Draft Outline*, pp. 256–257.

[14] See *Overseas Hindustan Times*, Feb. 23, 1967. This does not mean that all food-grain imports should cease by 1971. It refers only to "concessional imports" under P.L. 480. Since these represent by far the bulk of the food-grain imports, it means that the food deficit should be reduced to a very small amount which India could buy according to the international market conditions.

every hope. It required the establishment of a highly complex and efficient administrative machinery, a task which was, and remains, too ambitious, except in countries that are very advanced economically.

Within this field positive and worthy efforts have been made for some years to allow market mechanisms and private initiative to operate more efficiently, in both production and distribution, as well as in the matter of controls. Without going into all the details about the lack of cement, one of the factors responsible has been the heavy state controls, and a good deal of red tape. The abolition of controls in 1966 led to an improvement in the situation, with the result that production is now picking up.[15]

Fertilizers are experiencing the same flexibility. When I was in India they were distributed almost entirely by the public sector and by the cooperatives. With a view to stimulating both production and consumption, the government has authorized new private enterprises which are being set up, or are about to be, to fix their own prices on fertilizers and arrange for their marketing. Such a liberalization is welcome, judging from the experience of West Pakistan, where eight months after private enterprise had once again been authorized to sell chemical fertilizers in 1964, the surplus stock amounting to 250,000 tons of ammonium sulphate was sold out and dealers could not cope with the demand.[16]

Such measures take us away from dogmatism and back to practical realities. It is no longer a question of fortifying one's position with lofty principles but of seeking efficient formulas. Obviously the state has an important role to play, but it must limit its responsibilities to the things that it is capable of managing and organizing in a really efficient way.

The Blind Alleys

To these changes in the conception of development are added others concerned with the agricultural policy proper. The experience accumulated in the course of the three Five-Year Plans has made it possible to distinguish clearly between the true and the false remedies, the blind alleys and the roads leading to a faster growth. Again, in this field the temptation of the impossible has not completely disappeared.

In both the short and medium term there seem to be several blind alleys. At the risk of being taken for a reactionary, I shall quote further

[15] *Ibid.*, Dec. 20, 1966.
[16] See Etienne, *Progrès agricole et maîtrise de l'eau: le cas du Pakistan* (Paris, 1967), chap. 6.

agrarian reforms as an example. The present legal framework is no doubt inadequate, but new laws could not alter it fundamentally. More important is the near impossibility, under India's political situation, of having such laws really and thoroughly implemented. Only a violent revolution could achieve that end, and the prospects of a Communist take-over appear rather remote for India as a whole.

Besides, what is the real economic importance of sharecropping and/or other types of tenancy as well as that of small, uneconomic holdings? The conditions described in this book fit rather well into the global picture which emerges from all-India estimates.

In the highest bracket (20 ha. or 50 acres and above) there were in 1953/54, according to the National Sample Survey, 604,000 rural households owning 54 million acres, with an average of 36 hectares (90 acres). The land reforms that took place between 1953/54 and 1959/60 reduced the area by a third and the number of holdings also by about a third. At the bottom (zero to two hectares or five acres) there were 47.5 million holdings. The land reforms increased the number of such holdings from 60 to 63 percent of the total and the area from 15 to 19 percent. In the categories owning between two and 20 hectares, there was almost no change.[17]

It is clear from these figures that from an economic point of view the situation is not so bad. Uneconomic holdings cover only a small part of the cultivated area. Now, we must ascertain the minimum size of a holding that will allow an owner to meet his basic needs and still leave at least a small margin of savings, which can be invested and enlarged by credit, so that the process of growth can work: production—saving—increased investment—increased production, and so on.

From what has been observed in the field, in alluvial soil and at least fairly well irrigated areas, the minimum economic holding is around two hectares in wheat and one and a half in paddy zones. In the Deccan, where soil and irrigation conditions are often poor, the minimum economic holding may be around four hectares, or even more. Hence, one can assume from the figures of the N.S.S. that at least two-thirds of the cultivated land [18] is covered by holdings that are economic, or can be, provided that the cultivator shows at least some spirit of entrepreneurship.

From a social point of view the picture is, of course, entirely different, considering the very large proportion of uneconomic holdings;

---

[17] See M. L. Dantwala, "Problem of Subsistence Farm Economy: The Indian Case," *Honolulu Seminar,* 1965.

[18] See Appendix; around 66 percent of the cultivated area is above four hectares (ten acres), and 80 percent above two hectares (five acres).

but what can be done? Further land reforms would bring limited relief to a few of the poorest peasants, but production would be hit, with consequent hardship to millions of people in villages and cities. Today the food situation is so serious that production must increase at all costs.

Let us now look at another aspect of land reforms: the types of land tenures. There is no doubt that, as we have observed in Tanjore, sharecropping may often hinder agricultural growth; the same can be said of the *mafi* system in Benares, or of other types of tenancy which do not induce the tiller to work and invest more. But what is the real importance of the problem at national level? In a study based on the 1961 census, P. S. Sharma gives the following data: cultivating owners represent 76.3 percent of the cultivating households and 77.6 percent of the cultivated area. Pure tenancy involves 7.7 percent of the holdings and 4.2 percent of the area; mixed tenancy 15.5 percent of the households and 18.2 percent of the area.[19]

It must further be borne in mind that not all kinds of sharecropping are so adverse to agricultural progress. It is certainly the case when a fairly important owner splits his holding in favor of several sharecroppers, but the opposite is also by no means uncommon: a small landowner may, as we observed in Eksal, go to work in the city, leaving his land to a sharecropper who may already be a medium-sized farmer, at least. In such cases sharecropping helps to reduce the area of uneconomic holdings.

Although the figures quoted above should not be accepted without reservations, since accuracy is absolutely impossible in such complicated matters, they give a broad and fairly reliable idea of the pattern of ownership and tenancy. For this reason I fail to see what can really be gained, especially at the present stage, by re-opening the land reform issue.[20]

Another blind alley must be mentioned with reference to the Panchayati Raj: the idea of extending the powers of the panchayats at all three levels in the hope that production will increase thereby. One shudders to hear the views expressed by that otherwise highly respected

[19] P. S. Sharma, "A Study of the Structural and Tenurial Aspects of Rural Economy in the Light of the 1961 Census," *Indian Journal of Agricultural Economics*, No. 4, October–December, 1965.

[20] At the Conference of State Ministers for Community Development and Panchayati Raj in 1966 it was decided to set up a national committee to study the implementation of land reforms and the possible role of the panchayats in such a move. The latter point is particularly odd, since, as observed in the field, small farmers and tenants cannot have much influence on the panchayats. See *Overseas Hindustan Times*, Oct. 20, 1966.

person, Jayaprakash Narayan. Tarlok Singh and Shriman Narayan, then members of the Planning Commission, expressed a quite opposite opinion when they replied that before demanding any additional power, the panchayats should first fulfill the role originally assigned to them.[21] Nevertheless pressures and claims continue to be made.

A third blind alley is that of cooperative farming. In every region that I visited I got the same impressions as I had gathered at Unchagaon: the peasants do not want it and the experiments that have been made have failed with the exception of an extremely well-managed cooperative farm that I visited in the Coimbatore district. Certainly a system that is more or less collective offers some practical advantages, but if the great majority of the peasants, including a large number of very small peasants, are hostile to it, and if the government refuses to use force, it is difficult to see how the problem can be solved. The weaknesses of the system have been shown up fully by the Evaluation Committee on Co-operative Farming headed by Professor D. R. Gadgil. The report submitted in 1965 proposed the consolidation of the movement in areas where it has met with a relative success such as those districts mentioned in chapter 4. Such a suggestion could, as a last resort, be taken up, but one can hardly agree with the proposal to set up 10,000 cooperative farms during the Fourth Plan.[22]

Then there are the hopes placed in the *shramdan* and, more recently, in the village volunteer forces. The observations that I made in the Bulandshahr district were repeated in other districts and other states: either enthusiasm was restrained, or it had never existed. There is much to be said for the idea of human investment, but how far does the social and economic structure of the villages lend itself to the idea? In the previous chapter we looked at the arguments against it, on a large scale at least, and it would be dangerous to rely too much on this system to stimulate development at the present stage.

Another solution which has already been refuted is the multipurpose approach in community development. This sort of "deviationism" away from realistic planning dies hard. It is nourished by a broad international trend of opinion, encouraged in part by the United Nations.[23]

[21] See *Times of India,* July 7 and 21, 1964.

[22] See the criticisms in this connection of U. B. Panikkar, "Whither Indian Co-operative Farming," *Kurukshetra,* Annual No., 1966.

[23] In October, 1964, I visited a community development pilot scheme aided by the U.N. in Afghanistan. With remarkable perseverance they were repeating the errors so widely known in India at least since 1958.

Finally, let us remember the faith placed in primary and compulsory education as a factor for speeding up development. Here also the international climate lends itself to specious arguments.

The Right Remedies

There is an ever increasing call for the strengthening of agricultural policy in ways that will avoid the blind alleys described above. As B. Mehta writes: "Agriculture in this country, for quite some time, is going to remain primarily a problem of better organisation, organisation for supplies and better services, rather than any significant structural or institutional changes in the Panchayati Raj institutions" [24]— or, we might add, in other similar directions.

These explicit proposals are typical of the pragmatic way of thinking. The package program of 1960 having laid the trail, this policy broadened, later on through the efforts of Mr. Subramaniam.[25] Chemical fertilizers, minor irrigation, high-yield varieties of seeds, pesticides, better credit facilities—all received increased attention. In 1964 a formula was set in motion which derived from the package program but was more limited: the Intensive Agricultural Area Programme (I.A.A.P.) as mentioned in Madras (see chap. 18). Some 646 blocks have been selected in 75 districts for paddy, 356 blocks in 54 districts for millet, and 200 blocks in 30 districts for wheat. Thanks to these programs, 2.4 million hectares are profiting from high-yield varieties of seeds in 1966–1967, a figure that hopefully will be increased to 6 million hectares in 1967–1968.[26] This selective approach takes into account the fact that only 52 districts out of a round total of 330 produce a food surplus.[27] It is concerned with relatively advanced regions where there is a reasonable chance that progress will be quicker than in more backward areas.

Credit represents another source of noticeable influence. Many states are in a much less advanced stage than Maharashtra, which has simplified and broadened its cooperative credit, but progress can be achieved merely by instituting more adequate administrative rules. In addition, the practice of crop loans, which is so far being carried out in Maha-

[24] "Panchayati Raj and Agricultural Production," *Kurukshetra*, Annual No., 1966.
[25] Subramaniam was a victim of the Congress party's defeat in his state of Madras and was unfortunately not re-elected.
[26] *News from India* (Embassy of India, Berne), Mar. 10, 1967.
[27] *Times of India*, Feb. 23, 1966.

rashtra and a few other states, could produce profitable results if credit could be repaid without delay and without too great a percentage of loss. Loans granted with the future crop as security are much more within the means of the very small peasant than are loans with the usual personal securities. In 1966 it was decided to extend crop loans to the majority of states starting with the 1967 *kharif*. The loan will be disbursed in three stages: a cash component to take care of expenditures on traditional methods of cultivation, a component in kind (implements, fertilizers), and a further component in cash on account of the use of more costly inputs.[28]

Numerous steps are being taken to improve irrigation. The Fourth Plan will concentrate on consolidation of schemes already underway or already completed. There are plans for strengthening coordination between the department of irrigation and the department of agriculture so that the latter will draw up a program of agricultural development which will run parallel with the construction works of the department of irrigation. Within the field of hydraulic policy itself, minor irrigation is being more and more encouraged, as we have seen in the states surveyed. It should reach 1.6 million additional hectares, while the various major works already under construction should cover a similar area.

There is also greater recognition of the role of agricultural research than there was ten or fifteen years ago. This is directly linked to the program of high-yield varieties mentioned above. All agricultural research stations have been centralized under the control of the Indian Council of Agricultural Research, which has itself been reorganized. Equal encouragement is being given to research in other directions such as proper soil and water management.[29]

It would be difficult to question these measures and the selection of inputs. Care is taken to concentrate on measures aiming at quick results, and this is why it is only at a later stage that other improvements can be tackled on a really large scale, for example the modernization of implements, and massive progress in the field of cattle breeding [30] and poultry farming. The last is proving successful in parts of Maharashtra and in the Punjab, where markets are available and where the farmers take an interest in raising poultry. Implements and

[28] *Overseas Hindustan Times*, Oct. 20, 1966.

[29] *Fourth Five Year Plan, A Draft Outline*, pp. 196–199.

[30] In his book *L'Inde indépendante* (Paris, 1962), pp. 40–42, Professor Bettelheim shows with great insight the difficulty of the cattle question. The animals are both superfluous and, in the case of bullocks, indispensable to the peasants even if they are only mediocre in quality. It is hard to see a solution to the problem in the near future.

cattle, as we have observed in Khandoï (chap. 8), may involve rather heavy investments.

In this way one can draw up a fairly simple chart for development, by which the eyes of those in charge are concentrated on the fundamental points to which they devote all their care and ability.

This conception does not dismiss the social services out of hand; it simply insists on some priority services that are directly linked to production. Following these, come services involving family planning, drinking water, the anti-malaria campaign, and the operation and extension of primary schools.

The reorientation of agricultural development, whether latent or partly introduced, can never be achieved completely. There will always be politicians who, for the sake of their own power, wish to bring up such questions as electrifying the villages or speeding up primary education. This phenomenon is in the nature of things and no country in the world can escape it, much less a system of parliamentary and federal democracy. In the present circumstances it is a question of degree, and of limiting losses to the profit of the most practical solutions. If, in some cases, they clash with popular feeling and the immediate interests of the politicians, they will in the long run be of more benefit to the peasants and to the political parties than promises that cannot be kept.

All these measures would indicate an outright victory for pragmatism as well as adding up to an agricultural policy that is clear and coherent. Up to now (April, 1967) —and this is the irony of fate—it has only produced very limited results following the repeated and exceptionally severe natural calamities. But with a minimum of luck so far as the weather is concerned, the results should be sizable. That is why one should not give way to an excess of pessimism no matter how bad the present crisis.

It is obvious that the view stressed in this chapter is not in keeping with the ideas of social justice, for in the immediate future at least it will favor the medium farmers. But what other remedies are there? As we have already seen, under India's present political conditions, despite all the efforts made and reforms carried out, it would be impossible to improve overnight the conditions of the weaker sections of society. On the other hand, if during the first phase of development the medium farmers, or at least some of them, follow up their breakthrough, it would not be unreasonable to hope that the effects of the present economic movement will in the end reach those whose present lot is so very hard.

Postscript: Delhi, August, 1967

Being again in India in the summer of 1967, I should like to add some additional direct observations. The Fourth Plan would appear to be stillborn. Not only has it not yet been endorsed by the Parliament, but the *Draft Outline* of 1966 referred to above is far from being implemented. Instead of a full five-year plan, the Indian government is following a year-to-year approach, preparing an annual plan based on the available resources. For lack of financing, the outlay for 1966/67 was only 22.21 billion rupees, and for 1967/68 it should be around 22.46 billion for the public sector, although the total for the five years was set at some 160 billion for the public sector. Several ambitious projects, particularly in the heavy industries sector, are having to be postponed, and there is a growing concentration on existing projects—in itself certainly not a bad thing.

As for agricultural strategy, more and more emphasis is being given to minor irrigation, high-yield varieties, chemical fertilizers, and better credit facilities. Here again, one cannot expect immediate returns, because the implementation of these measures takes time and is far from simple. For instance, high-yield varieties have not always been as successful as expected: in certain areas they were ill-adapted to local conditions, and in others the additional chemical fertilizers needed were not available. As for the crop-loan formula, it is evident in Andhra that it is being introduced in the 1967 *kharif* only on a very limited basis, mainly because it involves many changes in the organization of the cooperative sector which cannot be introduced overnight. Finally, in progressive areas such as coastal Andhra the demand for chemical fertilizers is rising faster than the supply.

To sum up, all these measures are in the right direction, but it would be dangerous to overlook the unavoidable difficulties and delays of implementation. This, however, is not the main issue. The important point is that India's agriculture is really breaking through. There is also now a better awareness of agricultural problems in the districts.

CONCLUSION

Before considering what sort of future may lie ahead for the agriculture of India, we must return to the conditions under which an inquiry can be made in that country—specifically to see how conditions may affect the judgment of a foreign observer.

In many countries of the Third World the visitor can easily be influenced by official propaganda and organized tours with the result that, even when he is on his own, those positive features to which his attention has previously been drawn are more immediately evident than other aspects. India, however, keeps her records open for everyone to see. Official reports, newspapers, unrestricted traveling, all help to give the foreigner an opportunity to become closely acquainted with the true facts. This openness and freedom can turn against the Indians when the visitor takes an unfair advantage of them, and particularly when he only comes up against the weaknesses of the economy and of the political regime. I remember one foreign expert who came to see me at Khandoï and condemned community development and the cooperatives in a few devastating sentences. There are others who start by becoming annoyed with one rather weak official, go on to express their strong disapproval of the politicians and lack of reforms, and end by indicting the whole planning system. Such bitter criticism must be regarded as a sign of presumptuousness or of superficiality. In fact, when one goes to a village or block, or even into the Planning Commission offices, one's uppermost feeling ought to be one of humility. It is far too easy to criticize everything; one should first be completely aware of the myriad of contradictions between what is desirable and what is practicable.

Throughout this book I have tried to be as objective as possible by swinging the pendulum between these opposing forces. My hope is that I have succeeded in showing the extreme complexity of Indian development, and the relatively narrow working margin allowed by human nature and force of circumstances to those who lead India.

With new emerging political forces replacing the old guard who won independence, and with a much clearer idea than ever before of economic problems, India is entering upon a period of transition in which the future can be seen in the light of two main hypotheses.

According to the first, political power will crumble in the face of centrifugal forces, ending in confusion within and among the states. Some will manage to hold to the main task, but others will sink into chaos—not the chaos of a sudden crisis or revolution, but a slow rot. India could well repeat the experience of Pakistan during the years 1952–1958. In such an event, any hope of sound and steady economic progress would be seriously jeopardized. Agriculture would be particularly affected, for it, more than any other sector, depends on the support of the state. In Pakistan, political instability did not prevent a strong growth of industry before Marshal Ayub Khan came to power, but it was one of the principal causes of stagnation in the output of food grains.

The difficulties encountered by the Third Plan, the danger of famine and its eventual consequences, the dissensions within the Congress party, the lack of homogeneity among the Opposition, and the instability of several states are things that give cause for anxiety. Nor can one escape the a priori hypothesis of a shipwreck. Relevant in this respect is the speech of the President of the Republic, Dr. S. Radhakrishnan, on Republic Day, 1967: "The unruly behaviour of some members in our legislatures, the factions, the caste disputes and the political rivalries that have disrupted many a State . . . the riots and sabotage directed at almost everyone . . . have raised in many minds doubts about the stability of a united democratic India." Indeed, he continued: "Charges of corruption are frequently made against people at all levels of government," a fact he deplored: "We cannot forgive the widespread incompetence and gross mismanagement of our resources." M. R. Masani, a Swatantra party member who is leader of the opposition in the Lok Sabha, issued a similar warning a few months later: "All politicians are on trial today, and if we fail either on this side or on that side, then there is the danger of the whole lot of us being swept into the dustbin of history." [1]

Still, the die is not yet cast: the progressive reinforcement of economic structures is conceivable if a minimum of stability and political cohesion can be attained. In fact, new forces are appearing: at the summit they are represented by politicians who care about efficiency before anything else. In the I.A.S. young and able men are by no means lacking, and in industry, commerce, and higher education there are many extremely talented and competent persons. These men have

[1] See *News from India* (Berne) , Jan. 26, 1967, and the speech of M. R. Masani on March 21, 1967.

the interests of their country at heart and will not allow themselves to be blinded by dogmatism. The great question of the future is whether they will succeed in overcoming the adverse forces of shortsighted politicians, sowers of discord, and those who are ignorant of economic realities.

If this second hypothesis is borne out, agricultural progress will be stimulated, but, for reasons I have indicated, the improvement cannot be divided equally among the various social groups. In the preliminary phase the spearhead represented by the average dynamic cultivators will continue its breakthrough, and slowly, gradually, the landless laborers, lower down, will begin to benefit from the rise in production as their wages rise.

The same inequality will remain for an intermediate period between the areas that are really moving and those that are just beginning to wake up. Even with increased aid to the backward areas, this gap may well widen before it begins to narrow. Certainly such differences are regrettable, but what country in the world has not experienced this phenomenon?

Let us return now to the population problem. Is it, as is sometimes said, going to devour all economic progress? Will it in fact exceed output and cause a decline in living standards? This risk is linked to the political situation. If this is not too much endangered, progress per head of population is possible. It will not provide abundance, but it should improve the daily diet of large sections of the population. Moreover, once a certain stage has been passed, there is no reason why the rhythm of growth should not increase. Even in an advanced area like the Bulandshahr district, they are far from achieving maximum yields within their framework of semitraditional agriculture. There is nothing utopian in increasing the figures for wheat from 1,300 kg/ha to 2,000 kg/ha and above.

At the present time the future is unpredictable; only in the next few years will it begin to become clearer. Until it does, without yielding to the optimism of *Candide*'s Dr. Pangloss, it would seem premature to endorse the pessimistic views of those who forecast the complete chaos and economic stagnation of the Indian Union. If the political situation does not deteriorate any further, the agricultural policy implemented in the last few years should produce positive results.

I have made little reference, in the course of this survey of India, to other developing countries for fear of overloading what is already a rather heavy record. Now that I have come to the end of the book, I should like to enlarge on this issue. The *"Koi nahin sunta"* of the

Uttar Pradesh peasants (Nobody listens to us) is exaggerated as is proved by the efforts made for agriculture in the Five-Year Plans, but it expresses a feeling that is fairly widespread in the Third World.

In order to gain a better understanding of this reaction, let us remember a precedent far too often forgotten: the economic rise of Europe in the eighteenth century. By about 1750 Great Britain had already begun to progress smartly in agriculture. France, aware of its own delay, was fully preoccupied with the problem, and a wave of fresh, constructive thinking was brought to the situation: "The sovereign and the nation must never lose sight of the fact that the land is the only source of wealth, and that it is agriculture which causes it to multiply . . . men and their wealth can make agriculture progress, can extend commerce, and encourage the growth of industry." [2]

Dr. Quesnay can, in all fairness, be accused of what one might call agrarian extremism, and this is abundantly illustrated in his *Tableau économique*. Nonetheless, the leader of the physiocrats along with other economists of the period like Cantillon and Turgot fully understood the role of agriculture, and their theories were gradually translated into action. Thus an agricultural foundation was laid for the industrial revolution in France, on the heels of the revolution already well advanced on the other side of the Channel.

It would be a little absurd to apply the physiocrats' theses to the Third World today. The conditions are not the same; times, ideas, and techniques have changed; and, although recognizing the importance of agriculture, one cannot say that it is the only pole of development. On the other hand, one can only deplore the limited amount of space devoted to this sector in the enormous amount of works on development. Several Western authors—whether they call themselves liberals or socialists matters little—prefer studies of a more general nature and sometimes transpose the refinements of their own subject into a socioeconomic context which does not lend itself kindly to this sort of treatment. It would be really logical to have one agronomist or specialist in rural economy for everyone who generalizes about development.

In the Third World the problem is even more serious, for it is not only a question of studying, but of finding and applying concrete solutions. Too many economists underestimate agriculture, and the intelligentsia will have nothing to do with it. Some countries that possess a relatively long experience of development are making a worthy effort to reduce this breach. Certainly it is one of the main

[2] A maxim of François Quesnay quoted by P. Gemähling, *Les Grands économistes* (Paris, 1933), p. 52.

concerns of the Chinese, as is clearly shown by the insistence with which the press and the Party line constantly revert to the subject. In India, too, there are persons who are taking a more encouraging attitude. Elsewhere, the breach is in danger of widening into a gulf. It is, for example, impossible to open a book or a report on black Africa without coming across the leitmotiv of the rejection of the bush by the intelligentsia.[3] It is clear that if this situation continues, or grows worse, the lot of the Third World will not improve no matter how much foreign aid it receives.

To create a more favorable psychological climate for agriculture by rediscovering a small fragment at least of the "agromania" of eighteenth-century Europe is one thing, but to perfect a development policy is another. The reader will perhaps reproach me for having too often looked at Indian agriculture through a microscope. Is it not rather petty to count the number of shutters on the school at Kila Ulur, and to relate all those tales of badly cemented field channels, of officials being late, and of peasants not using the right amount of fertilizer?

In fact it is not very difficult to devise the broad lines of an agricultural plan; the critical point occurs at the level where the ideas are put into effect, mainly at district level, which is the first stage in the operation. It is here that these "miscellaneous doings" take on their full significance, and crucial delays and blockages occur. The speed with which development progresses will be determined by the extent to which some, at least, of these critical points can be eliminated. Thus it is important for the planners to have a thorough knowledge of practical problems in order to see what changes in the administrative structure and organization of output might improve the situation.

* * *

The rural life that I have described is not idyllic, and I have attempted to hide none of its weaknesses or defects. On the other hand, I have not stressed one aspect which, without being directly linked to development, is worthy of mention.

My long stay at Khandoï enabled me to observe a rural community at very close range. The villagers accepted us (my wife, my children, and myself) with a naturalness and confidence which made it possible for us to share their daily lives. It is difficult to describe the innate

---

[3] It would be unfair to criticize the educated African here, for many other men would act in the same way if they were in their place. In Africa, the breach between the traditional village society and the educated classes is often much greater than it is in Asia. Unlike some, at least, of the Asian intelligentsia, an educated African will seldom remain faithful to his spiritual heritage, especially if it is animist.

dignity of this civilization. Essentially agrarian, it has an invigorating quality not only in its farming techniques but also in its festivals and rites: the offerings to the mother-goddess in the courtyards of their houses, the ritual bath in the Ganges in December, the departure on a long pilgrimage to the Himalayas. Behind the agriculture there stretches a spiritual heritage of habits and customs which are without affectation and know nothing of the vulgarity that is the ever increasing taint of modern civilization.

Reference Material

APPENDIX: *Statistics*

I. POPULATION

	1951	1961	1967
Total population (% of increase, 1951–1961, 21.5%)	361 million	439 million	over 500
Death rate	27–31%	about 20%	million
Birth rate	41–43%	about 41%	
Life expectancy	32.1 years	41.2 years	

Rural population in 1961: 359 million
Active population in 1961: 188 million, including 130.9 million cultivators and landless laborers
Breakdown of the active population: in % (males only):

Cultivators	29.41%
Landless laborers	7.67
Persons engaged in plantations, forestry, fishing, hunting, mining, and quarrying	1.77
Cottage industry	3.26
Modern industry	3.17
Building	0.80
Trade	3.02
Transport, storage, and communications	1.30
Services	6.72
Total	57.12% of the total male population

Sex ratio: 941 females per 1,000 males (1961)

Age groups:	less than 15 years	402
	15 to 49 years	479
	50 years and above	119
	Total	1,000

Education (1961): literate people,	males	77.8 million
	females	27.5 million
	Total	105.3 million

Castes and tribes:

scheduled castes (mostly Harijans)	64 million (1961)
scheduled tribes (mostly aborigines)	30 million

SOURCE: *Census of India, Paper No. 1*, Vol. I, 1962.

II. LAND HOLDINGS AND AREA

Estimated number and cumulative percentage of households and area owned by size limits of household ownership holdings (1953–1954 crop season)

Holding size (acres)	No. of Households (000)	Area Owned (000 acres)	Cumulative Households	Percentage Area
(1) 0.001	14,669	—	23.09	—
(2) 0.01–0.99	15,360	4,166	47.26	1.37
(3) 1.00–2.49	8,879	14,839	61.24	6.23
(4) 2.50–4.99	8,569	30,821	74.73	16.32
(5) 5.00–7.49	4,966	30,411	82.55	26.28
(6) 7.50–9.99	2,972	25,766	87.23	34.72
(7) 10.00–14.99	3,207	39,053	92.28	47.50
(8) 15.00–19.99	1,690	29,253	94.94	57.08
(9) 20.00–24.99	929	20,623	96.40	63.84
(10) 25.00–29.99	636	17,480	97.40	69.55
(11) 30.00–49.99	1,051	39,439	99.06	82.46
(12) 50.00 and above	604	53,580	100.00	100.00
Total	63,532	305,431	—	—

SOURCE: *National Sample Survey Report on Land Holdings*, No. 36.

III. NATIONAL INCOME (at 1960–1961 prices)

Rate of increase, 1951–1961	42 percent
Increase per capita, 1951–1961	16 percent
National income in 1960/61	141,400 million rupees (net income)
Per capita income in 1960/61	326 rupees

	1964/65	*1965/66*
National income	166,300 million	159,300 (likely)
Per capita income	348	325

Breakdown of the national income:

Agriculture	46.5%
Mines and industries	16.7
Trade and transport	19.3
Services	17.5
Total	100 %

SOURCES: W. Malenbaum, *Prospects for Indian Development*, and *Fourth Five Year Plan, A Draft Outline.*

IV. FIVE-YEAR PLANS

Outlays (billions of rupees) *	1951–1956	1956–1961	1961–1966
Public sector	19.6	46	75
Private sector	18.	31	41
Total	37.6	77	116

* By development outlays, the Indian planners mean not only investments proper, but also operating expenses which are of a current account nature, and accompany an investment.

For the first two plans these are the achievements. For the third, these are the targets.

Investments (billions of rupees)	1956–1961			
	Public	Private	Total	%
Agriculture, community development, and cooperation	2.1	6.25	8.35	12
Irrigation (major and medium)	4.2	—	4.2	6
Power	4.45	0.4	4.85	7
Village and small industries	0.9	1.75	2.65	4
Organized industry and mining	8.7	6.75	15.45	23
Transport and communications	12.75	1.35	14.10	21
Social services and other programs	3.40	9.50	12.90	19
Inventories	—	5.00	5.00	8
Total	36.50	31.00	67.50	100

	1961–1966			
Agriculture, community development, and cooperation	6.60	8.00	14.60	14
Irrigation (major and medium)	6.50	—	6.50	6
Power	10.12	0.50	10.62	10
Village and small industries	1.50	2.75	4.25	4
Organized industry and mining	15.20	10.50	25.70	25
Transport and communications	14.86	2.50	17.36	17
Social services and other programs	6.22	10.75	16.97	16
Inventories	2.00	6.00	8.00	8
Total	63.00	41.00	104.00	100

For the Second Plan these are the actual investments, for the Third these are the targets. As mentioned in chap. 26, the investments and outlays in the public sector were expected to reach 75 billion, but in fact they amounted to 86.30 billion. For the private sector, results are not yet available. The largest differences appear in the following sectors: power, about 2 billion additional investments, and organized industry and mining, also about 2 billion additional.

Investments (billions of rupees)	1966–1971		
	Public	Private	Total
Agriculture, community development, and cooperation	15.75	9.00	24.75
Irrigation (major and medium)	9.64	—	9.64
Power	20.30	0.50	20.80
Village and small industries	2.30	3.20	5.50
Organized industry and mining	39.36	23.50	62.86
Transport and communications	30.10	6.30	36.40
Social services and other programs	18.55	16.00	34.55
Inventories	—	19.00	19.00
Total	136.00	77.50	213.50

SOURCES: *Third Five Year Plan* and *Fourth Five Year Plan, A Draft Outline.*

According to the latest reports from India (May, 1967) it appears quite possible that the total size of the Fourth Plan will be reduced. The total outlay in the public sector may be cut by 40 billion.

V. FOREIGN AID

[Rate of U.S. dollar: 4.75 rupees, predevaluation; 7.50 rupees, postdevaluation (June, 1966).]

Loans and grants excluding those under U.S. Public Law (billion rupees):
  1951–1961
    Authorizations during 1951–1961........................17.85
    Utilizations during 1951–1961..........................10.84
  1961–1966
    Balance available from 1951–1961............................. 7.01
    Authorizations...24.89
      Total...31.90
    Utilizations..20.27

U.S. Public Law Assistance
  1951–1961
    Authorizations.......................................11.47
    Utilizations.. 5.50
  1961–1966
    Balance available... 5.97
    Authorizations.. 4.50
      Total...10.47
    Utilizations.. 8.53

SOURCE: Govt. of India, *Economic Survey 1966–67.*

[Note: The figures on population are reasonably accurate, except perhaps so far as the exact breakdown of the active population is concerned. Figures on the national income are quite uncertain: size of subsistence economy, agricultural statistics, etc. Figures on investments and foreign aid are accurate.]

GLOSSARY

adhyaksh, president of the zila parishad, district council in Uttar Pradesh

A.D.O., assistant development officer,
assistant to the B.D.O., in charge of
one of the technical services of the
block: agriculture, cooperatives,
animal husbandry, etc.

asami, tenant with only a temporary
right of occupation of the land, a
right that was made permanent by
the abolition of the zamindari system in Uttar Pradesh

artha, Sanskrit term meaning profit or
material interest

bajra, pearl millet *(Pennisetum ty-
phoideum)*

bakshish, gift, present, in a wider
sense bribe for a corrupt purpose

bandhara, small dam built on a river
to retain water for irrigation (Maharashtra)

batai, metayage system, generally on
the basis of sharecropping the gross
product between the metayer and
the landlord

B.D.O., block development officer,
head of a development block grouping together about 60 to 100 villages

begar, compulsory, unpaid service due
the zamindar, in a wider sense
forced labor

Bhangi, ex-untouchable, scavenger or
sweeper

bigha, measure used in the north of
India, 1 *bigha pakha* = 1/4 ha.; 1
bigha kachcha = 1/16 ha.

Bhudan, movement founded by Vinoba Bhave advocating gifts of land

bhumidar, in actual fact a landowner
in Uttar Pradesh after the abolition
of the zamindari system

Brahmin, the highest *varna* (category) in Hindu society. Originally
Brahmins were especially responsible for the maintenance and trans-
mission of traditional and spiritual
values.

C.E.O., chief executive officer, an official of the I.A.S. with the rank of
collector, responsible for district development in Maharashtra

chak, plot, as indicated in the land
records

chakbandi, consolidation of holdings

Chamar, ex-untouchable, by tradition
one who deals with leathers and
skins but today often a farm
worker

collector, deputy commissioner or district magistrate, the government
representative at district level, head
of most of the district's administrative services

dharma, conformity, fidelity to spiritual traditions; in a wider sense,
roughly religion or religious duty

D.P.O., district planning officer (Uttar Pradesh) responsible for community development in a district

gaon or *gram sabha,* plenary assembly
of adults in a village

ghee, clarified butter

gram sewak, village-level worker; the
lowest rank in the block's personnel, in charge of a circle of villages,
a kind of rural organizer

gur, raw sugar, obtained by evaporat-
ing sugar-cane juice

Harijan, name given by Gandhi to the untouchables, literally people of the god Hari

I.A.S., Indian Administrative Service, cadre of high officials which replaced the British Indian Civil Service (I.C.S.)

inam, land exempt from tax, generally intended to provide income for a religious foundation

Jat, a farming caste from the northwest of India, whose rank is similar to the Kshatriyas

jowar, millet, sorgo (*Sorghum vulgare*)

Kallar, a caste (Sudra) in the Tamil country

karnam, village accountant, Madras

kharif, crop-growing season beginning with the monsoon (June–July) and ending between November and January

khasra, land record with classification by plots (Uttar Pradesh)

khatauni, land record classified according to the landowners in Uttar Pradesh (in addition to the *khasra,* whose plots are classified in serial order, according to their numbers)

khudkasht, land cultivated directly by the zamindar (Uttar Pradesh)

kolu, a kind of sugar-cane or oil press

Kshatriya, second category (*varna*) of Hindu society, by tradition engaged in military affairs and temporal power

kshetr samiti, council at development block level, instituted by the Panchayati Raj, Uttar Pradesh

Kurmi, a farming caste (Sudra)

kuruvai, rice crop planted at the end of June, harvested in September (Madras)

lekhpal, village accountant in Uttar Pradesh, known as *patwari* before 1953

Lodha-Rajput, a farming caste (Sudra)

mafi, temporary land tenancy in exchange for services rendered (Uttar Pradesh)

maund or *man,* Indian measure; 1 *maund* = 37.3 kg.

mot, irrigation well with leather or metal pails drawn by bullocks

munsif, collector of the land tax (Madras)

panchayat, arbitration council composed of five influential people. It used to exist either within each caste to judge infringements of caste rules, or at village level where for a long time it probably represented the power of the one dominant caste to which its members all belonged. Today it is an elected, multicaste, village council.

Panchayati Raj, lit. rule of the panchayats, an administrative reform instituted as a result of the *Mehta Report,* 1957

patwari, similar to *lekhpal,* but usually hereditary

pradhan, president of a village panchayat in Uttar Pradesh

pramukh, president of the *kshetr samiti* (Uttar Pradesh)

rabi, winter farming season beginning after the monsoon and ending in March or April

rahat, Persian wheel for drawing water from a well; it is rotated by two bullocks

rayatwari, a system by which the peasant (*rayat*) pays land tax direct to the state

samba, rice crop, sown in August, harvested in January (Madras)

settlement, an operation by which the British determined the land tax

shramdan, a gift in the form of work, a kind of human investment or mobilization of manpower

sirdar, tenant in Uttar Pradesh after the abolition of the zamindari system

Sudra, fourth category (*varna*) of Hindu society composed of workers or artisans

taccavi, state credit granted to agriculture

talathi, village accountant in Maharashtra

taluk or *tehsil,* administrative subdivision of the district

Thakur, a caste belonging to the Kshatriya category

thaladi, rice crop sown in October, harvested in February (southern India)

Vaisya, third category (*varna*) of Hindu society, composed of merchants and farmers

village volunteer force, a voluntary force created at the end of 1962, following the Sino-Indian conflict. Its purpose was threefold: to increase output, to promote education, and to ensure the defense of the village.

zamindar, landowner who was responsible for the collection of tax during British rule

zila parishad, district council, created by the Panchayati Raj

BIBLIOGRAPHY

[*A complete bibliography on India would fill several volumes. I have therefore limited myself to government publications and books cited in the various chapters, with the addition of a few other books which are of particular importance for our subject.*]

OFFICIAL PUBLICATIONS

I. Central Government Publications, New Delhi

The Constitution of India. 1963. 390 pp.
Census of India, 1951. Vol. I, 1953. 238 pp.
Census of India, 1961. Vol. I, 1962. 454 pp.
Ministry of Finance. *External Assistance 1960.* 75 pp.
Ministry of Community Development, Panchayati Raj, and Cooperation:
    Sahakari Samaj [On Cooperatives]. 1962. 335 pp.
    The Evolution of the Community Development Programme in India. 1963. 104 pp.
    The Scope of Extension. 1962. 22 pp.
    A Guide to Community Development. 1962. 180 pp.
Ministry of Food and Agriculture:
    Report on India's Food Crisis and Steps to Meet It. 1959. 258 pp. (Prepared by a team of experts of the Ford Foundation.)
    Intensive Agricultural District Programme Report 1961–63. 1963. 216 pp.
    Report of the Working Group on Inter-departmental and Institutional Co-ordination for Agricultural Production. 1963. 9 pp.
    Review of the Scarcity Situation and Measures to Meet It. 1966. 18 pp.
Planning Commission:
    The First Five Year Plan. 1952. 671 pp.
    Review of the First Five Year Plan. 1957. 479 pp.
    Second Five Year Plan. 1956. 653 pp.
    Third Five Year Plan. 1961. 774 pp.
    Third Plan, Mid-Term Appraisal. 1963. 179 pp.
    Report on Indian and State Administrative Services and Problems of District Administration. 1962, 108 pp. (Prepared by V. T. Krishnamachari.)
    Fourth Five Year Plan, A Draft Outline. 1966. 430 pp.
Programme Evaluation Organization:
    Evaluation Report on Working of Community Projects and N.E.S. Blocks for the years 1957, 1958, 1959, and 1960.
    Study of the Problems of Minor Irrigation. 1961.

National Sample Survey: *
  Report on Land Holdings, No. 30, 1960, and No. 59, 1962.
  Some Results of the Land Utilization Survey and Crop-Cutting Experiments, No, 73, 1963.
Committee on Plan Projects:
  Reports of the Team for the Study of Community Projects and National Extension Service. Vol. I, 1957. 175 pp. (*Mehta Report.*)
Reserve Bank:
  Rural Credit Follow Up Survey 1957–58. Bombay, 1961. 327 pp.

II. STATE PUBLICATIONS AND DOCUMENTS

[Documents in vernacular language are abridged as follows: H = Hindi, U = Urdu, T = Tamil, M = Marathi. Documents that are not printed are indicated: mimeo. = mimeographed; hand. = handwritten.]

UTTAR PRADESH

(*a*) *General Problems*

Laws:
  The Uttar Pradesh Zamindari Abolition and Land Reforms Act. 1950.
  The Uttar Pradesh Imposition of Ceiling on Land Holdings Act. 1960.
  The United Provinces Panchayat Raj Act. 1947.
  The Uttar Pradesh Kshetr Samitis and Zila Parishads Act. 1960.
Economic Development (Government of Uttar Pradesh, Lucknow) :
  Second Five Year Plan, Progress Review. 1962. 212 pp.
  Third Five Year Plan. Vol. I, 1961. 202 pp.
  Third Five Year Plan, The First Year. 1963. 181 pp.
  Third Five Year Plan, The Second Year. 1964. 272 pp.
  Annual Review of Development Activities for 1961–62 and 1962–63.
Planning, Research, and Action Institute:
  Report on the Study of Tube-well Irrigation Potential and Its Utilization with Special Reference to Eastern U.P. 1962. 61 pp.

(*b*) *District of Bulandshahr:*

  District Census Handbook, U.P., Bulandshahr. 1951.
  Bulandshahr Tisri Panchvarshiya Yojna ["Third Five Year Plan of Bulandshahr"]. 1961. (H.)
  Quarterly Progress Report. 1961–1964. (hand.)
  Unchagaon Tisri Panchvarshiya Yojna ["Third Five Year Plan of Unchagaon"]. 1961. (H.; hand.)
  Quarterly Progress Report. 1961–1964. (hand.)
  Khasra and *Khatauni* [land records]. 1860–1964. (U. & H.; hand. Hindi is used instead of Urdu after Independence.)
  Gaon Sabha ki Tisri Panchvarshiya Yojna ["Five Year Plan of the Village"]. 1961. (H.; hand.)
  Karyavahiyon ki Pustakon ka Farm [minutes of the panchayat]. 1954–1964. (H.; hand.)

---

* The P.E.O. is attached to the Planning Commission, the N.S.S. to the Cabinet Secretariat. Both are responsible, under much freedom of action and criticism, for surveys and evaluation reports.

(c) *District of Benares (Varanasi)* :

District Census Handbook, U.P., Banaras District. 1951.
Varanasi Tisri Panchvarshiya Zila Yojna ["Third Plan"]. 1961 (H.)
Quarterly Progress Report 1961–63, Pindra block. (hand.)
Khasra and *Khatauni* of Nahiyan. 1961–64. (H.; hand.)

MADRAS:

(a) *General Problems*

Laws:
The Madras Estates Abolition and Conversion into Ryotwari Act. 1948. (As modified up to April, 1961.)
The Madras Estates Land (Reduction of Rent) Act. 1947. (As modified up to November, 1957.)
The Madras Cultivating Tenants (Payment of Fair Rent) Act. 1956. (As modified up to August, 1962.)
The Madras Panchayats Act. 1958.
The Madras District Development Councils Act. 1958.
The Madras Act (Fixation of Ceiling on Agricultural Land Holdings). 1961.
Report of the Special Officer on Land Tenures in the Ryotwari Areas of Madras. 1947.
Guide Book on Panchayat Development in Madras State. 3 vols. 1961.
Economic Development (Government of Madras, Madras) :
Third Five Year Plan. 1961. 272 pp.
Third Five Year Plan, Mid-Term Review. 1964. 137 pp.
Madras State, Administration Report 1962. 1963. 214 pp.
Basic Agricultural Statistics. 1963. 45 pp. (mimeo.)
National Council of Applied Economic Research:
Techno-economic Survey of Madras. 1960. 286 pp.
Rural Development and Local Administration Department (Notes and reports on activities) :
G.O. No. 664, August 16, 1960.
G.O. No. 2460, September 8, 1961.
Demand No. XXVI, 1961–1962.
Demand No. XXIII, 1962–1963.
Demand No. XXIII, 1963–1964.
Demand No. XXIII, 1964–1965.

(b) *District of Tanjore (Thanjavur)*

The Intensive Agricultural District Programme (I.A.D.P.) :
A Brief Note on the Work Done 1960–63. (mimeo.)
District Plan 1963–64. (mimeo.)
Final Programme of Work 1964–65. (mimeo.)
Orathanad Block, I.A.D.P. 1964. (mimeo.)
Orathanad Panchayat Union, minutes, 1963–1964. (T.; hand.)
Descriptive Memoir of Kila Ulur Village, Resettlement 1924–25. Tanjore: Revenue Settlement Office, February 4, 1924.
Land Records, Kila Ulur, 1963–1964. (T.; hand.)
Minutes of the Panchayat of Kila Ulur, 1956–1964. (T.; hand.)

MAHARASHTRA

(a) General Problems

Laws:

The Bombay Tenancy and Agricultural Lands Act. 1948.
The Maharashtra Cooperatives Societies Act. 1960.
The Maharashtra Agricultural Lands (Ceiling on Holdings) Act. 1961.
The Bombay Village Panchayat Act. 1958.
The Maharashtra Zila Parishad and Panchayat Samiti Act. 1961.
Economic Development (Government of Maharashtra, Bombay) :
Third Five Year Plan. 1961. 265 pp.
Annual Plan for 1964–65. 1964. 108 pp.
Outline of Activities 1963–64 and 1964–65. 1964. 228 pp.
Report of the Committee on Democratic Decentralisation. 1961. 298 pp.
Basic and Current Agricultural Statistics. 1964. 114 pp.

(b) District of Satara

*Note on the Agricultural Activities in Satara District from 1955–56 to 1961–
62.* (mimeo.)
Annual Administration Report, 1962–1963 and 1963–1964. (mimeo.)
Satara Agricultural Production Programme 1963–64. (mimeo.)
Master Note on Progress Report 1963–64. (mimeo.)
Zila Parishad Satara, minutes, 1962–1964. (M.; hand.)
A Note on Development Activities of Koregaon Block, April 30, 1964.
(mimeo.)
Koregaon Panchayat Samiti, minutes, 1962–1964. (M.; hand.)
Eksal Gram Panchayat, minutes, 1957–1964. (M.; hand.)
Land Records of Eksal 1952–1964. (M.; hand.)

III. UNITED NATIONS REPORT

COLDWELL, M-J., R. DUMONT, and M. READ. *Report of a Community Development Evaluation Mission in India.* New York, 1959. (mimeo.)

GENERAL WORKS

ARAKERI, H. R., G. V. CHALAM, P. SATYANARAYANA, and R. L. DONAHUE. *Soil Man-
agement in India.* Bombay: Asia, 1962.
BETTELHEIM, C. *L'Inde indépendante.* Paris: Colin, 1962.
BRAIBANTI, R., and J. J. SPENCER (eds.). *Administration and Economic Develop-
ment in India.* Durham, N.C.: Duke University Press, 1963.
CHAMBARD, J. L. "Pour une sociologie phénoménologique de l'Inde," *Cahiers
Internationaux de Sociologie* (Paris), July, 1958.
DANDEKAR, V. M., and G. J. KHUDANPUR. *Working of Bombay Tenancy Act 1948.*
Poona: Gokhale Institute of Politics and Economics, 1957.
DANTWALA, M. L. *India's Food Problem.* Bombay: Asia, 1961.
———. *Problem of Subsistence Farm Economy: The Indian Case,* Honolulu:
Seminar on Subsistence and Peasant Economics, 1965.
DEY, S. K. *Panchayati Raj.* Bombay: Asia, 1962.
DODWELL, H. H., and R. R. SETHI (eds.). *The Cambridge History of India,* Vol.
VI. Delhi: S. Chand, 1964.

DUMONT, LOUIS. *La Civilisation indienne et nous*. Paris: Colin, 1964.

———. *Homo hierarchicus, essai sur le système des castes*. Paris: Gallimard, 1967.

EICHER, C. K., and L. W. WITT (eds.). *Agriculture in Economic Development*. New York: McGraw-Hill, 1964.

ETIENNE, GILBERT. "Le Recensement indien de 1961," *Population* (Paris), 1964, No. 2.

GEERTZ, C. (ed.). *Old Societies and New States*. New York: Free Press, 1963.

GOUROU, P. *L'Asie*. Paris: Hachette, 1953.

———. *Les Pays tropicaux*. Paris: Presses Universitaires de France, 1966.

HARRISON, SELIG S. *India, The Most Dangerous Decades*. Princeton, N.J.: Princeton University Press, 1960.

HICKS, URSULA. *Development from Below*. Oxford: Clarendon Press, 1961.

HUTTON, J. H. *Caste in India*. Cambridge: Cambridge University Press, 1946.

LEWIS, J. P. *Quiet Crisis in India*. Washington, D.C.: Brookings Institution, 1962.

MALENBAUM, W. *Prospects for Indian Development*. London: George Allen & Unwin, 1962.

MELLOR, J. W., and U. J. LELE. "Alternative Estimates of the Trend in Indian Foodgrains Production During the First Two Plans," *Economic Development and Cultural Change* (Chicago), No. 2, 1965.

NAIR, K. *Blossoms in the Dust*. New York: Praeger, 1961.

NANAVATI, M. B., and J. J. ANJARIA. *The Indian Rural Problem*. Bombay: Indian Society of Agricultural Economics, 1960.

RAO, V. K. R. V. (ed.). *Agricultural Labour in India*. Bombay: Asia, 1962.

REDDAWAY, W. B. *The Development of the Indian Economy*. London: George Allen & Unwin, 1962.

ROSEN, G. *Democracy and Economic Change in India*. Berkeley and Los Angeles: University of California Press, 1966.

SCHULTZ, T. W. *Transforming Traditional Agriculture*. New Haven, Conn., Yale University Press, 1964.

SINGER, H. W. *Problems of Social Development*. Geneva: U.N. Research Institute for Social Development, 1965. (mimeo.)

SINGH, B. *Next Step in Village India*. Bombay: Asia, 1961.

SOVANI, N. V. "Planning and Planners in India," *Indian Economic Journal*, No. 4, January–March, 1966.

SPATE, O. H. K. *India and Pakistan, A General and Regional Geography*. London: Methuen, 1964.

STAMP, L. D. *Asia*. London: Methuen, 1959.

TARLOK SINGH. *Poverty and Social Change*. London: Longmans Green & Co., 1945.

THORNER, DANIEL. *Land and Labour in India*. Bombay: Asia, 1962.

WEINER, M. *The Politics of Scarcity, Public Pressure and Political Response in India*. Chicago: University of Chicago Press, 1962.

WOODRUFF, P. *The Men Who Ruled India*. 2 vols. London: Jonathan Cape, 1963.

REGIONAL STUDIES

DUBE, S. C. *Indian Village*. London: Routledge and Kegan Paul, 1955.

———. *India's Changing Villages*. London: Routledge and Kegan Paul, 1960.

DUMONT, LOUIS. *Une Sous-caste de l'Inde du Sud.* Paris: Mouton, 1957.

GOUGH, E. KATHLEEN. "Caste in a Tanjore Village," in E. R. Leach (ed.), *Aspects of Caste in South India* (Cambridge Papers in Social Anthropology, No. 2, 1960).

LELE, J. K. *Local Government in India.* Cornell International Agricultural Development Bulletin No. 7, 1966. (On Maharashtra.)

LEWIS, OSCAR. *Village Life in Northern India.* New York: Random House, 1965.

MARRIOTT, MC KIM (ed.). *Village India.* Chicago: University of Chicago Press, 1960.

MAYER, A. C. *Caste and Kinship in Central India.* London: Routledge and Kegan Paul, 1960.

MAYER, A. et al. *Pilot Project India.* Berkeley and Los Angeles: University of California Press, 1959. (About Etawah.)

NEALE, W. C. *Economic Change in Rural India.* New Haven, Conn. Yale University Press, 1962. (On Uttar Pradesh.)

PURWAR, V. L. *Panchayats in Uttar Pradesh.* Lucknow: Universal Book, 1960.

SOVANI, N. V., and N. RATH. *Economics of a Multiple-Purpose River Dam.* Poona: Gokhale Institute of Politics and Economics, 1960.

WISER, WILLIAM, and CHARLOTTE WISER. *Behind Mud Walls, 1930–1960,* Berkeley and Los Angeles: University of California Press, 1963.

NEWSPAPERS AND PERIODICALS

The Eastern Economist, weekly, and its annual number. New Delhi.

The Economic Weekly Review. Bombay.

The Far Eastern Economic Review, weekly. Hong Kong.

The Hindu, daily, and its weekly edition, *The Hindu Weekly Review.* Madras.

The Hindustan Times, daily, New Delhi; and its weekly edition, *The Overseas Hindustan Times.*

The Indian Express, daily. New Delhi.

The Indian Journal of Agricultural Economics, quarterly. Bombay.

The Indian Journal of Public Administration, quarterly. New Delhi.

Kurukshetra, publication of the Ministry of Food and Agriculture, Community Development and Cooperation

The Statesman, daily, and its weekly edition, *The Statesman Overseas Weekly.* New Delhi and Calcutta.

Seminar, monthly. Bombay.

The Times of India, daily. New Delhi and Bombay.

INDEX

Administration, 6, 23, 28, 140, 141, 237, 292, 293; district, 166, 167, 294–296; state, 178, 179, 189, 197, 201

Administrative structure: under British rule, 132; after independence, 133

Agrarian reforms. *See* Land Reforms

Ambalakkarar, 205, 207, 213

Ambedkar, Dr., 35

Animal husbandry. *See* Bullocks; Cattle

Artisans, 92–94, 100, 207, 242. *See also* Jativ; Muslim

Asami, 59. *See also* Tenants and tenancy

Assistant development officer (A.D.O.). *See* Community development

Bajra. See Food grains

Bananas, 211, 212, 215, 247

Begar, 57, 60

Benares district, 5, 6, 45, 49, 50, 106, 288

Benares Irrigation Division, 166n

Bengal, famine of, 16

Bettelheim, C., 314n

Bhakra Dam, 26

Bhaktavatsalam, M., 202

Bhangi, 61, 77, 99, 276

Bhoodan, 39, 40

Bhumidar, 59, 60, 63, 87, 115, 117

Block development officer (B.D.O.). *See* Community development

Bombay Land Improvement Scheme Act, 263

Bombay Tenancy and Agricultural Lands Act (1948), 243

Bombay Village Panchayats Act of 1958, 237

Brahmins, 61–63, 71, 80, 85, 159, 242; prominent role of, due to traditional education, 281; repartition of land of, 67, 219; and sociological attitude, 223

Bulandshahr district, 5, 20, 49, 50, 55, 84

Bullocks, 54, 57, 71–88 *passim*, 94, 97, 115, 153–160 *passim*, 248

Cash crops, 155, 193, 233, 257. *See also* Cotton; Groundnuts; Sugar cane

Caste, 34, 61, 62, 162; dominant, 62, 63, 152, 207, 242, 300; and relation to land, 63, 100, 152, 218, 275; and social status, 88, 96, 98, 161, 215; and sociological attitude, 156, 276, 277. *See also* Enterprising spirit

Caste system: as an obstacle to development, 282; division into varna of, 61

Cattle, 54, 55, 78–96 *passim*, 112, 158–160, 211, 213, 247, 258; breeding of, 314, 315; quality of, 84

Cauvery delta, 24, 193

Cauvery Mettur Project (C.M.P.), 205, 206, 210, 211

Cement, 116n, 119, 120, 126, 144, 254, 264–266, 307, 309

Chamar, 159, 161. *See also* Jativ

Chana. See Food grains

Chemical fertilizers: consumption of, 54, 71, 76, 85, 88, 114, 129, 137–139, 174, 192, 196, 209, 221, 234, 244, 257, 259, 260, 269; distribution of, 28, 316; import of, 27; production of, 23, 27, 307, 309

Chief executive officer (C.E.O.), 238, 258, 267, 270, 289, 294

China, 21, 25, 36, 103, 112, 122, 130, 307n, 321

Cholas, 24

Civil Service, Indian. *See* Indian Civil Service

Civil Service, State, 133, 294

Coconut plantations, 206, 213, 269

Coimbatore, 194, 202, 223n, 248n, 312

Collector, 132–134, 141, 142, 227, 228, 257, 294

Communism, 40, 161, 162, 203, 288

Community development, 13; aims and achievements of, 32, 33, 140, 290–296 *passim*, 312; Assistant development